ASCENT®

CENTER FOR TECHNICAL KNOWLEDGE

AutoCAD® Civil 3D® 2017 (R1) for Surveyors

Student Guide

Metric - 1st Edition

AUTODESK.
Authorized Publisher

ASCENT - Center for Technical Knowledge®
AutoCAD® Civil 3D® 2017 (R1)
for Surveyors
Metric - 1st Edition

Prepared and produced by:

ASCENT Center for Technical Knowledge
630 Peter Jefferson Parkway, Suite 175
Charlottesville, VA 22911

866-527-2368
www.ASCENTed.com

Lead Contributor: Michelle Rasmussen

ASCENT - Center for Technical Knowledge is a division of Rand Worldwide, Inc., providing custom developed knowledge products and services for leading engineering software applications. ASCENT is focused on specializing in the creation of education programs that incorporate the best of classroom learning and technology-based training offerings.

We welcome any comments you may have regarding this student guide, or any of our products. To contact us please email: feedback@ASCENTed.com.

Contents

Preface

This in-depth *AutoCAD® Civil 3D® 2017 (R1) for Surveyors* student guide is for surveyors and survey technicians that do not necessarily need all of the functionality that is taught in AutoCAD Civil 3D Fundamentals. This student guide equips the surveyor with the basic knowledge required to use AutoCAD Civil 3D efficiently in a typical daily workflow. Students learn how to import the converted field equipment survey data into a standardized environment in AutoCAD Civil 3D and to use the automation tools to create an Existing Condition Plan. Data collection, and traverses are also covered. Other topics that help in increasing efficiency include styles, correct AutoCAD® drafting techniques, the methodology required to create linework effectively for variables used in defining symbology, surfaces, categorizing points, and importing imagery.

Topics Covered

- The AutoCAD Civil 3D Interface
- The Planning and Analysis workspace
- Points overview and styles
- Importing points and coordinate transformations
- Creating points and drafting
- Point groups, grips, and reports
- Point security and editing
- Introduction to data collection in the field
- Introduction to Civil 3D Survey and automated linework
- Survey networks
- Coordinate Geometry Editor for entering traverse information or legal descriptions
- Surface overview
- Surface editing
- Surface labels and analysis
- Point clouds and creating a surface from point cloud data

Note on Software Setup

This student guide assumes a standard installation of the software using the default preferences during installation. Lectures and practices use the standard software templates and default options for the Content Libraries.

Students and Educators can Access Free Autodesk Software and Resources

Autodesk challenges you to get started with free educational licenses for professional software and creativity apps used by millions of architects, engineers, designers, and hobbyists today. Bring Autodesk software into your classroom, studio, or workshop to learn, teach, and explore real-world design challenges the way professionals do.

Get started today - register at the Autodesk Education Community and download one of the many Autodesk software applications available.

Visit www.autodesk.com/joinedu/

Note: Free products are subject to the terms and conditions of the end-user license and services agreement that accompanies the software. The software is for personal use for education purposes and is not intended for classroom or lab use.

Lead Contributor: Michelle Rasmussen

Specializing in the civil engineering industry, Michelle authors training guides and provides instruction, support, and implementation on all Autodesk infrastructure solutions, in addition to general AutoCAD.

Michelle began her career in the Air Force working in the Civil Engineering unit as a surveyor, designer, and construction manager. She has also worked for municipalities and consulting engineering firms as an engineering/GIS technician. Michelle holds a Bachelor's of Science degree from the University of Utah along with a Master's of Business Administration from Kaplan University.

Michelle is an Autodesk Certified Instructor (ACI) as well as an Autodesk Certified Evaluator, teaching and evaluating other Autodesk Instructors for the ACI program. In addition, she holds the Autodesk Certified Professional certification for Civil 3D and is trained in Instructional Design.

As a skilled communicator, Michelle effectively leads classes, webcasts and consults with clients to achieve their business objectives.

Michelle Rasmussen has been the Lead Contributor for *AutoCAD Civil 3D for Surveyors* since 2011.

In this Guide

The following images highlight some of the features that can be found in this Student Guide.

Practice Files

To download the practice files for this student guide, use the following steps:

1. Type the URL shown below into the address bar of your Internet browser. The URL must be typed **exactly as shown**. If you are using an ASCENT ebook, you can click on the link to download the file

   Address bar

   http://www.ASCENTed.com/getfile?id=xxxxxxxx

   File   Edit   View   Favorites   Tools   Help

2. Press <Enter> to download the .ZIP file that contains the Practice Files

3. Once the download is complete, unzip the file to a local folder. The unzipped file contains an .EXE file

4. Double-click on the .EXE file and follow the instructions to automatically install the Practice Files on the C:\ drive of your computer.

   Do not change the location in which the Practice Files folder is installed. Doing so can cause errors when completing the practices in this student guide

http://www.ASCENTed.com/getfile?id=xxxxxxxx

Stay Informed!
Interested in receiving information about upcoming promotional offers, educational events, invitations to complimentary webcasts, and discounts? If so, please visit *www.ASCENTed.com/updates/*

Help us improve our product by completing the following survey:
www.ASCENTed.com/feedback
You can also contact us at: feedback@ASCENTed.com

FTP link for practice files

Practice Files

The Practice Files page tells you how to download and install the practice files that are provided with this student guide.

Chapter

1

Getting Started

In this chapter you learn how to start the AutoCAD® software, become familiar with the basic layout of the AutoCAD screen, how to access commands, use your pointing device, and understand the AutoCAD Cartesian workspace. You also learn how to open an existing drawing, view a drawing by zooming and panning, and save your work in the AutoCAD software.

Learning Objectives in this Chapter

- Launch the AutoCAD software and complete a basic initial setup of the drawing environment.
- Identify the basic layout and features of AutoCAD interface including the Ribbon, Drawing Window, and Application Menu.
- Locate commands and launch them using the Ribbon, shortcut menus, Application Menu and Quick Access Toolbar.
- Locate points in the AutoCAD Cartesian workspace.
- Open and close existing drawings and navigate to file locations.
- Move around a drawing using the mouse, the **Zoom** and **Pan** commands, and the Navigation Bar.
- Save drawings in various formats and set the automatic save options using the **Save** commands.

Learning Objectives for the chapter

Chapters

Each chapter begins with a brief introduction and a list of the chapter's Learning Objectives.

1.3 Working with Commands

Starting Commands

The main way to access commands in the AutoCAD software is to use the Ribbon. Several of the file commands are available in the Quick Access Toolbar or in the Application Menu. Some commands are available in the Status Bar or through shortcut menus. There are additional access methods, such as Tool Palettes. The names of all of the commands can also be typed in the Command Line. A table is included to help you to identify the various methods of accessing the commands.

When typing the name of a command in either the Command Line or Dynamic Input, the **AutoComplete** option automatically completes the entry when you pause as you type. It also supports mid-string search by displaying all of the commands that contain the word that you typed, as shown in Figure 1–12. You can then scroll through the list and select a command.

Figure 1–12

You can also click (Customize) to display the Input Settings for the AutoComplete feature.

To set specific options for the **AutoComplete** feature, right-click on the Command Line, expand Input Settings, and select from the various options, such as the ability to search for system variables or to set the delay response time, as shown in Figure 1–13.

Figure 1–13

If you need to stop a command, press <Esc> to cancel. You might need to press <Esc> more than once.

As you work in the AutoCAD software, the software prompts you for the information that is required to complete each command. These prompts are displayed in the drawing window near the cursor and in the Command Line. It is crucial that you read the command prompts as you work, as shown in Figure 1–14.

Instructional Content

Each chapter is split into a series of sections of instructional content on specific topics. These lectures include the descriptions, step-by-step procedures, figures, hints, and information you need to achieve the chapter's Learning Objectives.

Side notes

Side notes are hints or additional information for the current topic.

© 2015 ASCENT - Center for Technical Knowledge   1–9

Practice 1c   Saving a Drawing File

Practice Objectives
- Open and save a drawing.
- Modify the **Automatic Saves** option.

Estimated time for completion: under 5 minutes

In this practice you will open a drawing, save it, and modify the **Automatic saves** option, as shown in Figure 1–61.

Figure 1–61

1. Open **Building Valley-M.dwg** from your class files folder.
2. In the Quick Access Toolbar, click (Save). In the Command Line, _QSAVE displays indicating that the AutoCAD software has performed a quick save.
3. In the Application Menu, click [Options] to open the Options dialog box.
4. In the Open and Save tab, change the time for Automatic save to 15 minutes.

Practice Objectives

Practices

Practices enable you to use the software to perform a hands-on review of a topic.

Some practices require you to use prepared practice files, which can be downloaded from the link found on the Practice Files page.

Chapter Review Questions

1. How do you switch from the drawing window to the text window?
   a. Use the icons in the Status Bar.
   b. Press <Tab>.
   c. Press <F2>.
   d. Press the <Spacebar>.
2. How can you cancel a command using the keyboard?
   a. Press <F2>.
   b. Press <Esc>.
   c. Press <Ctrl>.
   d. Press <Delete>.
3. What is the quickest way to repeat a command?
   a. Press <Esc>.
   b. Press <F2>.
   c. Press <Enter>.
   d. Press <Ctrl>.
4. To display a specific Ribbon panel, you can right-click on the Ribbon and select the required panel in the shortcut menu.
   a. True
   b. False
5. How are points specified in the AutoCAD Cartesian workspace?
   a. X value x Y value

Chapter Review Questions

Chapter review questions, located at the end of each chapter, enable you to review the key concepts and learning objectives of the chapter.

Command Summary

The Command Summary is located at the end of each chapter. It contains a list of the software commands that are used throughout the chapter, and provides information on where the command is found in the software.

Autodesk Certification Exam Appendix

This appendix includes a list of the topics and objectives for the Autodesk Certification exams, and the chapter and section in which the relevant content can be found.

Icons in this Student Guide

The following icons are used to help you quickly and easily find helpful information.

New in 2017	Indicates items that are new in the Civil 3D 2017 (R1) software.
Enhanced in 2017	Indicates items that have been enhanced in the Civil 3D 2017 (R1) software.

Practice Files

To download the practice files for this student guide, use the following steps:

1. Type the URL shown below into the address bar of your Internet browser. The URL must be typed **exactly as shown**. If you are using an ASCENT ebook, you can click on the link to download the file.

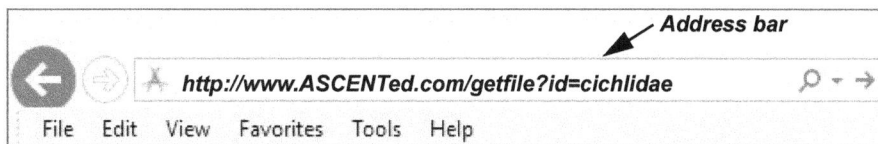

Address bar

http://www.ASCENTed.com/getfile?id=cichlidae

File   Edit   View   Favorites   Tools   Help

2. Press <Enter> to download the .ZIP file that contains the Practice Files.

3. Once the download is complete, unzip the file to a local folder. The unzipped file contains an .EXE file.

4. Double-click on the .EXE file and follow the instructions to automatically install the Practice Files on the C:\ drive of your computer.

   Do not change the location in which the Practice Files folder is installed. Doing so can cause errors when completing the practices in this student guide.

http://www.ASCENTed.com/getfile?id=cichlidae

Stay Informed!

Interested in receiving information about upcoming promotional offers, educational events, invitations to complimentary webcasts, and discounts? If so, please visit:

www.ASCENTed.com/updates/

Help us improve our product by completing the following survey:

www.ASCENTed.com/feedback

You can also contact us at: *feedback@ASCENTed.com*

The AutoCAD Civil 3D Interface

In this chapter, you learn about the AutoCAD® Civil 3D® software interface and terminology. You learn how to navigate the available workspaces, the Toolspace, and how to work in a dynamic model environment. You also learn how to use styles across multiple models, to ensure that your drawings adhere to specific standards.

Learning Objectives in this Chapter

- Switch between the AutoCAD Civil 3D tools, 2D drafting and annotation tools, 3D modeling tools, and planning and analysis tools by changing the workspace.
- Locate the basic features and commands of the AutoCAD Civil 3D software interface which include the Ribbon, Drawing Window, Command Line, Toolspace, etc.
- Access commands by right-clicking on an object or collection of objects in the Prospector and Settings tabs in the Toolspace.
- Access predefined reports and create custom reports to be able to share useful engineering data about AEC objects in a drawing.
- Create and assign object and label styles to correctly display AutoCAD Civil 3D objects for printing and other purposes.

1.1 Product Overview

The AutoCAD Civil 3D software supports a wide range of Survey and Civil Engineering tasks. It creates intelligent relationships between objects so that design changes can be updated dynamically.

- The AutoCAD Civil 3D software uses dynamic objects for points, alignments, profiles, terrain models, pipe networks, etc. Objects can update when data changes. For example, if an alignment changes, its associated profiles and sections update automatically. Commands can be safely undone in the software without the graphics becoming out-of-date with survey and design data.

- These objects are style-based and dynamic, which streamlines object creation and editing.

- AutoCAD Civil 3D objects (surfaces, alignments, etc.) are often stored directly inside drawing files. The only time they are not is when working with the Autodesk Data Management System (Vault), shortcuts, or a survey database.

- The AutoCAD Civil 3D software, unlike the AutoCAD® Land Desktop software, supports a multiple document interface. This means that more than one drawing file can be open in the same session of the AutoCAD Civil 3D software at the same time. Users of AutoCAD Land Desktop software who are going to use the AutoCAD Civil 3D software, should be aware that, by default, opening a second drawing does not automatically close any currently open drawings.

- The AutoCAD Civil 3D software can be launched by selecting its icon on the desktop or by accessing the command through the Start menu. Depending on the installed version of the software, the icon indicates Imperial or Metric, as shown in Figure 1-1. Once launched, the software initiates with the standard AutoCAD Civil 3D profile. You can also customize the shortcut to have the software launch with a project based setting. This is accomplished using a custom profile.

Civil 3D 2017
Metric

Figure 1–1

1.2 AutoCAD Civil 3D Workspaces

When the AutoCAD Civil 3D software is launched for the first time, a *Start* tab window displays, as shown in Figure 1–2. This window enables you to complete several actions:

- Create new drawings from template files (1)

- Open existing files (2)

- Open a sheet set (3)

- Download online templates (4)

- Open example drawings (5)

- Review and open recent documents (6)

- Sign in to the Autodesk 360 service (7)

- Send feedback to Autodesk about the AutoCAD Civil 3D software (8)

The *Start* tab is persistent even when other drawings are open. This makes it easier and faster to open or start new drawings.

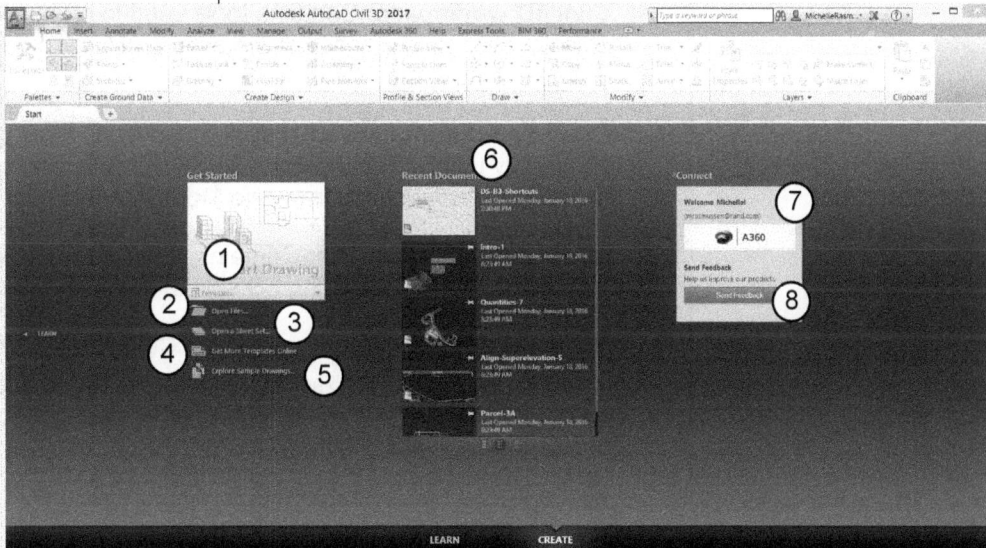

Figure 1–2

It is recommended that you stay in the Civil 3D workspace most of the time. As a review, AutoCAD® Workspaces are saved groupings of menus, toolbars, and palettes, which can be customized as required for specific tasks. You can modify the default Workspaces supplied with the AutoCAD Civil 3D software or create your own. In this material, you work with the Civil 3D workspace, which includes a complete list of AutoCAD Civil 3D-specific ribbons, drop-down menus, and tools.

Workspaces can be changed using the Workspaces switching icon in the lower right corner of the Status Bar, as shown in Figure 1–3. They can also be modified using the **CUI** command.

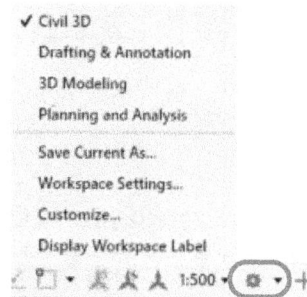

Figure 1–3

Each of the ribbons from the workspaces are shown in order in Figure 1–4 and include the following:

- **Civil 3D workspace:** Contains tools used to create AEC objects, such as surfaces, alignments, profiles, corridors, grading objects, etc.

- **Drafting & Annotation workspace:** Contains tools that are commonly used in the standard AutoCAD software, such as those in the *Home* tab>Draw and Modify panels.

- **3D Modeling workspace:** Contains standard AutoCAD 3D modeling tools for designing 3D solids, mesh surfaces, etc.

- **Planning and Analysis workspace:** Contains tools found in the AutoCAD® Map 3D® software that help you to attach and analyze GIS data for more efficient planning of projects before starting your design.

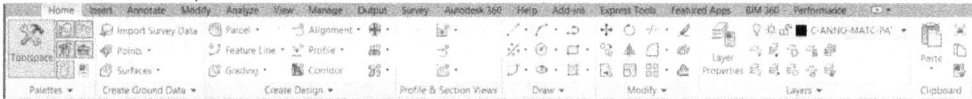

Civil 3D workspace

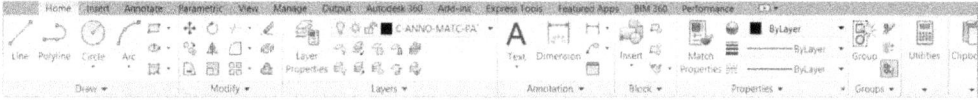

Drafting & Annotation workspace

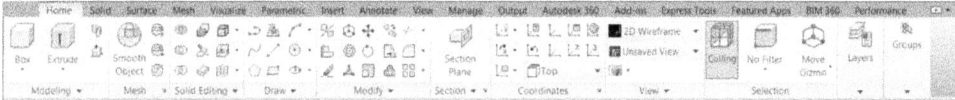

3D Modeling workspace

Planning and Analysis workspace

Figure 1–4

1.3 The AutoCAD Civil 3D User Interface

The AutoCAD Civil 3D software user interface is shown in Figure 1–5.

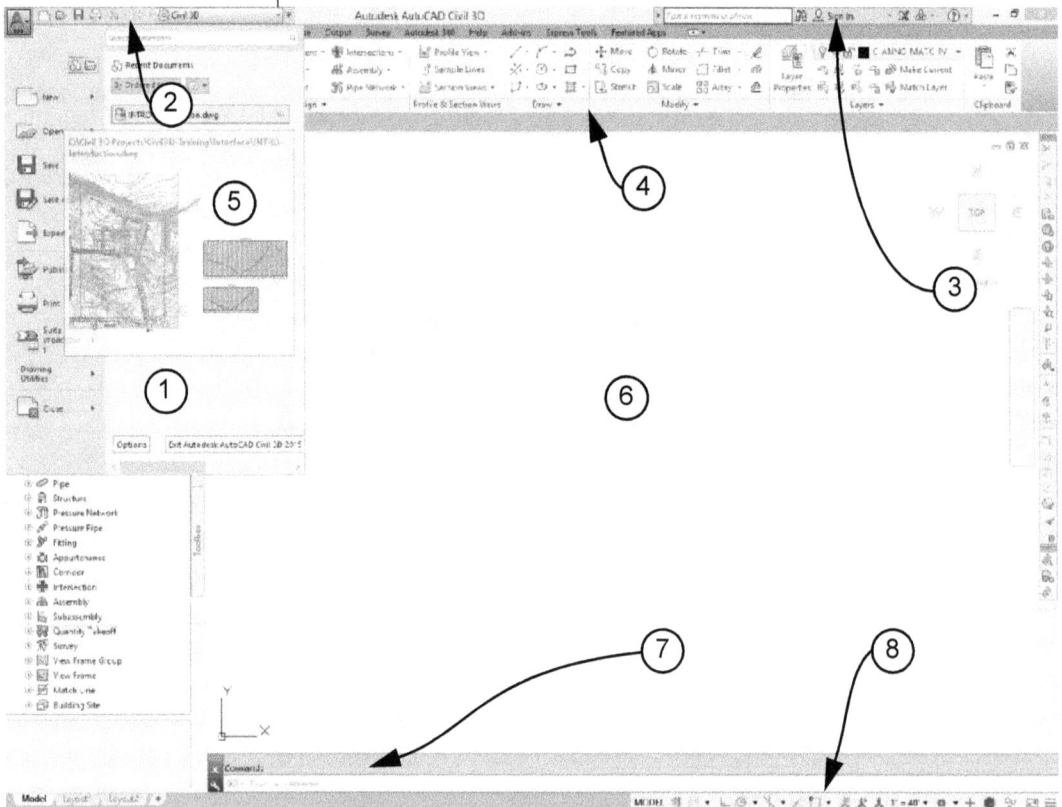

Figure 1–5

1. Application Menu	5. Tooltips
2. Quick Access Toolbar	6. Drawing Window
3. InfoCenter	7. Command Line
4. Ribbon	8. Status Bar

1. Application Menu

The *Application Menu* provides access to commands, settings, and documents, as shown in Figure 1–6. With the Application Menu you can:

- Browse the menus available in the AutoCAD Civil 3D software.

- Perform a search of menus, menu actions, tooltips, and command prompt text strings.

- Browse for recent documents, currently open documents, and commands you have recently executed.

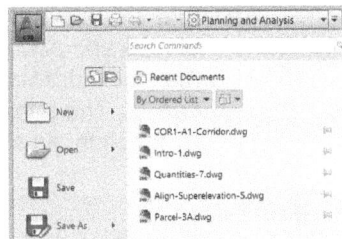

Figure 1–6

2. Quick Access Toolbar

The *Quick Access Toolbar* provides access to commonly used commands, such as **Open**, **Save**, **Print**, etc. You can add an unlimited number of tools to the Quick Access Toolbar by clicking the down arrow on the right, as shown in Figure 1–7.

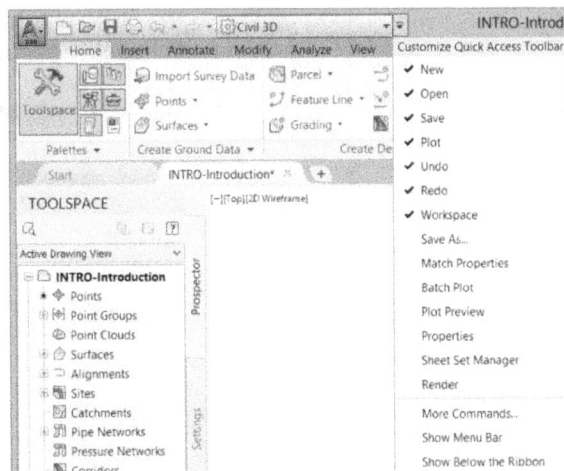

Figure 1–7

3. InfoCenter

The *InfoCenter* enables you to quickly search for help. You can specify which Help documents to search, and collapse or expand the search field (as shown in Figure 1–8) to save screen space. You can also sign in to the A360 service, where you can share files with other design team members using the cloud.

Figure 1–8

4. Ribbon

The *Ribbon* provides a single, compact location for *commands* that are relevant to the current task. It contains tools in a series of *tabs* and *panels* to reduce clutter in the application and maximize drawing space. Selecting a tab displays a series of panels. The panels contain a variety of tools, which are grouped by function, as shown in Figure 1–9.

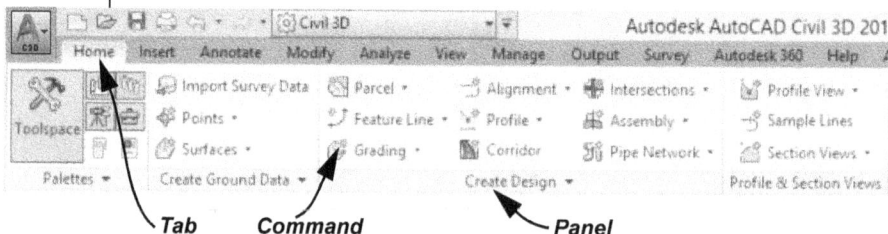

Figure 1–9

Clicking the drop-down arrow expands the panel to display additional tools, as shown in Figure 1–10. Clicking an arrow pointing to the bottom right opens the tool's dialog box, which contains additional options.

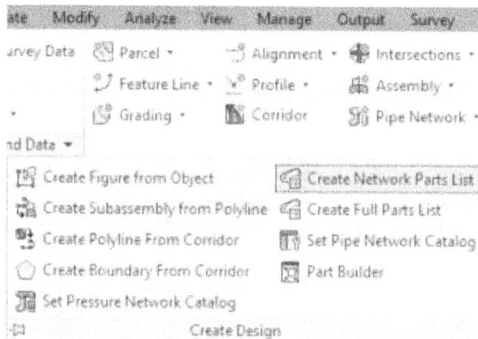

Figure 1–10

You can minimize the ribbon by clicking the arrow successively, as shown in Figure 1–11.

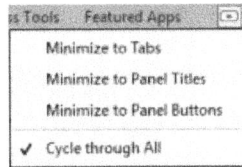

Figure 1–11

There are two classifications of ribbons: static and contextual.

• **Static ribbons:** Display the most commonly used tabs, panels, and commands.

• **Contextual ribbons:** Display the tabs, panels, and commands that are only applicable to the selected object. An example of a contextual ribbon is shown in Figure 1–12.

AEC ribbon

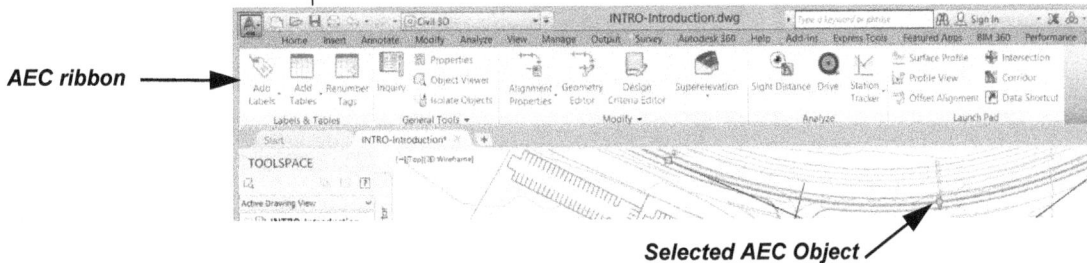

Selected AEC Object

Figure 1–12

Enhanced in 2017

5. Tooltips

Tooltips display the item's name, a short description, and sometimes a graphic. They provide information about tools, commands, and drawing objects, as shown in Figure 1–13.

Tooltips can be turned off and display delays can be set in the Options dialog box> Display tab.

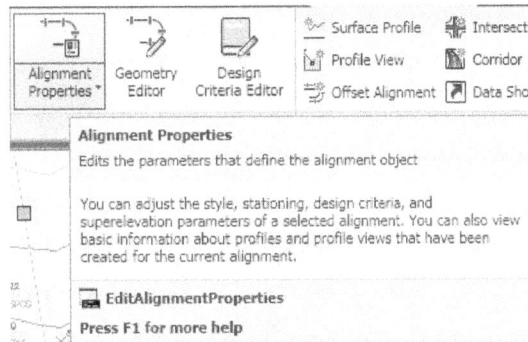

Figure 1–13

6. Drawing Window

The *Drawing Window* is the area of the screen where the drawing displays.

7. Command Line

The *Command Line* is a text window that is located at the bottom of the screen and displays command prompts and a history of commands, as shown in Figure 1–14.

To toggle the Command Line display on or off, press <Ctrl>+<9>.

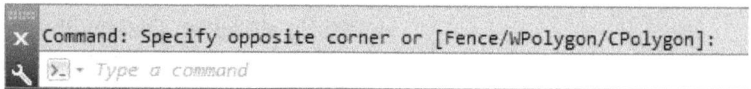

Command: Specify opposite corner or [Fence/WPolygon/CPolygon]:

Type a command

Figure 1–14

8. Status Bar

The *Status Bar* enables you to change many of AutoCAD's drafting settings, such as Snap, Grid, and Object Snap, as shown in Figure 1–15.

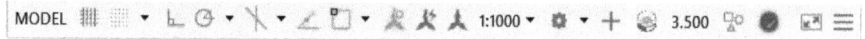

Figure 1–15

Practice 1a

Overview of the AutoCAD Civil 3D User Interface

Estimated time for completion: 5 minutes

Practice Objective

- Locate the basic features and commands of the AutoCAD Civil 3D software interface which includes the ribbon, Toolspace, Drawing Window, Command Line, etc.

In this practice you will become familiar with AutoCAD Civil 3D's capabilities and learn about its interface.

Task 1 - Set up the practice.

1. If required, start the AutoCAD Civil 3D software by double-clicking (Civil 3D 2017 Metric) on the desktop.

    You can add a folder shortcut in the pane on the left side of the dialog box. This enables you to quickly access the practice folder in the Open dialog box.

2. Click (Open) on the *Start* tab, or expand (Application Menu) and select **Open**. In the Select File dialog box, browse to the *C:\Civil 3D for Surveyors Practice Files* folder.

3. Expand the Tools drop-down list and select **Add Current Folder to Places**, as shown in Figure 1–16.

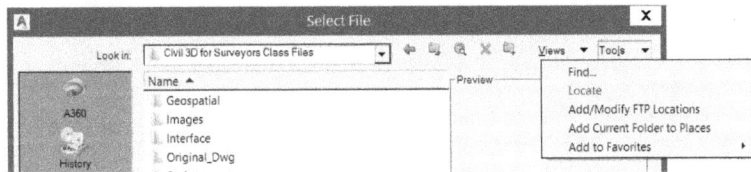

Figure 1–16

4. Double-click on the *Interface* folder to display its contents. Select **INTRO-Introduction.dwg** and then select **Open**.

*If prompted to save the changes to your Places List, click **Yes**.*

5. In the Status Bar, confirm that **Civil 3D** is the active Workspace. The Workspace icon is located in the Status Bar (at the bottom right of the interface) and in the Quick Access Toolbar (at the top left of the interface), as shown in Figure 1–17.

Figure 1–17

6. Select the *Home* tab and ensure that the Layers panel is displayed. If it is not, right-click anywhere on the ribbon and select **Layers**, as shown in Figure 1–18.

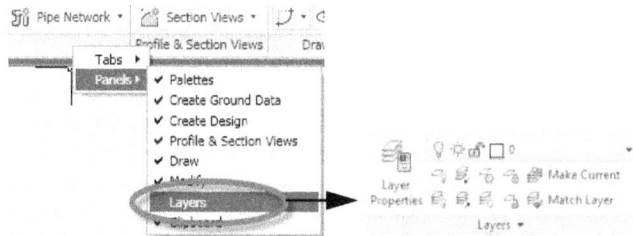

Figure 1–18

By default, the Toolspace is docked to the left side of your drawing window.

7. Locate the AutoCAD Civil 3D Toolspace (as shown in Figure 1–19). If you cannot find it, click ✎ (Toolspace) in the *Home* tab>Palettes panel.

Figure 1–19

8. Save the drawing as **Example 1.dwg**. Expand (Application Menu) and select **Save As**. In the *File Name* field, type **Example 1**, and click **Save**.

Task 2 - Review AutoCAD Civil 3D's Dynamic Object Model.

*Alternatively, select the View tab>Views panel, expand the Named Views drop-down list and select **Aln-Profile**.*

1. In the top-left corner of the drawing window, select **Top**, expand *Custom Model Views* and select **Aln-Profile**, as shown in Figure 1–20. This will zoom into a preset view of the alignment and the surface profile to the right.

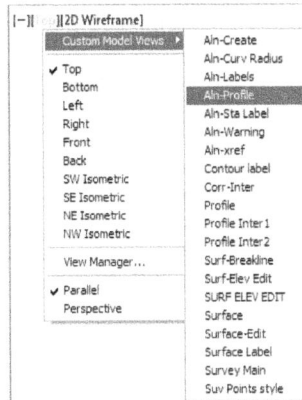

Figure 1–20

If the alignment is displaying labels, they also update.

2. Select the **Jeffries Ranch Rd** alignment to activate its grips, as shown in Figure 1–21. (If you have difficulty selecting the alignment, you might need to set the draw order so that it is on top of all of the other objects.) Select the eastern grip and reposition it. The alignment and profile both update.

Figure 1–21

3. Hover the cursor near the alignment in its new position. The station, offset, and surface elevation information are displayed through tooltips.

4. Close the drawing without saving.

1.4 AutoCAD Civil 3D Toolspace

The AutoCAD Civil 3D software uses a Toolspace to manage objects, settings, and styles. Each tab uses a hierarchical tree interface to manage objects, settings, and styles. Branches in these hierarchical trees are referred to in the AutoCAD Civil 3D software as *collections*. The Toolspace is an interactive data management tool.

Toolspace operates similar to an AutoCAD tool palette in that it can be resized, set to dock or float, and when floating can be set to auto-hide. The Toolspace is shown floating in Figure 1–22 and docked in Figure 1–23.

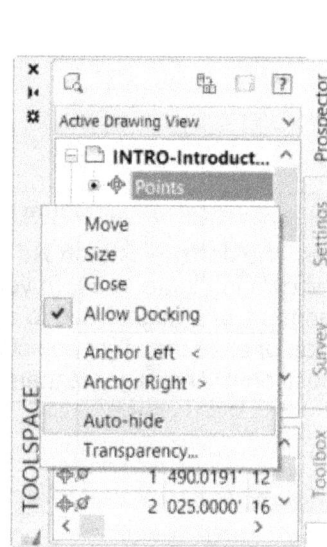

Figure 1–22

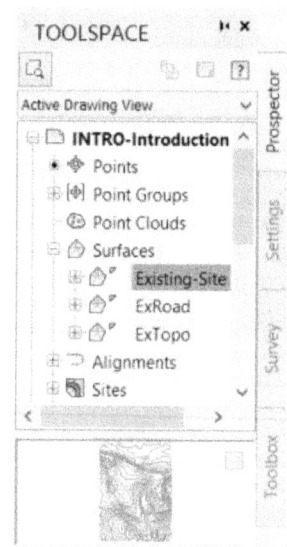

Figure 1–23

Right-clicking on a collection or on an individual object provides many commonly used commands in the shortcut menus.

- The Toolspace can be closed by selecting the **X** in the upper left or right corner.

- Once closed, it can be opened by clicking

  (Toolspace) in the *Home* tab>Palettes panel.

Prospector Tab

The *Prospector* tab lists the AutoCAD Civil 3D objects that are present in open drawings and other important information. Its hierarchical structure dynamically manages and displays objects and their data. As objects are created or deleted, they are removed from the *Prospector*. A drop-down list at the top contains the following options:

- **Active Drawing View:** Displays only the AutoCAD Civil 3D objects that are present in the active drawing. If you switch to another drawing, the tree updates to reflect the currently active drawing.

- **Master View:** Displays a list of all open drawings and their objects, project information, and a list of drawing templates. The name of the active drawing is highlighted.

The *Prospector* tab is shown in Figure 1–24.

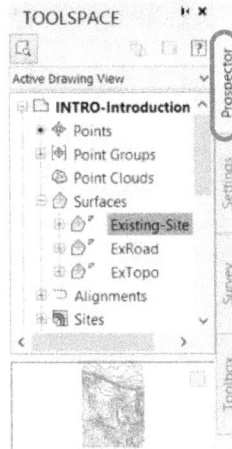

Figure 1–24

- To toggle the display of the *Prospector* tab on or off, click

  (Prospector) in the *Home* tab>Palettes panel.

- Each object type (Points, Point Groups, Alignments, Surfaces, etc.) is allotted a collection, and objects present in a drawing are listed below the respective collection.

- The bottom of the *Prospector* tab displays a list view of items in the highlighted collection or a preview of an object that has been selected in the Prospector.

- The icon at the top of the *Prospector* tab controls how items in the Prospector tree are displayed. Icons next to objects provide additional information about the object. A list of common icons is as follows:

	Toggles the Toolspace item preview on or off.
	Opens (or closes) the Panorama window. This window only opens if vistas are available to be displayed in the Panorama.
	Opens the AutoCAD Civil 3D Help system.
	Indicates that the object is currently locked for editing.
	Indicates that the object is referenced by another object. In the *Settings* tab, this also indicates that a style is in use in the current drawing.
	Indicates that the object is being referenced from another drawing file (such as through a shortcut or Vault reference).
	Indicates that the object is out of date and needs to be rebuilt, or is violating specified design constraints.
	Indicates that a project object (such as a point or surface) has been modified since it was included in the current drawing.
	Indicates that you have modified a project object in your current drawing and that those modifications have yet to be updated to the project.

Settings Tab

The *Settings* tab is used to configure how the AutoCAD Civil 3D software operates and the way AutoCAD Civil 3D objects are displayed and printed, as shown in Figure 1–25.

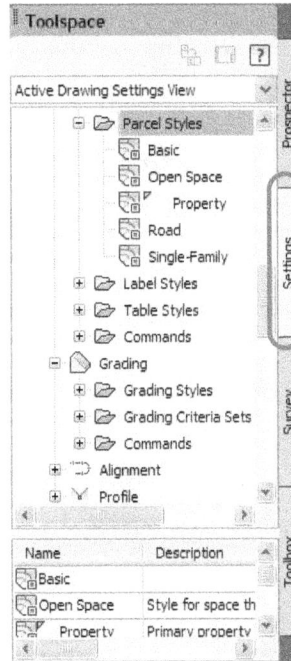

Figure 1–25

Different settings are accessed by right-clicking on the name of a drawing file or on one of the collections located inside the tab.

The collections (such as the **Parcel** collection shown in Figure 1–25) can contain object styles, label styles, command settings, and related controls.

Changes to settings affect all lower items in the tree. For example, assigning an overall text height in the drawing's Edit Label Style Defaults dialog box applies that height to all other settings and styles in the drawing. Applying the same setting in the **Surface** collection's Edit Label Style Defaults only applies the text height to the surface label styles. (Lower items in the tree and styles can be set to override these changes individually as required.)

- All drawing settings originate from the template used to create an AutoCAD Civil 3D drawing.

- To toggle the display of the *Settings* tab on or off, click

  (Settings) in the *Home* tab>Palettes panel.

Survey Tab

To toggle the Survey tab display on or off, click

🎥 *(Survey) in the Home tab>Palettes panel.*

The *Survey* tab is used to manage survey observations data, as shown in Figure 1–26. Selecting this tab enables you to create a survey database, a survey network, points, and figures, and import and edit survey observation data.

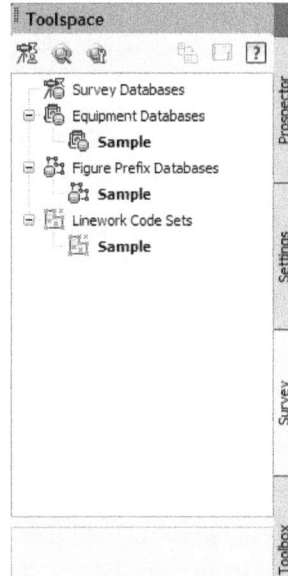

Figure 1–26

Toolbox Tab

The Toolbox can be toggled on and off by clicking

🧰 *(Toolbox) in the Home tab>Palettes panel.*

The *Toolbox* tab is used to access the Reports Manager and to add custom tools to the AutoCAD Civil 3D interface, as shown in Figure 1–27.

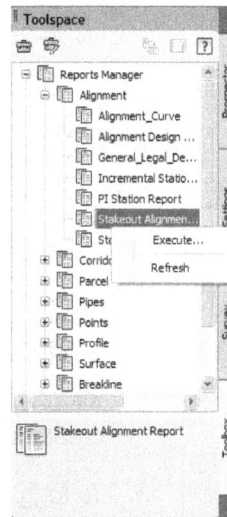

Figure 1–27

The Reports Manager, the only set of tools that displays in the toolbox by default, enables you to generate a large variety of survey and design reports. For example, to launch a Stakeout Alignment Report, right-click on it in the **Alignments** collection and select **Execute**.

The icons in the upper left area of the *Toolbox* tab enable you to:

	Open the Edit Report Settings dialog box, in which you can assign settings for all report types. These settings include items, such as the name to display in the report.
	Open the Toolbox Editor, in which you can add custom reports and other tools.

Once a report has been executed, it can be saved in multiple formats, including .HTML, .DOC, .XLS, .TXT, and .PDF. To save it in a format other than the default .HTML, expand Files of type and select the type of file required, as shown in Figure 1–28.

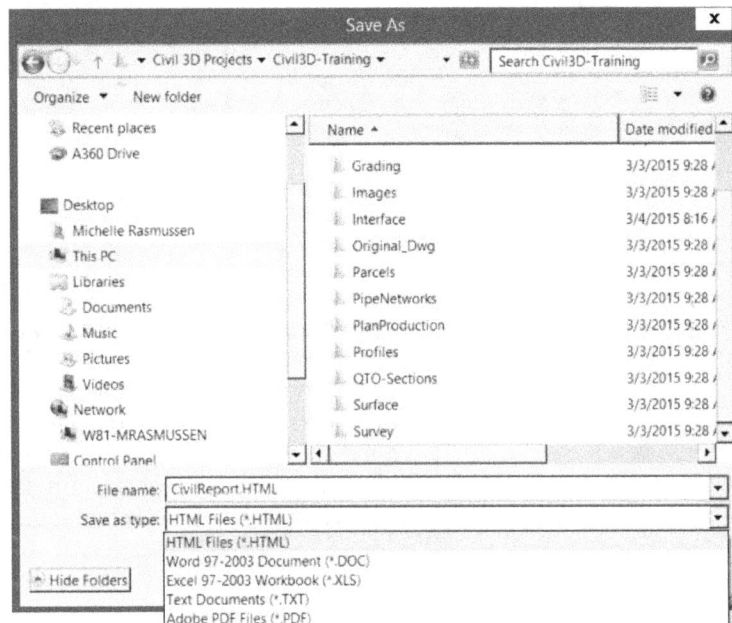

Figure 1–28

1.5 AutoCAD Civil 3D Panorama

The AutoCAD Civil 3D software includes a multi-purpose grid data viewer called the *Panorama window*. It is similar to an AutoCAD tool palette in that it can be docked or floating, and set to auto-hide. Each tab in the Panorama is called a *Vista*. The Panorama can be opened from the AutoCAD Civil 3D Toolspace by clicking (Panorama), and can be closed by selecting the **X** in the upper left or right corner of the window. You can only display the Panorama after launching a command that uses it, such as **Edit Points** (right-click on a Point Group in the *Prospector* tab in the Toolspace to access this option). The Panorama can display many different kinds of data, such as point properties, alignment, and profile data, as shown in Figure 1–29.

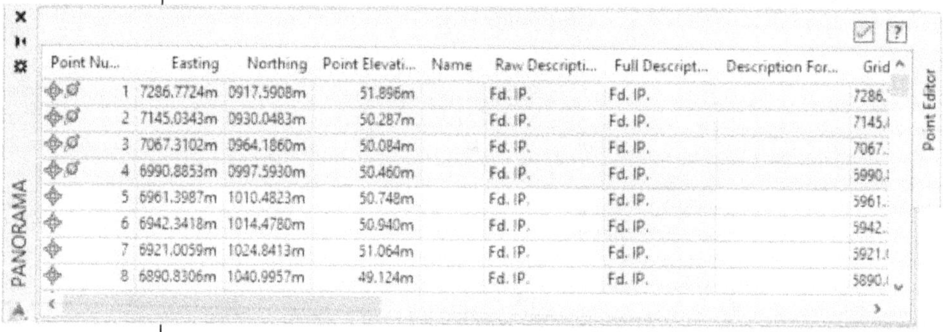

Figure 1–29

The Panorama can also display a special Vista called the *Event Viewer*, as shown in Figure 1–30. The *Event Viewer* opens prompting you about the status of the performed action. If every thing was successful, it displays a white circle containing a blue **i**, indicating that it is for informational purposes only. When there are items of interest or an item needs attention, a yellow triangle containing a black **!** (exclamation point) displays.

When the AutoCAD Civil 3D software encounters a processing error, such as when surface breaklines cross or a road model passes over the edge of the existing ground surface, a red circle containing a white **x** displays. When working through a large number of events, you can use **Action>Clear All Events** to clear all of the old entries in the Panorama.

*If a Panorama contains multiple Vistas, selecting a green checkmark only closes the current Vista. To close (hide) the Panorama, select the **X** in the top right or left corner.*

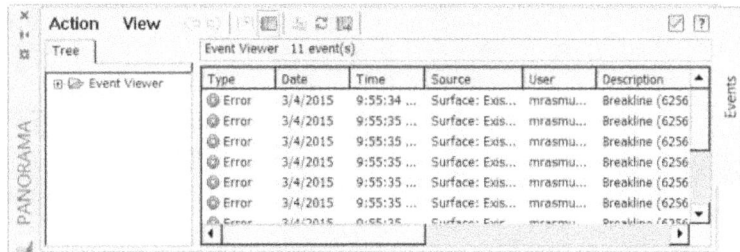

Figure 1–30

Practice 1b

AutoCAD Civil 3D Toolspace

Practice Objective

Estimated time for completion: 10 minutes

- Access commands and change the drawing using the AutoCAD Civil 3D Toolspace.

In this practice you will explore the tabs in the AutoCAD Civil 3D Toolspace.

Task 1 - Review the Prospector tab.

If the Toolspace is not displayed, click

✎ *(Toolspace) in the Home tab>Palettes panel.*

1. Open **INTRO-Introduction.dwg** from the *C:\Civil 3D for Surveyors Practice Files\Interface* folder.

2. Ensure that the AutoCAD Civil 3D Toolspace is displayed.

3. Select the *Prospector* tab to make it active. (The tabs are listed vertically along the right side of the Toolspace.)

4. Select the **+** signs to open the collections and the **-** signs to close them. Items displayed in the *Prospector* tab are the design data (also known as AEC objects) currently in the drawing file (such as points, alignments, and surfaces).

5. Collections, such as **Points**, do not have a **+** or **-** sign because they are not intended to be expanded in the tree view of the *Prospector*. Select the **Points** collection and the list view displays in the Preview area, describing the AutoCAD Civil 3D points that are currently in the drawing file.

6. Under the **Surfaces** collection, look for the surface called **ExTopo**. Expand its branch and the *Definition* area inside it. Highlight the items below (breaklines, boundaries, etc.) and note the components displayed in the list view.

7. With the **ExTopo** surface breaklines highlighted in the list view, right-click on **Ridge** and note the commands available in the shortcut menu, as shown on the left in Figure 1–31. Select **Zoom to**.

Similar shortcut menus are available for nearly all of the objects displayed in the Prospector tab.

8. Expand the **Point Groups** and select the **Boundary Pin Survey** point group. In the *Preview* area at the bottom, press <Shift> to select both point numbers **2** and **3**, as shown on the right in Figure 1–31. Right-click and select **Zoom To**. Although the points are not displayed, the software knows where they reside in the drawing.

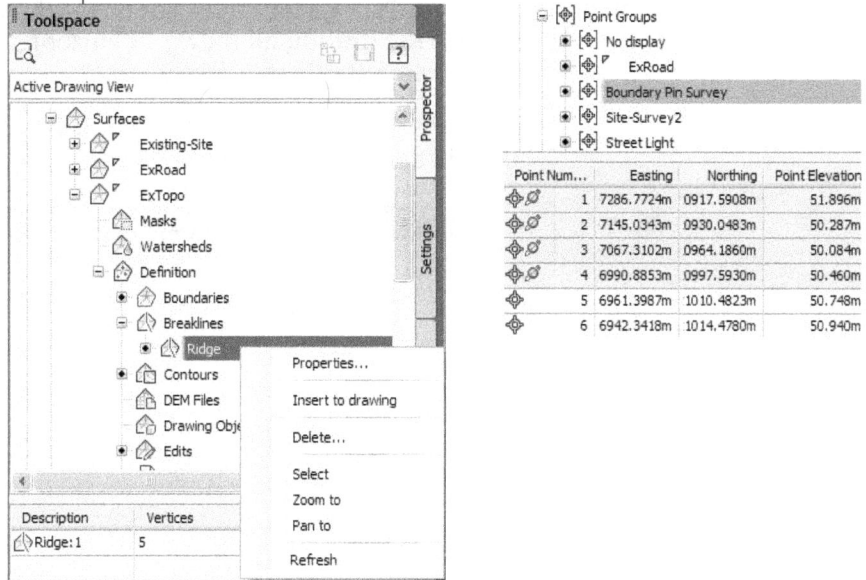

Figure 1–31

Task 2 - Review the Settings tab.

1. In the AutoCAD Civil 3D Toolspace, select the *Settings* tab, as shown in Figure 1–32.

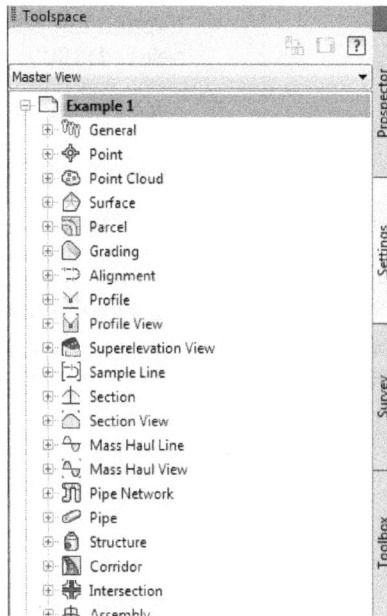

Figure 1–32

2. In the *Settings* tab, right-click on the drawing's name (**INTRO-Introduction.dwg**, at the top), and select **Edit Drawing Settings**.

3. In the Drawing Settings dialog box, select the *Units and Zone* tab, as shown in Figure 1–33.

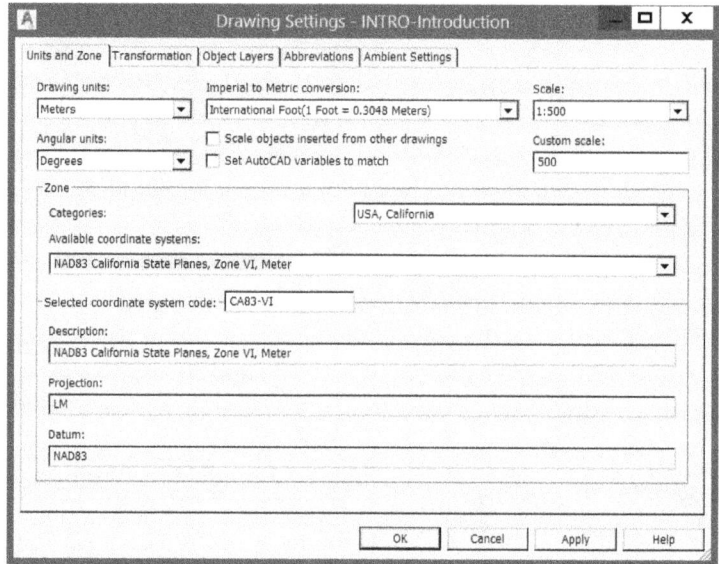

Figure 1–33

4. Expand the Scale drop-down list in the upper right corner and select **1:1000**.

5. Note the coordinate systems that are available in the *Zone* area, such as **CA83-VI**, **NAD83 California State Planes**, **Zone VI**, and **Meter**.

6. Click **OK** to close the dialog box.

7. You can also change the Model Space display scale using the **Annotation** icon in the Status Bar. Change it to read **1:500**. Note that as you change the scale, all of the labels also change in size, as shown in Figure 1–34.

Because AutoCAD Civil 3D labels are annotative, the label annotation size has changed to match the new Drawing Scale.

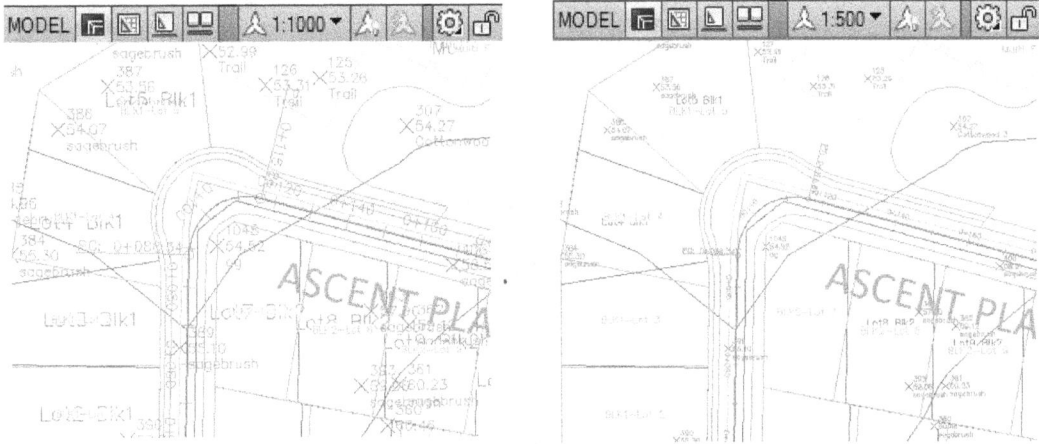

Figure 1–34

8. You can change the display of the contours by changing the style of the surface. In the drawing, select the surface object so that the contextual tab displays in the ribbon, as shown in Figure 1–35.

Figure 1–35

Alternatively, you can right-click and select **Surface Properties**

9. In the *Modify* tab, click [icon] (Surface Properties).

10. In the *Information* tab, select the drop-down arrow for the surface style, as shown in Figure 1–36. Select any of the predefined styles and click **Apply** to apply the selected style to the surface to preview the results before they are displayed in the dialog box.

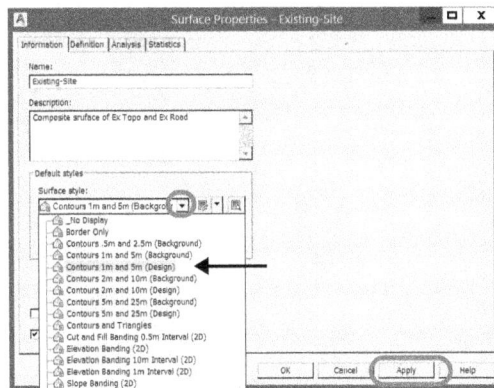

Figure 1–36

11. Click **OK** to exit the Surface Properties dialog box.

12. Save the drawing.

Task 3 - Review AutoCAD Civil 3D's Reports Manager.

1. In the *Toolbox* tab, expand Reports Manager>Alignment, then right-click on **PI Station Report**, and select **Execute,** as shown in Figure 1–37.

*As a shortcut, you can double-click to launch the **Report** without having to select the **Execute** command.*

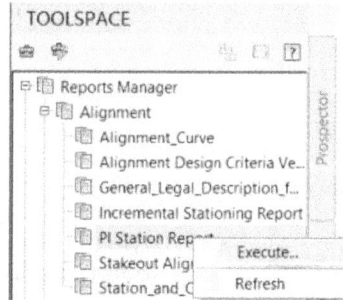

Figure 1–37

2. Accept all of the defaults and click **Create Report**. The report displays, as shown in Figure 1–38.

Alignment PI Station Report

Client:
Client
Client Company
Address 1
Date: 5/16/2012 1:03:36 PM

Prepared by:
Preparer
Your Company Name
123 Main Street

Alignment Name: Ascent PI
Description:
Station Range: Start: 0+000.00, End: 0+212.96

PI Station	Northing	Easting	Distance	Direction
0+000.00	620,770.0472m	1,906,991.4759m		
			107.646m	N1° 18' 05"E
0+107.65	620,877.6655m	1,906,993.9206m		
			116.413m	S75° 18' 32"E
0+212.96	620,848.1420m	1,907,106.5278m		

Figure 1–38

3. Expand the **Surface** collection. Select **Surface Report**, right-click, and select **Execute**, as shown in Figure 1–39.

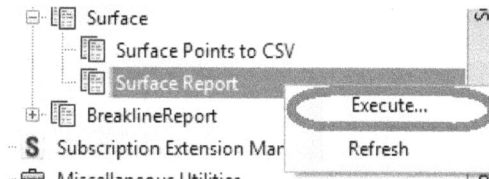

Figure 1–39

4. Accept all of the defaults and click **OK**. Type a filename for the saved report or accept the default. Expand the Files of type drop-down list, select **.XLS** and select **Save**. The report displays in Microsoft Excel, as shown in Figure 1–40. Review and close the report.

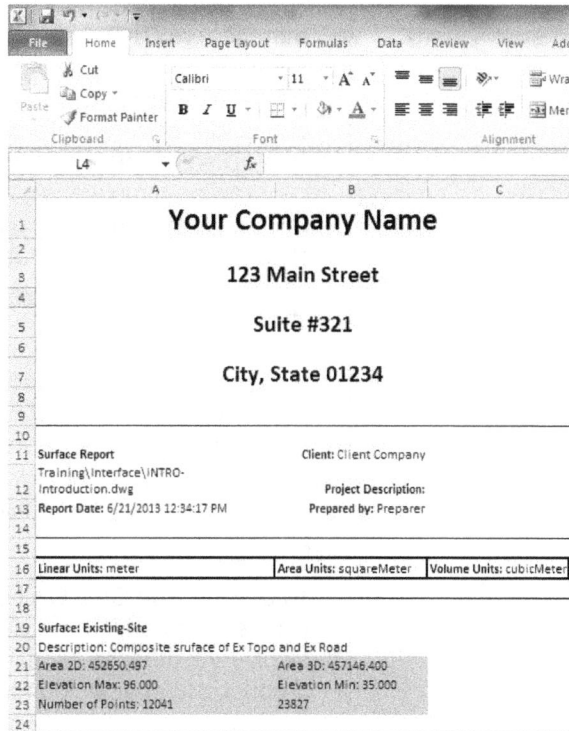

Figure 1–40

1.6 AutoCAD Civil 3D Templates, Settings, and Styles

A drawing template (.DWT extension) contains all blocks, Paper Space title sheets, settings, and layers for a new drawing. As with the AutoCAD software, a template (.DWT) file in the AutoCAD Civil 3D software is the source file from which new drawings acquire their settings, units, layers, blocks, text styles, etc., and therefore, enforces standardization. With the AutoCAD Civil 3D software, in addition to the AutoCAD components noted, the drawing template is also the source for specific AutoCAD Civil 3D styles and settings. As you learn, AutoCAD Civil 3D styles and settings (Feature and Command) have a profound impact on the appearance of objects, labels, and tables. These styles and settings also act as the primary mechanism that controls the behavior and default actions. Selecting the correct template for your intended design and standards needs is a significant component of fully using the benefits that the AutoCAD Civil 3D software offers. Therefore, it is highly recommended that all styles and setting be set up in the template file before you use the AutoCAD Civil 3D software in a project.

To use the AutoCAD Civil 3D software efficiently and effectively, you need to configure styles and settings to control the object display. All of these styles and settings affect the final delivered product and enable you to deliver a product with consistent quality.

To create a template file, use the **Save As** command and in the Save As dialog box, change the *File of Type* to **DWT**.

Drawing Settings in Detail

The values in Drawing Settings influence every aspect of the drafting environment. Each tab has values affecting a specific drawing area. For example, layer naming properties, coordinate systems, default precisions, input and output conventions, abbreviations for alignment, volume units, etc. After implementing the AutoCAD Civil 3D software, you only need to access the first two tabs.

To access Drawing Settings, in the *Settings* tab in Toolspace, select and right-click on the drawing name (at the top), and select **Edit Drawing Settings**.

Units and Zone

In the Drawing Settings dialog box, the *Units and Zone* tab (as shown in Figure 1–41), sets the Model Space plotting scale and coordinate zone for the drawing. The scale can be a custom value or selected from a drop-down list. A zone is selected from a drop-down list of worldwide categories and coordinate systems.

A drawing which has been assigned a coordinate system enables points to report their grid coordinates and/or their longitude and latitude. Conversely, when assigning a coordinate system, grid coordinates and Longitude and Latitude data can create points in a drawing.

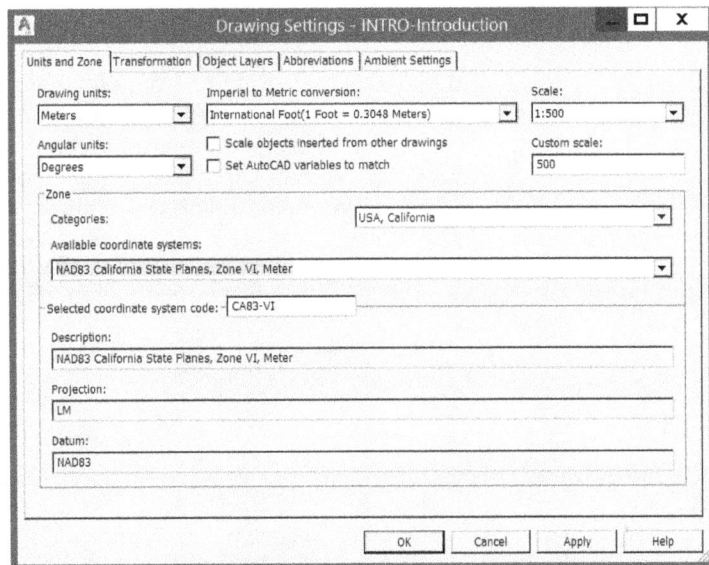

Figure 1–41

When plotting from the *Model* tab, the drawing scale in the upper right corner is the scale at which you would prefer the drawing to be printed. When in the *Model* tab, changing this scale automatically updates all AutoCAD Civil 3D annotations that are scale-dependent. (AutoCAD Civil 3D annotations are automatically resized for correct plotting in each viewport that displays them based on that viewport's scale.)

Changing the drawing scale does not automatically change the **ltscale** variable, since it assumes that you most often prefer to leave it at **ltscale = 1**. If this is not the case, you need to assign this variable manually. Refer to the AutoCAD User Guide if you need more information on variables, such as **ltscale**.

You can also set the drawing scale by assigning a different annotation scale in the Status Bar, as shown in Figure 1–42. In layouts you can change either the VP Scale or Annotation Scale and have both update.

Figure 1–42

Transformation

During the life of a project, there can be reasons to change local point coordinates to a coordinate system. The values in the *Transformation* tab (as shown in Figure 1–43), transform local coordinates to a State Plan Coordinate system, UTM system, or other defined planar system.

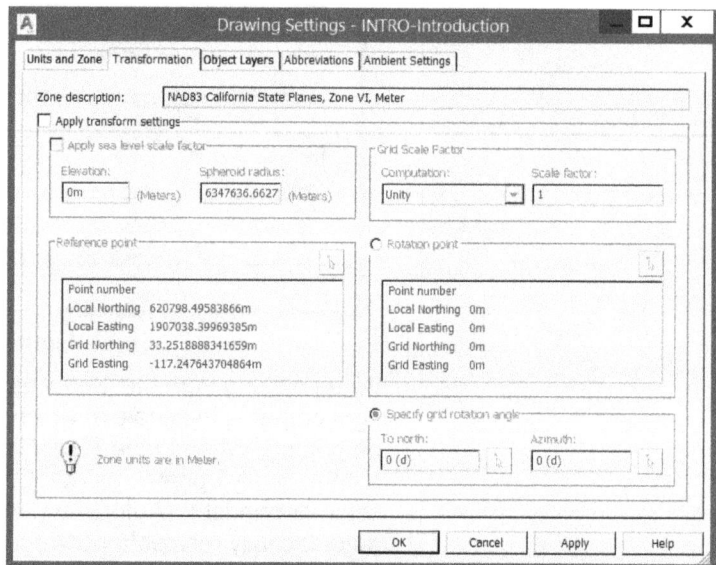

Figure 1–43

Object Layers

The *Object Layers* tab (shown in Figure 1–44), assigns layer names to AutoCAD Civil 3D objects. A modifier, which can be a prefix or a suffix, is associated with each layer's name. The value of the modifier can be anything that is typed into its *Value* field. Traditionally, the value is an * (asterisk) with a separator (a dash or underscore). The AutoCAD Civil 3D software replaces the asterisk with the name of the object of the same type. For example, the base surface layer name is **C-TOPO** with a suffix modifier of -* (a dash followed by an asterisk). When a surface named **Existing** is created, it is placed on the layer **C-TOPO-EXISTING**, and when a surface named **Base** is created it is placed on the layer **C-TOPO-BASE**.

The last column of the *Object Layers* tab enables you to lock the values. When a value is locked at this level, the AutoCAD Civil 3D software does not permit it to be changed by any lower style or setting.

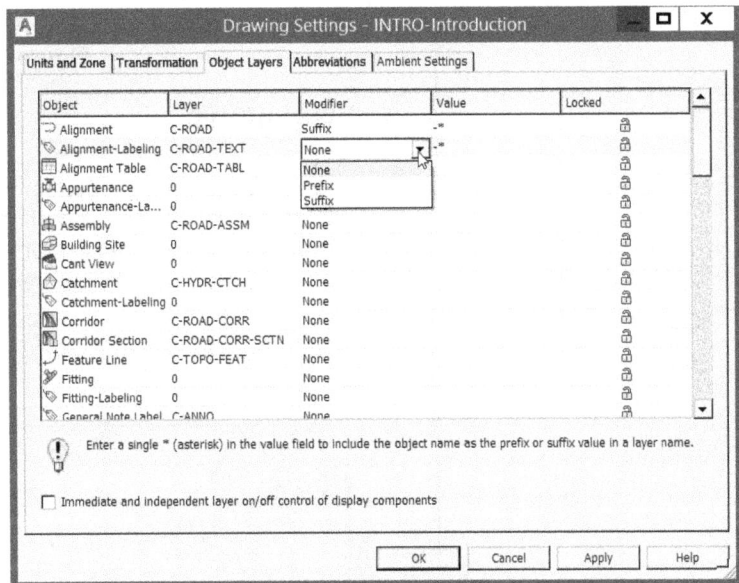

Figure 1–44

To change the listed object layers, double-click on a layer name. In the Layer Selection dialog box (shown in Figure 1–45), select the layer from the list. If the layer does not exist, click **New** in the Layer Selection dialog box. This opens a second dialog box, in which you can define a new layer for the object type.

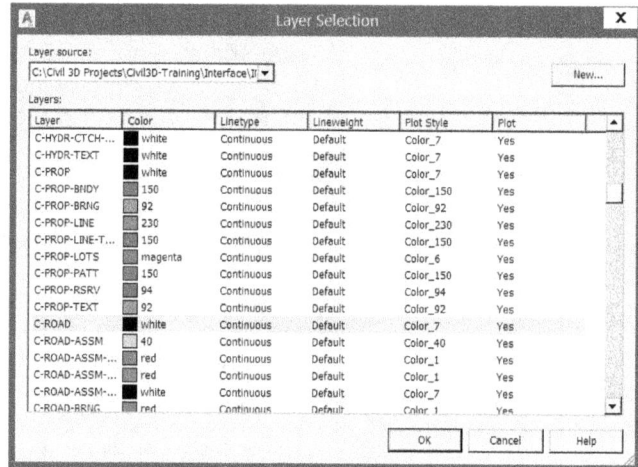

Figure 1–45

Abbreviations

The *Abbreviations* tab (shown in Figure 1–46), sets standard values for reports referencing alignment or profile data. Some entries in this panel have text format strings that define how the values associated with the abbreviation display in a label.

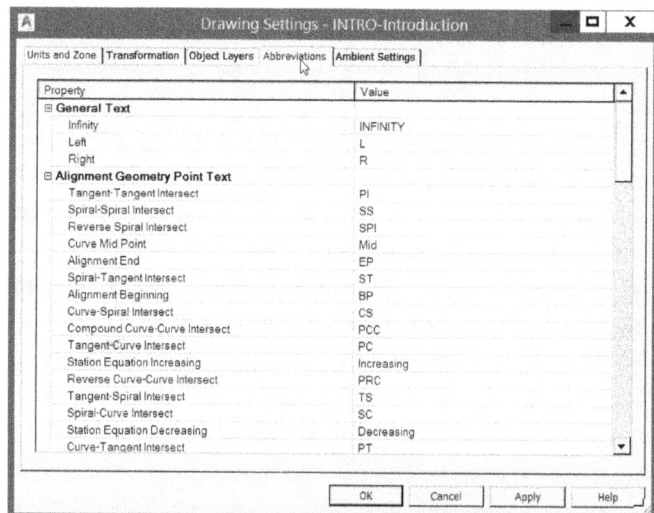

Figure 1–46

Ambient Settings

In the *Ambient Settings* tab (shown in Figure 1–47), the values influence prompting and reports. For example, the *Direction* area affects the prompting for direction input: **Decimal Degrees**, **Degrees Minutes and Seconds** (with or without spaces), or **Decimal Degrees Minutes and Seconds**. Any value set at this level affects everything (labels and commands) in the drawing.

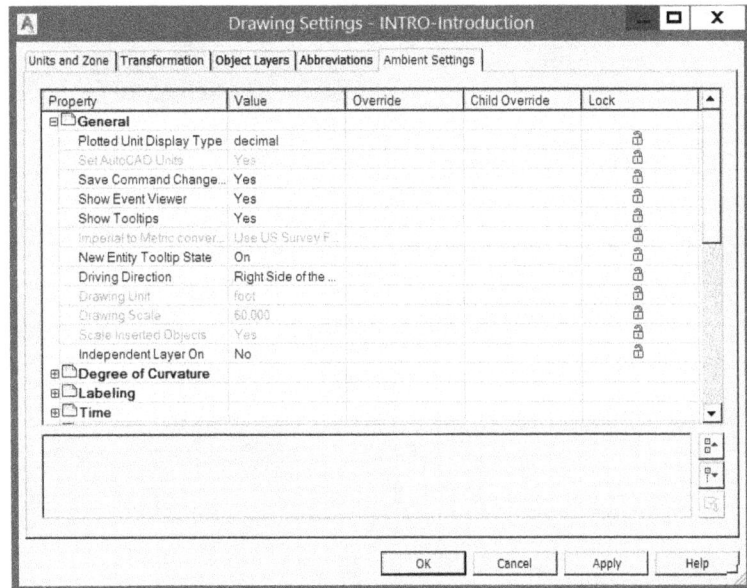

Figure 1–47

Edit Label Style Defaults

The values assigned in the Edit Label Style Defaults dialog box (shown in Figure 1–48), control text style, plan orientation, and the basic behavior of label styles. Similar to Feature Settings, this dialog box is available at the drawing level and at the individual objects level. Editing Label Style defaults at the drawing level affects all label styles in the drawing. Editing them at the object level (such as surfaces) only affects that object's labels.

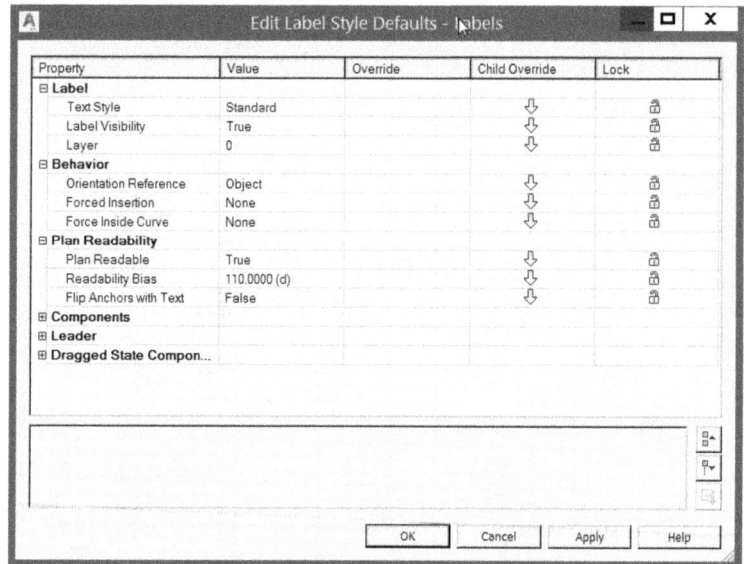

Property	Value	Override	Child Override	Lock
⊟ **Label**				
Text Style	Standard		⇩	🔒
Label Visibility	True		⇩	🔒
Layer	0		⇩	🔒
⊟ **Behavior**				
Orientation Reference	Object		⇩	🔒
Forced Insertion	None		⇩	🔒
Force Inside Curve	None		⇩	🔒
⊟ **Plan Readability**				
Plan Readable	True		⇩	🔒
Readability Bias	110.0000 (d)		⇩	🔒
Flip Anchors with Text	False		⇩	🔒
⊞ **Components**				
⊞ **Leader**				
⊞ **Dragged State Compon...**				

Figure 1–48

In the *Label, Behavior,* and *Plan Readability* areas, the values affect the overall visibility of labels, their default text style, label orientation, and the rotation angle that affects plan readability.

The values in the *Components, Leader,* and *Dragged State Components* areas affect the default text height for the label, colors for the text, leader, surrounding box, and type of leader. There are also several settings defining what happens to a label when you drag it from its original position.

Edit Autodesk LandXML Settings

The LandXML Settings dialog box (shown in Figure 1–49), provides settings that control how Autodesk LandXML data is imported and exported from the AutoCAD Civil 3D software. Autodesk LandXML is a universal format for storing Surveying and Civil Engineering data that enables you to transfer points, terrain models, alignments, etc., between different software platforms. For more information, see *www.landxml.org* and the AutoCAD Civil 3D Help system. The dialog box can be opened by right-clicking on Drawing Name in the *Settings* tab and selecting **Edit LandXMLSettings**.

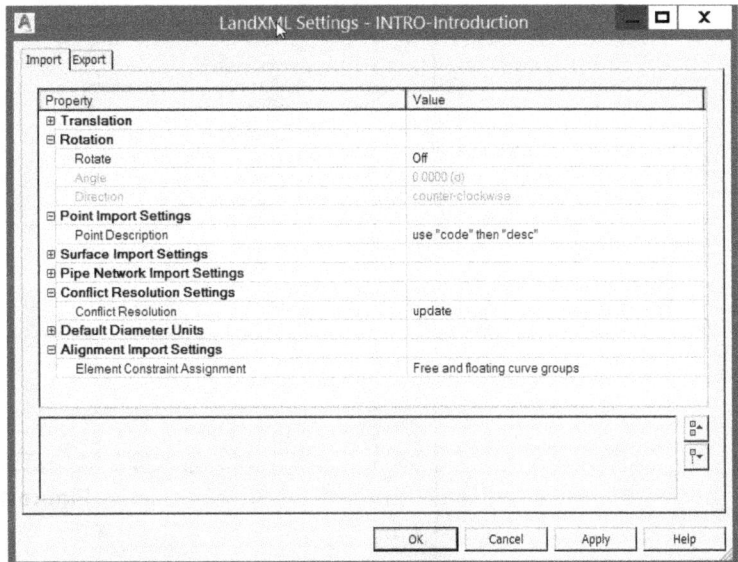

Figure 1–49

Feature Settings

In Settings, each object type collection has an Edit Feature Settings dialog box, as shown for Surface in Figure 1–50. Its main function is to assign default naming values, initial Object and Label styles, and overriding the default values found in Edit Drawing Settings for that object type. You can access the feature settings by right-clicking on the object tree in the *Settings* tab and selecting **Edit Feature Settings**.

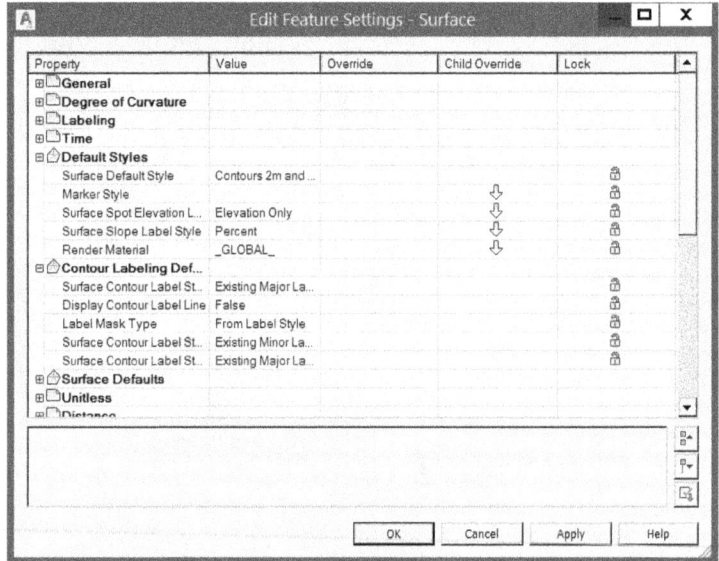

Figure 1–50

Command Settings

Similar to feature settings, in the Edit Command Settings dialog box (shown in Figure 1–51), you can set the default object and label styles used when creating objects with a specific command. Each object type contains a unique set of commands. Typical values in these dialog boxes include the name format (surface 1, parcel 1, etc.), design criteria (minimum area, frontage, length of vertical curve, and minimum horizontal curve), etc. To open the dialog box, expand a collection in Settings until the commands are displayed. Right-click on the command to which you want to assign default settings and select **Edit Command Settings**.

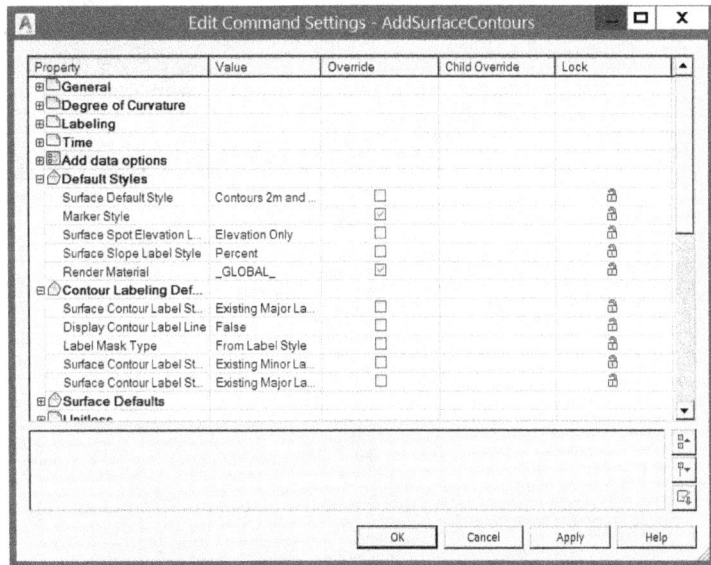

Figure 1–51

Hint: Style and Setting Overrides

In the Edit Label Style Defaults, Feature Settings and similar dialog boxes, a downward pointing arrow in the Child Override column indicates that a setting or style lower in the settings tree has a different value than the one displayed. Selecting the arrow (which creates a red **x** over the icon) and clicking **OK** removes the variant settings and makes all lower settings and styles match those assigned in the dialog box. This can be a quick way of standardizing multiple settings dialog boxes and styles at the same time.

For example, in the Surface Label Style defaults window (shown in Figure 1–52), some surface label styles are assigned a layer other than 0 and a visibility of false, because an arrow is present in the *Child Override* column. Since an arrow is not shown for the *Text Style* property, all surface label styles are using a text style of **Standard**.

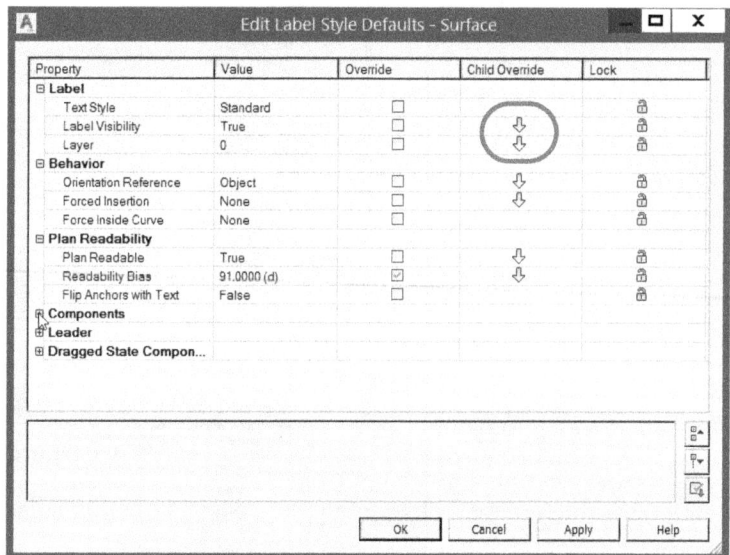

Figure 1–52

The *Override* column indicates whether a value in this window is overriding a higher settings dialog box. Clicking the **Lock** icon prevents you from changing that value in a lower setting's dialog box or style

Styles

Styles are preconfigured groups of settings specific to an individual object type or label that make the objects print the way you want them to print. For example, in the list of surface styles shown in Figure 1–53, each surface style is configured differently to display different features, such as contours at different intervals and on the correct layers. The display of a terrain model could be changed by swapping one surface style for another. Styles enable an organization to standardize the look of their graphics by providing preconfigured groupings of display settings.

Figure 1–53

The two categories of styles you work with most often are Object Styles and Label Styles. Some objects have table styles as well. Object styles control how AutoCAD Civil 3D objects (points, surfaces, alignments, etc.) display, what combination of components the object displays, which layers they display on, and many other settings. Label Styles are similar except that they control the text and other annotations associated with the objects.

For example, an alignment object style specifies many settings including the layers on which to draw tangents and curve segments (which might be different) and which symbols to add at certain points as required (such as a triangle at the PI point). Alignment label styles include major and minor station labels, the display of station equations, design speeds, and similar annotation. By separating object and label styles, you can mix and match the right combination for a specific object.

Styles are the lowest items in the Settings tree and are typically dependent on other settings above them. If a style is given a unique setting, different from feature settings or label style defaults (such as a different text height), then that style is considered to have an override.

Styles in Depth

Styles are central to the AutoCAD Civil 3D software. Their flexibility enables an Office or Company to create a unique *look* for their drawings. By changing the assigned style, you can change the composition of a profile view as shown in Figure 1–54.

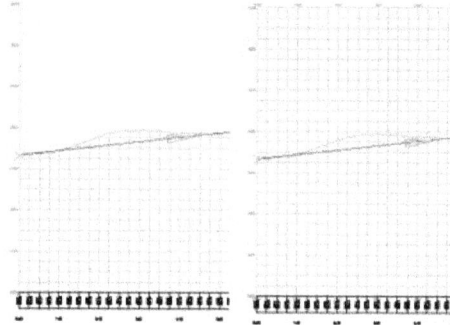

Figure 1–54

In the *Settings* tab in Toolspace, an object type branch identifies each style type and lists its styles below each heading. An example is shown in Figure 1–55.

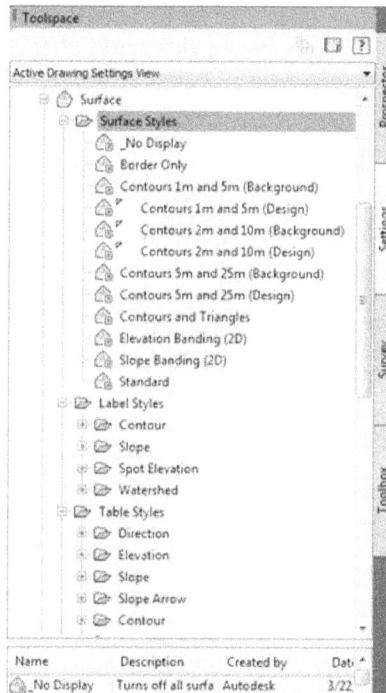

Figure 1–55

Object Styles

Object Styles stylize an object's data for display. To edit a style, in the *Settings* tab, right-click on the style and select **Edit**. Most of the work for all object styles is done in the *Display* tab. For certain objects, other tabs might need to be modified.

For example, in the Surface Style dialog box, the *Display* tab enables you to toggle on or off triangles, borders, contours, and other items as well as define the layer, color, linetype, etc. that are assigned to them, as shown in Figure 1–56. The *Contours* tab sets the contour interval, smoothing, and other settings, as shown in Figure 1–57.

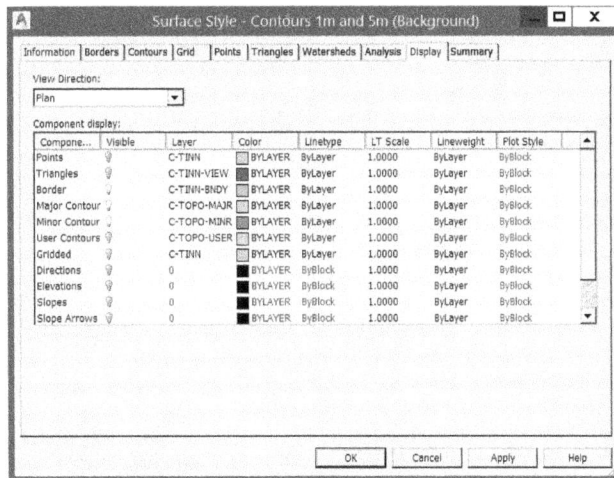

Figure 1–56

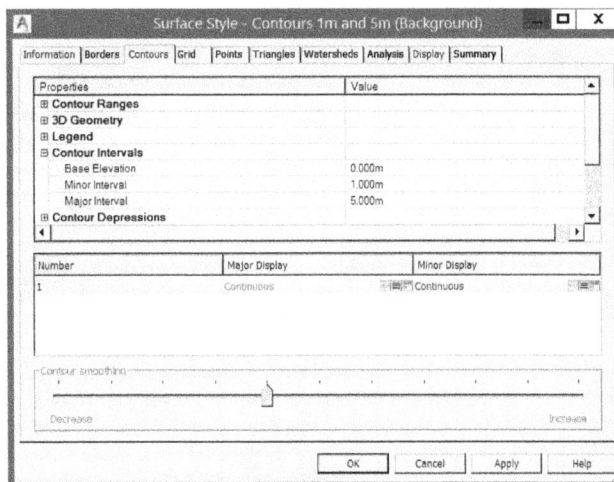

Figure 1–57

From the default AutoCAD Civil 3D template, the respective Parcel Style dialog box for Open Space, Road, or Single Family, (as shown in Figure 1–58), define how each displays their segments and hatching by assigning different layers for the components. The other tabs are rarely used for the Parcel styles.

Figure 1–58

An object style represents a specific task, view, type, or stage in a process. For example, a surface style for developing a surface, reviewing surface properties, or documenting surface elevations as contours for a submission. For Parcels, styles represent a type such as open space, commercial, easement, single family, etc. One style can cause an object to look different in various views. For instance, you might want to display both the point and the label in the plan view but only the point marker in a model (3D view). As shown in Figure 1–59, there are four view directions to consider when creating an object style.

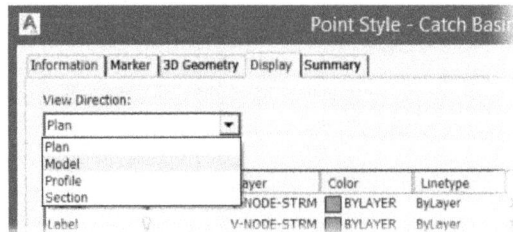

Figure 1–59

Label Styles

Label styles produce annotation of critical values from existing conditions or a design solution. A label annotates a contour's elevations, a parcel's number and area, an horizontal geometry point's station on an alignment, etc.

A label style can have text, vectors, AutoCAD blocks, and reference text. The content of a label depends on the selected object's components or properties. For instance, a Line label can annotate bearing, distance, and coordinates, and use a direction arrow. A Parcel Area label can contain a parcel's area, perimeter, address, and other pertinent values. A surface label can include a spot elevation and reference for an alignment's station and offset.

- To access the values of a label style, in *Settings*, select the style, right-click on its name, and select **Edit**.

- A style's initial values come from Edit Label Style Defaults and the style's definition.

- All labels use the same interface.

- The object properties available for each label vary by object type.

Each label style uses the same tabbed dialog box. The Information tab describes the style and who defined and last modified its contents. The values of the *General* tab affect all occurrences of the label in a drawing. For example, if Visibility is set to False, all labels of this style are hidden in the drawing. Other settings affect the label's text style, initial orientation, and reaction to a rotated view.

The *Layout* tab lists all of a label's components. A label component can be text, line, block, or tick. The Component name drop-down list (shown in Figure 1–60), contains all of the defined components for the style. When selecting a component name in the drop-down list, the panel displays information about the component's anchoring, justification, format, and border.

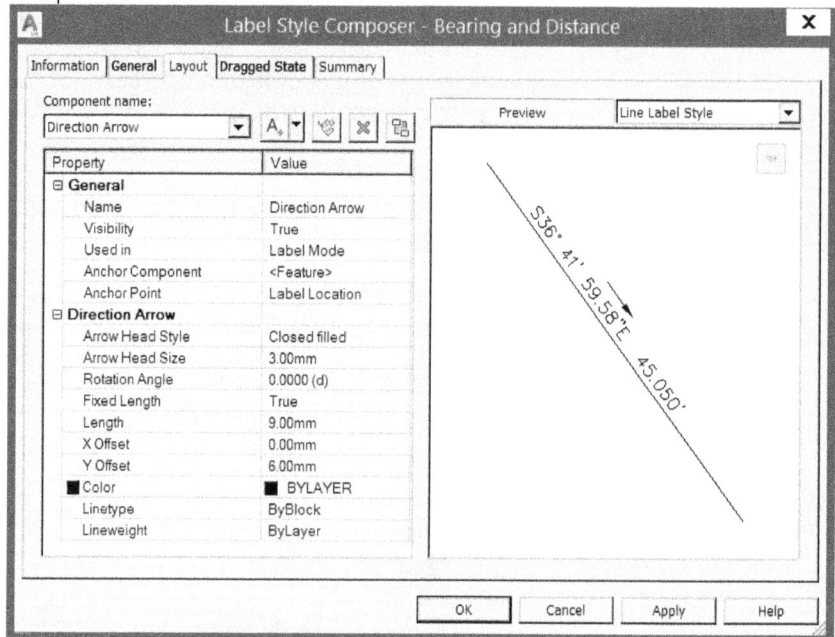

Figure 1–60

When defining a new text component, you assign it an object property by clicking ⬚ (Browse) for Contents. This opens the Text Component Editor dialog box, as shown in Figure 1–61. The Properties drop-down list displays the available object properties. The number and types of properties varies by object type. For example, a parcel area label has more and different properties than a line label does. Once a property has been selected, units, precision, and other settings can be set to display the property correctly in the label. Click ⬚ next to Properties to place the property in the label layout area to the right.

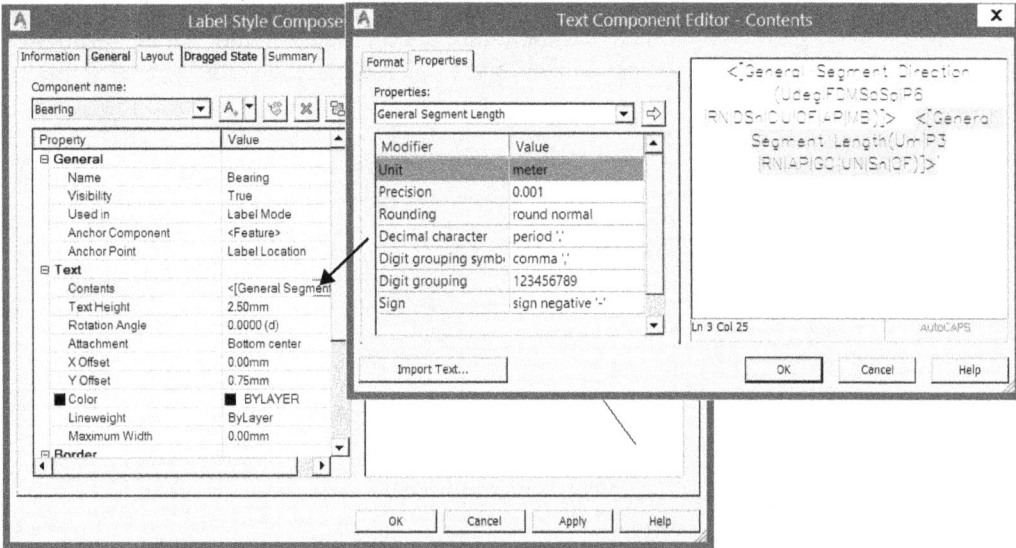

Figure 1–61

The values in the *Dragged State* tab define a label's behavior when it is dragged to a new location in the drawing.

The key to having the label display correctly when it is not in the dragged state, is to line up the Anchor Point of the component with the **Attachment** option for the text. Each has nine options from which to select. The options are shown in Figure 1–62.

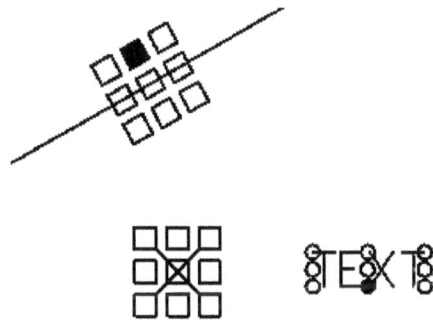

Figure 1–62

Lining up the square hatched Anchor Point with the circular hatched attachment option results in the text centered above the object similar to the bearing distance label shown in Figure 1–63.

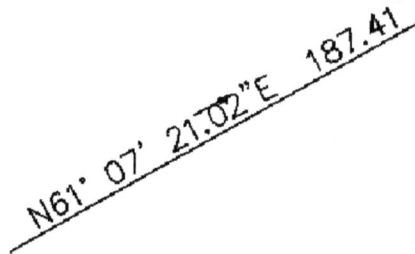

Figure 1–63

Templates

A drawing template (.DWT extension) contains all blocks, Paper Space title sheets, settings, layers, AutoCAD Civil 3D styles, and content-specific settings for a new drawing.

Creating Template Files

To use the AutoCAD Civil 3D software efficiently and effectively, you need to configure styles and settings to control the object display. All of these styles and settings affect the final delivered product and enable you to deliver a product with consistent CAD standards. Once all of the styles required for a set of drawings have been created, saving the file as a template enables you to use the same styles over and over in various projects. To create a template file, use the **Save As** command and in the Save As dialog box, change the *File of Type* to **DWT**. After giving it a name, the Template Options dialog box opens as shown in Figure 1–64. It enables you to enter a description, set the measurement units, and save new layers as reconciled or unreconciled.

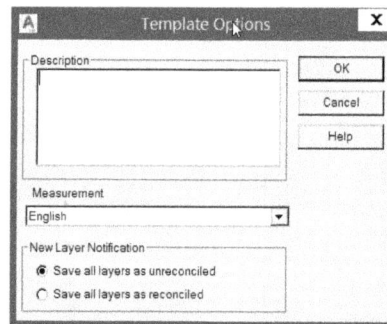

Figure 1–64

Once an AutoCAD Civil 3D style has been created, it can be transferred between drawings and templates by selecting the style and dragging it to the required file. When dragging a style to a drawing, any associated style layers also transfer.

There are three methods of managing styles in a drawing: **Import**, **Purge**, and **Reference**. These commands are located in the *Manage* tab>Styles panel, as shown in Figure 1–65.

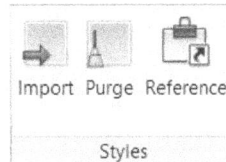

Figure 1–65

Import

The **Import** styles command enables you to import the styles from a source drawing into the current drawing. The Import Civil 3D Styles dialog box (shown in Figure 1–66) lists the styles that are available for import and also displays the style differences between the source and the current drawing. Each style collection lists three subcategories: styles to be added, styles to be deleted, and styles to be updated. When you use the **Import** command, the styles in the design file are overwritten. If the styles change in the DWG or DWT source file that you imported, the styles in the design file do not automatically update.

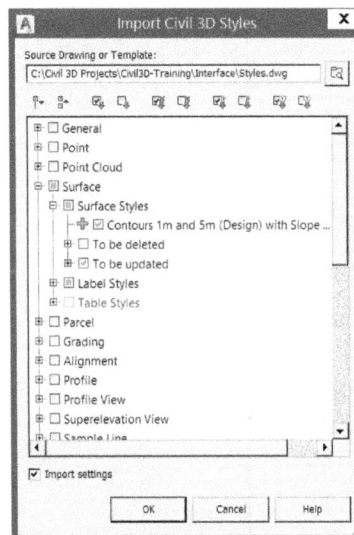

Figure 1–66

Purge

The **Purge** styles command enables you to purge all of the selected unused styles in a drawing. However, you might need to run this command more than once as there might be some styles that are used as parents to other styles. The purging information is displayed in the Style Purge Confirmation dialog box, as shown in Figure 1–67. The Command Line prompts you when there are no unused styles in the drawing.

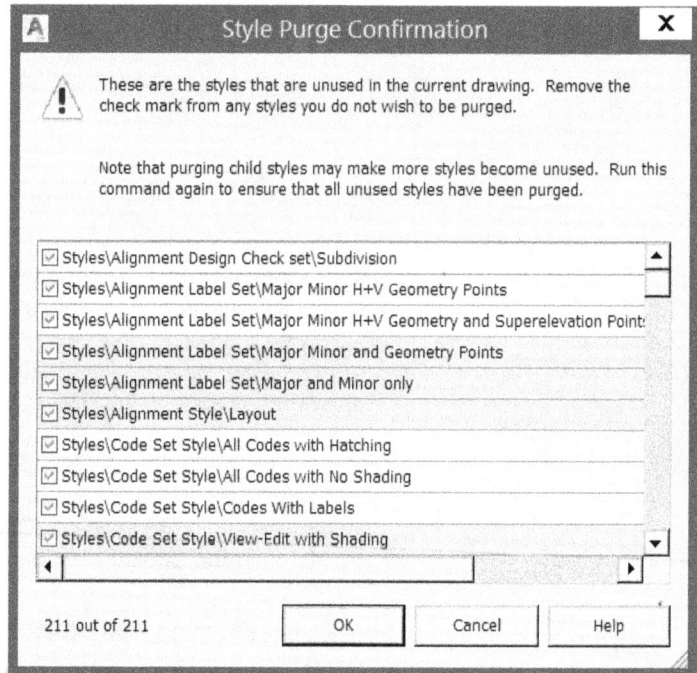

Figure 1–67

New in **2017**

Reference

The **Reference** styles command enables you to attach one or more DWG or DWT files to your design file. Styles that are in the attached files override styles with the same name in the design drawing. If the styles in the attached DWG or DWT file change, the styles in the design file also change. Using the **Reference** styles command enables you to maintain a consistent style across multiple drawings, and can be used to implement and maintain a company-wide CAD standard. Figure 1–68 shows the Attach Referenced Template dialog box.

- When multiple style templates are attached, you can set the priority using the arrows on the right of the Attach Referenced Template dialog box.

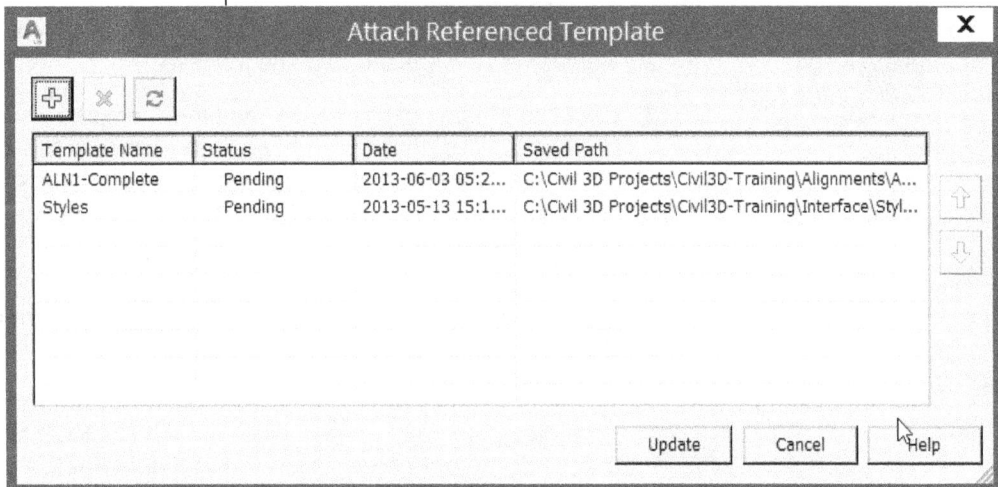

Template Name	Status	Date	Saved Path
ALN1-Complete	Pending	2013-06-03 05:2...	C:\Civil 3D Projects\Civil3D-Training\Alignments\A...
Styles	Pending	2013-05-13 15:1...	C:\Civil 3D Projects\Civil3D-Training\Interface\Styl...

Figure 1–68

Practice 1c

AutoCAD Civil 3D Styles

Practice Objectives

- Create an object and label style to be used in the drawing.
- Import object and label styles to be used in the drawing and purge any styles not being used.

Estimated time for completion: 10 minutes

In this practice you will create AutoCAD Civil 3D styles, import styles, and purge styles for both objects and labels.

Task 1 - Create an object style.

1. Continue working in the drawing from the last practice. If you closed it, open **INTRO-Introduction.dwg** from the *C:\Civil 3D for Surveyors Practice Files\Interface* folder.

2. Select the *Settings* tab to make it active.

The tabs are listed vertically along the right side of the Toolspace.

3. Click the **+** sign next to Parcel, and then click the **+** sign next to Parcel Styles. Five parcel styles are already in the drawing, but a new one needs to be created to designate blocks.

4. Right-click on **Parcel Styles** and select **New**. In the *Information* tab, set the *Name* to **Blocks**.

5. In the *Display* tab, highlight both the Parcel Segment and Parcel Area Fill (press <Shift> to select both), click **0** under the *Layer* column.

6. Click **New...** to create a new layer named **C-PROP-BLOCK** and set its *color* to **blue**, as shown in Figure 1–69.

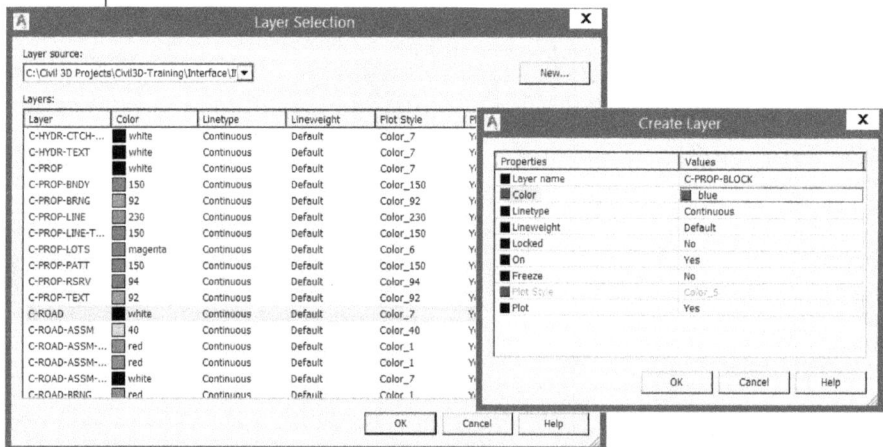

Figure 1–69

7. Click **OK** to exit the Create Layer dialog box. Click **OK** to exit the Layer Selection dialog box.

8. Verify that the light bulb is on for the Parcel Segment visibility and off for the Parcel Area Fill visibility, as shown in Figure 1–70.

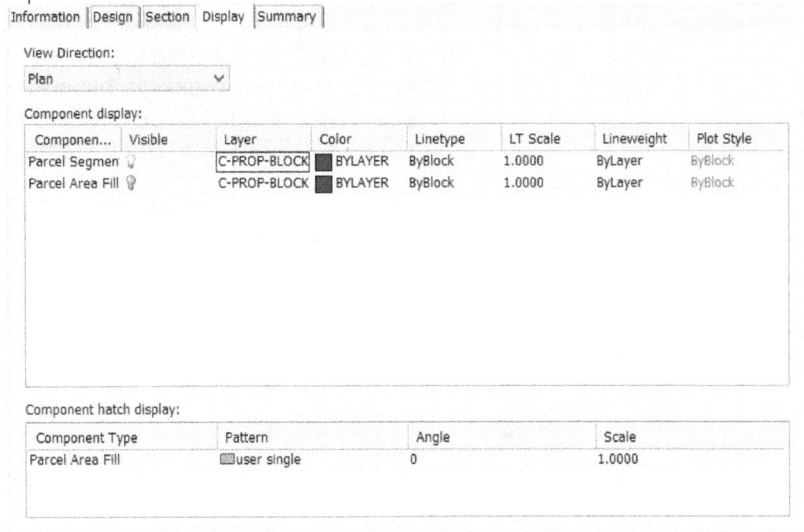

Information | Design | Section | Display | Summary

View Direction:
Plan

Component display:

Componen...	Visible	Layer	Color	Linetype	LT Scale	Lineweight	Plot Style
Parcel Segmen		C-PROP-BLOCK	BYLAYER	ByBlock	1.0000	ByLayer	ByBlock
Parcel Area Fill		C-PROP-BLOCK	BYLAYER	ByBlock	1.0000	ByLayer	ByBlock

Component hatch display:

Component Type	Pattern	Angle	Scale
Parcel Area Fill	user single	0	1.0000

Figure 1–70

9. Click **OK** to exit the Parcel Style dialog box.

10. Save the drawing.

Task 2 - Work with a label style.

1. Verify that the *Settings* tab is still active.

2. View the label style default. In the *View* tab>Views panel, expand the Named Views drop-down list and select **Contour label**. It will zoom to a preset view of the contour labels, as shown in Figure 1–71.

Figure 1–71

Note that the labels are not rotated to the correct drafting standards. The contour label style being used is rotating the text so that it remains plan readable (so they do not display upside down). The highlighted labels are rotated more than 90 degrees from horizontal. This is caused by the *Readability Bias* setting being larger than 90 degrees. This setting controls the viewing angle at which the contour text should be flipped.

3. If required, you can change the setting in this specific contour label style only. To assign this new value to all of the surface label styles, right-click on the **Surface** collection>*Settings* tab and select **Edit Label Style Defaults**.

4. Under the **Plan Readability** property, set the *Readability Bias* to **110°**, as shown in Figure 1–72. Click **OK**.

Property	Value	Override	Child Override	Lock
⊞ **Label**				
⊞ **Behavior**				
⊟ **Plan Readability**				
Plan Readable	True		⇩	🔓
Readability Bias	91.0000 (d)		⇩	🔓
Flip Anchors with Text	False		⇩	🔓
⊞ **Components**				
⊞ **Leader**				
⊞ **Dragged State Compone...**				

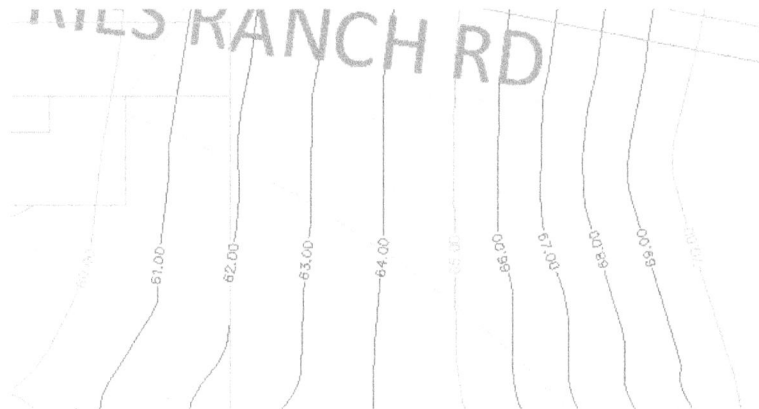

Figure 1–72

5. Click **+** next to Surface, and then click **+** next to Label Styles and Contour. Right-click on **Existing Major Labels** and select **Edit**.

6. In the *Layout* tab, click ⊡ (Browse) next to Contents to open the Text Component Editor. Delete all of the information in the content area to the right.

7. In the Properties drop-down list, select **Surface Elevation**, change the *Precision* to **1**, and click ⇨ to place it in the content area, as shown in Figure 1–73.

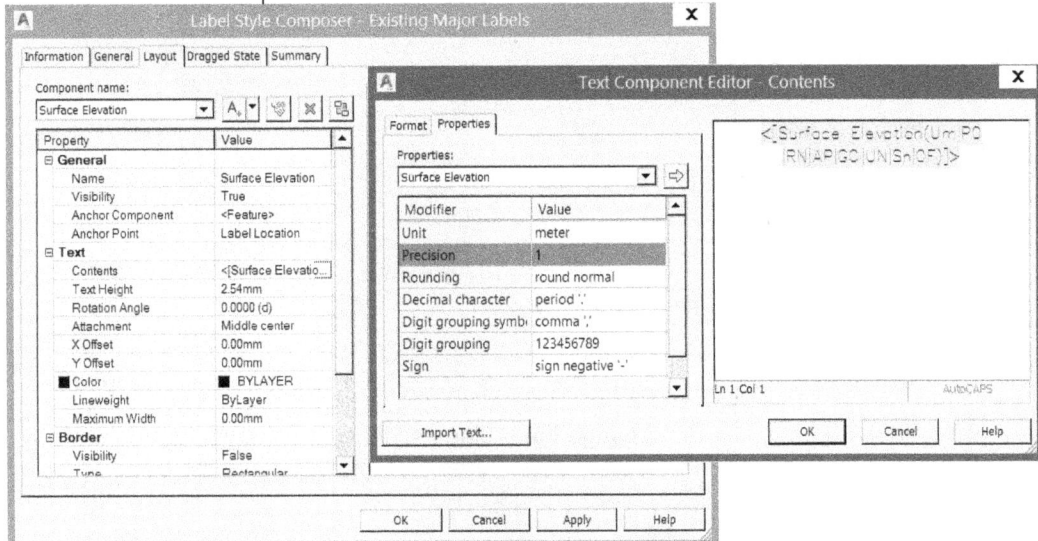

Figure 1–73

8. Click **OK** to exit the Text Component Editor dialog box. Click **OK** again to exit the Label Style Composer dialog box.

9. Repeat Steps 5 to 8 to change the **Existing Minor Labels** style in the same way.

10. Save the drawing.

Task 3 - Import and purge styles.

1. In the *Manage* tab>Styles panel, click ⇨ (Import).

2. Select and open the **Styles.dwg** file from the *C:\Civil 3D for Surveyors Practice Files\Interface* folder.

3. Expand *Surface Styles* and verify that **Contours 1m and 5m (Design) with Slope Arrows** is selected, as shown in Figure 1–74.

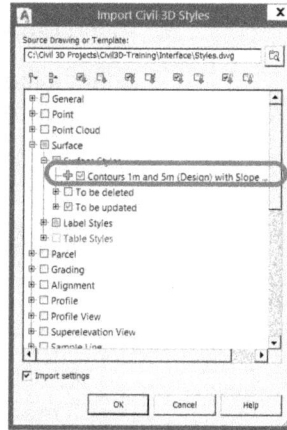

Figure 1–74

4. Click **OK** in the Warning dialog box regarding overwriting duplicate styles. Click **OK** in the Message dialog box.

5. Change the surface style to the newly imported style by changing the surface properties. Note the slope arrows shown in Figure 1–75.

Figure 1–75

6. In the *Manage* tab>Styles panel, click (Purge).

7. Clear any styles that you do not want to purge and click **OK**.

8. Save the drawing.

Task 4 - Attach a styles template

1. In the *Manage* tab>Styles panel, click ⬛ (Reference).

2. In the Attach Referenced Template dialog box, click
   ⊕ (Attach New Template).

3. In the *C:\Civil 3D Projects\Civil3D-Training\Interface* folder, select **Styles.dwg** and then click **Open**.

4. In the Attach Referenced Template dialog box (shown in Figure 1–76), click **Update**.

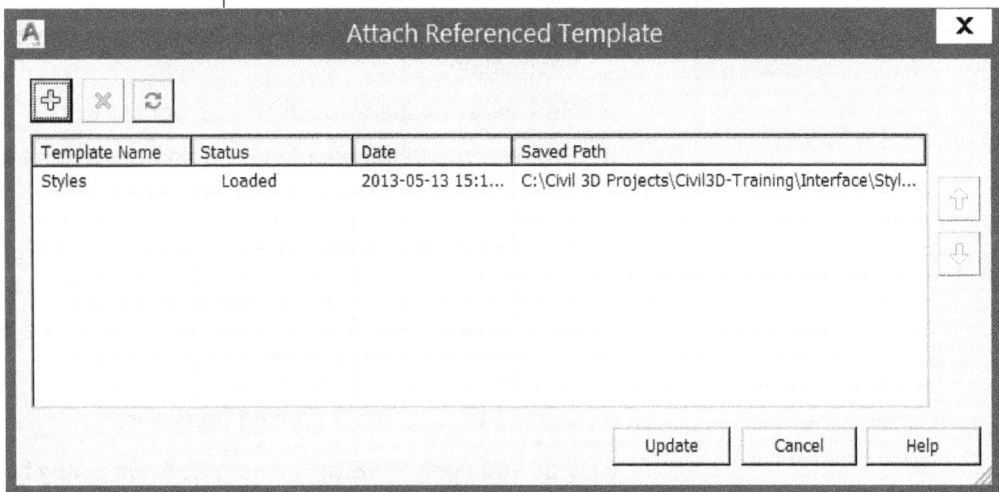

Template Name	Status	Date	Saved Path
Styles	Loaded	2013-05-13 15:1...	C:\Civil 3D Projects\Civil3D-Training\Interface\Styl...

Figure 1–76

5. Save and close the drawing.

Chapter Review Questions

1. Which Workspace should you be in if you want to create an AEC object (surfaces, alignments, profiles, etc)?

   a. 2D Drafting and Annotation

   b. 3D Modeling

   c. Civil 3D

   d. Planning and Analysis

2. What does the *Prospector* tab do?

   a. Sets the layers for AEC objects.

   b. Lists the AEC objects and provides access to their information.

   c. Sets the workspace in which you want to work.

   d. Enables you to connect to GIS data from a number of sources.

3. What does the *Settings* tab do?

   a. Sets the layers and display styles for AEC objects.

   b. Creates templates from which new drawings are based.

   c. Creates new drawings with references to data.

   d. Generates Sheets for printing purposes.

4. How do you open the Edit Drawing Settings dialog box?

   a. Type **CUI** in the Command Line to open the Customize User Interface dialog box.

   b. **Application menu>Drawing Utilities**.

   c. *Prospector* tab, right-click on the drawing name.

   d. *Settings* tab, right-click on the drawing name.

5. What is the main function of the Panorama window?

   a. Setting up styles for AEC objects.

   b. Reviewing and editing tabular AEC object data.

   c. Pan inside the drawing.

   d. Look at the AEC objects in 3D views.

6. How do you force the styles in a design file to update every time the CAD Manager makes a change to the styles in the company CAD Standards template file?

   a. In the *Manage* tab>Styles panel, click ⬛ (Reference).

   b. In the *Manage* tab>Styles panel, click 🔲 (Purge).

   c. In the *Manage* tab>Styles panel, click ➡ (Import).

   d. You must create a new style manually. There is no way to force an update to styles in an existing drawing.

Command Summary

Button	Command	Location
	Close	• **Drawing Window** • **Application Menu** • **Command Prompt:** close
	Close Current Drawing	• **Application Menu**
	Import Styles	• **Ribbon:** *Manage* tab>Styles panel • **Command Prompt:** importstylesandsettings
	Manager Reference Styles	• **Ribbon:** *Manage* tab>Styles panel • **Command Prompt:** AttachReferenceTemplate
	Open	• **Quick Access Toolbar** • **Application Menu** • **Command Prompt:** open, <Ctrl>+<O>
	Prospector	• **Ribbon:** *Home* tab>Palettes panel • **Command Prompt:** prospector
	Settings	• **Ribbon:** *Home* tab>Palettes panel • **Command Prompt:** settings
	Style Purge	• **Ribbon:** *Manage* tab>Styles panel • **Command Prompt:** purgestyles
	Surface Properties	• **Contextual Ribbon:** *Surface* tab> Modify panel • **Command Prompt:** editsurfaceproperties
	Survey	• **Ribbon:** *Home* tab>Palettes panel • **Command Prompt:** survey
	Toolbox	• **Ribbon:** *Home* tab>Palettes panel • **Command Prompt:** toolbox
	Toolspace	• **Ribbon:** *Home* tab>Palettes panel • **Command Prompt:** toolspace

Connecting to Geospatial Data

In this chapter, you will learn how to easily connect to existing geospatial data and create a surface from it. This process enables you to easily determine which data should be collected during the field survey.

Learning Objectives in this Chapter

- Identify where tools are found in the Planning and Analysis Workspace.
- Set the drawing coordinate system for a new drawing.
- Display the current conditions by connecting to GIS data.
- Create a surface from a shape file containing elevation data.

2.1 Introduction to the Planning and Analysis Workspace

The Planning and Analysis Workspace in the AutoCAD® Civil 3D® software contains tools that are also found in the AutoCAD® Map 3D® software. They help you to attach and analyze GIS data for more efficient planning of projects before starting a design.

Map Workflow

The following workflow is one of many workflows that can be used. It only covers a small portion of the AutoCAD Map 3D software capabilities.

1. Start a new drawing from a Civil 3D template that includes all of the required styles.
2. Assign a Coordinate System to the drawing file.
3. Attach Image and Digital Elevation Models (DEM) files using the **Data Connect** command.
4. Attach other source data using the **Data Connect** command. This includes file-based data sources (.SHP or .SDF files) and database data sources (Oracle or Microsoft SQL Server).
5. Create AutoCAD Civil 3D surfaces from source data.
6. Style the layers for presentation or publication purposes.
7. Analyze the data.
8. Create labels and legends to annotate the drawing.

Data can be queried as it is added to the drawing file to ensure that only the area of interest or items of interest are incorporated into the drawing file. Once data is included in the drawing, it can be displayed using themes and symbols for correct representation of the entities. Analysis can be done on the entities to determine which entities are within a specific distance of another (buffer analysis) or which entities overlay another (overlay analysis).

The *Map Setup* tab>Coordinate System panel is used to assign a coordinate system to the drawing file, as shown in Figure 2–1.

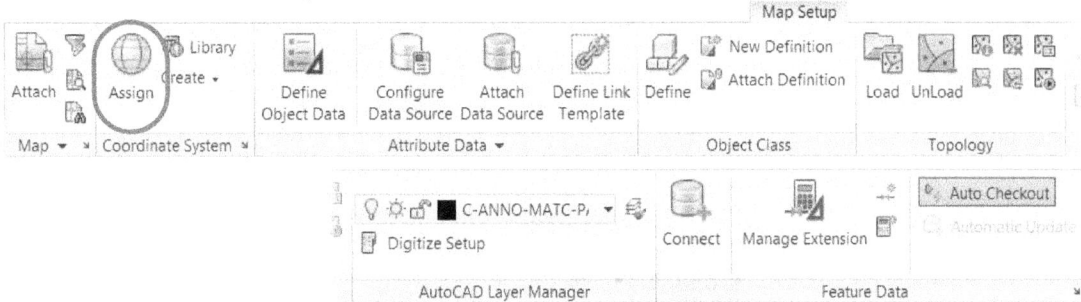

Figure 2–1

The *Home* tab>Data panel is used to connect to source data, such as images, file sources, and database sources, as shown in Figure 2–2.

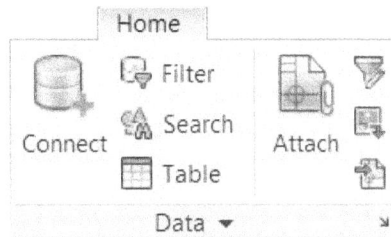

Figure 2–2

Creating a surface from source data is done using the Civil 3D workspace in the *Home* tab>Create Ground Data panel, as shown in Figure 2–3.

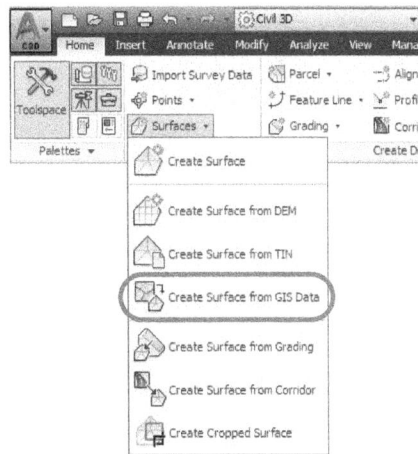

Figure 2–3

2.2 Coordinate Systems

Coordinate systems are used in engineering and mapping to uniquely identify the position of geographical elements. Various systems project elements differently to accommodate the curvature of the earth's surface. Therefore, it is vitally important to set the coordinate system for the drawing in which you plan to work.

Coordinate systems communicate to the computer where the project is located in the world, along with mathematical equations used to account for the curvature of the earth. Once the drawing coordinate system has been set, any GIS or Survey data that is connected to the drawing automatically re-projects and lines up correctly in the current drawing.

How To: Set the Drawing Coordinate System in the Planning and Analysis Workspace

1. In the Quick Access Toolbar, change the workspace to **Planning and Analysis**, as shown in Figure 2–4.

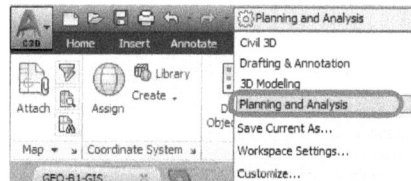

Figure 2–4

2. In the *Map Setup* tab>Coordinate System panel, click

   (Assign) to assign a coordinate system to the drawing file, as shown in Figure 2–5.

Figure 2–5

3. Search for the code required by your project and select it, as shown in Figure 2–6.

Figure 2–6

4. Click **Assign**.

How To: Set the Drawing Coordinate System in the Civil 3D Workspace

1. In the Quick Access Toolbar, change the workspace to **Civil 3D**, as shown in Figure 2–7.

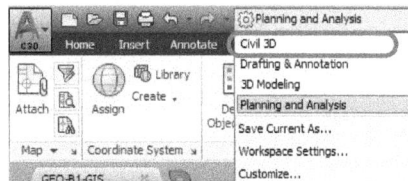

Figure 2–7

2. In the *Settings* tab in the Toolspace, right-click on the drawing name and select **Edit Drawing Settings**, as shown in Figure 2–8.

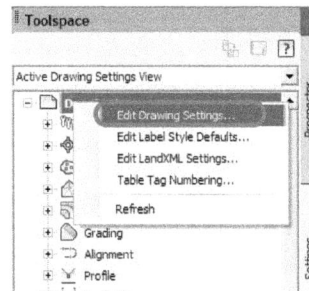

Figure 2–8

---

3. In the Drawing Setting dialog box, in the *Units and Zone* tab, select the category and coordinate system for the drawing, as shown in Figure 2–9. Click **OK**.

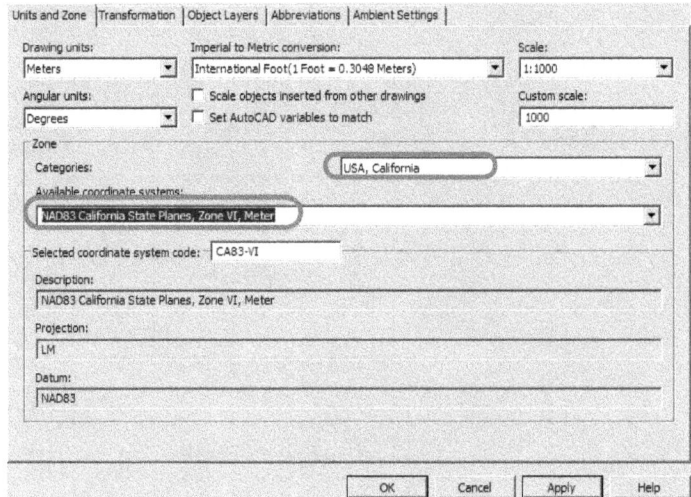

| Units and Zone | Transformation | Object Layers | Abbreviations | Ambient Settings |

Drawing units:
Meters

Imperial to Metric conversion:
International Foot(1 Foot = 0.3048 Meters)

Scale:
1:1000

Angular units:
Degrees

☐ Scale objects inserted from other drawings
☐ Set AutoCAD variables to match

Custom scale:
1000

Zone
Categories: USA, California
Available coordinate systems:
NAD83 California State Planes, Zone VI, Meter

Selected coordinate system code: CA83-VI

Description:
NAD83 California State Planes, Zone VI, Meter

Projection:
LM

Datum:
NAD83

OK   Cancel   Apply   Help

Figure 2–9

Practice 2a

Start a New Project

Practice Objective

- Display the current conditions by connecting to GIS data.

Estimated time for completion: 5 minutes

In this practice, you will create a new drawing and assign a coordinate system to the drawing.

Task 1 - Start a new file.

1. In the Start Tab, select the Templates drop-down list to start a new drawing file. Select **_AutoCAD Civil 3D (Metric) NCS.dwt**, which ships with the software, as shown in Figure 2–10.

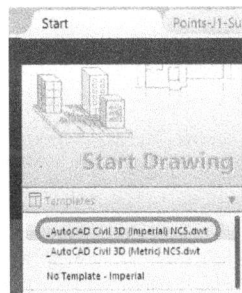

Figure 2–10

2. Click ▣ (Application Menu) and select **SaveAs**. Type **BaseMap** for the filename, browse to *C:\Civil 3D for Surveyors Practice Files* and click **Save**.

Task 2 - Set the drawing coordinates.

1. Continue working with the drawing from the previous task, or open **GEO-A2-GIS.dwg** from the *C:\Civil 3D for Surveyors Practice Files\Geospatial* folder.

2. In the Quick Access Toolbar, change the workspace to **Planning and Analysis**, as shown in Figure 2–11.

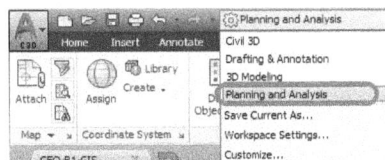

Figure 2–11

3. In the *Map Setup* tab>Coordinate System panel, click

   ⬚ (Assign) to assign a coordinate system to the drawing file, as shown in Figure 2–12.

Figure 2–12

4. In the *Search* field, type **CA83** and select **CA83-VI** from the list of code, as shown in Figure 2–13. Click **Assign**.

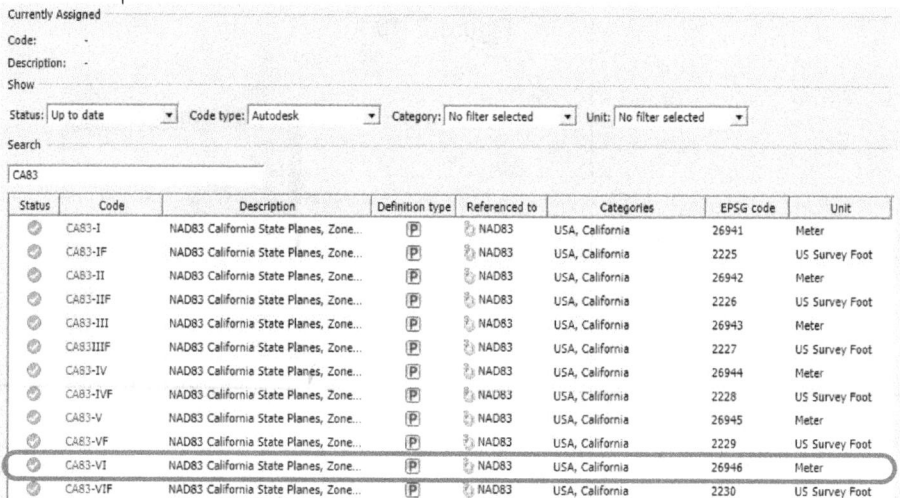

Currently Assigned
Code: -
Description: -
Show
Status: Up to date | Code type: Autodesk | Category: No filter selected | Unit: No filter selected
Search

CA83

Status	Code	Description	Definition type	Referenced to	Categories	EPSG code	Unit
✓	CA83-I	NAD83 California State Planes, Zone...	P	NAD83	USA, California	26941	Meter
✓	CA83-IF	NAD83 California State Planes, Zone...	P	NAD83	USA, California	2225	US Survey Foot
✓	CA83-II	NAD83 California State Planes, Zone...	P	NAD83	USA, California	26942	Meter
✓	CA83-IIF	NAD83 California State Planes, Zone...	P	NAD83	USA, California	2226	US Survey Foot
✓	CA83-III	NAD83 California State Planes, Zone...	P	NAD83	USA, California	26943	Meter
✓	CA83IIIF	NAD83 California State Planes, Zone...	P	NAD83	USA, California	2227	US Survey Foot
✓	CA83-IV	NAD83 California State Planes, Zone...	P	NAD83	USA, California	26944	Meter
✓	CA83-IVF	NAD83 California State Planes, Zone...	P	NAD83	USA, California	2228	US Survey Foot
✓	CA83-V	NAD83 California State Planes, Zone...	P	NAD83	USA, California	26945	Meter
✓	CA83-VF	NAD83 California State Planes, Zone...	P	NAD83	USA, California	2229	US Survey Foot
✓	CA83-VI	NAD83 California State Planes, Zone...	P	NAD83	USA, California	26946	Meter
✓	CA83-VIF	NAD83 California State Planes, Zone...	P	NAD83	USA, California	2230	US Survey Foot

Figure 2–13

5. Save the drawing.

2.3 Geospatial Data Connection

Geospatial data is collected and maintained by a large number of organizations using a variety of different software. The AutoCAD Civil 3D software can connect to many of these data sources using the Feature Data Object (FDO) connection in *Display Manager* tab of the AutoCAD Map 3D Task pane or the *Home* tab in the Planning and Analysis workspace. The types of data that can be connected include:

- ArcSDE
- MySQL
- ODBC
- SQLite
- WFS
- WMS

- Enterprise Industry Models
- Oracle
- PostgreSQL
- Raster Image or Surface
- Spatial Data Files (SDF)
- ESRI Shape files (SHP)
- SQL Server Spatial

Connect to GIS Data

The process of connecting to GIS data is similar among data types. First, you must select the type of data to which to connect. Then, select the number of files that are going to be connected at the same time. You can connect to one file at a time or to an entire directory of files at the same time. If a database connection is selected (such as Oracle or ArcSDE) you might need to input your login credentials, as shown in Figure 2–14.

Finally, you need to ensure that the coordinate system of the source file registers as you connect to it. If the coordinate system for the source file is listed as <unknown> (as shown in Figure 2–15), it did not register correctly. Therefore, you need to assign the source coordinate system manually so that it re-projects automatically in the drawing and displays in the correct location.

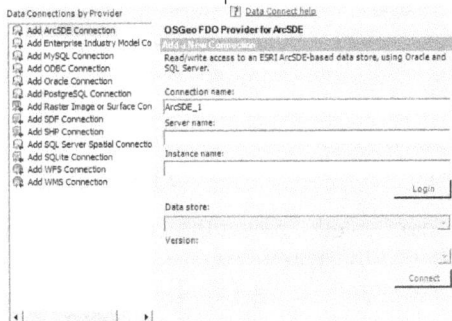

Figure 2–14

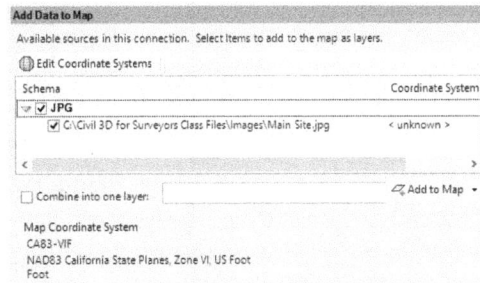

Figure 2–15

How To: Connect to GIS Data

There are multiple locations in which you can access the Data Connection palette. The first is the *Home* tab in the Planning and Analysis workspace, the second is in the Map Task pane.

1. In the *Home* tab>Data panel in the Planning and Analysis workspace, click ⬛ (Connect), as shown in Figure 2–16.

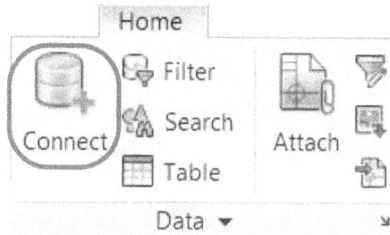

Figure 2–16

Alternatively, you can do the following:

- In the *Home* tab>expanded Palettes panel in the Civil 3D workspace, click ⬛ (Map Task Pane), as shown in Figure 2–17.
- In the *Display Manager* tab, in the Map Task Pane, click ⬛ (Data) and select **Connect to Data**, as shown in Figure 2–18.

Figure 2–17

Figure 2–18

2. In the Data Connect palette, select the correct connect type.

3. Type a name for the connection and click ▣ (Browse for source file) or ▢ (Browse for source folder), as shown in Figure 2–19.

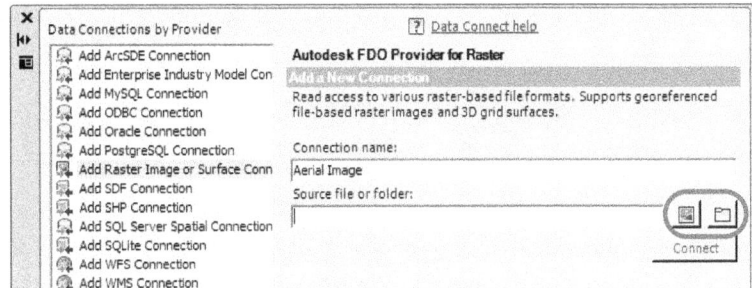

Figure 2–19

4. Select the file or folder and click **Open**.
5. In the Data Connect palette, click **Connect**.
6. In the *Coordinate System* column, double-click on **<unknown>** to edit the coordinate system that is registered with the source file, as shown in Figure 2–20.

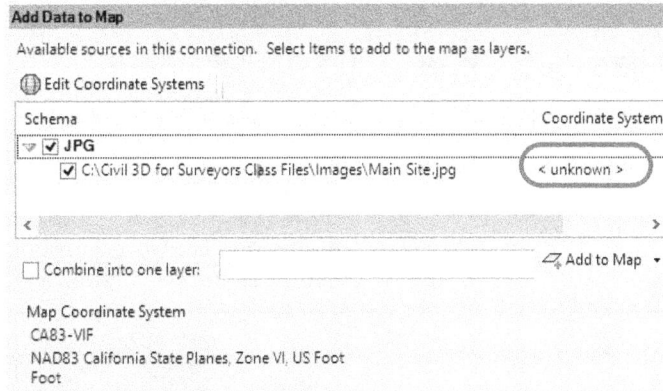

Figure 2–20

7. In the Edit Spatial Contexts dialog box, select **<unknown>** and click **Edit**, as shown in Figure 2–21.

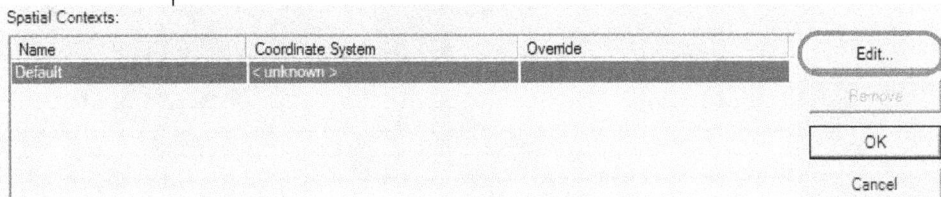

Figure 2–21

8. Select the required coordinate system from the list of codes, as shown in Figure 2–22. Click **Select**. Click **OK**.

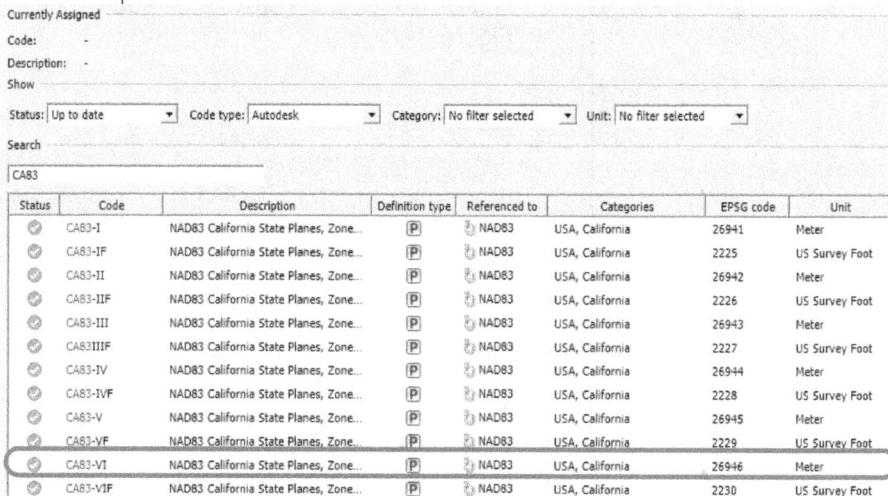

Currently Assigned
Code: -
Description: -
Show

| Status: | Up to date | ▼ | Code type: | Autodesk | ▼ | Category: | No filter selected | ▼ | Unit: | No filter selected | ▼ |

Search

CA83

Status	Code	Description	Definition type	Referenced to	Categories	EPSG code	Unit
✓	CA83-I	NAD83 California State Planes, Zone...	P	NAD83	USA, California	26941	Meter
✓	CA83-IF	NAD83 California State Planes, Zone...	P	NAD83	USA, California	2225	US Survey Foot
✓	CA83-II	NAD83 California State Planes, Zone...	P	NAD83	USA, California	26942	Meter
✓	CA83-IIF	NAD83 California State Planes, Zone...	P	NAD83	USA, California	2226	US Survey Foot
✓	CA83-III	NAD83 California State Planes, Zone...	P	NAD83	USA, California	26943	Meter
✓	CA83IIIF	NAD83 California State Planes, Zone...	P	NAD83	USA, California	2227	US Survey Foot
✓	CA83-IV	NAD83 California State Planes, Zone...	P	NAD83	USA, California	26944	Meter
✓	CA83-IVF	NAD83 California State Planes, Zone...	P	NAD83	USA, California	2228	US Survey Foot
✓	CA83-V	NAD83 California State Planes, Zone...	P	NAD83	USA, California	26945	Meter
✓	CA83-VF	NAD83 California State Planes, Zone...	P	NAD83	USA, California	2229	US Survey Foot
✓	CA83-VI	NAD83 California State Planes, Zone...	P	NAD83	USA, California	26946	Meter
✓	CA83-VIF	NAD83 California State Planes, Zone...	P	NAD83	USA, California	2230	US Survey Foot

Figure 2–22

9. In the Data Connect palette, click **Add to Map**.
10. Continue adding data sources, as required.

Stylize GIS Data

The available styles for a GIS layer depend on the type of GIS data being displayed. Point features (such as points of interest in a city) can use block symbols as the point style while linear features (such as roads) use linetypes and linewidths to communicate differences between feature types. If an area feature (such as a city boundary or parcel) is used, both hatch patterns and linetypes/linewidths are used to communicate differences between feature types, as shown in Figure 2–23.

Figure 2–23

How To: Modify an Area Style

1. In the *View* tab>Palettes panel, click ☐ (Map Task Pane), as shown in Figure 2–24.

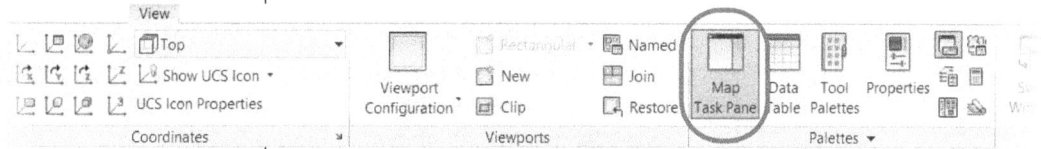

Figure 2–24

2. In the Task Pane>*Display Manager* tab, double-click on the area layer.
3. In the Style Editor palette, in the *Style* column, click

   ⋯ (Browse), as shown in Figure 2–25.

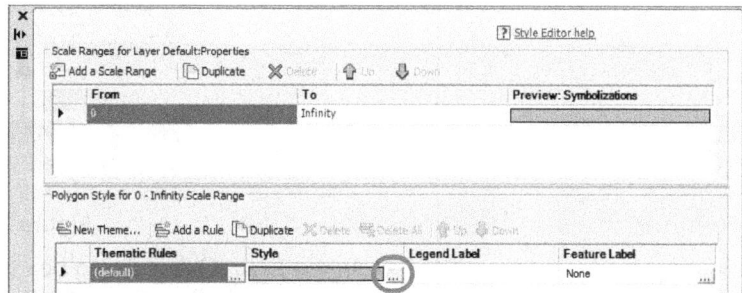

Figure 2–25

4. In the Style Polygon dialog box, change the border color and fill color or add additional borders and fills as required, as shown in Figure 2–26. Click **Apply** and close the Style Polygon dialog box and Style Editor palette.

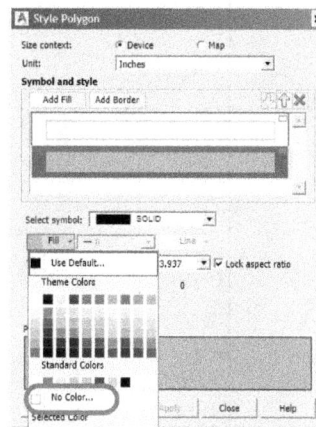

Figure 2–26

Draw Order

Setting the drawing order of the layer determines which layer is displayed on top of another. If an aerial photograph or other raster file is displayed, it is useful to move it to the background so that other layers are displayed.

How To: Change the Draw Order of GIS Layers

1. In the Task Pane>*Display Manager* tab, select **Draw Order** and drag the layers above or below the others to ensure that they all display, as shown in Figure 2–27.

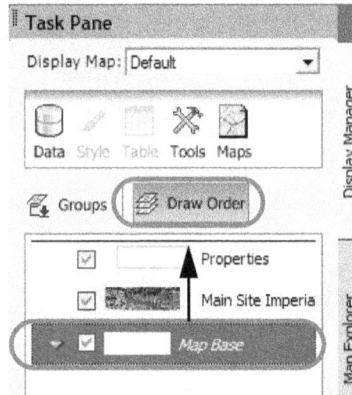

Figure 2–27

2. In the Draw Order dialog box that opens, select **Continue action and allow Draw Order to control layer position from now on**.

Practice 2b

Connect to GIS Data

Practice Objective

- Connect to an aerial image file using AutoCAD Map 3D tools.

Estimated time for completion: 10 minutes

In this practice, you will create a new drawing and assign a coordinate system to the drawing.

Task 1 - Connect to an image file.

1. Continue working with the drawing from the previous practice or open **GEO-B1-GIS.dwg** from the *C:\Civil 3D for Surveyors Practice Files\Geospatial* folder.

2. If required, change your workspace to **Planning and Analysis**.

3. In the *Home* tab>Data panel, click ⬚ (Connect), as shown in Figure 2–28.

Figure 2–28

4. In the Data Connect palette, select **Add Raster Image or Surface Connection**, set the *Connection name* to **Aerial Image** and click 🖳 (browse for image file), as shown in Figure 2–29.

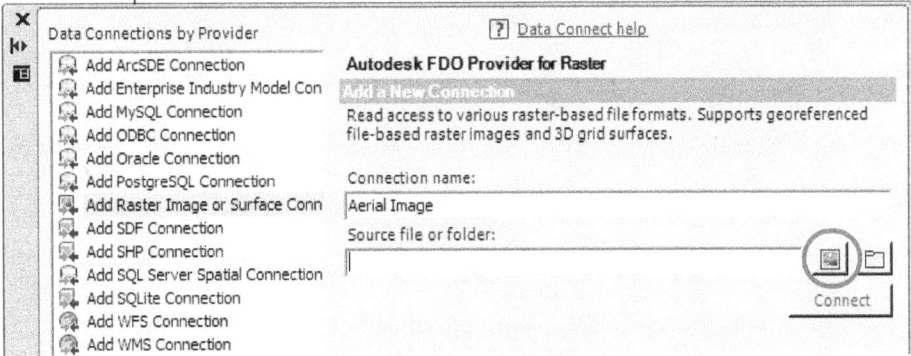

Figure 2–29

5. Select the **Main Site.jpg** in the *C:\Civil 3D for Surveyors Practice Files\Images* folder. Click **Open**.

6. In the Data Connect palette, click **Connect**.

7. In the *Coordinate System* column, double-click on **<unknown>** to edit the coordinate system that is registered with the image file.

8. In the Edit Spatial Contexts dialog box, select **<unknown>** and click **Edit**, as shown in Figure 2–30.

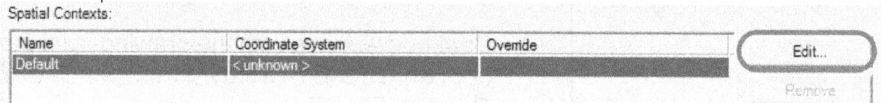

Figure 2–30

9. In the *Search* field, type **CA83**, and in the list of code, select **CA83-VI**. Click **Select**. Click **OK**.

10. In the Data Connect palette, click **Add to Map**, close the Data Connect palette, and save the drawing.

Task 2 - Connect to a Shape file.

---

1. Continue working with the drawing from the previous task or open **GEO-B2-GIS.dwg** from the *C:\Civil 3D for Surveyors Practice Files\Geospatial* folder.

2. If you closed the Data Connect palette, in the *Home* tab>Data panel, click 🗄 (Connect).

3. In the Data Connect palette, select **Add SHP Connection**.

   Set the *Connection name* to **Parcels** and click 🔲 (Browse for SHP file), as shown in Figure 2–31.

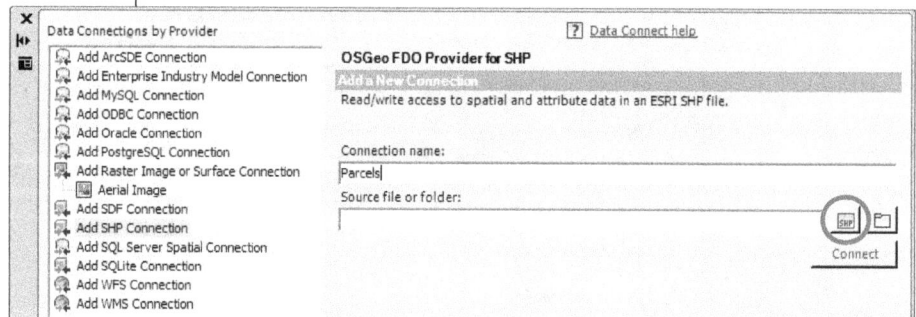

Figure 2–31

4. Select **Properties.shp** in *C:\Civil 3D for Surveyors Practice Files\Geospatial* folder. Click **Open**.

5. In the Data Connect palette, click **Connect**.

6. In the Data Connect palette, click **Add to Map**. Close the Data Connect palette and save the drawing.

7. If the Map Task Pane is not displayed, click (Map Task Pane) in the *View* tab>Palettes panel, as shown in Figure 2–32.

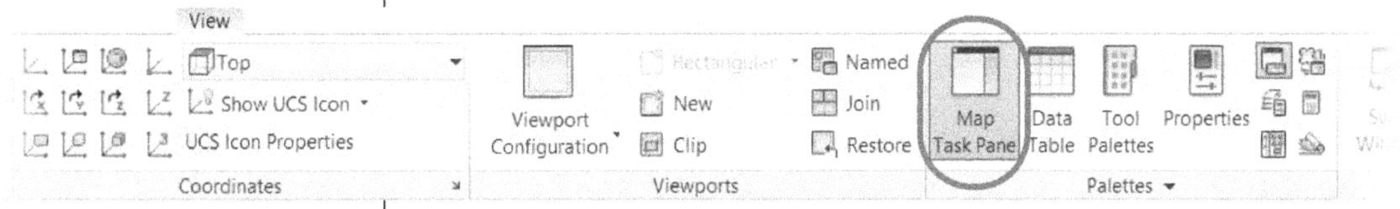

Figure 2–32

8. In the Task Pane>*Display Manager* tab, double-click on the **Properties** layer.

9. In the Style Editor palette, in the *Style* column, click (Browse), as shown in Figure 2–33.

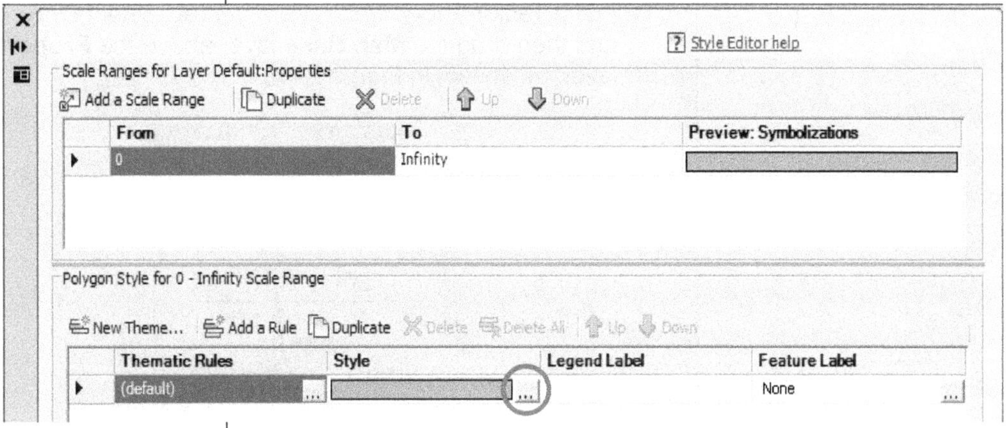

Figure 2–33

10. In the Style Polygon dialog box, change the *border color* to **Cyan** and the *fill color* to **No Color**, as shown in Figure 2–34. Click **Apply** and close the Style Polygon dialog box and Style Editor palette.

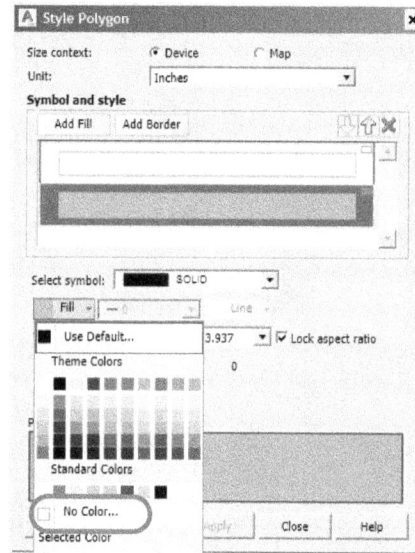

Figure 2–34

11. In the Task Pane>*Display Manager* tab, select **Draw Order** and then drag the **Map Base** layer above the **Properties** layer, as shown in Figure 2–35.

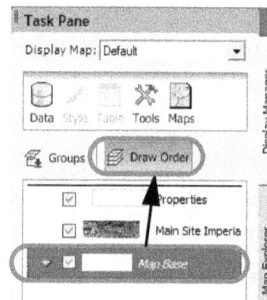

Figure 2–35

12. In the Draw Order dialog box that opens, select **Continue action and allow Draw Order to control layer position from now on**.

13. Save the drawing.

2.4 Create a Surface from GIS Data

An AutoCAD Civil 3D surface can be created from GIS data. Once created, the surface can be used to create surface profiles and act as a target for corridor models and grading groups. It is recommended that you request any available metadata when obtaining GIS layers that could be used for creating a 3D surface model. The metadata should indicate how accurate the data is and whether it can be used in detailed design drawings. GIS surfaces are not often used for detailed design because they are typically mapping grade rather than survey grade, but that is changing rapidly. Having a surface from GIS data can be useful in the project planning phase of a project, even if it is not survey grade. Data source types that can be used to create a surface include: ArcSDE, Oracle, and ESRI Shape Files.

How To: Create an AutoCAD Civil 3D Surface from SHP files

1. In the Quick Access Toolbar, select **Civil 3D** for the workspace.
2. In the *Home* tab>Create Ground Data panel, expand the Surfaces drop-down list and click 🖾 (Create Surface from GIS Data), as shown in Figure 2–36.

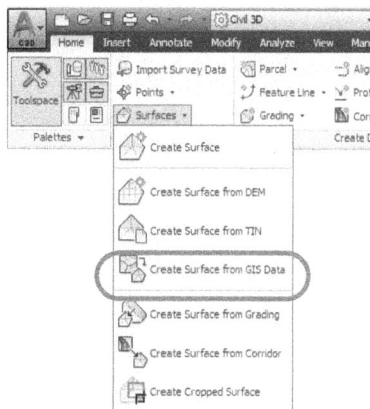

Figure 2–36

3. In the Object Options page, set the *Civil 3D object type* to **Surface**. Type a name and select the required styles for displaying the surface, as shown in Figure 2–37. Click **Next**.

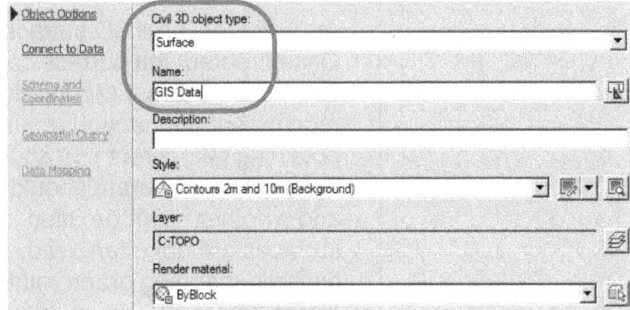

Figure 2–37

4. In the Connect to Data page, for the Data source type, select **SHP**, click ⌷ (Browse for file) and select a shape file that includes vector data for the contours and elevation data in the database file, as shown in Figure 2–38. Click **Open** and click **Login**.

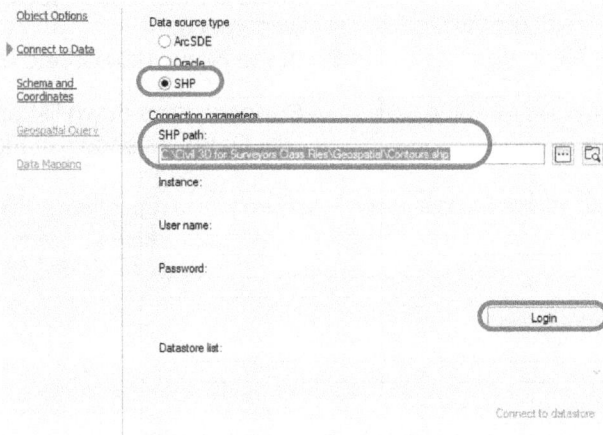

Figure 2–38

5. In the Schema and Coordinates page, select the **Contours** feature class and ensure that the *Contours Coordinate system* is set, as shown in Figure 2–39. Click **Next**.

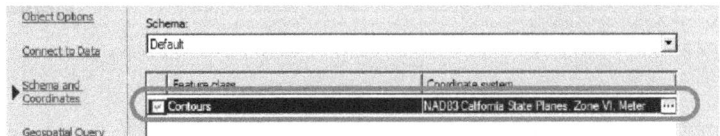

Figure 2–39

6. In the Geospatial Query page, clear the **Define area of interest** option so that the entire Contours shape file is used to create a surface, as shown in Figure 2–40. Click **Next**.

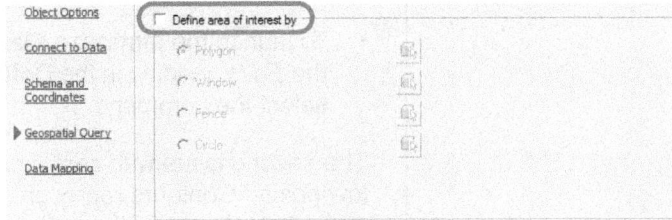

Figure 2–40

7. In the Data Mapping page, expand the drop-down list and select the field that holds the surface elevation values, as shown in Figure 2–41. Click **Finish**.

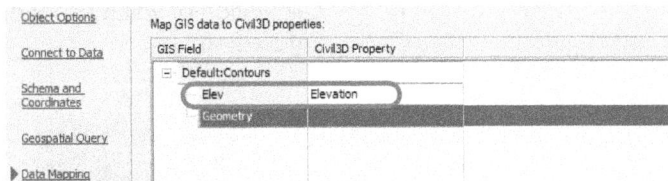

Figure 2–41

Contour data is available from many sources. Large sites are often surveyed using aerial photogrammetry, which provides contour polylines and spot elevations. When contour data is used from other GIS data types, the AutoCAD Civil 3D software interprets the imported linework as polylines with elevations.

In the AutoCAD Civil 3D software, polylines with elevation are useful as custom contour objects. Whether using polylines or other GIS contour objects, the AutoCAD Civil 3D software builds a surface by triangulating between contours. The end of each triangle side connects to a vertex of two different contours.

Contour Issues

Note the following issues when working with contour data: bays and peninsulas in the contours and the lack of high and low point elevations. These issues affect triangulation and the quality of a surface.

Bays and peninsulas in contours represent gullies or isolated high points on a surface. As long as there is data to work with, the AutoCAD Civil 3D software builds a surface by triangulating between contours of different elevations. When the software cannot triangulate between different contours, the triangulation switches to connecting vertices on the same contour.

The **Minimize Flat Faces** command helps mitigate this situation by forcing the triangulation to target different contours, as shown in Figure 2–42. However, this method, similar to the edge swap method, does not correct every problem on a contour surface.

- To launch the **Minimize Flat Faces** command, right-click on the *Edits* heading in the **Definition** collection of a surface and select the command.

The second issue with contour data regards the loss of high and low points. Contours represent an elevation interval (120, 122, 123, etc.). However, the top of a hill could be 123.04 or 136.92 and the only contours present are for the elevations of 123 or 136. Spot elevations are required in the surface data to help correctly resolve the high and low spots of a surface.

- Flat spots and the loss of high and low points affect the calculation of volumes for earthworks, as shown in Figure 2–43.

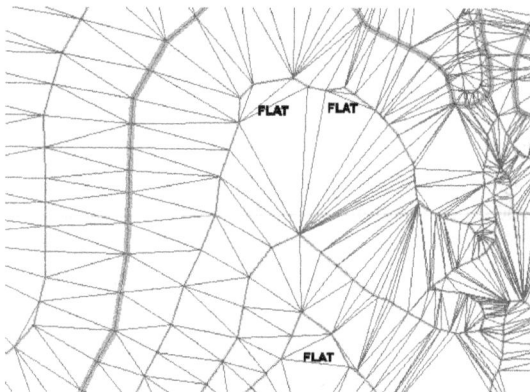

Figure 2–42

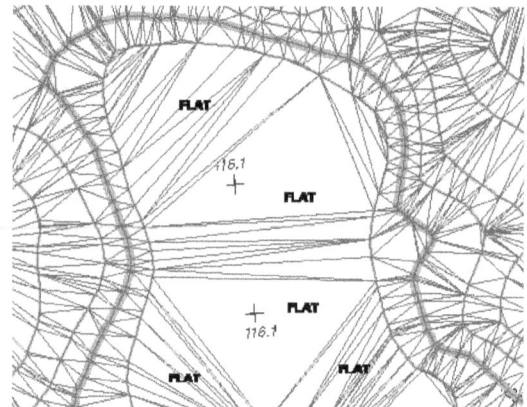

Figure 2–43

Minimizing Flat Triangle Strategies

By default, the **Minimize flat areas by:** options (shown in Figure 2–44) are selected in the Add Contour Data dialog box.

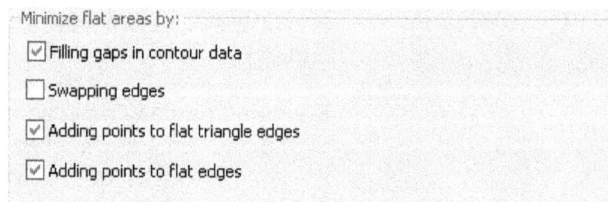

Minimize flat areas by:
☑ Filling gaps in contour data
☐ Swapping edges
☑ Adding points to flat triangle edges
☑ Adding points to flat edges

Figure 2–44

Together, these three methods attempt to detect and resolve peninsulas, bays, and other issues by adding additional points and filling in gaps based on surface trends. Generally, these provide the most expected results. The **Swapping edges** option is provided as a way of emulating how other terrain modeling software (such as AutoCAD Land Desktop) traditionally approached minimizing flat areas. The AutoCAD Civil 3D software automatically applies three of the four Minimize flat area options as it creates the surface from GIS data.

Draping Images on a Surface

Images and other 2D linework can be draped on a surface. Draping a 2D image on a surface gives it the appearance of being 3D and provides a better visualization of what is happening on the project site.

How To: Drape an Image on an AutoCAD Civil 3D Surface

1. In Model Space, select the **GIS Data** surface. In the contextual *Surface* tab>Surface Tools panel, click ⬠ (Drape Image), as shown in Figure 2–45.

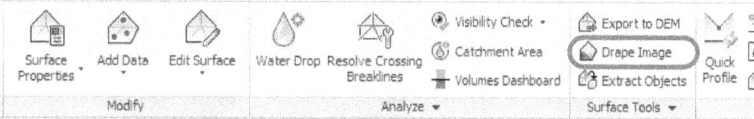

Figure 2–45

2. In the Drape Image dialog box, ensure that the **Main Site** image is selected and that the GIS Data surface is selected, as shown in Figure 2–46. Click **OK**.

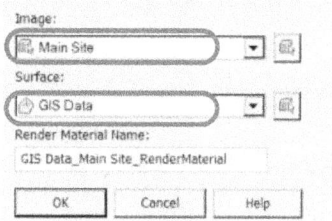

Figure 2–46

Practice 2c

Estimated time for completion: 5 minutes

Create a Surface from a Shape File

Practice Objective

- Create a surface from a shape file containing elevation data.

In this practice, you will create a new drawing and assign a coordinate system to the drawing.

Task 1 - Create a surface from a Shape file.

1. Continue working with the drawing from the previous practice or open **GEO-C1-GIS.dwg** from the *C:\Civil 3D for Surveyors Practice Files\Geospatial* folder.

2. In the Quick Access Toolbar, select **Civil 3D** for the workspace.

3. In the *Home* tab>Create Ground Data panel, expand the Surfaces drop-down list and click (Create Surface from GIS Data), as shown in Figure 2–47.

Figure 2–47

4. In the Object Options page, for the *Name*, type **GIS Data**. Leave all of the other settings as their defaults, as shown in Figure 2–48. Click **Next**.

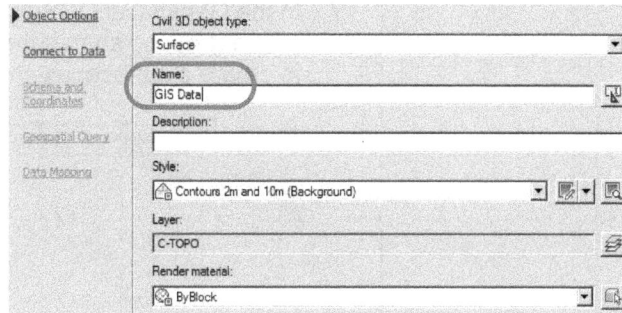

Figure 2–48

5. In the Connect to Data page, set the *Data source type* to

   SHP. Click ▦ (Browse for file) and select **Contours.shp** in the *C:\Civil 3D for Surveyors Practice Files\Geospatial* folder, as shown in Figure 2–49. Click **Open**. Then, click **Login**.

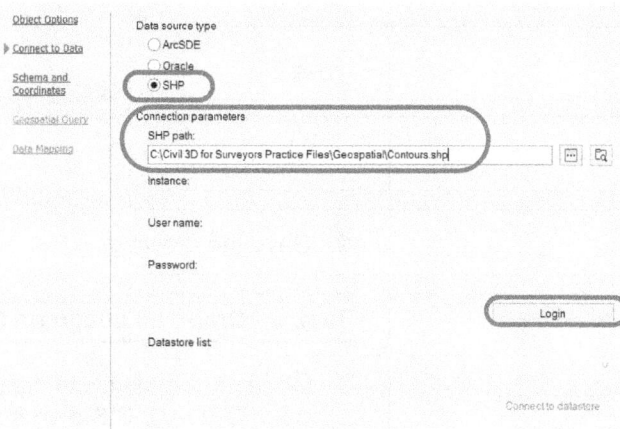

Figure 2–49

6. On the Schema and Coordinates page, select the **Contours** feature class and ensure that the *Contours Coordinate system* is set to **NAD83 California State Planes, Zone VI**, as shown in Figure 2–50. Click **Next**.

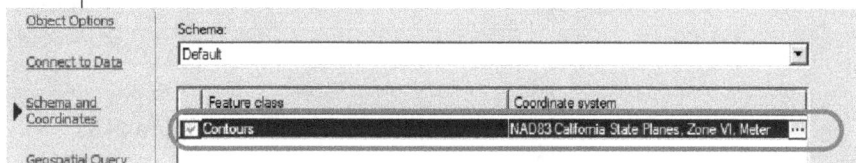

Figure 2–50

7. In the Geospatial Query page, clear the **Define area of interest** option so that the entire Contours shape file is used to create a surface, as shown in Figure 2–51. Click **Next**.

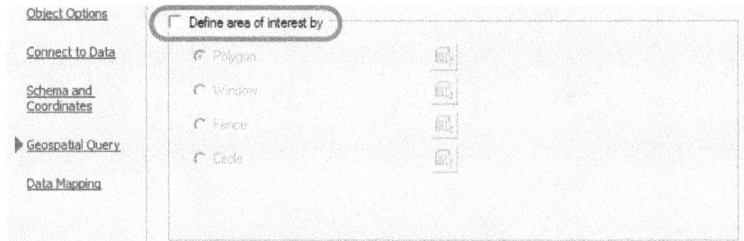

Figure 2–51

8. In the Data Mapping page, expand the Elev drop-down list and select **Elevation**, as shown in Figure 2–52. Click **Finish**.

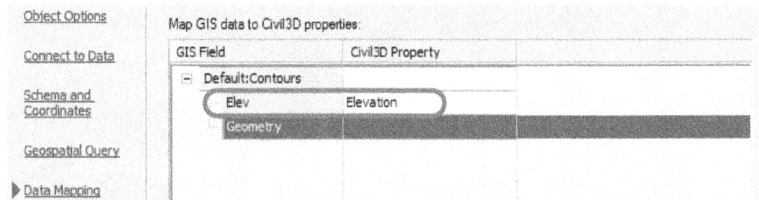

Figure 2–52

9. Save the drawing.

Task 2 - Drape an image on the surface.

1. Continue working with the drawing from the previous task or open **GEO-C2-GIS.dwg** from the *C:\Civil 3D for Surveyors Practice Files\Geospatial* folder.

2. In Model Space, select the **GIS Data** surface. In the contextual *Surface* tab>Surface Tools panel, click ◇ (Drape Image), as shown in Figure 2–53.

Figure 2–53

*The image might not look the same in the object view. Use **3D Orbit** to display the results of draping an image.*

3. In the Drape Image dialog box, ensure that the **Main Site** image is selected and that the GIS Data surface is selected, as shown in Figure 2–54. Click **OK**, then press <Esc> to clear the surface selection.

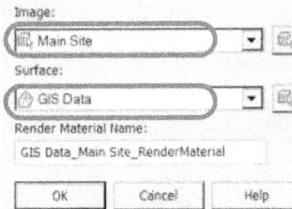

Figure 2–54

4. In the *View* tab>Navigate 2D panel, click ⚓ (Orbit). Orbit the drawing as shown in Figure 2–55. Press <Esc>.

Figure 2–55

5. Save the drawing.

Chapter Review Questions

1. In which workspace is the Coordinate System panel located?

   a. Civil 3D

   b. 2D Drafting and Annotation

   c. 3D Modeling

   d. Planning and Analysis

2. What type of data cannot be connected using the Data Connection palette?

   a. ArcSDE

   b. Oracle

   c. Microstation DGN file

   d. ESRI Shape File

3. You have to be in the Planning and Analysis workspace to access the Data Connect palette.

   a. True

   b. False

4. In which workspace is the **Create Surface from GIS Data** command located?

   a. Civil 3D

   b. 2D Drafting and Annotation

   c. 3D Modeling

   d. Planning and Analysis

5. What toolspace do you need to be in to drape an image on a surface?

   a. Civil 3D

   b. 3D Modeling

   c. Planning and Analysis

   d. It does not matter because the *Surface* contextual tab displays when you select a surface no matter which workspace you are using.

Command Summary

Button	Command	Location
	Assign	• **Workspace**: Planning and Analysis • **Ribbon**: *Map Setup* tab>Coordinate System panel • **Command Prompt:** MAPCSASSIGN
	Create Surface from GIS Data	• **Workspace**: Civil 3D • **Ribbon**: *Home* tab>Create Ground Data panel • **Command Prompt:** CreateSurfaceFromGISData
	Data Connect	• **Workspace**: Planning and Analysis • **Ribbon**: *Home* tab>Data panel • **Command Prompt:** MAPCONNECT
	Drape Image	• **Ribbon**: Contextual *Surface* tab>Surface Tools panel
	Map Task Pane	• **Workspace**: Civil 3D, or Planning and Analysis • **Ribbon**: *Home* tab>Expanded Palettes panel, or *View* tab>Palettes panel • **Command Prompt:** MapWSpace

Survey Setup

Every good survey begins with research of the property to be developed before ever stepping foot on the property. Evidence plays a key role in determining where the true boundary lies. This evidence can be found in deeds, contracts, maps, wills, or other legal documents. In this chapter, you learn how to prepare the model for importing survey data by creating a figure database and figure styles. Next, you learn how to successfully create a new survey database for storing survey data and to create linework from a legal description of a property.

Accuracy is one of the most important factors of a land survey. Inaccuracies can eventually lead to legal issues. For that reason, a traverse is important to reduce closure errors. In this chapter, you learn how to create a traverse and run a Map check on it to find closure errors.

Learning Objectives in this Chapter

- List the steps in a typical survey workflow that are going to be used to create linework from coordinate files.
- Display the Survey Toolspace and content that is listed under each of its trees.
- Create a figure prefix database for stylizing linework automatically on importing field book or ASCII files.
- Create a new survey database in the required working folder.
- Draw Parcels from a legal description.
- Create a traverse by entering data manually.
- Find the error of closure by running a mapcheck.

3.1 Survey Workflow Overview

This course focuses on automated **Field to Finish** tools that aid in drafting an accurate and efficient *Existing Conditions Plan*. These tools create a correct existing topography, property lines, right-of-way, and center line locations.

Workflow

The survey workflow can be broken into three distinctive phases: **Prepare for survey data**, **Obtain and create survey data**, and **Adjust, analyze, and output survey data** as shown in Figure 3–1.

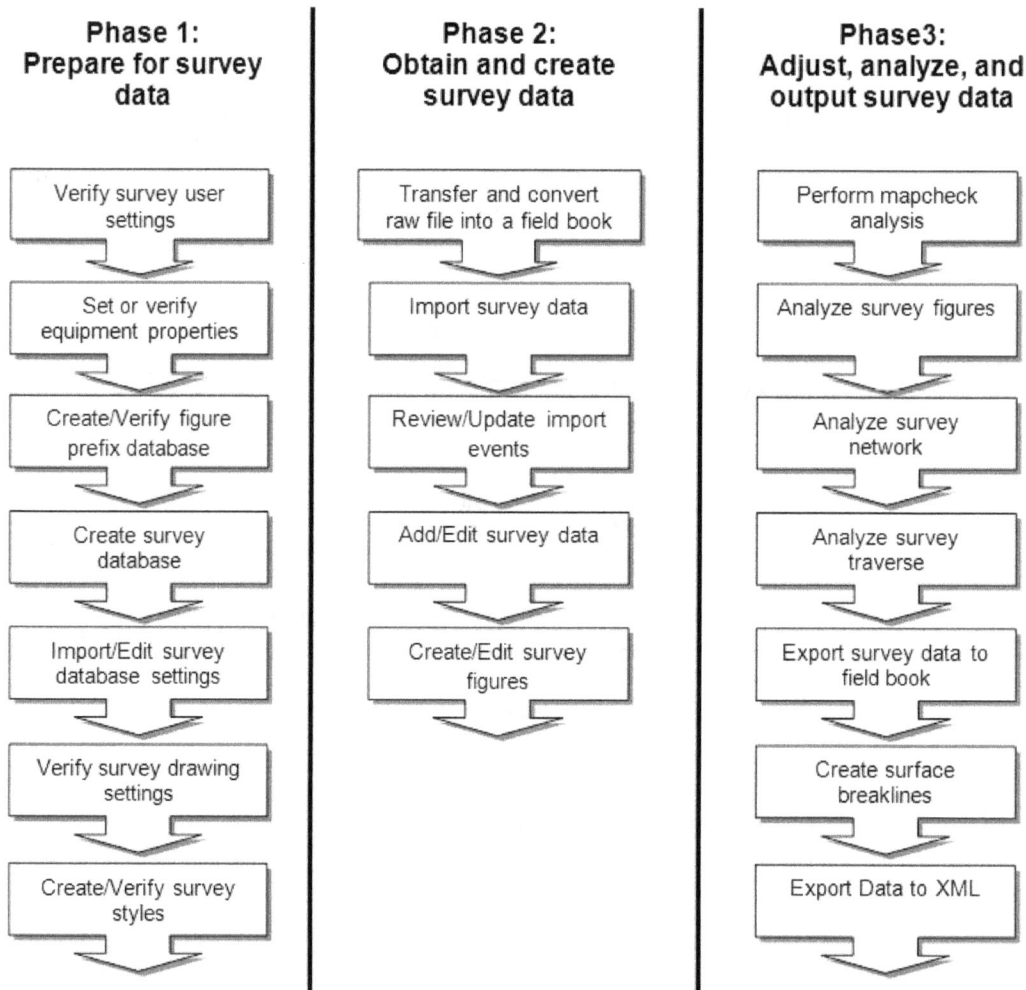

Phase 1: Prepare for survey data	Phase 2: Obtain and create survey data	Phase3: Adjust, analyze, and output survey data
Verify survey user settings	Transfer and convert raw file into a field book	Perform mapcheck analysis
Set or verify equipment properties	Import survey data	Analyze survey figures
Create/Verify figure prefix database	Review/Update import events	Analyze survey network
Create survey database	Add/Edit survey data	Analyze survey traverse
Import/Edit survey database settings	Create/Edit survey figures	Export survey data to field book
Verify survey drawing settings		Create surface breaklines
Create/Verify survey styles		Export Data to XML

Figure 3–1

The first stage in standardizing the survey workflow is to research, understand, establish, and put into practice the resources available to you. When using the data collector, you need to determine the format into which the data needs to be converted.

In addition, the AutoCAD® Civil 3D® Styles and Settings must be set up in advance and saved as a Template (*.DWT) for the required automation to work correctly.

Some factors that should be addressed so that you can maximize your productivity when using the automation, tools, and extensions in the AutoCAD Civil 3D software are as follows:

- Are the survey field crews responsible for reducing their field notes on site?

- What software is used to analyze the survey data, if not the AutoCAD Civil 3D software?

- Is the data analyzed before it is imported into the AutoCAD Civil 3D software?

- What type of data format is being used?

- Are point code description and line code connective used?

- When should you import points into the drawing using the Prospector or the Survey Database?

- Should the figure commands be placed before or after the code?

- Does the field crew know the correct keystrokes to enter into the data collector and how that input affects the linework, symbology, or breaklines for the office surveyors and draftsman?

3.2 Collecting Field Data

Before collecting field data, it is important to determine which file formats can be used when importing survey data. Both field books and point text files can be used. Depending on which ASCII format is used, point descriptions are coded differently in the field. The following three commonly used survey data files can be imported into AutoCAD Civil 3D:

- Point files

- Point files with connective codes

- Field book files

Point Files

Point files consist of a simple ASCII file containing the point number, northing, easting, elevation, and description, as shown in Figure 3–2. This format has been commonly used since the early days of CAD. Surveyors reduced their survey notes, modified the data as required, and output the point file that was imported into a CAD program.

```
306,620951.2129,1906947.2537,52.8633,Cottonwood 1
307,620891.4575,1907051.6193,54.2706,Cottonwood 3
308,620947.5148,1907001.1980,51.6455,Cottonwood 2
309,620929.0278,1907005.9716,52.2365,Cottonwood 1
310,620918.3755,1907041.4409,53.0132,Pine 2
311,620924.0094,1907055.0640,52.4753,Pine 1
312,620929.4085,1907070.0964,52.3893,Pine 1
313,620939.2678,1907131.8701,49.9998,Pine 1
314,620938.7983,1907117.7772,50.5543,Pine 2
315,620893.9387,1907122.4070,54.4228,Pine 2
```

Point Description

Figure 3–2

Point files with connective codes

A point file with connective codes contains the point number, northing, easting, elevation, description, and line connective codes, as shown in Figure 3–3. Line connective codes are appended to the point description. The connective code is a line command code that indicates whether the line is a beginning, continuation, end, curve segment, or line segment.

In the AutoCAD Civil 3D software, the syntax of the field code corresponds to a previously defined linework code set. The correspondence between the field codes and the linework code set permits the following:

- Automatic assignment of point properties, such as **Layer**, **Symbol**, and **Label**.

- Automatic assignment of line feature properties, such as **Layer**, **Color**, **Linetype**, and **Lineweight**.

- Line connectivity between the surveyed points.

```
1,5000.0000,10000.0000,77.2507,FdIP
2,5047.4285,9999.5818,78.6023,FencePost B
3,5047.6924,9987.9653,77.7915,FencePost
4,5047.1646,9974.7648,76.7385,FencePost
5,5047.1646,9957.3400,75.3846,FencePost
6,5046.9007,9945.4595,74.4644,FencePost
7,5046.9007,9933.8430,73.6032,FencePost
8,5047.1646,9921.4345,72.7112,FencePost E
9,5044.7895,9960.7722,75.5783,pool B BC
10,5045.0534,9954.6999,75.1165,pool
11,5042.6783,9950.4757,74.7183,pool
```

Connective Code

Point Description

Connective Code

Figure 3–3

Field Book File

A field book file typically contains all of the data that was used during the survey field pickup by a total station (e.g., setups, backsites, instrument height, prism height, turned angles, side shots, etc.). The difference between a field book file and a point file with connective codes is that, in the field, the connective code is added as a note which is separate from the point description. However, the point description and the connective codes must match, as shown in Figure 3–4.

Connective Code Must Match the Point Description

Connective Code

```
Begin Trail
NE SS 517 620921.1043 1907193.029 50.1765 "Trail"
NE SS 518 620925.7005 1907169.268 50.1039 "Trail"
NE SS 519 620931.0628 1907129.794 50.7929 "Trail"
MCS
NE SS 520 620927.9986 1907091.471 51.9004 "Trail"
NE SS 521 620916.8912 1907054.68 52.8681 "Trail"
NE SS 522 620903.8686 1907028.619 53.2647 "Trail"
```

Point Description

Figure 3–4

3.3 Introduction to the Survey Toolspace

The Survey Toolspace displays a panel through which all surveys are processed. Survey uses graphics to display field book imports, figure and network previews, and points. If you toggle off these graphics, you can process a survey without a drawing being open. If you want to display these graphics, you need to have a drawing open. Survey prompts you to open a drawing if you do not have one open.

The Survey Toolspace contains Survey settings, Equipment defaults, Figure Prefixes, and Linework Code Sets. Survey's settings can be on a local or network folder. Using a network folder is preferred for larger offices because all users can then standardize the file values.

How To: Display the Survey Toolspace

Click ﹅ (Survey Toolspace) in the *Home* tab>Palettes panel, as shown in Figure 3–5.

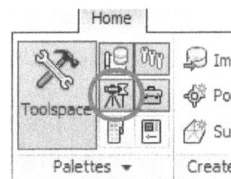

Figure 3–5

Typical Survey Database Settings

Surveys are either in a predefined, local Coordinate system or an assumed coordinate system (e.g., 5000 for Northing and 5000 for Easting). Either of these coordinates systems are typed in a data collector at the first survey control found by the field crew. In the AutoCAD Civil 3D software, these different settings can be stored as definitions that are assigned when creating a database, or are assigned by editing a survey's settings.

3.4 Survey Figures

Survey figures consist of linework generated by coding and placed in a file that is imported into the Survey Database. A figure represents linear features (edge-of-pavement, toe-of-slopes, etc.)

Therefore, a figure has many functions, as follows:

- A figure displays linework in a drawing.

- All preset figures in a drawing can be defined as breaklines for a surface definition with one step.

- All preset figures in a drawing can be defined as parcel lines.

- A figure can be drawn as a pipe run. For example, a surveyor notices that only one pipe comes through a manhole. The surveyor then invokes a figure command to draw a survey figure that denotes the location of a pipe run. The Elevation Editor in the AutoCAD Civil 3D software enables you to lower each survey figure at each manhole to the distance of what was measured in the field, and what was written on the manhole field notes as the flow elevation at the invert of the pipe run. The pipe functionality can make this line represent various types of locations within the circumference of the cross-sectional pipe and convert the survey figure into an existing pipe run.

- All figures can be targets for *Width* or *Offset Targets* in a Corridor.

- All figures can be targets for *Slope* or *Elevation Targets* in a Corridor (e.g., limits of construction for a road rehab project might be to the face of walk, which exists in the drawing as a Survey Figure, hence a target).

- The Figure Prefix database and figure styles should be set up before importing any survey data to obtain the required entities in a drawing. As point and label styles and the Description Key Set need to exist before importing points, figure styles and entries in the Figure Prefix database need to exist before importing survey data.

Drawing Settings

The Drawing Settings dialog box (shown in Figure 3–6), sets a universal layer for figures. You can access these settings by selecting the drawing name in the *Settings* tab, right-clicking, and selecting **Edit Drawing Settings…** When selecting the *Object Layer* tab and scrolling to the bottom of the list, the default layer names are displayed.

Your company might have one or more default layers for each of the linework types. For example, edge-of-pavement, sidewalk, etc., each have their own layers in the drawing. To accomplish this, you need to define figure styles.

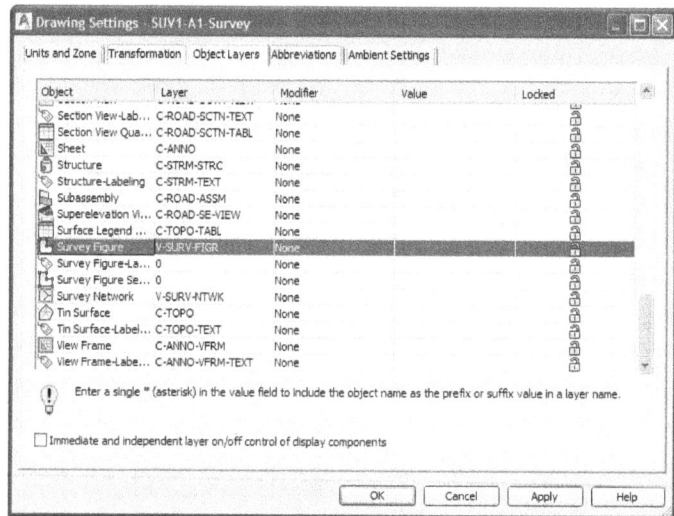

Figure 3–6

Figure Styles

Figure styles (found in the *Settings* tab in the Toolspace) affect how the survey linework displays in a drawing. They should be part of your template file. These styles are not critical. However, to make figures work, you should define the layers they use in the drawing.

- Figure styles are tied to the Figure Prefix database.

- The Figure Prefix database assigns a figure style to a figure that is imported into a drawing.

- A figure style includes the layers for its linework and markers.

- A marker is a symbol placed on the figure's segment midpoints and end points. They call attention to the figure's geometry. Although a figure style includes marker definitions, they do not need to display.

Figures can be 3D and use the layers set in the *Display* tab in the Figure Style dialog box. The *Information* tab assigns a name to a style. The *Plan*, *Profile*, and *Section* tabs define how the marker displays in each of these views. The Figure Style dialog box is shown in Figure 3–7.

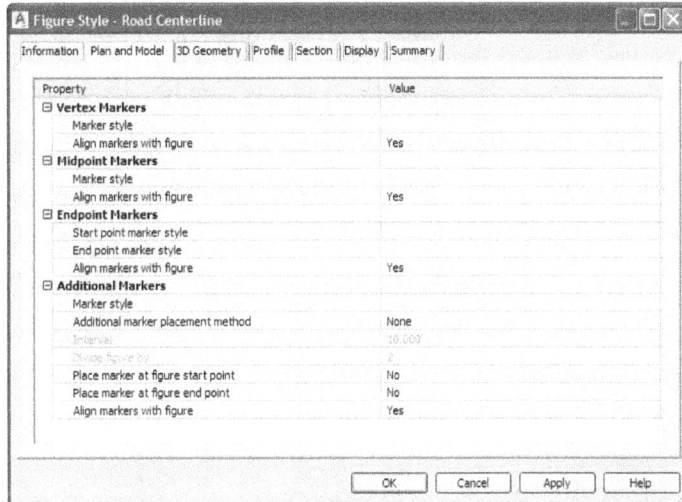

Figure 3–7

The *3D Geometry* tab defines a figure's vertical behavior. By default, the elevation of the point defines the figure. The *Display* tab defines which figure's components display and which layers they use for plan, profile, and section views, as shown in Figure 3–8.

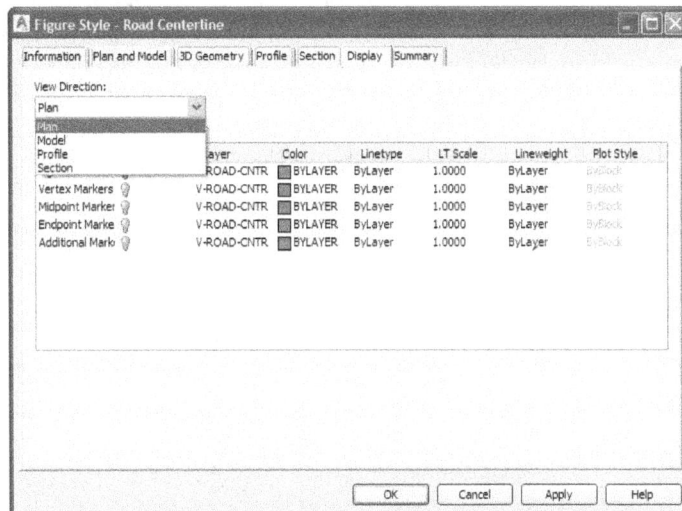

Figure 3–8

Figure Prefix Database

The Figure Prefix database, found in the *Survey* tab of the Toolspace, does the following, as shown in Figure 3–9:

- Assigns the figure a style.

- Assigns the figure a layer. If you did not define any figure styles, you should at least assign a layer to correctly place the figure in the drawing.

- Defines whether the figure is a surface breakline. Toggling on the *Breakline* property enables you select all of the tagged survey figures and assign them to a surface without having to insert or select from a drawing

- Defines whether the figure is a lot line (parcel segment). Toggling on the *Lot Line* property creates a parcel segment from the figure in the drawing and, if there is a closed polygon, assigns a parcel label and an entry in the survey site.

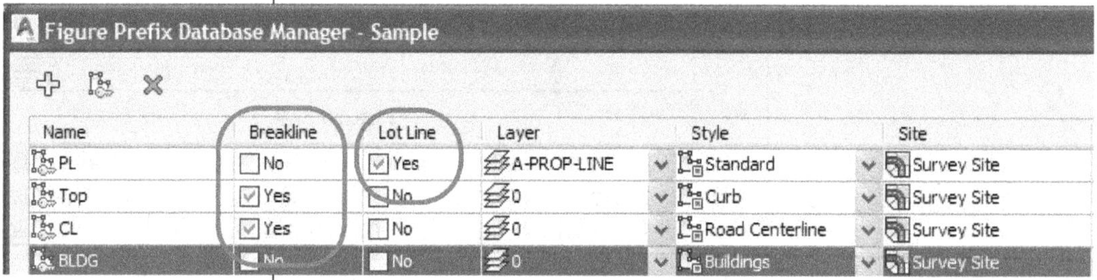

Figure 3–9

If the *Name* is **PL** (as shown in Figure 3–9), any figure starting with PL uses these settings. This is similar to using a Description Key Set, except that the entry in the Figure Prefix database does not need an asterisk (*). The entry **GUT** matches PL1 through PL100. When inserting survey figures in the drawing, Survey checks the Figure Prefix database for style or layer values.

Practice 3a

Creating Figure Prefixes

Practice Objective

- Create a figure database for automatically stylizing linework on importing field book or ASCII files.

Estimated time for completion: 5 minutes

1. Open **Setup-A1-Survey.dwg**, from the *C:\Civil 3D for Surveyors Practice Files\Survey* folder.

2. If required, change your workspace to Civil 3D.

3. In the *Home* tab>expanded Palettes panel, click ⬚ (Map Task Pane).

4. When prompted, select **ON**.

5. In the Task pane, *Display Manager* tab, clear the **Main Site** layer, as shown in Figure 3–10. Close the Map Task pane.

The aerial images used in this chapter were attached using the AutoCAD® Map 3D FDO connection. You toggle off the aerial images in order to make working with the survey data easier.

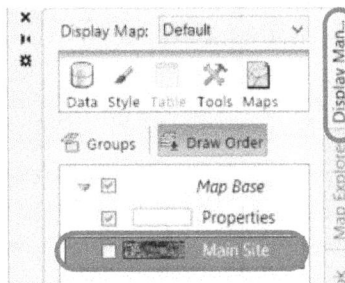

Figure 3–10

6. In the Toolspace, select the *Survey* tab. Right-click on Figure Prefix Databases, and select **New...**. Set the *Name* to **C3D Training**.

7. Right-click on the newly created **C3D Training** Figure Prefix database, and select **Make Current**.

8. Right-click on the C3D Training Figure Prefix database again, and select **Manage Figure Prefix Database...**.

9. Click ✛ to create a new Figure definition. The AutoCAD Civil 3D software creates a default Figure. Do the following, as shown in Figure 3–11:

   - Change the *Name* to **Trail**.
   - Set the *Breakline* to **Yes**.
   - Set the *Style* to **Road Centerline**.

Any figure starting with **Trail** will now be selectable for a surface breakline and will use the style **Road Centerline**. As noted earlier, unlike the Description Key Set, an asterisk (*) is not required to match Trail1, Trail2, etc.

Name	Breakline	Lot Line	Layer	Style	Site
Trail	✓ Yes	☐ No	0	Road Centerline	Survey Site

Figure 3–11

10. Click ✛ to create a new Figure definition and then do the following:

- Change the name to **Building**.
- Verify that *Breakline* is set to **No**.
- Set the *Style* to **Buildings**.
- Click **OK** to exit the dialog box.

11. Save the drawing.

3.5 The Survey Database

The Survey forking folder is the location for all of the Survey Databases and can be local or on the network. The preferred location is a network folder, in which you place the local Survey Databases. The Survey User Settings dialog box sets the defaults for all new Survey Databases. It is recommended to set them before starting Survey.

How To: Set the Working Folder for the Survey Database

1. In the *Survey* tab, select **Survey Databases**.
2. Right-click and select **Set working folder...**, as shown in Figure 3–12.

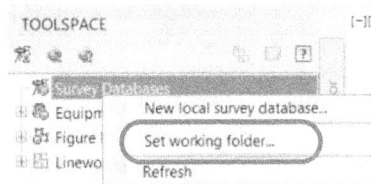

Figure 3–12

Survey Database

Survey Database Folders cannot be deleted in the AutoCAD Civil 3D Survey software. If you want to delete the working folder, it must be done manually external to the AutoCAD Civil 3D software.

A Survey Database is a subfolder in the working folder, as shown on the right in Figure 3–13. The Survey Working Folder contains the Survey's settings and the observation database. The database contains Survey's Networks, Figures, and Survey Points.

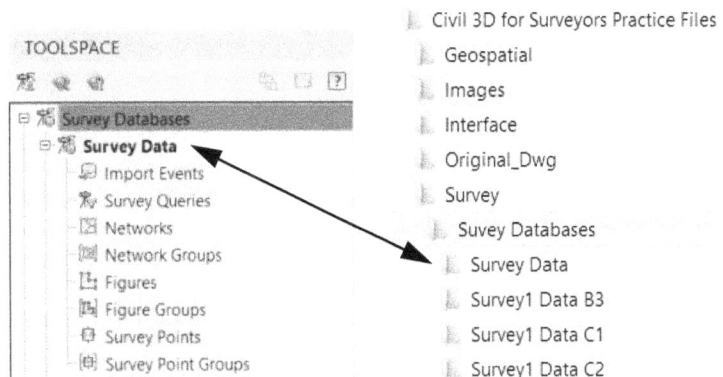

Figure 3–13

Each local Survey Database references files to perform some of its tasks.

- The Equipment Database is an *.EDB file. The Equipment settings file contains values to estimate errors for the Least Squares adjustment process.

- The Figure Prefix Database is an *. FDB file. The Figure Prefix Database lists definitions for Survey figures (figure style and layers). The default location for these files is *C:\Documents and Settings\All Users\Application Data\ Autodesk\C3D 2017\enu\Survey\.*

Survey has four nodes: **Import Events**, **Networks**, **Figures**, and **Survey Points**. **Import Events** is where files are imported into the Survey's networks. The files can be a coordinate, field book, LandXML file, and points from a drawing. When importing a file, depending on its contents, the import results in figures and points. Information in the file also populates portions of Survey's Network. When importing a coordinate or field book file containing only coordinates, the Figures and Survey Points nodes are used. When processing a file with observations, turned angles, zenith angles, slope distances, and setups, you use the network and its nodes.

How To: Create an Equipment Database

1. In the *Home* tab>Palettes panel, click 🔭 (Survey Toolspace) to display the *Survey* tab, as shown in Figure 3–14.

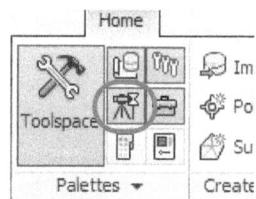

Figure 3–14

2. In the Toolspace, select the *Survey* tab.

3. Right-click on **Equipment Database** and select **New**, as shown in Figure 3–15. Enter an equipment database name, then click **OK** to accept and close the dialog box.

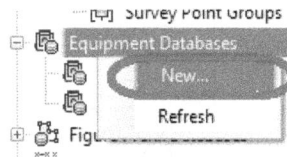

Figure 3–15

4. To open the Equipment Properties dialog box, select the equipment database, right-click, and select **Manage Equipment database...**
5. Review the settings. When done, click **OK** to close the dialog box.
6. The AutoCAD Civil 3D software saves the Equipment database files in the folder shown in Figure 3–16. To change the path to a network drive, click 🔭 (Survey User Setting), scroll down to *Equipment Defaults*, and browse for a new path.

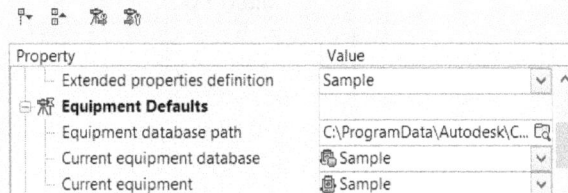

Figure 3–16

7. Review the settings. When done, click **OK** to close the dialog box.

By default, the AutoCAD Civil 3D software saves the Equipment database files in the folder C:\ProgramData\Autodesk\C3D 2017\enu\Survey\.

How To: Create a Survey Database Using the Import Survey Data Command

1. In the *Home* tab>Create Ground Data panel, click 🖳 (Import Survey Data).
2. In the Import Survey Data dialog box, click **Create New Survey Database**. Enter a name and click **OK**.
3. In the Import Survey Data dialog box, select the new survey database and click **Edit Survey Database Settings**.

Note that the survey can be done in any coordinate system even if it does not match the project coordinate system. The AutoCAD Civil 3D software converts the coordinates and units in the drawing.

4. In the dialog box, under *Units*, for the *Coordinate Zone*, click ⊡ and select a coordinate system, as shown in Figure 3–17. Click **OK**.

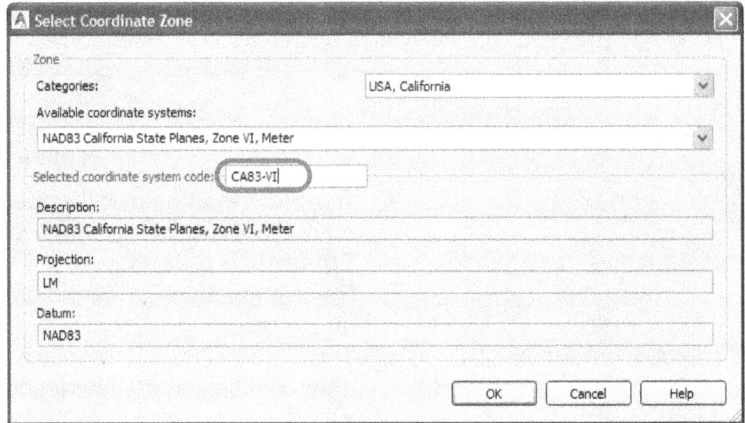

Figure 3–17

5. Set the *Direction*, *Temperature*, *Pressure* and other settings, as shown in Figure 3–18. When done, click **OK** to close the dialog box.

Property	Value
⊟ 🔭 **Units**	
Coordinate zone	CA83-VI
Distance	Meter
Angle	Degrees DMS (DDD.MMSSS)
Direction	North Azimuths
Temperature	Celsius
Pressure	Millimeters Hg

Figure 3–18

6. In the Import Survey Data dialog box, click **Next**.
7. Select the Data source type and browse for the file. Then click **Next**.
   • If the Data source type is set to **Point File**, specify the file format.
   • If the Data source type is set to **Points From Drawing**, click **Select points in current drawing**. Then, draw a selection window around the appropriate points and press <Enter>.
8. If a control network is required, click **Create New Network**. Then click **Next**.
   • If a control network in not required, just click **Next**.
9. Set the appropriate *Import Options* and click **Finish**.

How To: Create a Survey Database Without Importing Data at the Same Time

1. In the *Home* tab>Palettes panel, click 🔭 (Survey Toolspace) to display the *Survey* tab.
2. In the Toolspace, select the *Survey* tab.
3. Right-click on **Survey Databases** and select **New local survey database**.
4. Enter a name for the new database and click **OK**.

Open a Survey Database for Editing

Only one Survey Database can be opened at a time. When opened for editing, this prepares the survey for reading and writing. There are options to set the path or location for the Survey Database project files, as well as all of the settings. When you create a new Survey Database, a Windows folder is created with the same name. If you close a drawing with a survey open, the Survey Database closes automatically. You must start a new drawing and then open the required Survey Database.

How To: Open a Survey Database

1. Expand the **Survey Database** branch.
2. Select the survey database that you want to open, right-click and select **Open for edit** or **Open for read-only**, depending on your requirements, as shown in Figure 3–19.

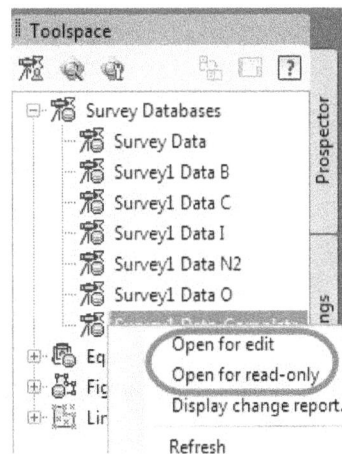

Figure 3–19

Practice 3b

Create a Survey Database

Estimated time for completion: 10 minutes

Practice Objective

- Create a survey database in preparation for importing survey data.

Task 1 - Create the Survey Database.

1. Open **Setup-B1-Survey.dwg** from the *C:\Civil 3D for Surveyors Practice Files\Survey* folder.

2. If the Survey Toolspace is not visible, in the *Home* tab>Palettes panel, click 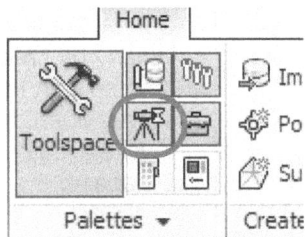 (Survey Toolspace), as shown in Figure 3–20.

Figure 3–20

3. In the Toolspace, select the *Survey* tab.

4. To create an Equipment database, right-click on **Equipment Database** and select **New**, as shown in Figure 3–21.

   - For the equipment database name, type **Training**, as shown in Figure 3–22.
   - Click **OK** to accept and close the dialog box.

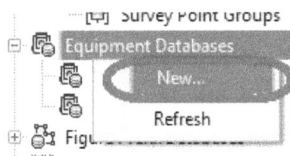

Figure 3–21

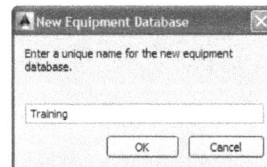

Figure 3–22

5. To open the Equipment Properties dialog box, select **Training**, right-click, and select **Manage Equipment database...**

6. Review the settings. When done, click **OK** to close the dialog box.

7. In the *Survey* tab, right-click on **Survey Databases**, and select **Set working folder…**, as shown in Figure 3–23.

   - Browse and select the *C:\Civil 3D for Surveyors Practice Files\Survey\ Survey Databases* folder, as shown in Figure 3–24.

   - When done, click **OK** to close the dialog box.

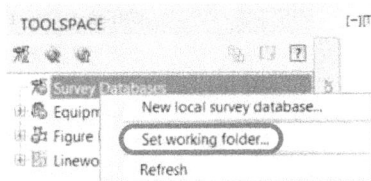

Figure 3–23

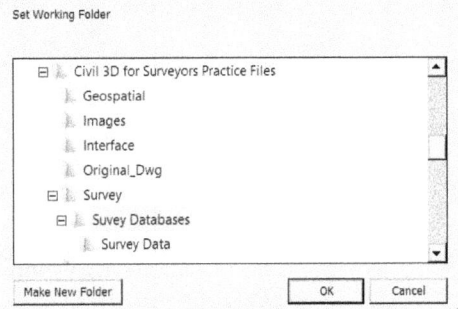

Figure 3–24

8. In the *Survey* tab of the Toolspace, right-click on **Survey Databases** and select **New local survey database**.

9. Set the *Name* to **Survey Data** and click **OK**.

10. Right-click on the **Survey Data** database and select **Edit Survey Database Settings**.

11. In the dialog box, under *Units*, for the *Coordinate Zone*, click

    ⸬ and select **NAD83 California State Planes, Zone VI, Meter**, as shown in Figure 3–25, and click **OK**.

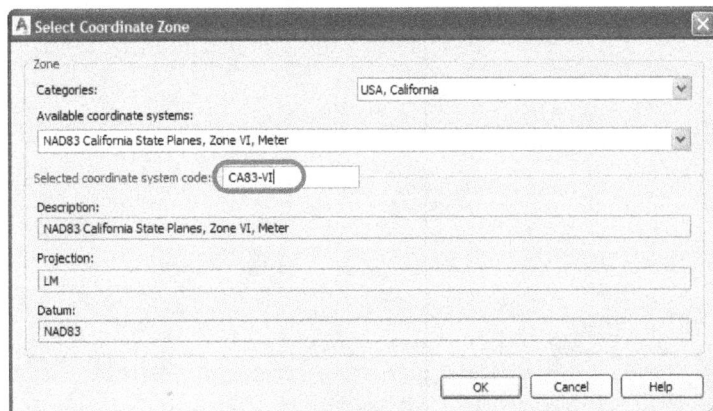

Figure 3–25

12. Set the following, as shown in Figure 3–26.
    - *Direction*: **North Azimuths**
    - *Temperature:* **Celsius**
    - *Pressure:* **Millimeters Hg**

Property	Value
⊟ 𝍪 **Units**	
Coordinate zone	CA83-VI
Distance	Meter
Angle	Degrees DMS (DDD.MMSSS)
Direction	North Azimuths
Temperature	Celsius
Pressure	Millimeters Hg

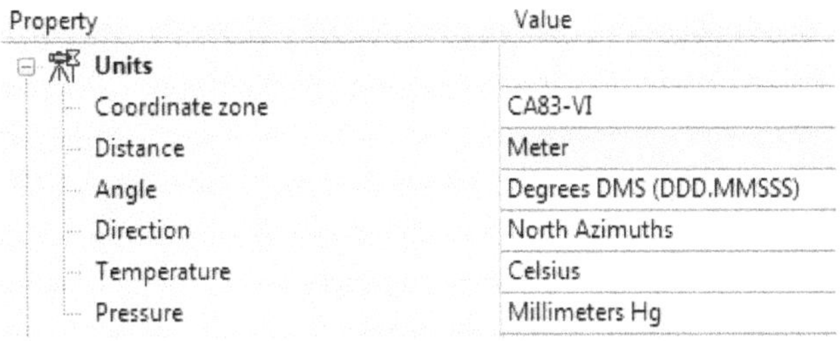

Figure 3–26

13. When done, click **OK** to close the dialog box.

14. Save the drawing.

3.6 Lines and Curves

Often, the first thing that has to be drawn up is the legal description of the property being developed. Designers need to enter into the computer, in the form of lines and curves, what they are given in a text description. The AutoCAD Civil 3D software makes this task easy with the many options under the **Lines** and **Curves** commands in the *Home* tab>Draw panel. Expanding the lines or curves commands displays several new options that are not found in the AutoCAD® software, as shown in Figure 3–27.

Figure 3–27

A second option is to use transparent commands. These are similar to Object Snaps because they can only be accessed while in another drawing command. Once the required command has been started, you can click the **Transparent** tool or type an apostrophe letter combination in the Command Line for the required **Transparent** command.

The benefit to using these to draw parcels over the **Lines** and **Curves** options (shown in Figure 3–27) is that a **Polyline** command can be used to create one entity rather than many individual lines that would need to be joined later.

Transparent Commands

Icon	Command Line	Description
	'AD	Angle Distance: Specifies a point location at an angle and distance from a known point and direction.
	'BD	Bearing Distance: Specifies a point location at a bearing and distance from a known point (or the last point occupied).
	'ZD	Azimuth Distance: Specifies a point location at an azimuth and distance from a known point (or the last point occupied).
	'DD	Deflection Distance: Specifies a point location at an angle and distance from a known point and previous direction.
	'NE	Northing Easting: Specifies a point location using northing and easting coordinates.
	'GN	Grid Northing Grid Easting: Specifies a point location using a grid northing and grid easting. (Note: You must have the drawing zone, coordinate system, and transformations set for grids.)
	'LL	Latitude Longitude: Specifies a point location using latitude and longitude. (Note: You must have the drawing zone, coordinate system, and transformations set.)
	'PN	Point Number: Specifies a point location using a point number found in the drawing or active project.
	'PA	Point Name: Specifies a point location using a point name found in the drawing or active project.
	'PO	Point Object: Specifies a point location by picking any part of an existing COGO point in the drawing.
	'ZTP	Zoom to Point: Zooms to a point in the drawing or active project by specifying the point number or name.
	'SS	Side Shot: Specifies a point location at an angle and distance from a known point and direction (uses the last two entered points to set the reference line).
	'SO	Station Offset: Specifies a point location at a station and an offset from an alignment in the current drawing.
	.g	Point Object Filter: Specifies a point location by picking any part of an existing COGO point in the drawing.

	'STAE	Profile Station from Plan: Specifies a profile view point location by specifying an alignment station in plan and an elevation.
	'SSE	Profile Station and Elevation from Plan: Specifies a profile view point location by specifying a surface, an alignment station, and a point in plan view.
	'SPE	Profile Station and Elevation from COGO Point: Specifies a profile view point location by specifying a COGO point and an alignment station in plan view.
	'PSE	Profile Station Elevation: Specifies a profile view point location by specifying a station and an elevation.
	'PGS	Profile Grade Station: Specifies a profile view point location using grade and station values from a known point.
	'PGE	Profile Grade Elevation: Specifies a profile view point location using grade and elevation values from a known point.
	'PGL	Profile Grade Length: Specifies a profile view point location using grade and length values from a known point (or the last point occupied).
	'MR	Match Radius: Specifies a radius equal to that of an existing object.
	'ML	Match Length: Specifies a length equal to that of an existing object.
	'CCALC	Curve Calculator: Calculates curve parameters based on input.

Practice 3c

Estimated time for completion: 20 minutes

Input the Project Boundary

Practice Objective

- Draw a parcel from a legal description.

In this practice you will use the legal description below to draw a parcel. Later you will create a traverse from the linework.

From the **POINT OF BEGINNING**; thence, S 00° 26' 42.2" W for a distance of 281.1517 m to a point on a line. Thence, S 00° 24' 20.8" W for a distance of 154.9449 m to a point on a line. Thence, S 66° 03' 35.8" W for a distance of 28.0978 m to the beginning of a curve.

Said curve turning to the right through 42° 35' 49.2", having a radius of 191.1641 m, and whose long chord bears S 87° 21' 30.4" W for a distance of 138.6165 m to the beginning of another curve.

Said curve turning to the left through an angle of 19° 13' 40.4", having a radius of 47.0864 m, and whose long chord bears N 80° 57' 25.2" W for a distance of 15.7277 m.

Thence, S 89° 25' 44.6" W for a distance of 220.9630 m to a point on a line. Thence, N 00° 11' 09.9" E for a distance of 580.4199 m to a point on a line. Thence, S 61° 50' 15.3" E for a distance of 41.4234 m to a point on a line. Thence, S 64° 05' 35.8" E for a distance of 23.7196 m to a point on a line. Thence, S 78° 09' 29.2" E for a distance of 19.4713 m to a point on a line. Thence, S 66° 23' 19.5" E for a distance of 115.8577 m to a point on a line. Thence, S 66° 17' 17.4" E for a distance of 84.8905 m to a point on a line. Thence S 84° 58' 37.7" E a distance of 142.2843 m to the **POINT OF BEGINNING.**

Task 1 - Draw a parcel from a legal description.

1. Open **Setup-C1-Parcels.dwg** from the *C:\Civil 3D for Surveyors Practice Files\Survey* folder.

2. Start the **Line** command. For the starting point, type **1907286.901,620917.57**.

3. In the Transparent Command toolbar, click ⬚ (Bearing Distance).

The legal description at the beginning of the practice was used to find the bearings and distances to type.

4. For the first line, do the following:
   - Type **3** for the southwest quadrant.
   - Type **0.26422** for the bearing.
   - Type **281.1517** for the distance.

5. Stay in the **Line** command with the **Bearing Distance Transparent** command running for the next few lines.
   - For the next two line segments, use the following values:

Quadrant	Bearing	Distance
3	0.24208	**154.9449**
3	66.03358	**28.0978**

6. Press <Esc> twice to end the command.

7. In the *Home* tab>Draw panel, click (Create Curve from End of Object). Then do the following:
   - Select the last line that was drawn using the **Bearing Distance** command.
   - Select **Radius** from the command options.
   - Set the *radius* to **191.1641**.
   - Select **Chord** from the command options.
   - Set the *chord length* to **138.6165**.

8. In the *Home* tab>Draw panel, click (Create Reverse or Compound Curve) and do the following:
   - Select the last curve drawn.
   - Select **Reverse** from the command options.
   - Set the *radius* to **47.4828**.
   - Select **Chord** from the command options.
   - Set the *chord length* to **15.7277**.

9. Start the **Line** command. For the starting point, pick the endpoint of the last arc drawn. Then do the following:

   - In the Transparent Command toolbar, click ◿ (Bearing Distance).
   - For the remaining line segments:, use the following values:

Quadrant	Bearing	Distance
3	89.25446	220.9630
1	0.11099	580.4199
2	61.50153	41.4234
2	64.05358	23.7169
2	78.09292	19.4713
2	66.23195	115.8577
2	66.17174	84.8905

10. Press <Esc> once to exit the **Bearing Distance** command. Hold <Ctrl> as you right-click and select **Endpoint**, select the starting point of the parcel to close on the point of beginning.

11. Start the **Polyline Edit** command by typing **PE**. In the model, select one of the lines or curves you just created and press <Enter> to turn it into a polyline.

This prevents closure errors from occurring later.

12. Select the **Join** option and then select all the lines and curves you just created. Press <Enter> to create one closed polyline. Press <Esc> to end the command.

13. Save the drawing.

3.7 Coordinate Geometry Editor

Before the areas of a piece of land can be computed, it is required to have a closed traverse. The Coordinate Geometry Editor (shown in Figure 3–28) assists in entering, editing, and outputting 2D traverse data. In addition, it can be used to enter a legal description of a property in table format making it easier to find and fix errors in data entry. Traverse data can be created in the following ways:

- From existing COGO data.

- By loading it from a polyline.

- By manually entering known data.

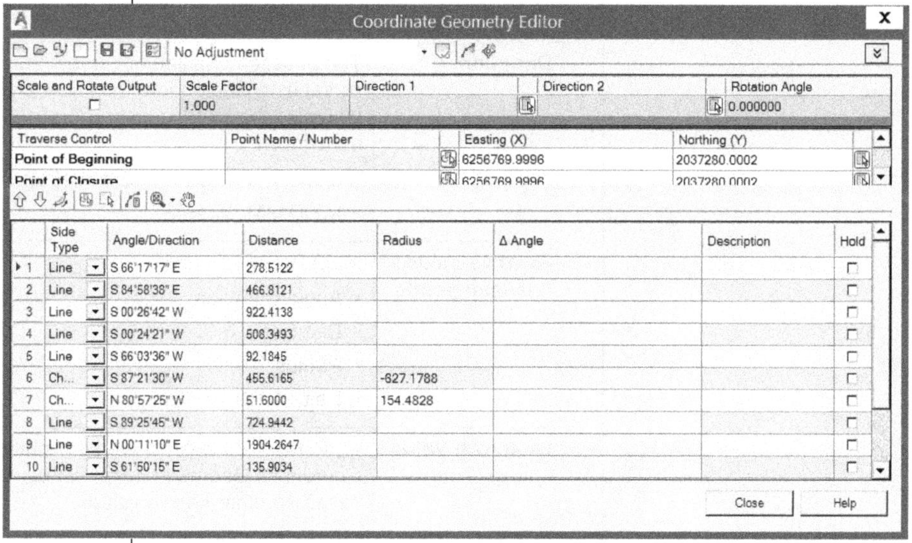

Figure 3–28

Manually Entering COGO Data

Traverse data can be entered using a variety of formats and mathematical equations. The key when defining a traverse is to start by defining a point of beginning and a point of closure. Then, the sides of the traverse are defined. When entering data, keep the following guidelines in mind:

- The tab key is used to navigate between cells.

- Any data that in red is considered invalid.

- Entered data is not affected if the traverse is adjusted, scaled, or rotated.

- Units of measure different from the project can be entered by typing **'** (feet) or **m** (meters). Once entered, the software converts the measurement to the project units.

Data Entry

Each vertex in a traverse can be manually entered or selected from the model. The following data types can be entered using the formats listed for each.

Points	The point of beginning or point of closure can be entered using the Latitude/Longitude to set the *x* and *y* values. When typing the values, use any of the following formats: • DDMMSS.ss • DD MM SS.ss • DD.MMSSss
Direction	The direction of a line or curve from the last point can be set using the quadrant number and then the angle or by typing the bearing just as it is listed in the legal description. • Quadrant..Angle (1..45 = N 45 E) • N DD MM SS.ss E
Relative Values between points	Multiple cells can be: • Angle/Direction • Distance • Radius • Delta Angle
Unknown Value	Up to two values per traverse might be unknown. The Coordinate Geometry Editor will calculate the values based on other known values. • Enter **U** in the cell.
Mathematical equations	A variety of mathematical equations can be entered to calculate a traverse parameter value. This allows you to calculate relative values based on known information. The following are valid operators: • + • - • / • * • ()

Side Type	The side type field determines which fields become available for entering data. For Example: If the Line option is selected, the Radius and Delta Angle fields become gray which indicates they cannot be modified. Five side types are available as follows: • Line • Tangent Curve • Cord Curve • Radial Curve • Side Shot

How To: Create a Traverse by Entering Data Manually

1. In the *Survey* tab>Analyze panel, click ![icon] (Coordinate Geometry Editor).
2. To clear any existing data in the Coordinate Geometry Editor, click ![icon] (New Traverse).
3. Type in an **Easting (X)** and a **Northing (Y)** for both the *Point of Beginning* and the *Point of Closure*.
4. In the Side Type drop-down list, select the appropriate option (as shown in Figure 3–29), and fill in the required cells to the right of it.

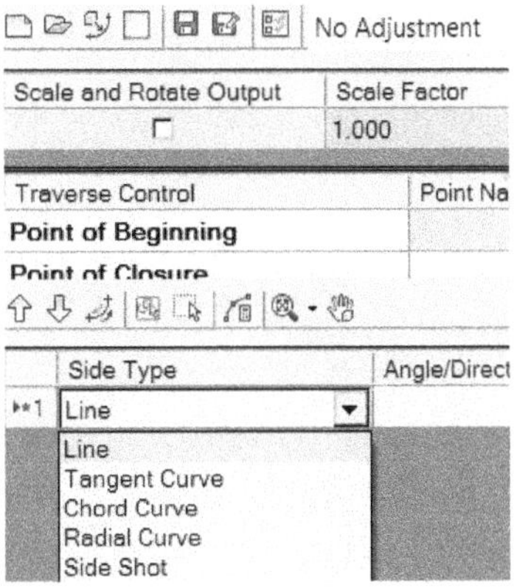

Alternatively, you can click ![icon] (Select COGO point) and select an existing point in the model.

Figure 3–29

5. Repeat step 4 until all segments of the traverse are entered.
6. To draw the traverse in the model, in the Coordinate Geometry Editor dialog box, click ![icon] (Create Polyline from Traverse).

7. To create points in the model from the traverse, in the
    Coordinate Geometry Editor dialog box, click (Add
    COGO Points to Drawing).

8. To see a report for the traverse, in the Coordinate Geometry
    Editor dialog box, click (Display Traverse Closure and
    Adjustment Reports).

    *   After you have run the report and/or drawn the traverse in
        the model, you might realize that you inadvertently typed
        a segment in the wrong order or missed a segment all
        together. In cases such as this one, you can change the
        order of segments by using the / (Move Selection
        Up/Down) tools in the Coordinate Geometry Editor dialog
        box.

9. Add in any missed segments.

10. Select the segment that was missing, click (Move
    Selection Up) until it is in its correct position in the traverse.

Practice 3d

Coordinate Geometry Editor

Practice Objective

- Add the property boundary to the model by typing in the legal description into the Coordinate Geometry Editor.

Estimated time for completion: 20 minutes

In this practice, you will create a polyline from the legal description of a property boundary using COGO tools, as shown in Figure 3–30. After realizing you missed a line of text in the legal description, you make edits to the boundary and import the polyline to the model.

Figure 3–30

Task 1 - Manually enter a traverse boundary.

1. Open **Setup-D1-Traverse.dwg** from the *C:\Civil 3D for Surveyors Practice Files\Survey* folder.

2. In the *Survey* tab>Analyze panel, click ▦ (Coordinate Geometry Editor).

3. To clear any existing data in the Coordinate Geometry Editor, click 🗋 (New Traverse).

---

4. For the Traverse Control, type **1907286.901** in the *Easting* field and **620917.57** in the *Northing* field for both the *Point of Beginning* and the *Point of Closure*.

5. In the Side Type drop-down list, select **Line**, as shown in Figure 3–31.

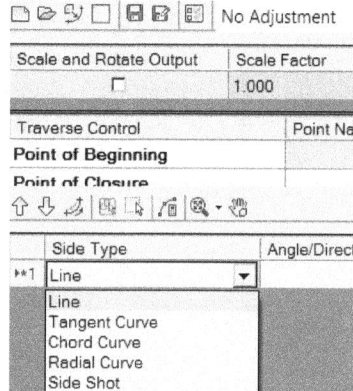

Figure 3–31

6. Then, set the following:

    *   *Angle/Direction*: **S 00 26 42.2 W**
    *   *Distance*: **281.1517**

7. Use the following table to set the remaining segments:

Side Type	Angle/ Direction	Distance	Radius	Delta Angle
Line	S 00 24 20.8 W	154.9449		
Line	S 66 03 35.8 W	28.0978		
Tangent Curve			191.1641	42 35 49
Line	S 89 25 44.6 W	220.9630		
Line	N 00 11 9.9 E	580.4199		
Line	S 61 50 15.3 E	41.4234		
Line	S 64 05 35.8 W	23.7169		
Line	S 78 09 29.2 E	19.4713		
Line	S 66 23 19.5 E	115.8577		
Line	S 66 17 17.4 E	84.8905		

| Chord Curve | S 76 22 12 E | 41.1489 | 340.4616 | |
| Tangent Curve | | | 344.5679 | 17 |

8. To see a report for the traverse, in the Coordinate Geometry Editor dialog box, click 🖑 (Display Traverse Closure and Adjustment Reports).

9. In the Coordinate Geometry Editor dialog box, click 🖫 (Save Traverse to File As).

10. Browse to the practice files directory and type a name for the traverse file. Click **Save**.

11. Close the Coordinate Geometry Editor.

Task 2 - Make corrections to the traverse.

After you have run the report and/or drawn the traverse in the model, you might realize that you inadvertently missed a segment and put in the wrong angle/direction for another segment. In this task, you will add the missing segment and make any other corrections.

1. Continue working in the **Setup-D1-Traverse.dwg** from the last task.

2. On the *Survey* tab>Analyze panel, click 🖳 (Coordinate Geometry Editor).

If you did not save the file, select NeedsCorrections.trvx from the C:\Civil 3D for Surveyors Practice Files\Survey folder.

3. In the Coordinate Geometry Editor, click 🗁 (Load Traverse from File). Select the file you save in the last task.

4. Click **OK** twice to acknowledge the messages that display.

5. Note that the curve in line 4 is going in the wrong direction and that line 8 has a miss-typed the bearing. Correct it by doing the following:

   • In the *Radius* field of line 4, type - (negative) in front of the value to change the direction of the curve without changing the direction of the tangent.

   • In the *Angle/Direction* field of line 8, change the *Bearing* to **S 64 05 35.8 E**.

6. Also note that the reverse curve is missing after line 4. To correct it, add a segment at the end and move it up by doing the following:

   - Change the *Side Type* of line 14 to **Tangent Curve.**
   - Set the *Radius* to **47.4828**.
   - Set the *Delta Angle* to **19 13 40**.
   - Select the **Tangent Curve** in line 14 that was missing and click ⇧ (Move Selection Up) multiple times until it is in Line 5.

7. In the Coordinate Geometry Editor dialog box, click 🖫 (Save Traverse to File)

8. Then, click ⬇ (Display Traverse Closure and Adjustment Reports) to view the new closure error. Close the report.

9. Click 🖾 (Create Polyline from Traverse) and click **OK**.

10. Close the Coordinate Geometry Editor dialog box and save the drawing.

Chapter Review Questions

1. What is the biggest difference between using a field book file and point file with connective codes for importing survey data? (Select all that apply.)

   a. There is no difference and they can be used interchangeably.

   b. When using a field book file, in the field, the connective code is added as a note which is separate from the point description. When using a point file with connective codes, the connective codes are entered in the same line as the point description.

   c. A field book file must be post processed where as a point file with connective codes can be directly imported.

   d. A point file with connective codes contains all of the data that was used during the survey field pickup by a total station (e.g., setups, back-sites, instrument height, prism height, turned angles, side shots, etc.)

2. What is the Figure Prefix Database used for? (Select all that apply.)

   a. To assign a layer to a figure.

   b. To add symbols to the drawing according to the point description.

   c. To determine whether a figure become a break line.

   d. To determine whether a figure becomes a lot line.

3. Why would you want to create an Equipment Database?

   a. The Equipment settings file contains values to estimate errors for the Least Squares adjustment process.

   b. The working folder is set inside the Equipment Database settings.

   c. The survey database coordinate system is set in the Equipment Database settings.

4. The survey database coordinate system must match the drawing coordinate system.

   a. True

   b. False

5. What is the best way to find and fix errors when inputting a property boundary from a legal description?

    a. When an error is made, it is always required to undo the linework and start over at the beginning of the legal description.

    b. Use Transparent command tools.

    c. Use expanded line or curve tools.

    d. Use the Coordinate Geometry Editor.

Command Summary

Button	Command	Location
	Bearing Distance	• **Toolbar:** Transparent Commands • **Command Prompt:** 'bd
	Coordinate Geometry Editor	• **Ribbon:** *Survey* tab>Analyze panel • **Command Prompt:** _AeccCogoEditor
	Create Curve from End of Object	• **Ribbon:** *Home* tab>Draw panel • **Command Prompt:** CurveFromEndOfObject
	Create Reverse or Compound Curve	• **Ribbon:** *Home* tab>Draw panel • **Command Prompt:** ReverseOrCompound
	Survey Toolspace	• **Ribbon**: *Home* tab>Palettes panel
	Survey User Settings	• **Toolspace**: *Survey* tab

Points

Points are a very important part of every construction project. They help layout the existing conditions plan as well as determine where stakes are placed for proposed features of the final design. In this chapter, you learn how to effectively create point styles, create various points in the model, and assign styles to points. This is done by importing points and creating points manually.

Learning Objectives in this Chapter

- Create a point marker style to ensure that the correct symbol is assigned to specific points.
- Create a point label style for annotating groups of points with the required information.
- Set the appropriate point creation values and next available point number.
- Create additional points using the Create Points toolbar for points that were not imported from the survey data.
- Assign point symbols, labels, layers, etc., automatically when importing points by setting up Description Key Sets.
- Import points from and export points to ASCII files created from the field survey.
- Group points together using common properties, such as name, elevation, description, etc.
- Review and edit points using the Panorama window to ensure accuracy.
- Prevent unwanted edits to points by locking them.
- Share information about points used for error checking or staking out points using predefined reports.

4.1 Points Overview

Points are often most heavily used at the beginning and end of a project. Surveyors collect data about existing site conditions (elevations, utilities, ownership, etc.) and stake out the points for those who are going to build the design. Their world is coordinates, which are represented by points. Each point has a unique number (or name) and a label containing additional information (usually the elevation at the coordinate and a short coded description).

There are no national standards for point descriptions in the Surveying industry. Each company or survey crew needs to work out its own conventions. There are no standards for symbols either. Each firm can have its own set of symbols. The symbols used in a submission set can be specified by the firm contracting the services.

The lack of standard descriptions and symbols adds time to preparing and converting contracted work. At the end of the design process, points can be used to represent critical coordinates of the design. These points and their coordinates become the cornerstone of the design construction process.

AutoCAD® Civil® 3D cogo points are a single object with two elements: a point style and a point label style. A cogo point definition is shown in Figure 4–1.

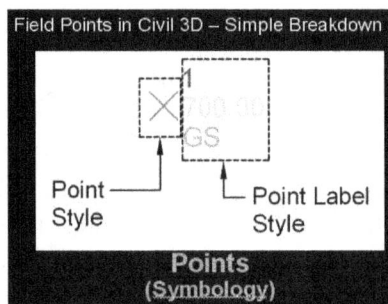

Figure 4–1

The following is important cogo point information:

*   A point style (no matter what it displays) is selectable with an AutoCAD Node object snap.

*   Points can be displayed as AutoCAD nodes, custom markers, or blocks.

A point label is not limited to the point's number, elevation, and description. A point label can contain lines, blocks, and other point properties. For example, point labels might only display an elevation or description. This text can be manually overridden (as shown in Figure 4–2) or it can consist of intelligent variables that represent point characteristics (such as its convergence angle). In state plane coordinate systems, the convergence angle is the difference between a geodetic azimuth and the projection of that azimuth onto a grid (grid azimuth) of a given point.

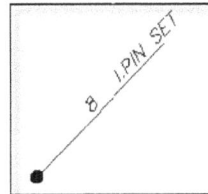

Figure 4–2

Creating the first point automatically creates a point group named **_All Points**. This point group is similar to layer **0**. It cannot be renamed or deleted. Every imported or created drawing point is located in this point group.

Additional point groups can use all or a subset of drawing points. Usually, additional point groups contain a subset of all points. Each of these groups can display the originally assigned point style and label, or change one or both using overrides.

The **Point** collection in the Settings panel manages all of the styles affecting points: *Point Styles, Label Styles, Description Key Sets, Table Styles,* and *Commands,* as shown in Figure 4–3.

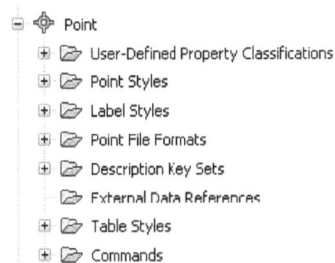

Figure 4–3

The AutoCAD Civil 3D software point styles define a cogo point's visibility, layer, color, and linetype. A style can use the layer properties or override them. To use AutoCAD layer properties, a style sets the properties' value to **ByLayer**, as shown at the top in Figure 4–4. To have the style control layer properties, the style sets a specific color, linetype, etc., as shown at the bottom in Figure 4–4.

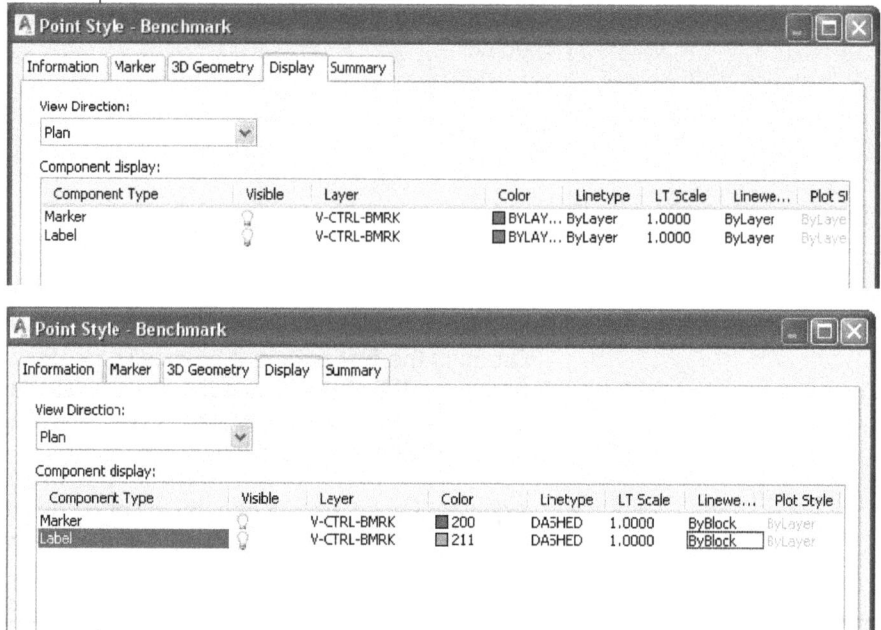

Figure 4–4

Point Marker Styles

A point style defines a point's display, its 3D elevation, and its coordinate marker size. In the example shown in Figure 4–5, the point style is an X for a ground shot.

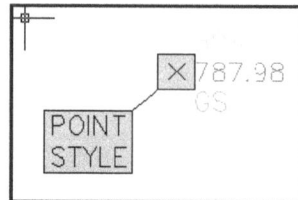

Figure 4–5

If opening a drawing without any AutoCAD Civil 3D content, or starting a drawing from a template without any AutoCAD Civil 3D content, the AutoCAD Civil 3D software provides a single style (Standard) using one layer (**0**). Every new style starts from this point style and can be edited, copied, and renamed.

The AutoCAD Civil 3D software provides metric and imperial template files that contain several point styles: AutoCAD Civil 3D Imperial (NCS) and AutoCAD Civil 3D Metric (NCS). These two templates use the National CAD standards for their layers and provide examples of styles that can be used in a project. To customize these styles, expand the list of point styles and double-click on each to modify them. The Point Style dialog box has five tabs:

- The *Information* tab sets the point style's name and description, as shown in Figure 4–6.

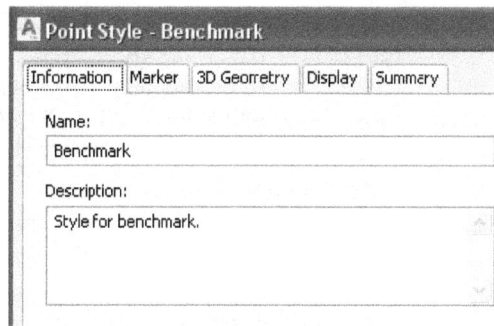

Figure 4–6

- The *Marker* tab supports three marker definition methods, as shown in Figure 4–7.

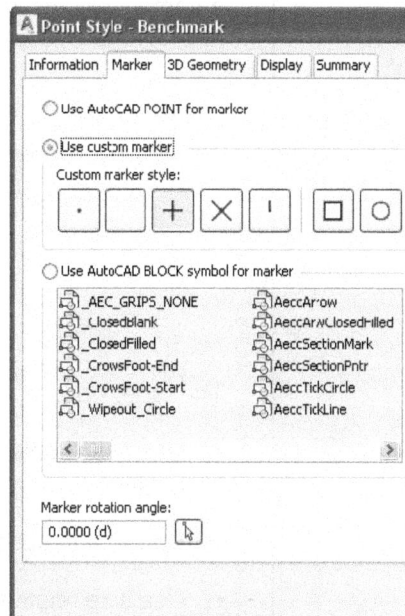

Figure 4–7

Use AutoCAD POINT [node] for marker	All points in the drawing follow AutoCAD's PDMODE and PDSIZE system variables. You do not have independent control over points using this option.
Use custom marker	This option creates markers similar to an AutoCAD point (node). However, the marker is under the AutoCAD Civil 3D software's control, and each point style can display a different combination of marker styles. When using this option, you select the components of the style from the list of Custom marker style shapes. A custom marker can have shapes from the left and right sides. The first comes from one of the five icons on the style's left side, and you can optionally add one or both shapes from the right.
Use AutoCAD BLOCK symbol for marker	This option defines the marker using a block (symbol). The blocks listed represent definitions in the drawing. When the cursor is in this area and you right-click, you can browse to a location containing drawings that you want to include as point markers

Hint: Scale Options

Options for scaling the marker are displayed in the marker panel's top right corner. The most common option is **Use drawing scale** (as shown in Figure 4–8), which takes the marker size (0.100) and multiplies it by the current drawing's annotation scale, resulting in the final marker size. When the annotation scale changes, the AutoCAD Civil 3D software automatically resizes the markers and their labels to be the appropriate size for the scale.

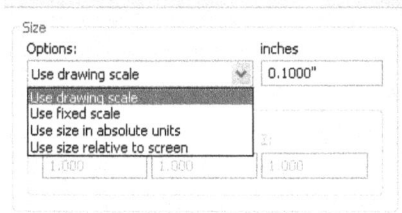

Figure 4–8

The other options are as follows:

- Use fixed scale: Specifies user-defined X, Y, and Z scale values.

- Use size in absolute units: Specifies a user-defined size.

- Use size relative to screen: Specifies a user-defined percentage of the screen.

- The *3D Geometry* tab affects the point's elevation. The default option is **Use Point Elevation** (as shown in Figure 4–9), which displays the point at its actual elevation value.

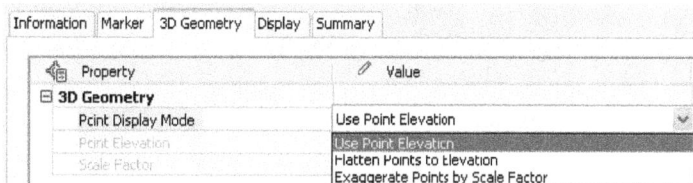

| Information | Marker | 3D Geometry | Display | Summary |

🔲 Property	🖉 Value
⊟ **3D Geometry**	
Pcint Display Mode	Use Point Elevation
Point Elevation	Use Point Elevation
Scale Factor	Flatten Points to Elevation
	Exaggerate Points by Scale Factor

Figure 4–9

- The other options are described as follows:

Flatten Points to Elevation	Specifies the elevation to which the point is projected (flattened). The Point Elevation cell highlights if this option is selected and is 0 elevation by default. When using an AutoCAD object snap to select a marker using this option, the resulting entity's elevation is the default elevation of 0. If selecting by point number or point object, the resulting entity is the point's actual elevation.
Exaggerate Points by Scale Factor	Exaggerates the point's elevation by a specified scale factor. When selecting this option, the Scale Factor cell highlights.

- The *Display* tab assigns the marker and label layers, and sets their visibility and properties. Setting the property to **ByLayer** uses the layer's properties. Alternatively, you can override the original layer properties by setting a specific color, linetype, or lineweight.

  - A style's view direction value affects how the point and label components display in the plan, model, profile, and section views, as shown in Figure 4–10.

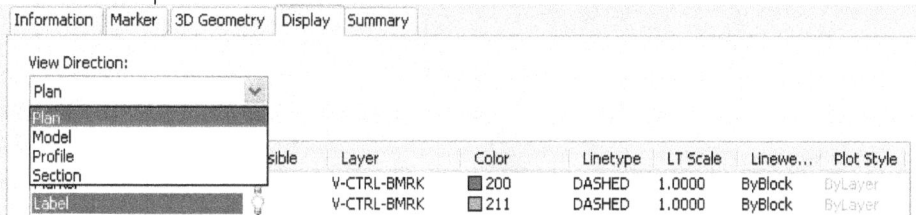

| Information | Marker | 3D Geometry | Display | Summary |

View Direction:

| Plan |

Plan
Model
Profile
Section
Label

	sible	Layer	Color	Linetype	LT Scale	Linewe...	Plot Style
		V-CTRL-BMRK	◼ 200	DASHED	1.0000	ByBlock	ByLayer
		V-CTRL-BMRK	◻ 211	DASHED	1.0000	ByBlock	ByLayer

Figure 4–10

- The *Summary* tab is a report of all of the style's settings. Controlling a leader arrow from a label in the dragged state, points to the boundary of the marker (yes) or the center of the marker (no). You can also edit style variables in this tab.

Practice 4a

Point Marker Styles

Estimated time for completion: 15 minutes

Practice Objective

- Create a point marker style to ensure that the correct symbol is assigned to specific points.

In this practice you will create a new point style and apply it to an existing group of points.

Task 1 - Add a Block Symbol.

1. Open **Points-A1-Survey.dwg** from the *C:\Civil 3D for Surveyors Practice Files\Survey* folder.

2. In the Toolspace, select the *Settings* tab and expand the **Point** collection until *Point Styles* is displayed. Expand the **Point Styles** collection.

3. Review the *Point Styles* list and note that there is no light pole style.

4. In the *Point Styles* list, select the **Guy pole** style, right-click, and select **Copy...**

5. In the *Information* tab, change the point style's name to **Light Pole** and set the *Description* to **Style for street light pole**, as shown in Figure 4–11.

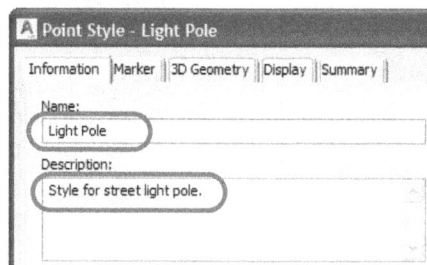

Figure 4–11

6. Select the *Marker* tab. Select the **Use AutoCAD BLOCK symbol for marker** option. In the block list, scroll across as required and select the AutoCAD block **ST-Light**, as shown in Figure 4–12.

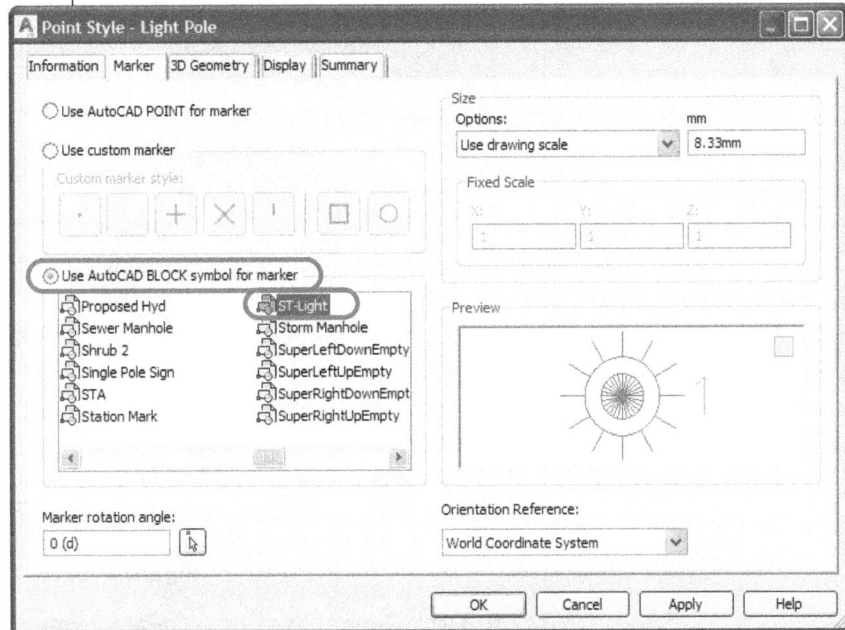

Figure 4–12

7. Select the *Display* tab and note that the layer settings are from the Guy Pole point style, as shown in Figure 4–13.

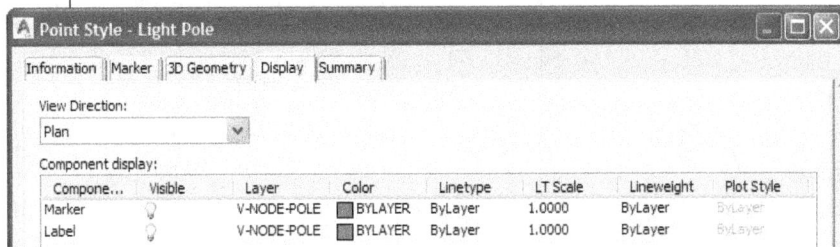

Figure 4–13

8. You can reassign the marker and/or label layer by selecting the layer name. Select the layer name to display the drawing layer list.

9. If you need to create a new layer, click **New** in the top right corner of the Layer Selection dialog box. The Create Layer dialog box opens (as shown in Figure 4–14), enabling you to create new layers without having to use the Layer Manager.

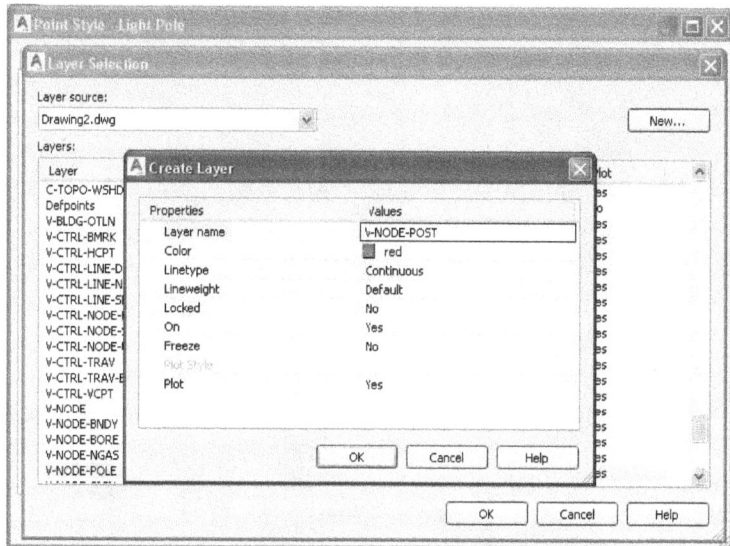

Figure 4–14

10. Click **Cancel** to exit the Create Layer dialog box. Click **Cancel** to exit the Layer Selection dialog box.

11. Click **OK** to create the point style.

12. Review the *Point Styles* list and note that Light Pole is now a point style, as shown in Figure 4–15.

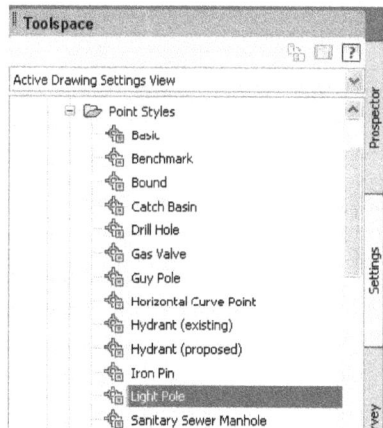

Figure 4–15

13. Save the drawing.

Task 2 - Apply the point style.

Alternatively, you can select the view in the View tab>Views panel.

1. Continue working with the drawing from the previous task or open **Points-A2-Survey.dwg** from the *C:\Civil 3D for Surveyors Practice Files\Survey* folder.

2. In the top-left corner of the drawing window, select **Top**. In the flyout, select **Custom Model Views** and select the preset view **Suv Points style**, as shown in Figure 4–16.

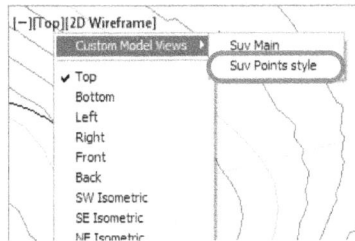

Figure 4–16

3. In the Toolspace, select the *Prospector* tab, expand the **Point Groups** collection until the *Street Light* point group displays. Select the **Street Light** group, right-click, and select **Properties**.

4. In the *Information* tab, in the *Default styles* area, select **Light Pole** in the Point style drop-down list, as shown in Figure 4–17.

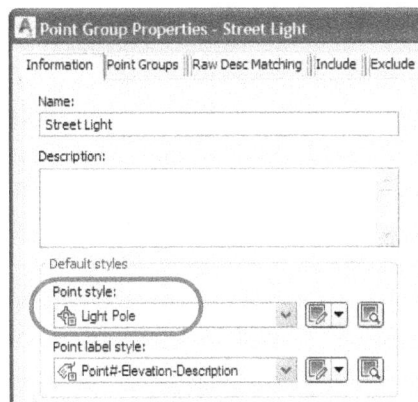

Figure 4–17

5. Click **OK** to accept the changes and close the dialog box. The symbols for the Light pole points have now been changed.

If you see ⚠ *next to the StreetLights point group, right-click on* **StreetLights** *and select* **Update**.

6. Save the drawing.

4.2 Point Label Styles

The AutoCAD Civil 3D point label style annotates point properties beyond the typical point number, elevation and description. A typical point label style is shown in Figure 4–18.

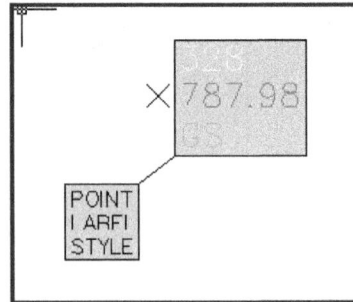

Figure 4–18

All AutoCAD Civil 3D label style dialog boxes are the same. The basic behaviors for a label are in the settings in the Edit Label Style Defaults dialog box. The values in this dialog box define the label layer, text style, orientation, plan readability, size, dragged state behaviors, etc.

In the *Settings* tab, the drawing name and object collections control these values for the entire drawing (at the drawing name level) or for the selected collection (*Surface*, *Alignment*, *Point*, etc.) To open the Edit Label Style Defaults dialog box, select the drawing name or a heading, right-click, and select **Edit Label Style Defaults...**, as shown in Figure 4–19.

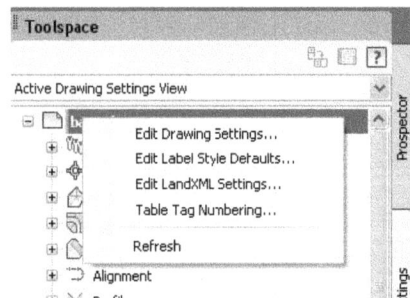

Figure 4–19

The Label Style Composer dialog box contains five tabs, each defining specific label behaviors: *Information*, *General*, *Layout*, *Dragged State*, and *Summary*.

Information Tab

The *Information* tab names the style, as shown in Figure 4–20.

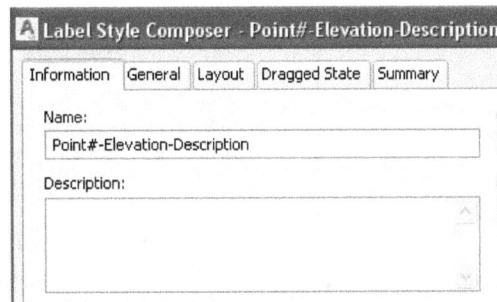

Figure 4–20

General Tab

The *General* tab contains three properties, as shown in Figure 4–21:

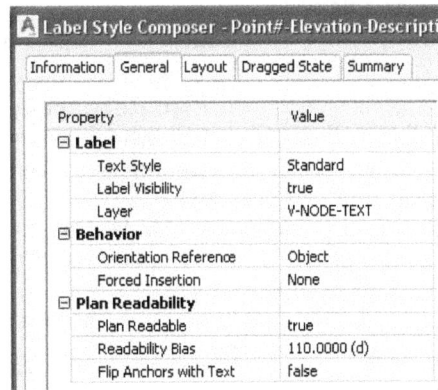

Figure 4–21

Select the *Value* cell next to any property to open browsers and change their values. (Selecting the *Label Visibility* cell displays a drop-down list containing the options **true** and **false**.)

- **Label***: sets the *Text Style*, *Label Visibility*, and the label's *Layer*.

- **Behavior***: sets two variables that control the label's location.

    - The *Orientation Reference* variable contains the following three label orientation options:

Object	Rotates labels relative to the object's zero direction. The object's zero direction is based on its start to end vector. If the vector changes at the label's anchor point, the orientation updates automatically. This is the default setting.

View	Forces labels to realign relative to a screen-view orientation in both model and layout views. This method assumes that the zero angle is horizontal, regardless of the UCS or Dview twist. If the view changes, the label orientation updates as well.
World Coordinate System	Labels read left to right using the WCS X-axis. Changing the view or current UCS does not affect label rotation. The label always references the world coordinate system.

- The **Forced Insertion** variable has three optional values that specify the label's position relative to an object. This setting only applies when the *Orientation Reference* is set to **Object** and the objects are lines, arcs, or spline segments.

Note that if you select Top or Bottom, the value of Plan Readable should be True.

None	Maintains label position as composed relative to the object.
Top	Adjusts label position to be above an object.
Bottom	Adjusts label position to be below an object.

- **Plan Readability**: has three variables that affect how text flips when rotating a drawing view. The result of these settings is to flip text to be left-to-right readable.

  - Under this property, the *Plan Readable* variable has two options available:

True	Enables text to rotate to maintain left-to-right readability.
False	Does not permit text to flip. The resulting text might be upside down or read from right to left.

  - The *Readability Bias* variable is the amount of rotation required to flip a label to become left-to-right readable. The angle is measured counter-clockwise from the WCS 0 (zero) direction.
  - The *Flip Anchors with Text* variable has two options.

True	If the text flips, the text anchor point also flips.
False	The label flips, but maintains the original anchor point. The behavior is similar to mirroring the original text.

Layout Tab

The *Layout* tab defines the label contents. A label component is an object property that it labels. Point properties include northing, easting, raw description, etc. A label might have one component with several properties, or several components each containing an object property.

A point style label component can be text, lines, or blocks. Other object type label styles can include additional components, such as reference text, tics, directional arrows, etc. To add a component, expand the drop-down list as shown in Figure 4–22 and select the component type.

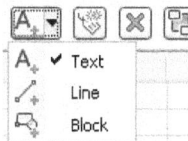

Figure 4–22

The remaining tools in the *Layout* tab are described as follows:

	Copies the current component and its properties.
	Deletes the current component.
	Changes a label's components display order. For example, use this icon to change the draw order of the label's components (such as text above a mask).

Depending on the label component type, it might have any combination of three elements: **General**, **Text**, and **Border**. **General** defines how the label attaches to the object or other label components, its visibility, and its anchor point.

If the label component is text, the **Text** property values affect how it displays its object property. To set or modify a label's text value, select the cell next to *Contents* to display ⸬ (shown in Figure 4–23). Click ⸬ to open the Text Component Editor dialog box.

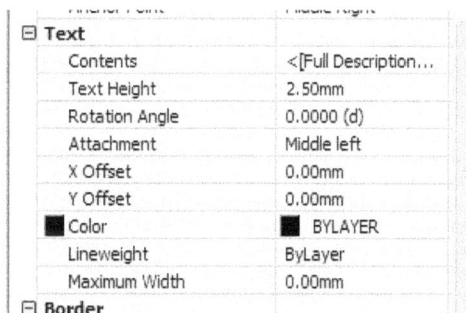

Figure 4–23

The Text Component Editor dialog box (shown in Figure 4–24), defines the properties that the label annotates. When creating a label component, use the following steps:

1. Double-click on the text in the right side panel to highlight it.
2. Select the property to add from the left side panel
3. Set the property's format values.
4. Click ⏩ to add the new property to the label component.

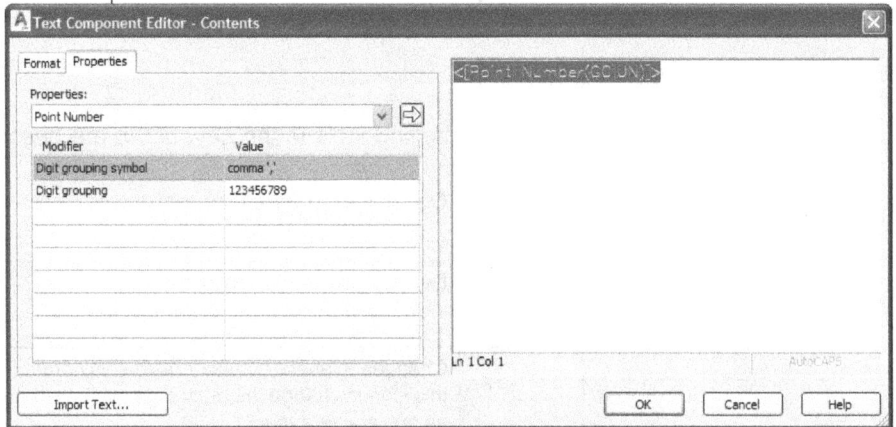

Figure 4–24

It is important to maintain the process order and to remember that the text on the right in brackets needs to be highlighted before revising its format values on the left.

Dragged State Tab

The *Dragged State* tab has two properties: **Leader** and **Dragged State Components**, as shown in Figure 4–25. This tab defines how a label behaves when you are dragging a label from its original insertion point.

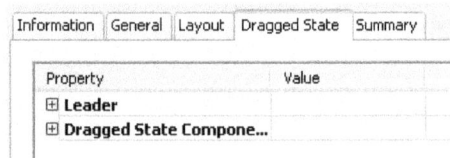

Figure 4–25

The **Leader** property defines whether a leader displays and what properties it displays. You can use the label's layer properties in the *General* tab (**ByLayer**) or override them by specifying a color, as shown in Figure 4–26.

The **Dragged State Components** property defines the label component's display after it is dragged from its original position. Select the cell next to *Display* to view the two display options, as shown in Figure 4–27.

Property	Value
⊟ **Leader**	
Arrow Head Style	Closed filled
Arrow Head Size	0.1000"
Visibility	true
Type	Straight Leader
■ Color	■ BYLAYER
Linetype	ByBlock
Lineweight	ByLayer
⊞ **Dragged State Compone...**	

Figure 4–26

Information | General | Layout | Dragged State | Summary

Property	Value
⊞ **Leader**	
⊟ **Dragged State Compone...**	
Display	Stacked Text
Border Visibility	As Composed
Border Type	Stacked Text
Background Mask	False
Border and Leader Gap	0.75mm
Text Height	2.50mm
Leader Attachment	Middle
Leader Justification	True
■ Color	■ BYLAYER
Linetype	ByBlock
Lineweight	ByLayer
Maximum Text Width	0.00mm

Figure 4–27

As Composed	The label maintains its original definition and orientation from the settings in the Layout panel. When you select **As Composed**, all of the other values become unavailable for editing.
Stacked Text	The label text becomes left-justified and label components are stacked in the order listed in Layout's Component Name list. When you select **Stacked Text**, all blocks, lines, ticks, and direction arrows are removed and all text becomes the same height.

Summary Tab

The *Summary* tab lists the label component, general, and dragged state values for the label style. The label components are listed numerically in the order in which they were defined and report all of the current values.

Practice 4b

Point Label Styles

Practice Objective

- Create a point label style for annotating groups of points with the required information.

Estimated time for completion: 20 minutes

In this practice, you will create a label style and use it with a point style.

Task 1 - Create a Point Label Style's Components.

1. Continue working with the drawing from the previous practice, or open **Points-B1-Survey.dwg** from the *C:\Civil 3D for Surveyors Practice Files\Survey* folder.

2. Select the *Settings* tab. Expand the **Point** collection until the *Label Styles* list displays.

3. From the list of point styles, select **Point#-Elevation-Description**, right-click, and select **Copy**.

4. In the *Information* tab, change the name to **Point#-Description-N-E**.

5. Select the *Layout* tab and set the following, as shown in Figure 4–28. This will attach the bottom left of the label to the top right of the point object:.
    - Component name drop-down list: **Point Number**
    - *Anchor Component*: **<Feature>**
    - *Anchor Point*: **Top Right**
    - *Attachment*: **Bottom left**

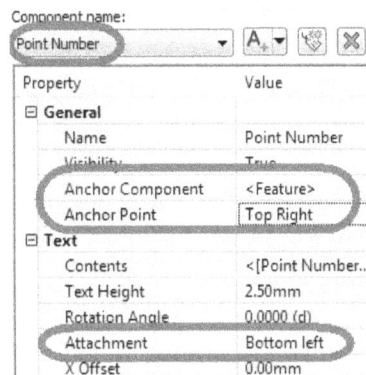

Figure 4–28

6. In the Component name drop-down list, select **Point Elev** and click [X], as shown in Figure 4–29. At the *Do you want to delete it?* prompt, click **Yes**.

You do not need the elevation label.

Figure 4–29

7. Set the properties for the description label by setting the following, as shown in Figure 4–30:
   - Component name drop-down list: **Point Description**
   - *Anchor Component*: **Point Number**
   - *Anchor Point*: **Bottom Left**
   - *Attachment*: **Top left**

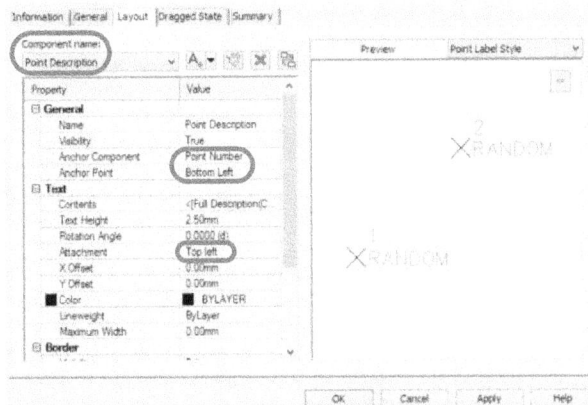

Figure 4–30

8. You will now add a new text component to display the Northing and Easting. Expand the **Create Text Component** flyout (shown in Figure 4–31) and select **Text** to create a text component.

The AutoCAD Civil 3D software creates a text component with some default values.

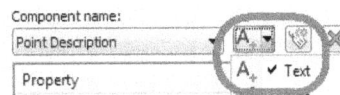

Figure 4–31

9. Make the following changes to the new text component:
   - Change the default *Name text.1* to **Coordinates**
   - *Anchor Component:* **Point Description**
   - *Anchor Point:* **Bottom Left**
   - *Attachment:* **Top left**

10. Click ⸬ in the *Contents* cell, next to *Label Text*, as shown in Figure 4–32.

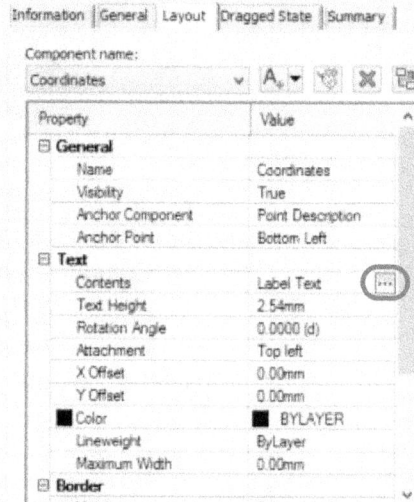

Figure 4–32

11. In the Text Component Editor dialog box, do the following:

- Double-click on the text in the right side panel to highlight it and type **N**.

- In the Properties drop-down list, select **Northing**.

- Change the *Precision* to **0.001**.

- Click ⇨ to add the code to display the northing, as shown in Figure 4–33.

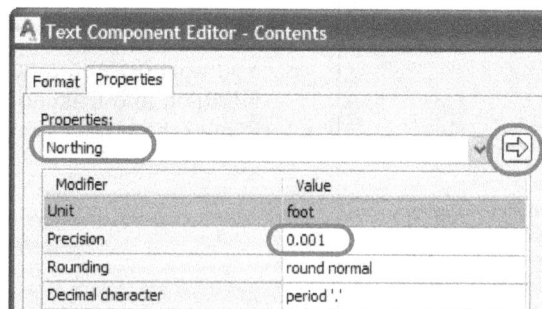

Figure 4–33

- Click at the end of the code.

- Press <Enter> to insert a new line and type **E**

- In the Properties drop-down list, select **Easting**.

- Click ⇨ to post the code in the right side panel. The following should be displayed:

  N<[Northing(Uft|P3|RN|AP|GC|UN|Sn|OF)]>

  E<[Easting(Uft|P4|RN|AP|GC|UN|Sn|OF)]>

  In the easting, the value will be displayed to the 4th decimal, *P4*. You need to change it so that it matches the northing. The only way to do this is re-insert the code. The AutoCAD Civil 3D software does not yet have the ability to edit or add a specific section of code.

12. Select all of the code for the easting. Change the *Precision* to **0.001** and click ⇨ to revise the easting code.

13. In the right side, select all the text

14. Select the *Format* tab and verify that *Justification* is set to **Left**.

15. Click **OK** to accept the changes in the Text Component Editor dialog box, and click **OK** again to accept the changes in the Label Style Composer.

16. Save the drawing.

Task 2 - Apply a Point Label Style's Components.

---

1. Continue working with the drawing from the previous task or open **Points-B2-Survey.dwg** from the *C:\Civil 3D for Surveyors Practice Files\Survey* folder.

2. In the Toolspace, select the *Prospector* tab and expand the **Point Groups** collection until the *Street Light* point group displays. Select the **Street Light** group, right-click, and select **Properties**.

3. In the *Information* tab, select **Point#-Description-N-E** in the Point label style drop-down list, as shown in Figure 4–34.

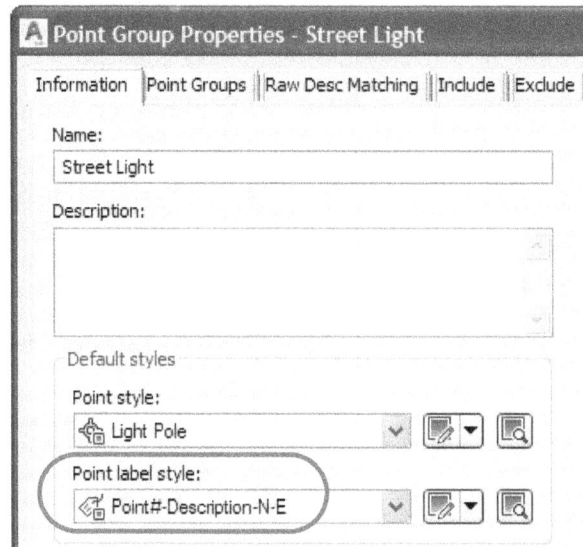

Figure 4–34

4. Click **OK** to accept the changes and close the dialog box.

   The symbols for the Light pole points have now been changed. Additionally, both the point symbols and point labels are annotative.

5. In the Status Bar, expand the Annotation Scale drop-down list and change the scale of the drawing from *1:1000* to **1:500**, as shown in Figure 4–35. The size of the labels and point symbols change.

Figure 4–35

6. Save the drawing.

4.3 Point Settings

When creating new points, you must determine the next point number, as well as which elevations and descriptions to assign and how to assign them. To set the current point number, default elevations, descriptions, and other similar settings, use the Create Points toolbar's expanded area. Display this area by clicking ⩗ in the Create Points toolbar. The two areas, *Points Creation* (shown in Figure 4–36) and *Point Identity* (shown in Figure 4–37), contain the most commonly used values.

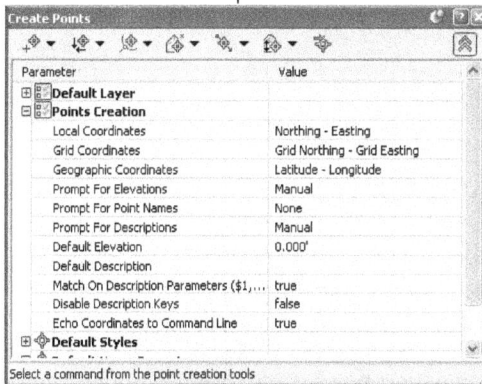

Figure 4–36

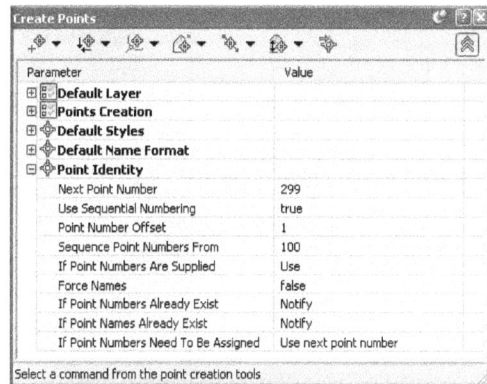

Figure 4–37

- Alternatively, you can select the *Settings* tab and expand the **Commands** collection, under the **Point** collection. Select **CreatePoints**, right-click, and select **Edit Command Settings...**, as shown in Figure 4–38.

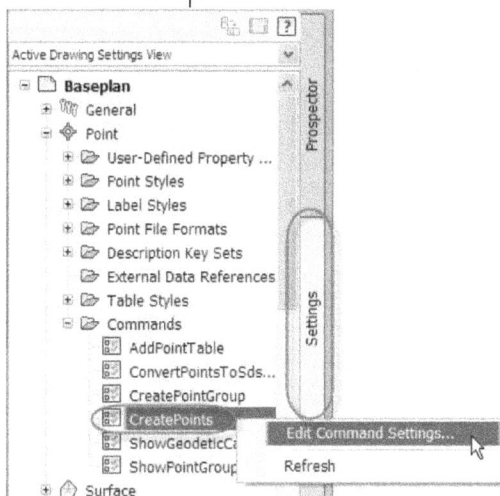

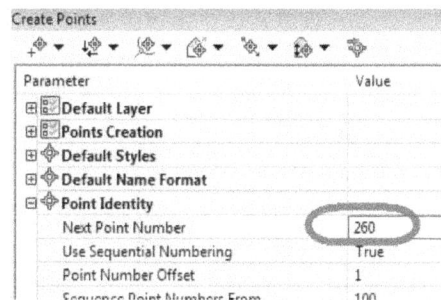

Figure 4–38

Points Creation Values

The *Points Creation* area affects prompting for elevations and/or descriptions. The two properties in this area are *Prompt For Elevations* and *Prompt For Descriptions*. These properties can be set as follows:

None	Does not prompt for an elevation or description.
Manual	Prompts for an elevation or description.
Automatic	Uses the **Default Elevation** or **Default Description** value when creating a point.
Automatic-O bject	Creates points along an alignment whose description consists of the **Alignment name** and **Station**. This description is not dynamic and does not update if the alignment changes or the point is moved.

Point Identity Values

The *Point Identity* area sets the default method of handling duplicate point numbers. If there are duplicate point numbers, there are three ways to resolve the duplication.

• Overwrite the existing point data.

• Ignore the new point.

• Assign it a new number.

This area's most critical property is *Next Point Number*. It is set to the first available number in the point list. If a file of imported point data uses point numbers 1-131 and 152-264, the current point number is 132 after importing the file. This value should be set manually to the next required point number before creating new points with the Create Points toolbar.

4.4 Creating Points

Points can be created using the commands in the Create Points toolbar. These commands include:

- **Miscellaneous - Manual:** Creates a new point at specified coordinates.

- **Alignments - Station/Offset:** Creates a point at an alignment's specific station and offset. These points and their descriptions do not update if the alignment is modified or the point is moved. If you prefer a dynamic station and offset labels, consider using an Alignment label instead.

- **Alignments - Measure Alignment:** Creates point objects at a set interval, which is useful for construction staking. Again, these points do not update if the alignment changes.

- **Surface - Random Points:** Creates points whose elevation is from a specified surface. These points do update, but you must manually force the update. If you prefer a dynamic spot label, consider a Surface label instead.

Each icon in the Create Points toolbar has a drop-down list. If expanded, a command from the list can be selected to run, as shown in Figure 4–39.

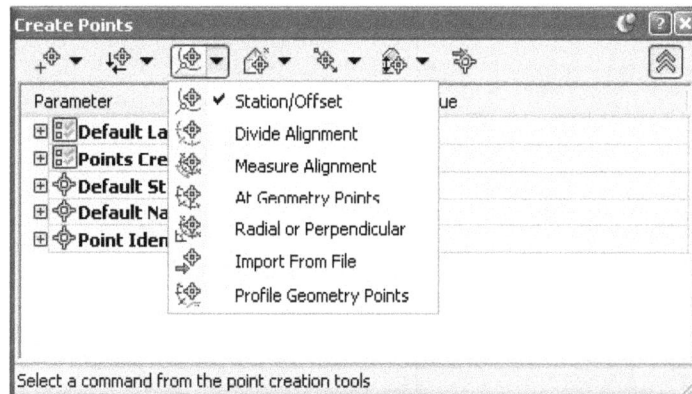

Figure 4–39

4.5 Transparent Command

Several methods of placing points can use other existing points to help define the location of a new point. For example, you might want to locate a new point at specific distances from two existing points. The AutoCAD Civil 3D software uses the point filters in the Transparent Commands toolbar to reference point objects in a drawing. The Transparent Command toolbar is shown in Figure 4–40.

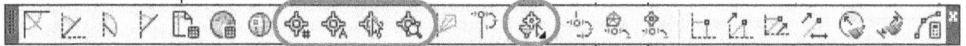

Figure 4–40

The point filters reference points by Point Name or Point Number, or by selecting a point on the screen (Point Object). You can access the transparent commands from their respective toolbars or type an apostrophe letter pair: **'PA** for Point Name, **'PN** for Point Number, **'PO** for Point Object, and **'ZTP** for Zoom to Point. Point Object is the easiest, because you only need to select a point on the screen.

The AutoCAD Civil 3D transparent commands work with most AutoCAD Civil 3D and AutoCAD commands that can use a point's coordinates. AutoCAD commands using transparent commands include **Line**, **Pline**, and **Circle**. To exit a transparent command, press <Esc> or <Enter>.

Practice 4c

Estimated time for completion: 10 minutes

Creating AutoCAD Civil 3D Points

Practice Objective

- Create a point manually then zoom to it using transparent commands.

In this practice, a fire hydrant was located by GPS. You will add a point object to locate it manually.

1. Continue working with the drawing from the previous practice, or open **Points-C1-Survey.dwg** from the *C:\Civil 3D for Surveyors Practice Files/Survey* folder.

2. In the *Home* tab>Create Ground Data panel, select **Points-Point Creation Tools** to display the Create Points toolbar.

3. Expand the toolbar by clicking ⊗, as shown in Figure 4–41.

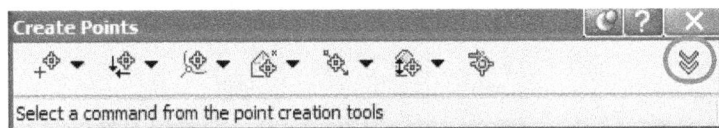

Figure 4–41

4. In the *Point Identity* area in the dialog box, set the *Next Point Number* to **260** and collapse the toolbar by clicking ⊗ .

5. Select the **Manual** option in the miscellaneous group in the toolbar, as shown in Figure 4–42.

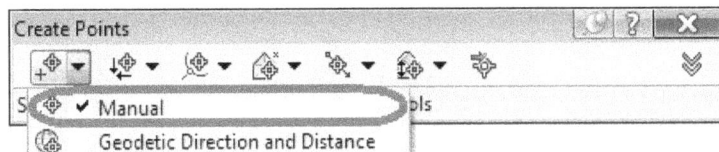

Figure 4–42

6. When prompted for a location, type **1906852.13,620768.56** and press <Enter> at the Command Line.

7. When prompted for a description, type **HYD** and press <Enter>.

The period is a placeholder for the elevation field. Typing a zero is incorrect because 0 is a valid elevation.

8. When prompted for an elevation, press <Enter> to accept the default value of **<.>** (period), because it is unknown.

9. Press <Enter> again to finish the command.

10. In the Transparent Command toolbar, click (Zoom to Point), and type **260**.

11. Save the drawing.

4.6 Description Key Sets

Description Keys categorize points by their field descriptions (raw description). If a point matches a Description Key entry, the point is assigned a point and label style, and a full description (possibly a translation of the raw description). Description Key Sets can also scale and rotate points. The **Description Key Sets** collection is shown in Figure 4–43.

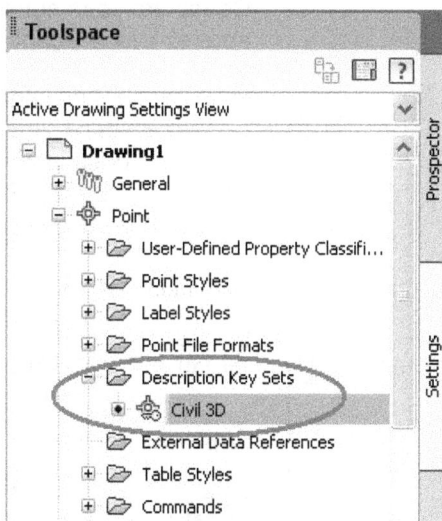

Figure 4–43

The Description Key's first five columns are the most used entries, as shown in Figure 4–44.

Figure 4–44

- To create a new Description Key row, select an existing code, right-click, and select **New**.

- To edit a code, double-click in the cell.

Code, Point, and Label Style

Description code is a significant part of data collection. Codes assigned to a raw description triggers action by the Description Key Set. Each entry in the set represents all of the possible descriptions that a field crew would use while surveying a job. When a raw description matches a code entry, the Key Set assigns all of the row's values to the matching point's point and label styles, translates the raw description, and assigns a layer. Codes are case-sensitive and must match the field collector's entered raw description.

- A code might contain wildcards to match raw descriptions that contain numbering or additional material beyond the point's description. For example, MH* would match MH1, MH2, etc. and UP* would match UP 2245 14.4Kv Verizon. Common wild keys are as follows:

# (pound)	Matches any single numeric digit. (T# matches T1 through T9.)
@ (at)	Matches any alphabetic character. (1@ matches 1A through 1Z.)
. (period)	Matches any non-alphanumeric character. (T. matches T- or T+.)
* (asterisk)	Matches any string of characters. (T* matches TREE, TR-Aspen, Topo, or Trench.)
? (question mark)	Matches any single character. (?BC matches TBC or 3BC.)

- Matching a Key Set entry for the code assigns a *Point Style* at the point's coordinates. If the *Point Style* is set to **Default**, the *Settings* tab's Point feature *Point Style* is used (set in the Edit Feature Settings dialog box), as shown in Figure 4–45.

- Matching a Key Set entry for the code assigns a point label style to annotate important point values. This is usually a number, elevation, and description. If the *Point Style* is set to **Default**, the *Settings* tab's Point feature *Point Label Style* is used (set in the Edit Feature Settings dialog box), as shown in Figure 4–45.

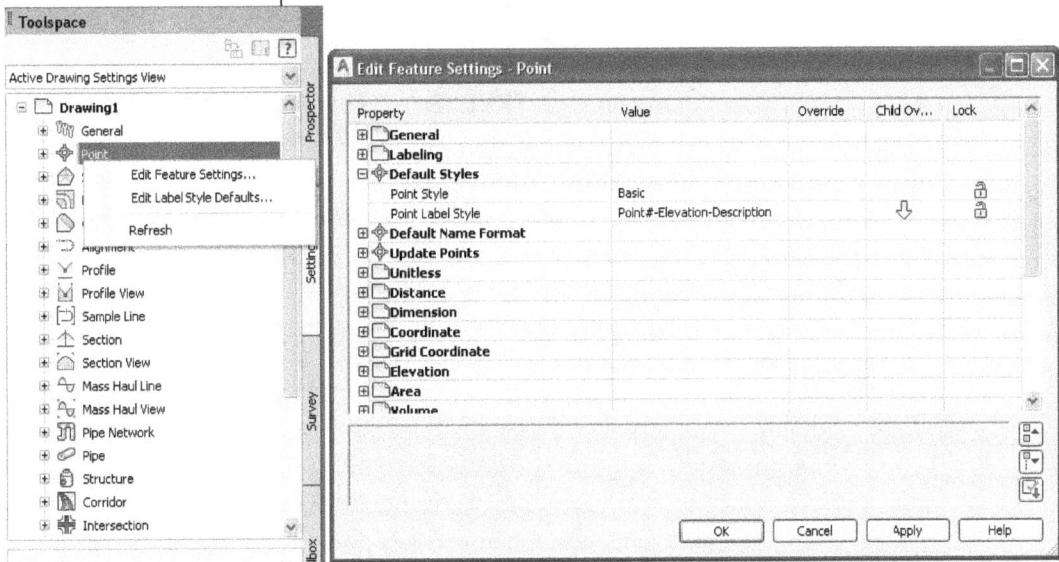

Figure 4–45

Format

The *Format* column translates the raw description (what the surveyor typed) into a full description (what you want it to read). When including spaces in a raw description, the AutoCAD Civil 3D software assigns parameter numbers to each description element. Parameters are represented by a $ sign followed by a number. For example, the description *PINE 6* has two elements: PINE and 6, with PINE as parameter 0 ($0) and 6 as parameter 1 ($1). To use the raw description as the full description, the *Format* column contains $* (use the raw description as the full description). The *Format* column can reorder the parameters and add characters to create a full description. For example, the raw description *PINE 6* can be translated to 6 PINE by entering **$1 $0**.

The function of parameters in the *Format* column is to translate a cryptic raw description into a more readable full description. Parameters are defined by spaces in a raw description. The first element is assigned **$0** and the maximum number of elements is 9 (i.e., **$0...$9**). A complex raw description is as follows:

TREE D MAPLE 3

For the raw description to match the Description Key Set entry, the entry **TREE** must have an asterisk (*) after **TREE** (as shown in Figure 4–46). The raw description elements and their parameters are **TREE** ($0), **D** ($1), **Maple** ($2), and **3** ($3). The *Format* column entry of **$3 $2 $0** creates a full description of **3mm MAPLE TREE**.

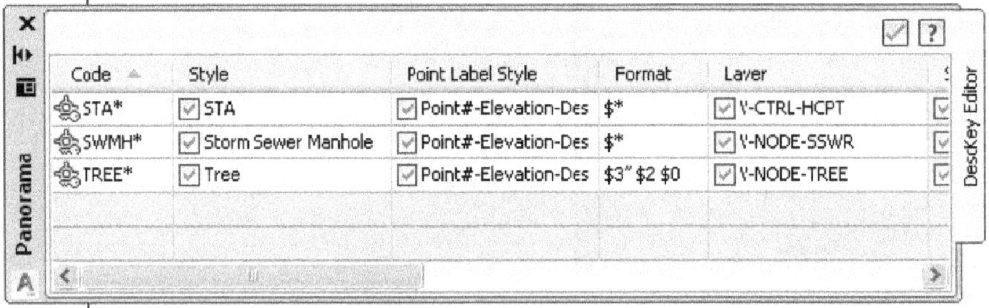

Code	Style	Point Label Style	Format	Layer	
STA*	☑ STA	☑ Point#-Elevation-Des	$*	☑ V-CTRL-HCPT	☑
SWMH*	☑ Storm Sewer Manhole	☑ Point#-Elevation-Des	$*	☑ V-NODE-SSWR	☑
TREE*	☑ Tree	☑ Point#-Elevation-Des	$3" $2 $0	☑ V-NODE-TREE	☑

Figure 4–46

If a point does not match any Description Key Set entry, it receives the default styles assigned by the **_All Points** group. The *Layer* column assigns a layer to the matching point. If the Point Style already has a marker and label layer, this entry should be toggled off. The Description Key Set also contains the *Scale* and *Rotate Parameter* columns. In the example shown in Figure 4–46, the **3** for the trunk diameter can also be a tree symbol scaling factor when applied to the symbol's X-Y.

Practice 4d

Estimated time for completion: 25 minutes

Creating a Description Key Set

Practice Objective

- Assign point symbols, labels, layers, etc., on importing by setting up Description Key Sets.

In this practice you will learn to create a new Description Key Set entry and apply it to an existing point. In addition you will update the Description Key Set to use parameters.

Task 1 - Create a new Description Key Set entry.

1. Continue working with the drawing from the previous practice, or open **Points-D1-Survey.dwg** from the *C:\Civil 3D for Surveyors Practice Files\Survey* folder.

2. In the Toolspace, select the *Settings* tab, and expand the **Point** collection until the **Description Key Set** collection and its list are displayed.

3. Select **Civil 3D**, right-click, and select **Edit Keys…**.

4. Right-click in any *Code* cell and select **New…**, as shown in Figure 4–47.

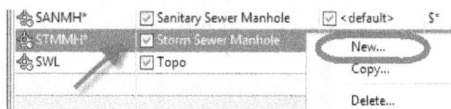

Figure 4–47

5. Double-click slowly in the *Code* cell in the newly created row and type **HYD**, as shown in Figure 4–48.

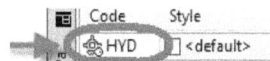

Figure 4–48

6. In the *Style* cell, toggle on the Point Style and select the **Style** cell to open the Point Style dialog box, as shown in Figure 4–49. In the drop-down list, select **Hydrant (existing)** and click **OK** to assign the style to the code.

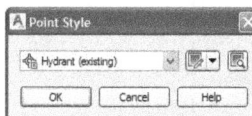

Figure 4–49

7. Make the following changes to the **HYD** description key, as shown in Figure 4–50:

   - *Point Label Style:* **<default>**
   - *Format:* **$*** (This means the label will be the same as the one entered by the surveyor.)
   - *Layer:* leave check box toggled off
   - *Use drawing scale:* **Yes**
   - *Scale Parameter:* clear check box

Code	Style	Point Label ...	F...	Layer	Scale Param...	Fixed ...	Use dra
⚙ HYD	☑ Hydrant (existing)	☑ <default>	$*	☐	☐ Parameter 1	☐ 1.000	☑ Yes

Figure 4–50

8. Close the *DescKey Editor* of the Panorama by clicking ☑ in the top right corner of the dialog box, as shown in Figure 4–51.

Figure 4–51

Task 2 - Apply the new Description Key Set to an existing point.

---

1. Continue working with the drawing from the previous practice or open **Points-D2-Survey.dwg** from the *C:\Civil 3D for Surveyors Practice Files\Survey* folder.

2. In the Transparent Command toolbar, click 🔍 (Zoom to Point) and type **260**.

3. In the *Prospector* tab, select the **_All Points** group, right-click, and select **Apply Description Keys**. The point updates to display the Hydrant symbol and its new description, as shown in Figure 4–52.

Figure 4–52

4. Save the drawing.

Task 3 - Update the Description Key Set to use parameters.

In this task you will use the Parameters feature to control the display properties of symbols in your drawings. The most common parameter is the **Scale** parameter. With this parameter, a surveyor will enter the size of a tree as part of the description and the description key file will insert a symbol scaled to the value provided by the surveyor. In this case, you want the pumpers on the hydrant to display correctly (i.e., running parallel to the road).

1. Continue working with the drawing from the previous task or open **Points-D3-Survey.dwg** from the *C:\Civil 3D for Surveyors Practice Files\Survey* folder.

2. In the *Settings* tab, expand the **Point** collection and expand the **Description Key Sets** collection. Select **Civil 3D**, right-click, and select **Edit Keys...**, as shown in Figure 4–53.

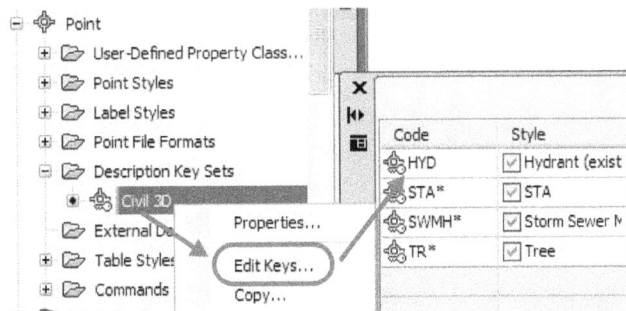

Figure 4–53

3. In the *HYD* row, *Code* column, type **HYD***. The asterisk symbolizes a wildcard, (i.e., any character after the letters HYD). In this example it is -5, parameter1, which you will enter in Step 6.

4. In the *HYD* row, select the check box in the *Marker Rotate* column, select the cell, and then select **Parameter1** in the drop-down list. The selected parameter is shown in Figure 4–54.

Figure 4–54

The -5 indicates the required rotation.

5. Click ☑ in the top right corner of the dialog box to close the Panorama view.

6. In Model Space, select the Hydrant point object, right-click, and select **Edit Points**. Change the *Raw Description* from *HYD* to **HYD -5**.

7. Select the row, right-click, and select **Apply Description Keys**, as shown in Figure 4–55.

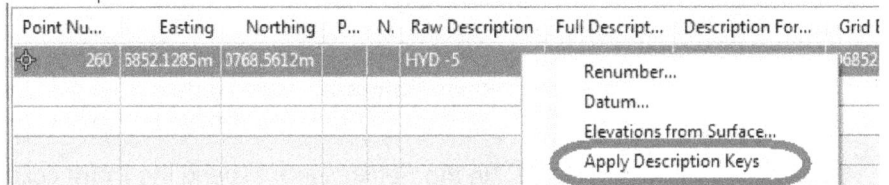

Point Nu...	Easting	Northing	P...	N.	Raw Description	Full Descript...	Description For...	Grid E
⊕ 260	5852.1285m	0768.5612m			HYD -5			06852
						Renumber...		
						Datum...		
						Elevations from Surface...		
						Apply Description Keys		

Figure 4–55

8. Click ☑ in the top right corner of the dialog box to close the Panorama view.

9. The hydrant has now been rotated to display the hydrant pumpers following the rotation of the road, as shown in Figure 4–56.

Figure 4–56

The label also displays the rotation angle text -5, which you do not want.

10. In the *Settings* tab, expand the **Point** collection and expand the **Description Key Sets** collection. Select **Civil 3D**, right-click, and select **Edit Keys...**

11. In the *HYD* row, change the *Format* from $* to **HYDRANT**, as shown in Figure 4–57.

Code	Style	Point Label ...	Format	Layer	Scale Para...	Fixed Scale ...	Use
⊕ HYD*	☑ Hydrant (existing)	☑ <default>	HYDRANT	☐	☐ Parameter	☐ 1.000	☑ Y
⊕ STA*	☑ STA	☑ Point#-Elev	$*	☑ V-C	☑ Parameter	☐ 1.000	☐ N
⊕ SWMH*	☑ Storm Sewer Manh	☑ Point#-Elev	$*	☑ V-N	☑ Parameter	☐ 1.000	☐ N

Figure 4–57

12. Click [✓] in the top right corner of the dialog box to close the Panorama view.

You still need to apply the changes.

13. In Model Space, select the Hydrant point object, right-click, and select **Apply Description Keys**. The changes are now applied, as shown in Figure 4–58.

Figure 4–58

14. Save the drawing.

4.7 Importing and Exporting Points

The AutoCAD Civil 3D software has methods to import point data from ASCII text files, AutoCAD Land Desktop point databases, and Autodesk LandXML files, as well as methods to convert AutoCAD Land Desktop points to AutoCAD Civil 3D points. The *Survey* tab also inserts points from a survey to a drawing.

To Import Points

There are two methods of launching the import point feature, one is by using the *Insert* tab and the other is using the **Points** creation toolbar in the *Prospector* tab.

How To: Use the *Insert* tab method

Alternatively, you can click ✥ (Import Points) in the Create Points toolbar.

1. In the *Insert* tab, select **Points from File**.
2. In the Import Points dialog box, do the following:
   - Set the file format.
   - Select the files to import.
   - Set any advanced options.
   - Click **OK** to import the points.

How To: Use the Point Creation tools method

1. In the *Home* tab>Create Gound Data panel, expand the Points drop-down list and select **Point Creation Tools**, as shown in Figure 4–59.
   - Alternatively, in the *Prospector* tab, select **Points**, right-click and select **Create...**, as shown in Figure 4–60.

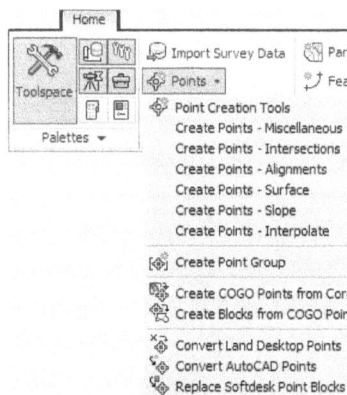

Figure 4–59

Figure 4–60

- All commands in the Points drop-down list can also be accessed in the Create Points toolbar, as shown in Figure 4–61.

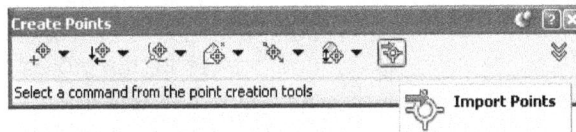

Figure 4–61

2. Click (Import Points) to open the Import Points dialog box. The Import Points dialog box is shown in Figure 4–62.
3. In the Import Points dialog box, expand the Format drop-down list and select a point file format.

4. After setting the format, click on the right to open the Select Source File dialog box.
5. In the Select Source File dialog box, browse to the import point file, select it, and select **Open**.

- You can select multiple files with the same file format.
- You can assign the imported points to a new or existing point group by selecting the **Add Points to Point Group** option and selecting the point group in the drop-down list.
- Select any **Advanced options**, as required.
- Click **OK** when done.

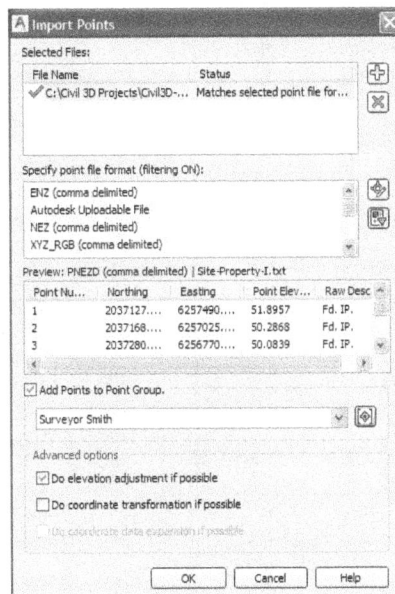

Figure 4–62

• The Duplicate Point Number dialog box opens if there is a conflict between point numbers in the ASCII file and the drawing (e.g., both contain Point Number 1).

To import points directly from an AutoCAD Land Desktop point database, select the **External Project Point Database** format and browse for the project's COGO subfolder. Then locate and select the **Points.mdb** file.

If a drawing contains all or a subset of all points, you only need to convert the points into AutoCAD Civil 3D cogo points.

Duplicate Point Numbers

If an imported file creates duplicate point numbers, AutoCAD Civil 3D software overwrites, merges, or reassigns them during the import process. When encountering duplicate point numbers, the AutoCAD Civil 3D software can assign the next available number, add an offset (add 5000 to each point number that conflicts), overwrite (replaces the current point values with the file's values), or merge (add the file's values to an existing point's values). If using the offset method, the new point numbers are kept unique in the drawing. If using the next available number method, the new points blend into the original points and are difficult to identify.

The offset method is preferred when resolving duplicate point numbers. When importing points that will potentially duplicate point numbers, the Create Points toolbar's *Point Identity* settings (shown in Figure 4–63) is the default when handling duplicate point numbers.

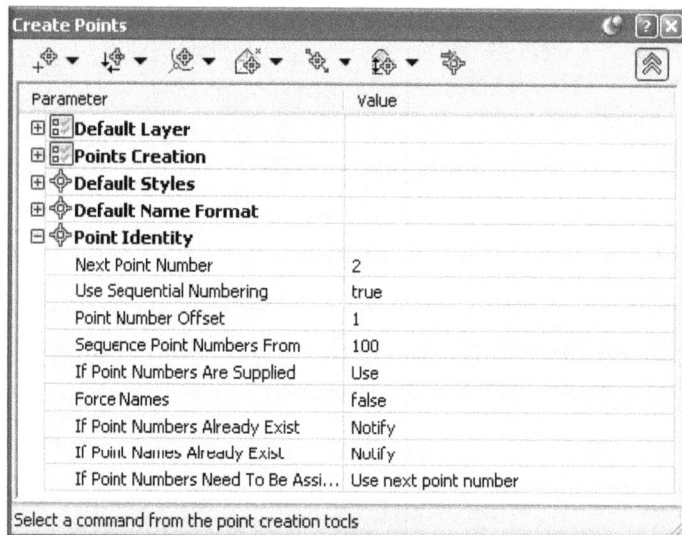

Parameter	Value
⊞ ☑ **Default Layer**	
⊞ ☑ **Points Creation**	
⊞ **Default Styles**	
⊞ **Default Name Format**	
⊟ **Point Identity**	
Next Point Number	2
Use Sequential Numbering	true
Point Number Offset	1
Sequence Point Numbers From	100
If Point Numbers Are Supplied	Use
Force Names	false
If Point Numbers Already Exist	Notify
If Point Names Already Exist	Notify
If Point Numbers Need To Be Assi...	Use next point number

Select a command from the point creation tools

Figure 4–63

In the *Point Identity* settings, set the duplicate point resolution method for the *If Point Numbers Already Exist* variable. The four methods are **Renumber**, **Merge**, **Overwrite**, and **Notify**, as shown in Figure 4–64. The import process never overwrites point data unless you specify that it should do so.

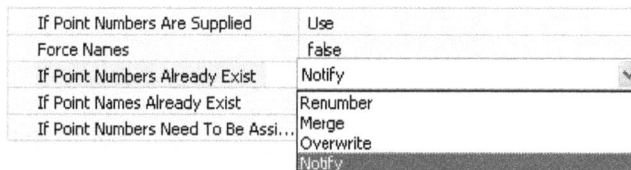

If Point Numbers Are Supplied	Use
Force Names	false
If Point Numbers Already Exist	Notify
If Point Names Already Exist	Renumber
If Point Numbers Need To Be Assi...	Merge
	Overwrite
	Notify

Figure 4–64

When encountering a duplicate point, the Duplicate Point Number dialog box opens. After you define a resolution, it can be assigned to the current duplicate point or to all encountered duplicate points.

Transforming Points on Import or Export

When importing points, the assumption is that the file's and drawing's points are in the same coordinate system. When the file's points are in a different coordinate system, you must define a point file format identifying the point file's coordinate system.

To identify that a point file contains coordinates from a different system, you must define a new point file format. When using this file to import points, the import routine knows that the points are from one system and that the drawing is assigned another. Therefore, when importing the points, it transforms them to the drawing's coordinate system.

When using the file format to export points, the export routine transforms the points from the drawing's coordinate system to the point file format's coordinate system.

The point file format must have two values: the coordinate system and the keywords Grid Northing and Grid Easting.

The coordinate system assignment is similar to assigning a system to a drawing. In the Point File Format dialog box, toggle on the **Coordinate zone transform** option and click 🌐 next to the *Zone* field.

In the Select Coordinate Zone dialog box, set the category and coordinate system, as shown at the bottom in Figure 4–65.

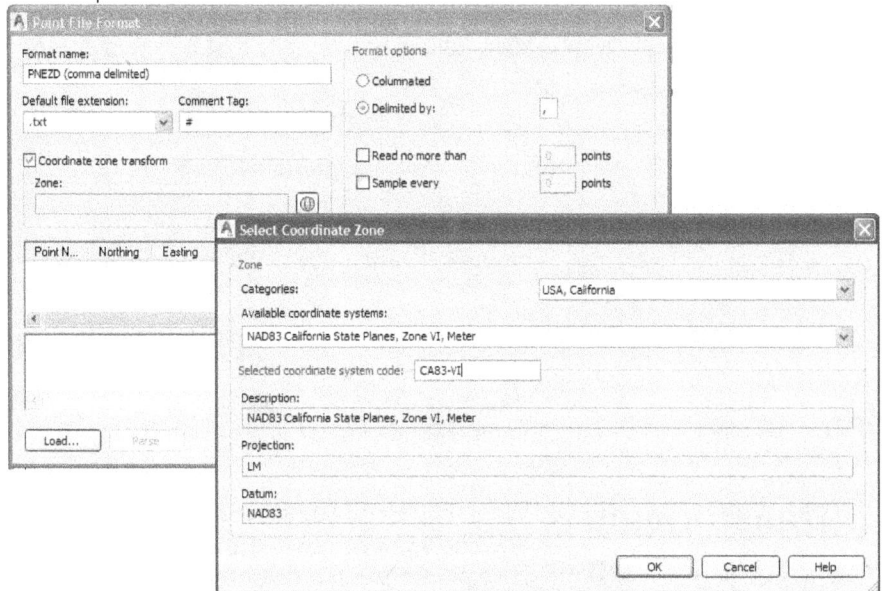

Figure 4–65

You then need to change the Northing and Easting headings to Grid Northing and Grid Easting. Select the heading and in the Select Column Name dialog box, select the new heading: **Grid Northing** or **Grid Easting**, as shown in Figure 4–66.

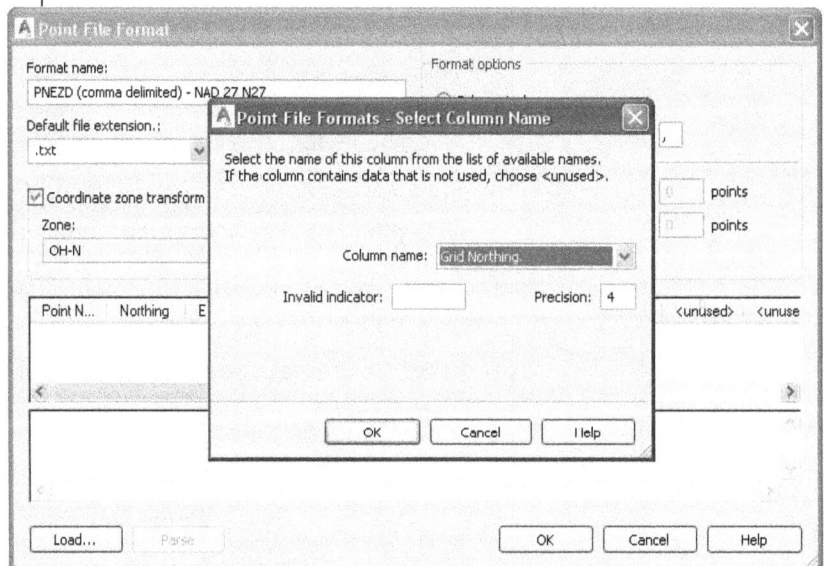

Figure 4–66

Practice 4e

Estimated time for completion: 25 minutes

Importing and Exporting Points Part I

Practice Objective

- Import points from and export points to ASCII files created from the field survey.

In this practice you will import an ASCII file created in the field.

Task 1 - Import an ASCII file using the Create Points toolbar.

1. Continue working with the drawing from the previous practice or open **Points-E1-Survey.dwg** from the *C:\Civil 3D for Surveyors Practice Files\Survey* folder.

2. In the *Home* tab, click (Points) and in the drop-down list, select the **Point Creation tools**.

3. Click (Import Points) in the toolbar.

4. Click and in the *Selected Files* area in the dialog box, browse to the ASCII file's location in the *C:\Civil 3D for Surveyors Practice Files\Survey* folder. Select the survey of the property pins, **Site-Property-M.txt**, as the file you want to import.

5. In the Import Points dialog box, expand the Specify point file format (filtering on) drop-down list and select **PNEZD (comma delimited)**, as shown in Figure 4–67.

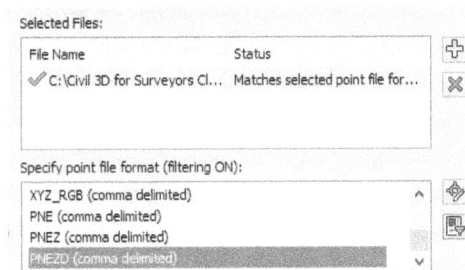

Selected Files:

File Name	Status	
✓ C:\Civil 3D for Surveyors Cl...	Matches selected point file for...	

Specify point file format (filtering ON):

XYZ_RGB (comma delimited)	
PNE (comma delimited)	
PNEZ (comma delimited)	
PNEZD (comma delimited)	

Figure 4–67

6. Click **OK** to import the file. When done, click **X** to close the Create Points toolbar.

7. Save the drawing.

Task 2 - Review points.

1. Continue working with the drawing from the previous practice or open **Points-E2-Survey.dwg** from the *C:\Civil 3D for Surveyors Practice Files\Survey* folder.

2. In the *Prospector* tab, select **Points** to preview the points in the *Prospector's* preview area.

3. In the Transparent Command toolbar, click (Zoom to Point), and type **249**.

4. In the model, select point **249** and press **<Delete>** on the keyboard.

5. In the *View* tab>Views panel, select the preset view **Suv Main**.

6. Save the drawing.

Task 3 - Create a new point file format.

In the AutoCAD Civil 3D software, you can create an output format based on an independent coordinate system. Using this output file, you can then open multiple drawings that each have their own coordinate systems and export the points to one common coordinate system.

1. Continue working with the drawing from the previous practice or open **Points-E3-Survey.dwg** from the *C:\Civil 3D for Surveyors Practice Files\Survey* folder.

2. Select the *Settings* tab.

3. Expand the **Point** collection until the **Point File Formats** collection and its format list display. Expand the Point File Formats drop-down list, select **PNEZD** (Comma delimited), right-click, and select **Copy...**

4. In the Point File Format dialog box, change the format name to **PNEZD (Comma delimited) Lat-Long**.

5. Select the **Coordinate zone transform** option and click next the *Zone* field.

6. In the Select Coordinate Zone dialog box, set the following, as shown in Figure 4–68:

   - *Categories*: **World/Continental**
   - *Available coordinate systems*: **WGS84 datum, Latitude-Longitude; Degrees**

Zone

| Categories: | World/Continental ∨ |

Available coordinate systems:

| WGS84 datum, Latitude-Longitude; Degrees | ∨ |

Selected coordinate system code: LL84

Description:

| WGS84 datum, Latitude-Longitude; Degrees |

Figure 4–68

7. Click **OK** to return to the Point File Format dialog box.

   Note that there are two WG84 Coordinate Systems. Verify that the selected coordinate system code is set to **LL84** after selecting the coordinate system. Alternatively, you can type the value rather than selecting it from the list.

8. Select the **Northing** heading, as shown in Figure 4–69. In the Select Column Name dialog box, expand the Column name drop-down list, select **Latitude**, and click **OK**.

9. Select the **Easting** heading, as shown in Figure 4–69. In the Select Column Name dialog box, expand the Column name drop-down list, select **Longitude**, and click **OK**.

Point File Format

Format name:

PNEZD (comma delimited) Lat-Long

Default file extension: Comment Tag:

.txt   #

☑ Coordinate zone transform

Zone:

LL84

| Point N... | Latitude | Longitude | Point El... | Raw De... |

Figure 4–69

10. Click **OK** to create the new point file format.

11. Save the drawing.

Task 4 - Export a Lat Longs point file.

1. Continue working with the drawing from the previous practice or open **Points-E4-Survey.dwg** from the *C:\Civil 3D for Surveyors Practice Files\Survey* folder.

2. Select the *Prospector* tab.

3. If required, expand the **Point Groups** collection.

4. Expand the list of point groups, select **_All Points**, right-click, and select **Export Points...** to open the Export Points dialog box.

5. In the Export Points dialog box, change the file format to **PNEZD Comma delimited) Lat-Long**.

6. Click to open the Select Destination File dialog box.

7. Browse to the *C:\Civil 3D for Surveyors Practice Files\Survey* folder. Type **Site-Lat-Long** for the filename and click **Open** to create the file.

8. In the Export Points dialog box, select the **Limit to Points in Point Group** option, expand the drop-down list on the left and select **Street Light**.

9. Select the **Do coordinate transformation if possible** option, and click **OK** to export the points.

10. Open Windows Explorer and browse to the *C:\Civil 3D for Surveyors Practice Files\Survey* folder. Open the file **Site-Lat-Long.txt** using Notepad and review its lat and long coordinates.

Practice 4f

Importing and Exporting Points Part II

Practice Objective

- Import points from an ASCII file into the survey database.

Estimated time for completion: 5 minutes

One method of importing points is to import a points file directly into the AutoCAD Civil 3D software. In this practice you will examine another method. You will use the Survey Database features to import a points file.

Task 1 - Set the Survey Database and import points.

1. Continue working with the drawing from the previous practice or open the file **Points-F1-Survey.dwg** from *C:\Civil 3D for Surveyors Practice Files\Survey* folder.

Refer to Appendix A-1 Open a Survey Database, on how to open a survey database.

2. Open the previously created database **Survey Data**. If you did not complete the previous practice where you created this database, open **Survey Data Points**.

3. Select the opened current survey database, right-click, and select **Import>Import point file**, as shown in Figure 4–70.

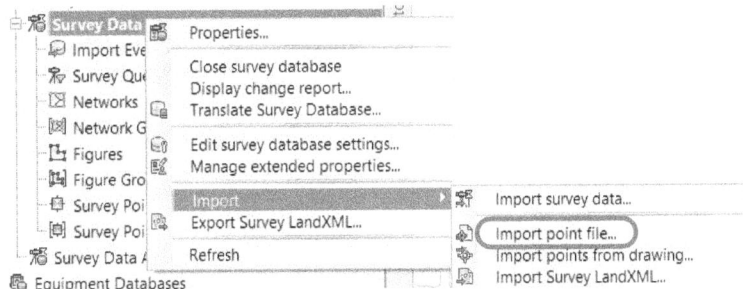

Figure 4–70

4. In the Select Source File, browse to the *C:\Civil 3D for Surveyors Practice Files\Survey* folder and select **Site-Survey2.txt** to open it. For the Specify Point file format, select **PNEZD (comma delimited)**. Check the option to Insert survey points and clear other selections, as shown in Figure 4–71. Click **OK** when done.

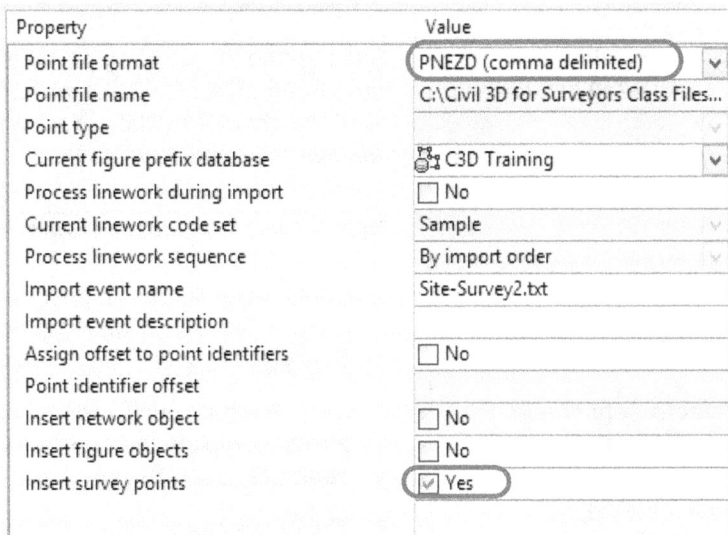

Property	Value
Point file format	PNEZD (comma delimited) ⌄
Point file name	C:\Civil 3D for Surveyors Class Files...
Point type	⌄
Current figure prefix database	🖧 C3D Training ⌄
Process linework during import	☐ No
Current linework code set	Sample ⌄
Process linework sequence	By import order ⌄
Import event name	Site-Survey2.txt
Import event description	
Assign offset to point identifiers	☐ No
Point identifier offset	
Insert network object	☐ No
Insert figure objects	☐ No
Insert survey points	☑ Yes

Figure 4–71

- Note that the AutoCAD Civil 3D software has created an import event that can be used to re-process the points files when changes are made to them, as shown in Figure 4–72.

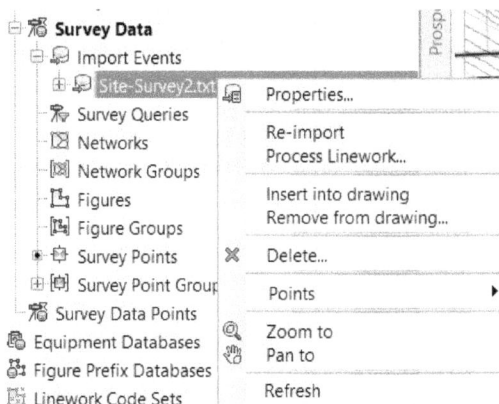

Figure 4–72

5. Save the drawing.

4.8 Point Groups

Point groups organize points that share common descriptions and characteristics (such as existing storm, gas lines, building corners, etc.). Point groups also enable points to display different point or label styles. For example, a Landscape Architect needs to display different symbols for each tree species, while an Engineer only needs to display a generic tree symbol. The **Description Key Set** enables you to assign the tree species symbols for the Landscape Architect, and a point group enables generic tree symbols to override the symbols for the Engineer. Another function of a point group is to hide all of the points.

In the AutoCAD Civil 3D software, point groups can be defined in the template along with a Description Key Set. When creating a new drawing from this template and importing points, they are assigned their symbols and can be sorted into point groups.

All points in a drawing belong to the **_All Points** point group. Consider this point group as the point database. It cannot be deleted and initially is not in a drawing until you add points. All new point groups include all drawing points or a subset of drawing points (copied points from the **_All Points** point group).

Defining Point Groups

To create a new point group, select the *Prospector* tab, right-click on the **Point Groups** collection and select **New...** Alternatively, in the *Home* tab, expand **Points** and select **Create Point Group**.

When you select **New...** or **Create Point Group**, the Point Group Properties dialog box opens. It has nine tabs, most of them affecting the point group's definition.

- The *Point Groups*, *Raw Desc Matching*, *Include*, and *Query Builder* tabs add points to the point group. The *Exclude* tab removes points from a point group.

- The *Information* tab defines the point group's name. The *Point style* and *Point label style* should remain at their defaults, unless you want to use either style to override the assigned styles of the points in the point group. The points in the point group display their originally assigned styles until you toggle on the override.

A point group can be locked by toggling on the **Object locked** option to prevent any changes to the group. The Point Group Properties dialog box opens as shown in Figure 4–73.

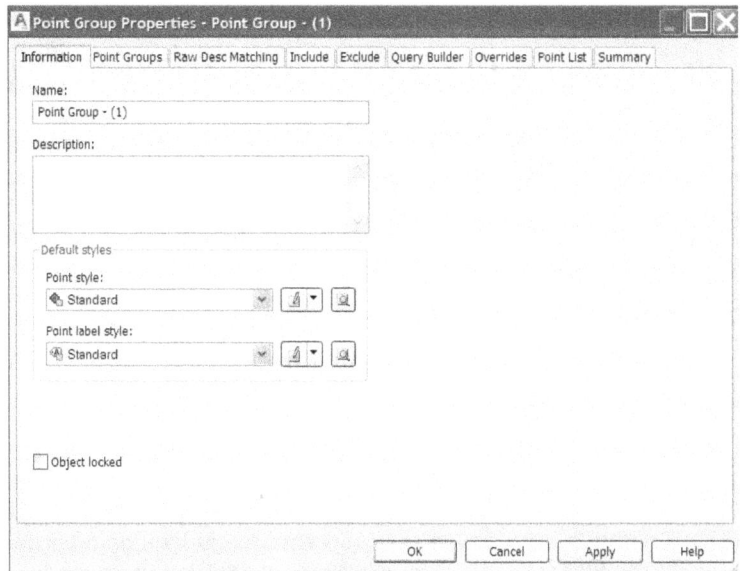

Figure 4–73

- The *Point Groups* tab lists the drawing's groups. A point group can be created from other point groups. When you select a point group name, the group and its points become members of the new point group. For example, the point group **Trees** is created from the point groups *Maple*, *Walnut*, *Oak*, etc.

- The *Raw Desc Matching* tab lists codes from the Description Key Code set. When you toggle on the code, any point matching the code becomes part of the point group.

- If you cannot select a point with the previous two methods, the *Include* tab enables you to include points by specifically entering in the selection criteria. The criteria include the point number (point number list or by selection), elevation, name, raw description, full description, and all points.

With numbers matching	Selects points by a point number range or list. When creating a list, sequential point numbers are hyphenated (1-20) and individual numbers are in a comma delimited list. A point list can include sequential and individual points (1-20, 14, 44, 50-60). Select **Selection Set in Drawing** to select the points in the drawing and list their point numbers at the top of the *Include* tab.

With elevations matching	Enables you to select points by entering a specific elevation or by specifying a minimum and/or maximum elevation. For example, valid entries include >100,<400, and >100. The first entry only includes points whose elevation is above 100, but less than 400. The second entry only includes points whose elevation is greater than 100. A point without an elevation cannot be selected using this method. An elevation range, defined by separating the start and end numbers with a hyphen, includes points whose elevation falls within the range (1-100). This can be combined with greater or less than symbols.
With names matching	Selects points based on matching their point names. Enter one or more point names separated by commas.
With raw/full descriptions matching	Selects points based on matching an entered raw or full description. Enter one or more descriptions separated by commas. You can use the same wildcards as the Description Key Set. Generally, this method uses the asterisk (*) as the wildcard after the description (e.g., PINE*, CTV*, CL*, etc.).
Include all points	Assigns all points in the drawing to the point group. When this option is toggled on, all other **Include** options are disabled.

- The *Exclude* tab has the same options as the *Include* tab, except for the **Include All Points** option.

- The *Query Builder* tab creates one or more expressions to select points. Each query is a row selecting points. As with all SQL queries, you combine expressions using the operators AND, OR, and NOT. You can also use parentheses to group expressions.

- The *Overrides* tab overrides the points in the point group's raw description, elevation, point style, and/or point label style. For example, you can override specific tree species symbols with a generic tree symbol, override a label style when displaying this group, or override the point and label style with none (to hide all points).

  The point group display order affects points and their overrides. To change how the point groups display, modify the Point Group display order.

- The *Point List* tab displays the point group's points. This tab enables you to review points that are currently in the point group. The *Summary* tab displays the point group's settings. You can print this tab as a report by cutting and pasting it into a document.

Updating Out of Date Point Groups

After defining point groups and adding points to a drawing, the group becomes out of date before assigning the points to the group. This enables you to verify that the point(s) should become part of the group. To review why a group is out of date, select the group, right-click, and select **Show Changes...** If the changes are correct, select **Update** to add the points to the group. If you know that all of the groups displaying as out of date should be updated, right-click on the **Point Groups** collection and select **Update**. At this level, the command updates all of the point groups.

Overriding Point Group Properties

If a Description Key Set exists in the file, the points take on the symbol and label style assigned by the Description Key Set unless a point group override is toggled on. When working with points, you might want them to display different labels, have them not be visible, or display different symbols. Each required change is a function of a point group override. A point group that contains all of the points and overrides their symbols and labels with none does not display any points. This is similar to freezing all of the layers involved with points. A point group that changes the symbols that a group displays overrides the label styles assigned to the point in the point group. To display a different symbol, the point group overrides the assigned point styles. To set the style and override the assigned styles, toggle on the point group in the *Overrides* tab and set the styles in the *Override* column of the point group, as shown in Figure 4–74.

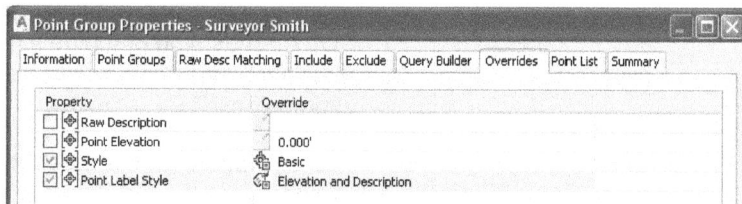

Figure 4–74

Point Groups Display Properties

When creating a point group, it is placed at the top of the point group list. The point group list is more than a list of point groups; it is also the AutoCAD Civil 3D's point draw order. The AutoCAD Civil 3D software draws the point groups starting from the bottom of the list to the top. If **_All Points** is the first drawn point group and the remaining point groups are subsets of all points, the individual point group does not display, but all of the points display.

To display point groups that are a subset of all points, you must create a point group whose purpose is to hide all points. This popular point group is commonly called **No Display**. With this group, any point group drawn after it displays its members without *seeing* the other points.

The AutoCAD Civil 3D software draws point groups from the bottom to the top of the list. To manipulate the display order, right-click on the **Point Groups** collection in the *Prospector* tab and select **Properties**. The Point Groups dialog box opens, enabling you to modify the point group display order using the arrows on the right, as shown in Figure 4–75.

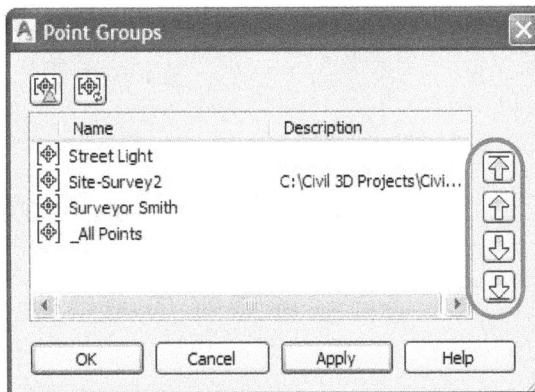

Figure 4–75

These arrows enable you to select the required point group and move it up or down in the list (or all the way to the top or bottom of the list with one click,) in the hierarchy for display purposes. The Point Groups dialog box has two additional icons at the top. The first icon displays the difference between point groups and the second icon updates them all.

If you use Description Key Sets, a point displays the assigned point and label style when it is part of any point group. The only time the point displays another style is when you override the style (in the Point Group Properties dialog box, in the *Overrides* tab).

With the Description Key Set and display order shown in Figure 4–76, the points display their originally assigned point label styles.

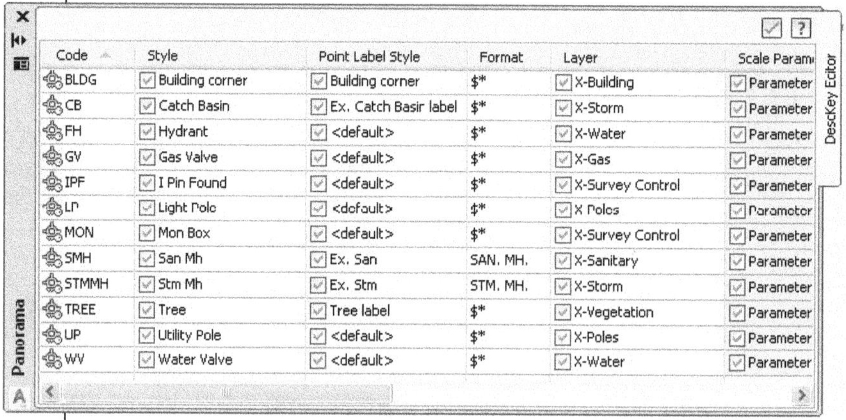

Figure 4–76

The **No Display** point group includes all of the points, but overrides the originally assigned point style and point label styles with **<none>**. When **No Display** is moved to the list's top, no points display. The Point Groups dialog box is shown in Figure 4–77.

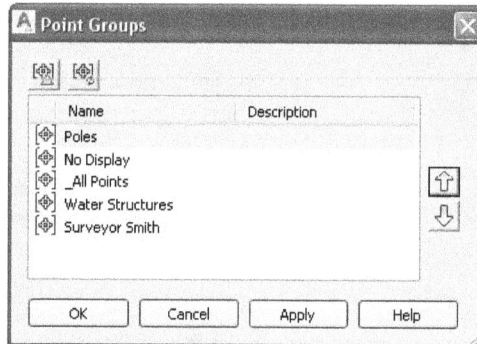

Figure 4–77

Practice 4g

Estimated time for completion: 10 minutes

Creating Point Groups

Practice Objective

- Draw Parcels from a legal description using lines and curves or polylines and transparent commands.

In this practice you will create point groups.

Task 1 - Create Point Groups (Boundary Pin Survey).

1. Continue working with the drawing from the previous practice or open **Points-G1-Survey.dwg** from the *C:\Civil 3D for Surveyors Practice Files\Survey* folder.

2. In the *Prospector* tab, select **Point Groups**, right-click, and select **New...**, as shown in Figure 4–78.

Figure 4–78

3. In the Point Group Properties dialog box, in the *Information* tab, set the following, as shown in Figure 4–79.

- *Name:* **Boundary Pin Survey**
- *Point style*: **Iron Pin**
- *Point label style*: **Elevation and Description**

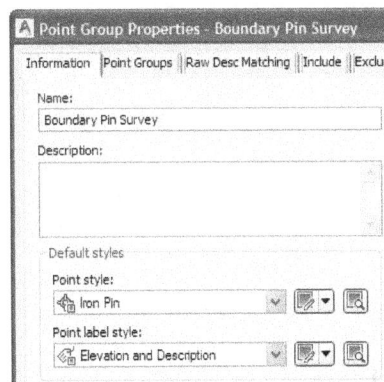

Figure 4–79

4. Select the *Include* tab. Select the **With raw description matching** option. Type ***IP.** (verify that a period follows IP) in the field to select all of the points that have the last three characters *IP.* (iron pin). You can confirm this in the *Point List* tab, as shown in Figure 4–80.

	Point Num...	Easting	Northing	Point Elevation	Name	Raw Description	Full Description	Description Forma
✧	1	7286.7724m	0917.5908m	51.896m		Fd. IP.	Fd. IP.	
✧	2	7145.0343m	0930.0483m	50.287m		Fd. IP.	Fd. IP.	
✧	3	7067.3102m	0964.1860m	50.084m		Fd. IP.	Fd. IP.	
✧	4	6990.8853m	0997.5930m	50.460m		Fd. IP.	Fd. IP.	
✧	5	6961.3987m	1010.4823m	50.748m		Fd. IP.	Fd. IP.	
✧	6	6942.3418m	1014.4780m	50.940m		Fd. IP.	Fd. IP.	
✧	7	6921.0059m	1024.8413m	51.064m		Fd. IP.	Fd. IP.	
✧	8	6890.8306m	1040.9957m	49.124m		Fd. IP.	Fd. IP.	

Information | Point Groups | Raw Desc Matching | Include | Exclude | Query Builder | Overrides | Point List | Summary

Figure 4–80

5. Click **OK** to close the dialog box and apply the changes.

Task 2 - Create point groups (No display).

Continue working with the drawing from the previous task. In this task you will use the point group to control the points display. Not only will you be able to display the same point differently, but you will also be able to control the visibility of the points. This eliminates needing to use the Layer command to thaw and freeze layers.

1. Select **Point Groups**, right-click, and select **New...** to create a new point group. In the *Information* tab, set the *Name* to **No display**.

2. Select **<none>** for both the *Point style* and the *Point label style*, as shown in Figure 4–81.

Default styles

Point style:

<none>

Point label style:

<none>

Figure 4–81

3. Select the *Overrides* tab and select **Style** and **Point Label Style**, as shown in Figure 4–82.

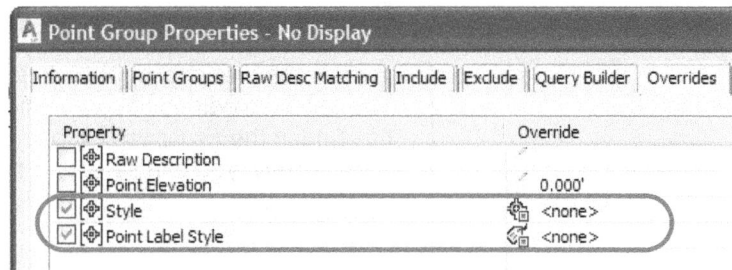

Figure 4–82

4. In the *Include* tab, select the **Include all points** option. Select the *Point List* tab to confirm that all of the points have been included.

5. Click **OK** to create the point group. Note that the points have disappeared.

6. To control the hierarchy and the display of the point group style, select the *Prospector* tab, select **Point Groups**, right-click, and select **Properties**.

7. In the Point Groups dialog box, select the **No display** point group and move it to the top of the list by clicking ⬆. Select the **Boundary Pin Survey** point group and move it to the top of the list by clicking ⬆. Click **OK** to apply the changes. Only the points in the Boundary Pin point group are displayed. You might need to type **regen** in the Command Line (type **RE**, and press <Enter).

8. Experiment with moving point groups up and down the list to control the display of points.

9. Save the drawing.

4.9 Reviewing and Editing Points

Reviewing and editing point data occurs throughout the AutoCAD Civil 3D environment. It is as simple as selecting a point in the drawing, right-clicking, and selecting **Edit Points...** You can also edit points using the shortcut menu in the *Points* heading in the *Prospector* tab, as shown in Figure 4–83. Alternatively, you can select a point entry in the *Prospector's* preview area.

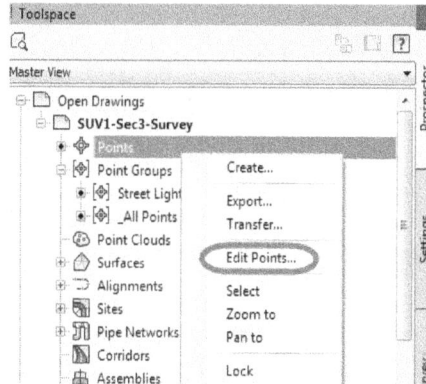

Figure 4–83

When selecting **Edit Points...**, the AutoCAD Civil 3D software displays the *Point Editor* tab inside the Panorama, as shown in Figure 4–84.

Figure 4–84

Repositioning Point Labels

Each point label style has **Dragged State** parameters. These parameters affect the label's behavior when moving the label from its original label position. Depending on the **Dragged State** parameters, a label can change completely (Stacked text) or display as it was originally defined (As composed). An example of a dragged label is shown in Figure 4–85.

Figure 4–85

When selecting a point, it displays multiple grips. Select the move point grip when you want to relocate the label.

A point displays three grips when selected.

- The **Rectangle** label grip to Move, Rotate, and Toggle sub item grips, and to Reset the label.

- The Diamond point object grip to Move and Rotate both the label and marker, Rotate just the marker, reset marker rotation, and Reset all.

- The third grip is a + (plus) symbol that enables you to add vertices to the leader, as shown in Figure 4–86.

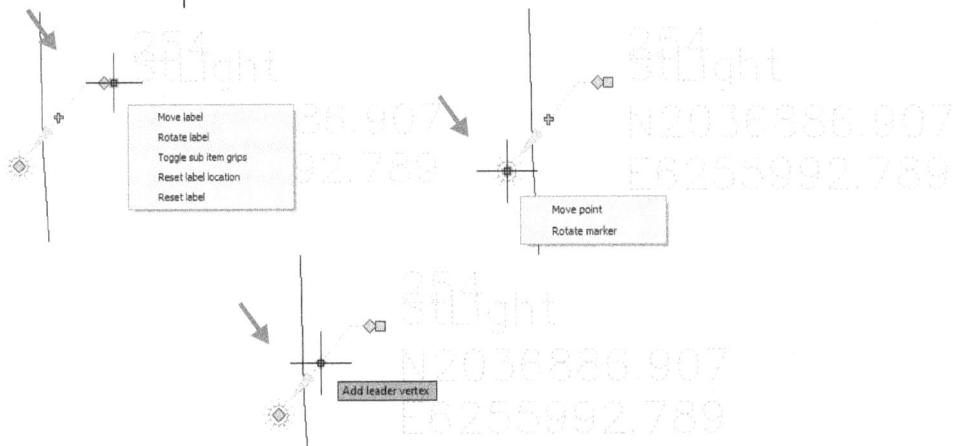

Figure 4–86

Each label component can be modified and the change is only for that point.

Point objects can be set to automatically rotate to match the current view using style settings. If this is not preferred, they can have a rotation assigned directly through the AutoCAD Properties dialog box.

You can reset a label to its original position by selecting the point, right-clicking, and selecting **Reset Label**.

Practice 4h

Manipulating Points

Practice Objective

- Modify the label position for points to ensure that the plan is readable.

Estimated time for completion: 5 minutes

Task 1 - Modify the position of the labels.

1. Continue working with the drawing from the previous practice or open **Points-H1-Survey.dwg** from the *C:\Civil 3D for Surveyors Practice Files\Survey* folder.

2. In the *Prospector* tab, right-click on **Point Group** and select **Properties**.

3. Select the **No display** point group and press <Down Arrow> to move it to the bottom of the list.

This positions the point at the center of the screen.

4. In the preview point list, scroll down until the point number **260** displays. Select it, right-click, and select **Zoom to**.

5. In the Status Bar, ensure that the *Annotation Scale* is set to **1:500** (as shown in Figure 4–87) to change the point size in the drawing.

Figure 4–87

6. Select point **260** to display its grips. Select the Drag Label grip, as shown in Figure 4–88, to relocate the label.

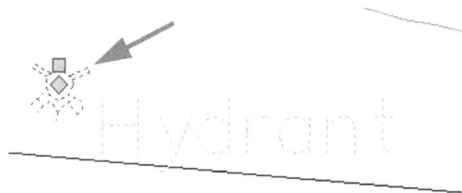

Figure 4–88

7. With the label still displaying grips, hover on the Rectangle grip and select **Reset Label**.

8. With the label still displaying grips, hover over the Square label grip to display the options for moving, rotating, and additional sub item grips, as shown in Figure 4–89. Select **Rotate label** and rotate the label.

9. With the label still displaying grips, hover over the diamond point grip to display the options to move, rotate label and marker, and Rotate marker, as shown in Figure 4–90. Select **Rotate marker** and rotate the marker.

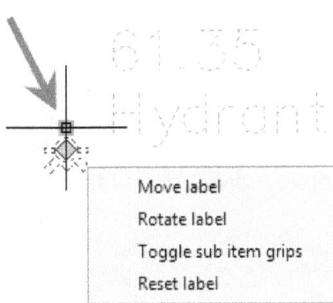

Figure 4–89

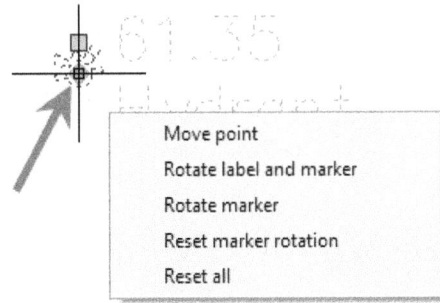

Figure 4–90

10. Save the drawing.

4.10 Locking/Unlocking Points

The AutoCAD Civil 3D software has point locking, which protects its properties from edits. A locked point displays ✎ (Lock).

To lock all of the points, select **Points** in the *Prospector* tab, right-click, and select **Lock**, as shown on the left in Figure 4–91. You can also lock points in a point group. To lock individual points, select the point, right-click, and select **Lock**, as shown on the right. You can also select points in a drawing and use the right-click method to lock them.

You can select a range of points by selecting a point in the list and while holding <Shift>, and then selecting another point in the list. This selects all of the points between the first and second selected points. Select individual points by holding <Ctrl> and selecting points.

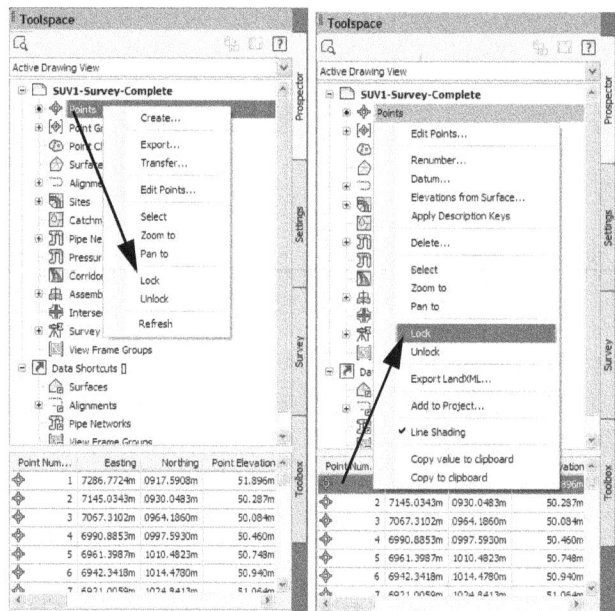

Figure 4–91

Reviewing/Editing Points

Review and/or edit points using one of the following methods: Use the tools in the *Modify* tab>Points panel, select the **Points** heading, right-click, and select **Edit Points...**, or select points in a drawing, right-click, and select **Edit Points...** These commands enable you to edit all or selected points, revise the points' elevation, reassign point elevations from a surface, or renumber the points.

In the Point Editor, use <Shift> or <Ctrl> to a select a range or set of individual points. After selecting the points, right-click and select the required editing option, as shown in Figure 4–92. You can also select points graphically and then right-click to edit the points.

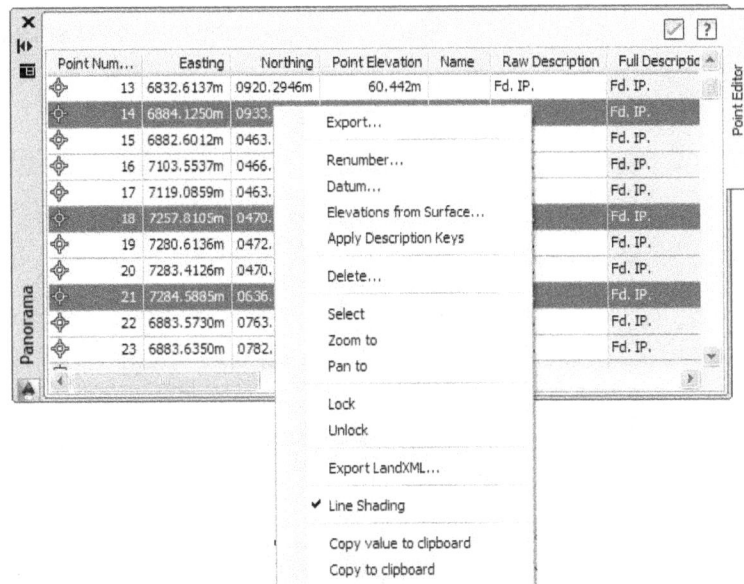

Figure 4–92

Practice 4i

Point Locking and Editing

Practice Objective

Estimated time for completion: 5 minutes

- Prevent unwanted edits to points by locking them.

1. Continue working with the drawing from the previous practice or open **Points-I1-Survey.dwg** from the *C:\Civil 3D for Surveyors Practice Files\Survey* folder.

2. In the *Prospector* tab, select **Points** to display a point list in the *Prospector's* preview area.

3. Scroll through the list, select point number **10**, right-click, and select **Zoom to**.

4. In the drawing, select point **10** and note the move grip that displays at its marker, as shown in Figure 4–93.

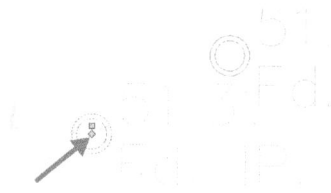

Figure 4–93

5. In the *Prospector* tab, select **Points**, right-click, and select **Lock**, as shown on the left in Figure 4–94. Note that the points in the *Prospector's* preview area now display the **Lock** icon, as shown on the right.

Figure 4–94

6. In the model, select point **10** and note that although the move grip is displayed, you cannot move the point, as shown in Figure 4–95.

Figure 4–95

7. In the *Prospector* tab, select **Points**. Right-click and select **Edit Points.....** The points display the **Lock** icon and the editor now has a gray background, as shown in Figure 4–96.

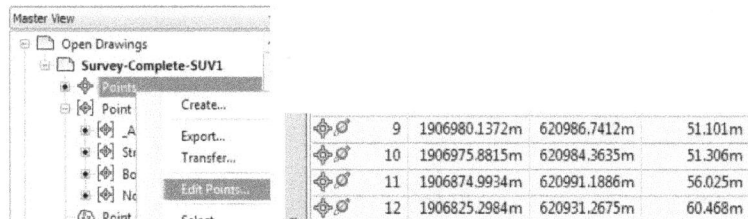

Figure 4–96

8. Select point **5** from the list of points. Scroll down the list, press <Shift> and select point **10**.

9. With points **5** to **10** highlighted right-click, and select **Unlock**. Note that the points no longer display the **Lock** icon and have a white background, as shown in Figure 4–97. These two things indicate that the points are available for editing.

r	Easting	Northing	Point Elevati...	Nan
3	7067.3102m	0964.1860m	50.084m	
4	5990.8853m	0997.5930m	50.460m	
5	5961.3987m	1010.4823m	50.748m	
6	5942.3418m	1014.4780m	50.940m	
7	5921.0059m	1024.8413m	51.064m	
8	5890.8306m	1040.9957m	49.124m	
9	5980.1372m	0986.7412m	51.101m	
10	5975.8815m	0984.3635m	51.306m	
11	5874.9934m	0991.1886m	56.025m	
12	5825.2984m	0931.2675m	60.468m	
13	5822.6127m	0930.2046m	60.442m	

Point Number		Easting	Northing	Point Elevati...	Nan
	3	7067.3102m	0964.1860m	50.084m	
	4	5990.8853m	0997.5930m	50.460m	
	5	5961.3987m	1010.4823m	50.748m	
	6	5942.3418m	1014.4780m	50.940m	
	7	5921.0059m	1024.8413m	51.064m	
	8	5890.8306m	1040.9957m	49.124m	
	9	5980.1372m	0986.7412m	51.101m	
	10	5975.8815m	0984.3635m	51.306m	
	11	5874.9934m	0991.1886m	56.025m	
	12	5825.2984m	0931.2675m	60.468m	
	13	5822.6127m	0930.2046m	60.442m	

Figure 4–97

10. In the Point Editor Panorama, double-click on point **10**. The cell switches to edit mode now that it has been unlocked.

11. Close the Panorama by clicking [✓] in the top right corner without making any changes.

12. In the drawing, select point **10**, right-click, and review the editing options in the shortcut menu.

13. Review the commands displayed in the ribbon. Because this is a contextual object, all of the entries are tools that are applicable to a point.

14. Save the drawing.

4.11 Point Reports

The surveyor needs to produce point reports. These can include a record list for the project, a checklist to find errors, reference for field crews, stakeout, etc. Incorporating survey data with an AutoCAD Civil 3D engineering project is unique in that it relies on connection and communication with third party survey equipment and software.

AutoCAD Civil 3D points can be exported and then uploaded to the survey equipment without relying on manually created lists. However, a documented point list might be required. There are several ways to create reports about points.

Point Reports - Reports Manager

The AutoCAD Civil 3D Reports Manager produces several point reports. To create reports from the Reports Manager, the *Toolbox* tab must be available in the Toolspace. To display the *Toolbox* tab, go to the *Home* tab, expand the Palettes drop-down list, and select **Toolbox**. Then select the *Toolbox* tab and expand the **Reports Manager** collection to display a list of object type reports, as shown in Figure 4–98.

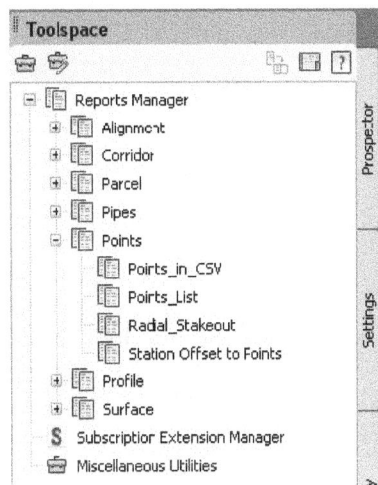

Figure 4–98

Points are easily organized into a convenient, legible list that displays the point number, northing, easting, elevation, and full description (as shown in Figure 4–99). Another point report lists the points' station and offset values relative to an alignment. Another report calculates distances and angles from an occupied and a backsight. You can transfer points to Microsoft Excel spreadsheets using a CSV report.

To create these reports, select the report's name, right-click, and select **Execute...**

Number	Northing	Easting	Elevation	Description
1	632055.919	2208068.041	900.655	MON
2	631396.467	2207989.483	900.171	MON
3	630834.659	2207979.534	898.369	MON
4	631382.131	2207989.229	900.174	MON

Figure 4–99

Point Editor Reports

Another report method is to use the *Point Editor* tab of the Panorama. In the *Prospector* tab, select **Points**, right-click, and select **Edit...** to display the *Point Editor* tab of the Panorama, as shown in Figure 4–100.

Point Nu...	Easting	Northing	Point E...	N..	Raw ...	Full ...	D..	Grid Easting	Grid Northing	Longitude	Latitude	Scale Fac...	Converge...	S...
1	7286.7724m	0917.5908m	51.896m		Fd. IP.	Fd. IP.	S*	1907286.7724m	620917.5908m	W117° 14' 41.97"	N33° 15' 10.74"	1.000	0° 32' 48.35"	Iror
2	7145.0343m	0930.0483m	50.287m		Fd. IP.	Fd. IP.	S*	1907145.0343m	620930.0483m	W117° 14' 47.45"	N33° 15' 11.10"	1.000	0° 32' 51.36"	Iror
3	7067.3102m	0964.1860m	50.084m		Fd. IP.	Fd. IP.	S*	1907067.3102m	620964.1860m	W117° 14' 50.46"	N33° 15' 12.19"	1.000	0° 32' 53.02"	Iror
4	5990.8853m	0997.5930m	50.460m		Fd. IP.	Fd. IP.	S*	1906990.8853m	620997.5930m	W117° 14' 53.43"	N33° 15' 13.25"	1.000	0° 32' 54.65"	Iror
5	5961.3987m	1010.4823m	50.748m		Fd. IP.	Fd. IP.	S*	1906961.3987m	621010.4823m	W117° 14' 54.57"	N33° 15' 13.66"	1.000	0° 32' 55.28"	Iror
6	5942.3418m	1014.4780m	50.940m		Fd. IP.	Fd. IP.	S*	1906942.3418m	621014.4780m	W117° 14' 55.31"	N33° 15' 13.78"	1.000	0° 32' 55.69"	Iror
7	5921.0059m	1024.8413m	51.064m		Fd. IP.	Fd. IP.	S*	1906921.0059m	621024.8413m	W117° 14' 56.14"	N33° 15' 14.11"	1.000	0° 32' 56.14"	Iror

Figure 4–100

In the Panorama, you can select individual points using <Ctrl> or select blocks of points using <Shift>. When done selecting points, right-click and select **Copy to clipboard**. You can then paste the copied points into Microsoft Excel, Notepad, or any application that accepts the points, as shown in Figure 4–101.

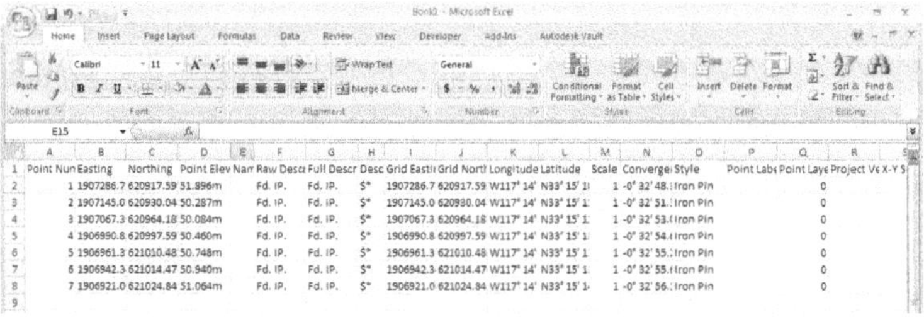

Figure 4–101

Practice 4j

Point Reports

Practice Objective

- Share information about points used for error checking or staking out points using predefined reports.

Estimated time for completion: 5 minutes

Task 1 - Create Point Reports.

1. Continue working with the drawing from the previous practice or open **Points-J1-Survey.dwg** from the *C:\Civil 3D for Surveyors Practice Files\Survey* folder.

2. If the *Toolbox* tab is not displayed in the Toolspace, select the *Home* tab and click (Toolbox), as shown in Figure 4–102 to display the *Toolbox* tab.

Figure 4–102

3. Select the *Toolbox* tab and expand the **Reports Manager** collection to display the list of object type reports. Expand the **Points** collection, as shown in Figure 4–103.

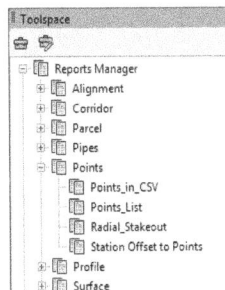

Figure 4–103

4. Select **Point List**, right-click, and select **Execute**.

5. In the Export to LandXML dialog box, click **OK** to generate the report. In the Save As dialog box, type a filename or accept the default **CivilReport.html**, and save the file. If the file exists, you will be prompted to replace it.

6. The point list is displayed in Internet Explorer. Review the report and when done, close it.

Chapter Review Questions

1. Which tab in the Point Label Style Composer dialog box controls the appearance of a point label when the point label grip is selected in the drawing and moved away from the point itself?

   a. *General* tab

   b. *Layout* tab

   c. *Dragged State* tab

   d. *Summary* tab

2. How do you control the next point number to be used in a drawing?

   a. The Point Identity parameters located in the expanded area in the Create Points toolbar.

   b. Under Label Styles, in the *Settings* tab in the Toolspace.

   c. In the *Survey* tab, right-click on **Survey Points**.

   d. In the *Prospector* tab, right-click on **Survey Points**.

3. Can the **_All Points** point group be deleted?

   a. Yes

   b. No

4. Can a point group be made out of other point groups?

   a. Yes

   b. No

5. When points are locked, the point label can still be dragged to another location.

   a. True

   b. False

Command Summary

Button	Command	Location
	Create Points	• **Ribbon**: *Home* tab>Create Ground Data panel
	Import Points from File	• **Ribbon**: *Insert* tab>Import panel • **Toolbar**: Create Points • **Command Prompt:** ImportPoints
	Import Survey Data	• **Ribbon**: *Home* tab>Create Ground Data panel • **Command Prompt:** ImportSurveyData
	Survey User Settings	• **Toolspace**: *Survey* tab
	Toolbox	• **Ribbon**: *Home* tab>Palettes panel
	Zoom To Points	• **Toolbar**: Transparent Commands • **Command Prompt:** 'ZTP

Chapter 5

Points with Connective Codes

Importing points with line connectivity codes enable you to create figures from survey data. In this chapter, you will learn how to work with connective codes. First you will import points, then you will modify linework as required. Finally, you will learn how to transpose a survey database so that points and figures fall in the correct locations.

Learning Objectives in this Chapter

- List some basic syntax coding rules used in the AutoCAD® Civil 3D® software.
- Describe how survey figures are used in the AutoCAD Civil 3D software.
- Edit the Linework Code Set to insure coding used in the field survey will create linework upon import into the drawing.
- Move survey data from an assumed location to a known location using the translation wizard.

5.1 Field Codes

During the survey pickup for each point, the surveyor assigns a field code that describes the point or line feature. This information is saved in the data collector and is output as an ASCII file. A line feature or connective code can be appended to a point description and indicates whether the feature line is a line segment or curve segment, and whether it is the beginning, continuation, or end of a segment.

Example

310,620918.3755,1907041.4409,53.0132, CL1 B

In this example, CL1 B is the field code in which:

- CL = An abbreviation that represents a center line.

- 1 = The center line number.

- B = The code in the linework code that is set to begin a figure.

Note that when you import the survey data, you can omit the Begin code if the feature name matches a figure prefix that is defined in the current figure prefix database. If the feature name does not match a figure prefix, you must specify a Begin code.

Field codes are associated with both the Figure Prefix database and the description keys in the current drawing. If **CL** has been defined in the Figure Prefix Database (as shown in Figure 5–1), CL1 matches CL and is assigned the properties of the CL figure prefix, such as **Layer**, **Figure Style**, and **Breakline**.

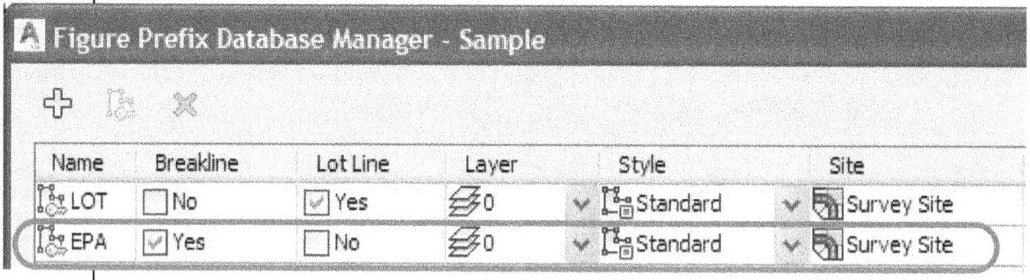

Figure 5–1

If the survey point with the description CL1 B is placed in a drawing that has a description key of CL* (as shown in Figure 5–2), CL1 B matches the description key CL* and is assigned the point properties defined in the CL* description key, such as **Layer**, **Point Style**, and **Point Label Style**.

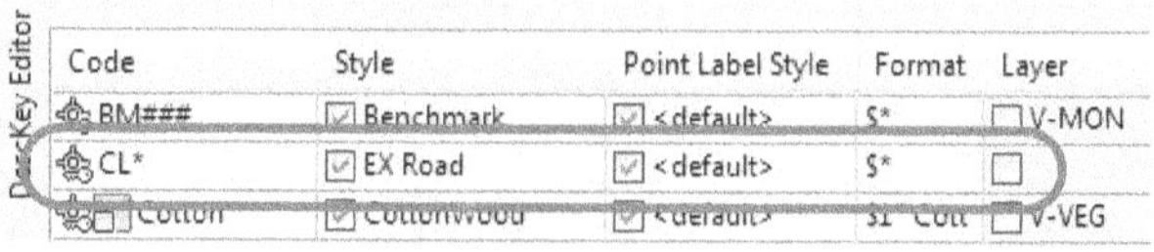

Figure 5–2

Linework Codes: Coding syntax

Some basic coding syntax rules are as follows:

CL1 B	It is recommended that you use <space> as the Field/Code delimiter property value (i.e., the <space> between the description CL1 and the B).
CL1 B/ Start of the centerline	A / <forward slash> is the recommended escape field code. It indicates that anything entered after the escape indicator is a comment.
CL1 B	Select **Yes** to specify that in CL1 B, CL1 matches the figure prefix of CL, and B is the Begin code. Select **No**, if you do not want the first instance of CL1 to automatically start a new figure named CL.

Linework Codes: Special Codes

CL1 B SW1 B B CL1 B SW1	**B** = Begin CL1 and SW1 are figure names. The letter B is the special code that is used to begin new figures named CL1 and SW1.
CL1 C SW1	**C** = Continue CL1 is a figure name. C continues the active figure named CL1. If the field code does not contain an explicit <Continue> code and the figure name in the field code matches an active figure, the figure is continued.
CL1 E SW1 B	**E** = End E is the End code. It continues an active figure with the name CL1 to this point and is then terminated (it is no longer an active). However, figure SW1 with the B code is starts at this point.
CL1 SW1 CLS	**CLS** = Close CLS is the Close code. A line segment is closed back to the starting vertex for the figure SW1. However, figure CL1 is still active and continues.
1,500,490,100.0 1,BC1 B H-4 V.1 H.5 H.75 V-.7 H2.25 V-.35	**H** = Horizontal offset H is the <Horizontal offset> code and -4 is the value for the first horizontal. **V** = Vertical Offset V is the <Vertical offset> code and .1 is the first vertical offset value, etc., for each of the remaining 3 offsets.
7,500,550,100.0 7,BC1 SO	**SO** = Stop offsets SO is the <Stop Offset> code. It terminates the offset for this figure.

Note that there are no spaces between RPN, CPN, or RECT, and the point number.

Linework Codes: Line Segment Codes

CL1 RPN CL1 RPN101	**RPN** = Recall point RPN is the Recall Point code. If a point is not supplied, it connects from the previous point to the current point and inserts a segment before the current point. If a point is supplied, as in the code CL1 RPN101, it connects from the current point to the indicated point.
CL1 B **CPN**101	**CPN** = Connect point A new figure CL1 is created at the current point, and a new figure with a single line segment is drawn to point 101 and called CL1.CPN101.
BLD1 RECT40	**RECT** = Rectangle A positive number indicates an offset to the right and a negative number indicates an offset to the left, which is relative to the direction of the line segment coming into the current point. If a number does not follow the Rectangle code, the code closes the figure by performing a perpendicular/ perpendicular line intersection between the previous segment coming into the current point and the first segment of the figure.
BLD1 RT X10.1 5 -12.2 -5 -12.2	**RT** = Right Turn Continues an active figure BLD1 to the current point, extends the current segment 10.1 units, and then draws perpendicular segments for each value
BLD1 X15.5	**X** = Extend BLD1 continues an active figure, X is the Extend code, and 15.5 is the value that the figure line segment is extended through the current point.

Linework Codes: Curve Segment Codes

CL1 BC	**BC** = Begin Curve BC indicates that the current point is the beginning of the curve segments.
CL1 EC	**EC** = End Curve EC indicates that the current point is the end of curve segments. You can have multiple figure points between the Begin and End curve segment codes.
CL1 CIR5.0	**CIR** = Circle CIR is the <Circle> code. It creates a new circular figure in which the current point is the radius point and 5.0 is the circle radius value.
CL1 OC	**OC** = Point On Curve OC is the Point On Curve code. The figure is continued and the point is evaluated as a point residing on a curve.

5.2 Survey Data - Figures

A Survey Figure is a line that is defined and coded during the field data pick up process. The name of the Survey Figure in the AutoCAD Civil 3D software is defined based on the description code assigned to the point in the survey data file. When importing a points line coded connective file through the Survey Database, if the Linework Code Set "B" is appended to the description code, defining the beginning of a line, GUT B begins a Survey Figure and the Survey Figure is named GUT in the drawing.

The Figure Prefix Database Manager is set up in advance so that rows are tagged analogous to the Description Key Set and a Figure Style can be assigned to define the Figure. Survey Figures are an improvement in the advance of Survey technology in that they are not just AutoCAD lines connecting points; they contain all of the properties of intelligent survey data that can be used by other tools in the AutoCAD Civil 3D software. These survey figures can be edited using the feature line tools to not only edit the data geographically but also perform design calculations to the vertical aspect of the survey line.

Both office and field personnel need to be consistent when using the set of standards that result from the preset naming conventions. The conventions can assign multiple figures as breaklines or as lot lines in a parcel. For example, all figures that are preset as breaklines, populate the Breaklines variable in the Surface.

When using figures, you might need to create a Survey Figure of a building measure with a tape. A surveyor only needs to pick up a few key reference points and either enter the turned measured distances into the survey data file or edit the survey figure in the AutoCAD Civil 3D software to enter the turned measured distance. However, it must be noted that using this method assumes that the turned angles are 90 degrees.

Practice 5a

Importing Data - Figures

Practice Objective

- Import figures from survey data and create new figures interactively.

In this practice you will import data using figures. The surveyor has used a local coordinate system for the survey pickup. Therefore, you will open a drawing and a survey project database without an established coordinate zone.

Estimated time for completion: 20 minutes

Task 1 - Set up a network and Import a survey.

1. Open the file **LineCodes-A1-Survey.dwg** from the *C:\Civil 3D for Surveyors Practice Files\Survey* folder.

2. For the survey database, continue working in the **Survey Data** database created earlier or open **Survey Data A**.

If not already set, refer to Appendix A-1: Open a Survey Database, on how to open a survey database.

3. Expand the survey database collection and then right-click on the **Networks** collection. Select **New**.

4. In the New Network dialog box, set the *Name to* **Figures-LineCodes**. Click **OK**.

5. Right-click on **Figures-LineCodes** and select **Import> Import point file** to import the ASCII file, as shown in Figure 5–3.

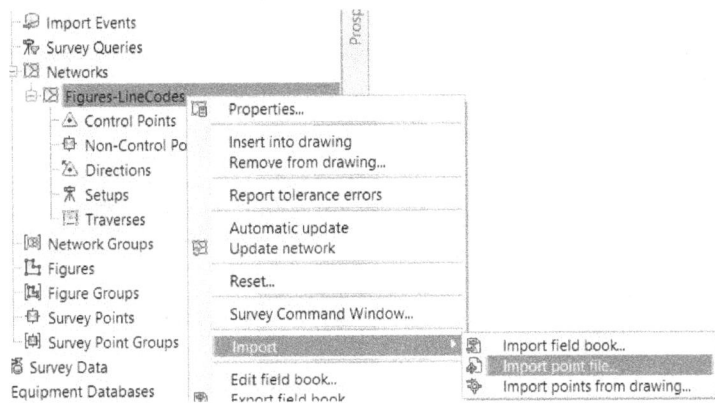

Figure 5–3

6. Select the field book file **Figures-LineCodes.txt** from the *C:\Civil 3D for Surveyors Practice Files\Survey* folder and click **Open**.

7. In the Import Point File dialog box, *Point file format* drop-down list, select **PNEZD (comma delimited)**. Verify that all of the other checkboxes are selected, as shown in Figure 5–4. Click **OK**.

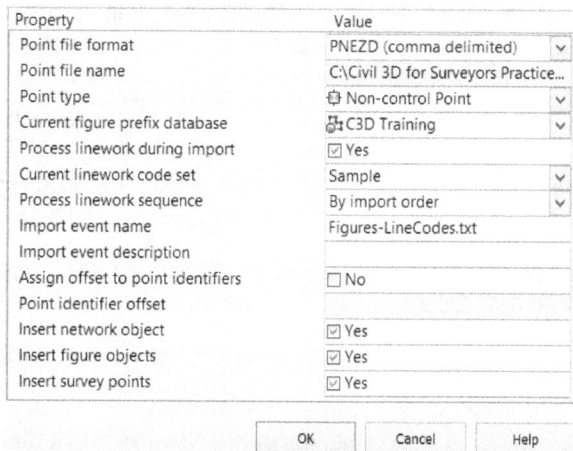

Property	Value
Point file format	PNEZD (comma delimited)
Point file name	C:\Civil 3D for Surveyors Practice...
Point type	Non-control Point
Current figure prefix database	C3D Training
Process linework during import	☑ Yes
Current linework code set	Sample
Process linework sequence	By import order
Import event name	Figures-LineCodes.txt
Import event description	
Assign offset to point identifiers	☐ No
Point identifier offset	
Insert network object	☑ Yes
Insert figure objects	☑ Yes
Insert survey points	☑ Yes

OK   Cancel   Help

Figure 5–4

8. Save the drawing.

Task 2 - Review the survey data.

In this task, you will review the survey data without making any changes. To make it easier to view, you will change the Annotative scale.

1. Continue working with the drawing from the previous practice or open the file **LineCodes-A2-Survey.dwg** from the *C:\Civil 3D for Surveyors Practice Files\Survey* folder.

Refer to Appendix A-1: Open a Survey Database, on how to open a survey database.

2. Continue with the previously opened database or open **Survey Data A2**.

In reviewing your imported points file (as shown in Figure 5–5), there are a number of errors that need to be fixed. The errors dealing with Line Code will be fixed in the next section. Additionally, there are a number of solutions to fixing the missing figure.

Missing figure **Line code errors**

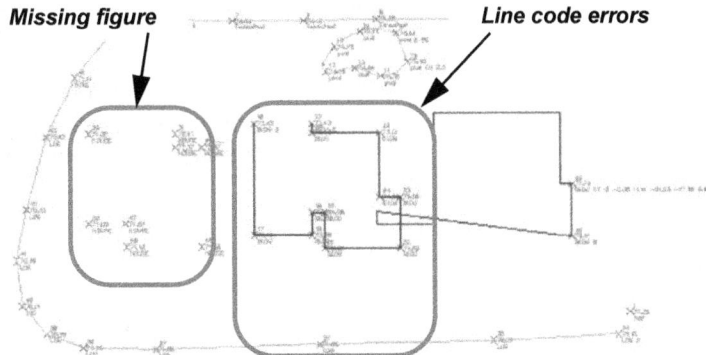

Figure 5–5

In addition to adding **B** and **CLS** line code connective to your survey data file, you can also change the survey data description from *House* to **BLDG**, as shown in Figure 5–6. As a BLDG is defined in the Figure prefix database, on re-import, a BLDG figure will be created.

```
28,5010.5005,9928.7677,72.4282,HOUSE
29,5026.5950,9928.7677,72.7032,HOUSE
30,5026.5950,9924.3764,72.3679,HOUSE
```

```
28,5010.5005,9928.7677,72.4282,BLDG  B
29,5026.5950,9928.7677,72.7032,BLDG
30,5026.5950,9924.3764,72.3679,BLDG
```

Figure 5–6

You can also create a new figure definition in the Figure prefix database, as shown in Figure 5–7.

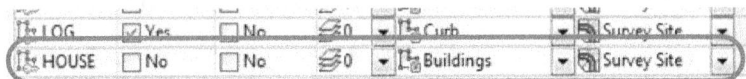

Figure 5–7

Alternatively, you can draw a figure manually, based on the survey points. For demonstration purposes, you will use this method.

3. In the Status Bar, change the view scale to **1:200**, as shown in Figure 5–8.

Figure 5–8

4. Save the drawing.

Task 3 - Create a survey figure.

1. Continue working with the drawing from the previous practice or open **LineCodes-A3-Survey.dwg** from the *C:\Civil 3D for Surveyors Practice Files\Survey* folder.

Refer to Appendix A-1: Open a Survey Database, on how to open a survey database.

2. Continue with the previously opened database or **Survey Data A2**.

3. In the Survey toolspace, in the current open survey database, right-click on the **Figures** collection and select **Create figure interactively**, as shown in Figure 5–9.

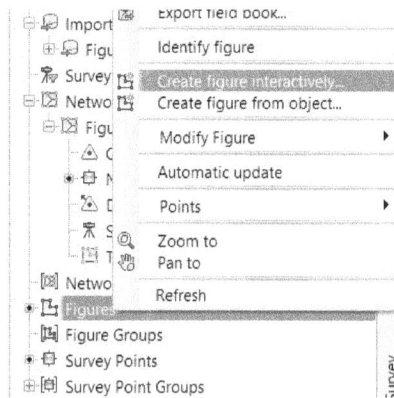

Figure 5–9

You can also use some of the AutoCAD Civil 3D tools, such as the transparent tools.

4. In the New figure dialog box, type **W. Building** for the figure name, as shown in Figure 5–10 and click **OK**.

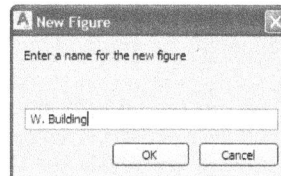

Figure 5–10

5. When prompted, select the point objects, select points **2028-2033, 2047, and 2048** in order and press <Enter>.

6. In the Figure Properties dialog box, set the following, as shown in Figure 5–11:

   - *Style*: **Buildings**
   - *Closed*: **Yes**

7. Click **OK**.

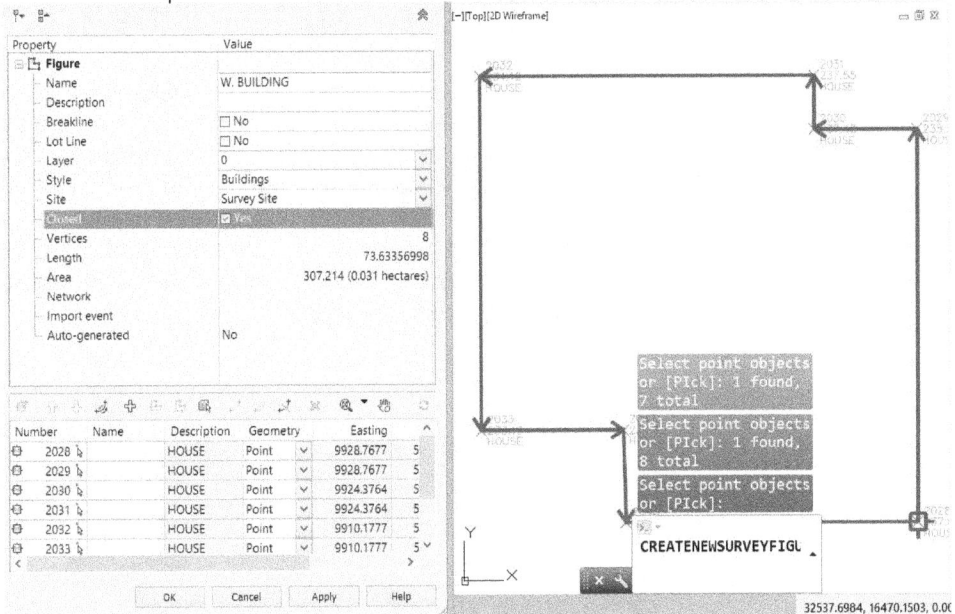

Figure 5–11

8. In the Survey toolspace, in the survey database, select the **Figures** collection. In the list of figures below, right-click on the newly created figure **W. Building** and select **Insert into drawing**, as shown in Figure 5–12.

*The figure might display as not closed. Reselect the figure in the survey figures panorama window, and select **Properties**. The screen will refresh and the figure will be displayed as closed.*

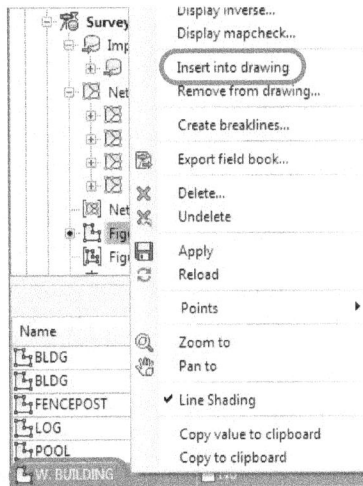

Figure 5–12

9. Save the drawing.

5.3 Survey Data - Line Code

Linework Code Set can be used to customize the language used to create the linework geometry. The Sample Linework Code Set shown in Figure 5–13 requires that the field crew enter the Figure commands in the Value cells to create a variety of geometry. You can modify this to use your Survey company's standard methodology to create automated linework as was done in legacy Civil/Survey software before the AutoCAD Civil 3D software was available.

Property	Value
Information	
Name	Sample
Description	
Coding Methods	
Feature/Code delimiter	<Space>
Field code escape	/
Start in comment mode	☐ No
Automatic begin on figure prefix ma...	☑ Yes
Special Codes	
Begin	B
Continue	C
End	E
Close	CLS
Horizontal offset	H
Vertical offset	V
Stop offsets	SO
Line Segment Codes	
Recall point	RPN
Connect point	CPN
Rectangle	RECT
Right turn	RT
Extend	X
Curve Segment Codes	
Begin curve	BC
End curve	EC
Circle	CIR
Point on curve	OC

Figure 5–13

Select the **Automatic begin on figure prefix match** option to enable a Survey Figure to be created if a code in the point file matches a code in the Figure Prefix Database. The Survey Figure begins at the first instance at which the point codes match and continues until the matching point codes no longer occur. The Survey Figure then ends.

If a project contains multiple figures of the same name, it is important to use the **End Figure** command. You can also add an alpha or numeric suffix (depending on whether you are using alpha or numeric codes). For example, GUT B starts the figure GUT for the left side. Using the Zorro method for survey pickup, where an entire station cross-section from left to right is surveyed before proceeding to the next station, the right side of the street is usually entered as GUT1 B. If 59 is the numeric code for a gutter shot, then 59 B starts the figure 59 and the other side of the street is 59A B.

The AutoCAD Civil 3D software enables you to use double coding methodology. For example, in GUT APR B a gutter shot is taken and an apron figure is started.

In earlier releases of the AutoCAD Civil 3D software, a curve had to be completed before a different shot was taken. This caused problems in the field with large curves. You can now use the **Begin Curve** figure command when one shot is taken on the curve and ends with the **End Curve** command. Alternatively, if you shoot at least two incoming tangent shots and at least two outgoing tangent shots, only one **Point on Curve** command shot is required.

For example, if a survey crew conducts a field survey on an existing parking lot that contains many raised islands, a large number of figures with the same names might be created for the gutter shots. Large parking lots can contain many islands and multiple aprons for entering and exiting the site. You sometimes need to use the End figure command to keep track of the multiple sequencing suffixes. An example of this geometry is shown in Figure 5–14.

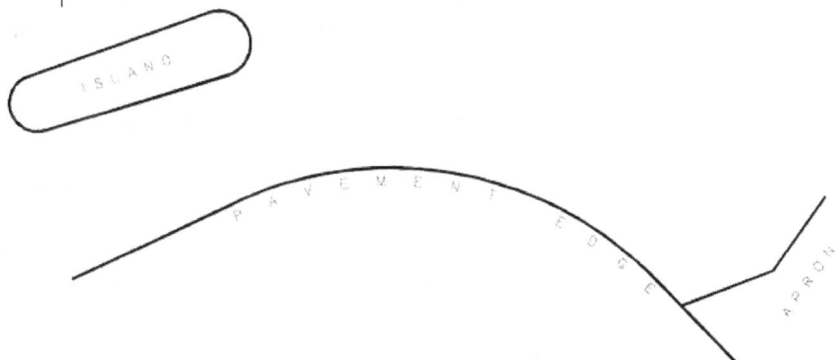

Figure 5–14

*This process replaces the **MCS** and **MCE** commands from previous releases of Civil 3D.*

For the island, you can use the **Begin Curve** command to start the figure and then use the **End Curve** and **Close** figure commands as shown in Figure 5–15. At least one point on the curve must be shot between the **Begin Curve** and **End Curve** commands. Shoot as many points as required between the commands, to create an accurate curve.

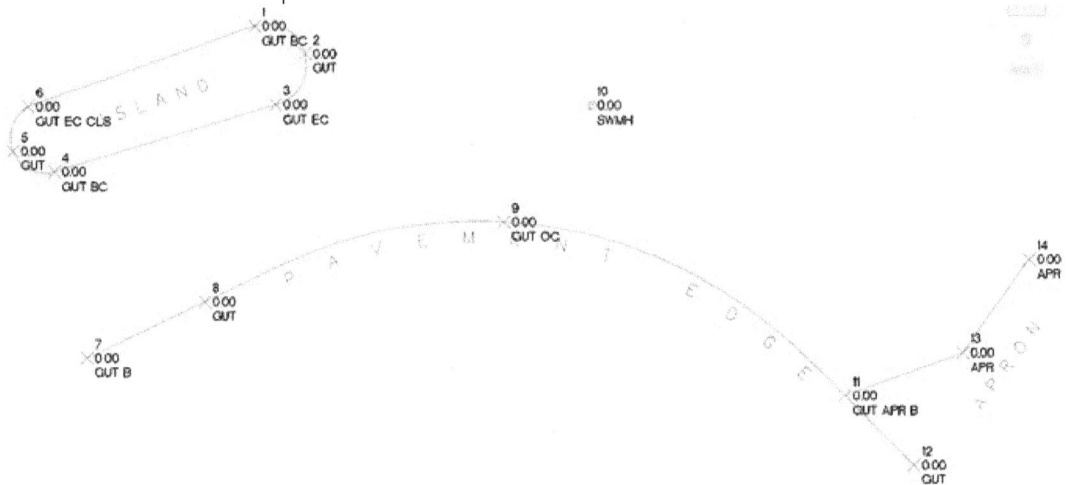

Figure 5–15

Use the **Begin** figure command to create the pavement edge. If you shoot at least two incoming tangents and two outgoing tangents, you only need to use one **Point on Curve (OC)** figure command.

In Figure 5–15, point #10 defines a SWMH manhole and was shot before the curve ended. There is double-coding for the gutter and apron shot. The P.C. and P.T. of the curve for the pavement edge was not required because the two shots that define the bearing for the incoming and outgoing tangents were taken.

In the Linework Code Set defining the custom figure commands, you can also create horizontal and vertical offsets from a Survey Figure. For example, the horizontal offset and vertical offset commands can be used if a segment of a length of an area within the project limits is defined by consistent cross-sectional geometry, such as an existing curb.

In defining an offset survey figure, as shown in Figure 5–16, point #7 starts the pavement edge and is then defined by GUT B H-.1 V.5 H-.5. The AutoCAD Civil 3D software then creates another gutter figure that has a horizontal offset to the left of 0.1 units (H-.1) and a vertical offset of 0.5 units (V.5). This creates the top face of the curb. Another gutter figure is then created at 0.5 units to the left (H-.5). Since another vertical callout is not listed, the AutoCAD Civil 3D software uses the same vertical offset of 0.5 units (V.5). This creates the top back of a 6" high curb that is 6" wide. This is a fast and accurate methods of creating breaklines for existing surfaces.

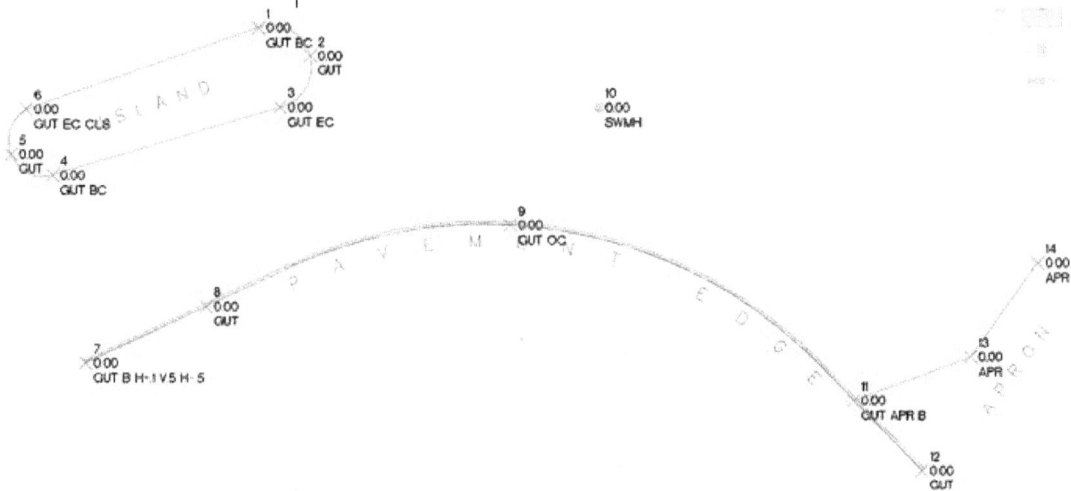

Figure 5–16

In the Toolspace, the two offset figures are named GUT.1 and GUT.2. They become a subset of the original GUT figure as shown in Figure 5–17.

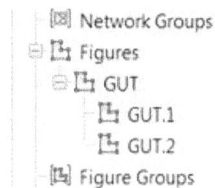

Figure 5–17

Practice 5b

Line Code

Estimated time for completion: 10 minutes

Practice Objective

- Correct errors in survey figures by editing the line code connotative file.

Task 1 - Review the survey data.

In this task, you review the errors that you will fix in the next task.

1. Continue working with the drawing from the previous practice or open **LineCodes-B1-Survey.dwg** from the *C:\Civil 3D for Surveyors Practice Files\Survey* folder.

2. Continue with the previously opened database or open **Survey Data B**.

3. Review the imported points file and note the errors that need to be fixed as shown in Figure 5–18.

   - Close the building figure (A).
   - Correct the linecode in the imported points file (B).
   - Create an offset line to display the back of the sidewalk (C).

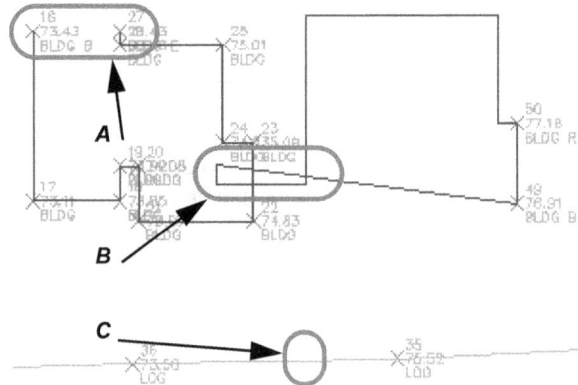

Figure 5–18

Task 2 - Fix the line code survey file.

In this task you will fix the error in the line code file.

1. Using a text editor such as Notepad, open and edit the survey points file **Figures-LineCodes.txt**. from the *C:\Civil 3D for Surveyors Practice Files\Survey* folder.

2. At point 2027, after **E** in the description, and type **CLS** as shown in Figure 5–19. This fixes error "A" by closing building error 1 from point **2016** to point **2027**.

```
2026,5028.9361,9946.7723,73.4284,BLDG
2027,5030.3992,9946.7723,73.4284,BLDG E CLS
2028,5010.5005,9928.7677,72.4282,HOUSE
```

Figure 5–19

3. In the line for point **2050**, after the west edge of the building, -17.85 in a south direction, change *9.66* to **-9.66**, as shown in Figure 5–20. This will fix the building error "B".

```
2049,5012.1099,9990.2467,76.9132,BLDG B
2050,5020.5961,9990.2467,77.1798,BLDG RT x0 -2.05 11.41 -21.23 -17.85 -9.66 2.05 CLS
```

Figure 5–20

4. To create a back of sidewalk offset line, you will add a horizontal and vertical offset. The sidewalk only runs from the BC of the curb return. Starting at point **2038**, add the code for a horizontal offset of **2** and a vertical offset of **0.25** to the LOG to create an offset that represents the back of the walk, as shown in Figure 5–21.

```
2037,4994.2704,9921.0427,71.5496,LOG
2038,4994.5600,9909.1654,70.6753,LOG BC H2 V0.25
2039,4996.7317,9903.0819,70.2459,LOG
```

Figure 5–21

5. At point **2046**, add **SO** to end the offset, as shown in Figure 5–22.

```
2045,5045.8125,9914.6695,72.1788,LOG
2046,5051.8933,9921.7669,72.8921,LOG EC SO
2047,5014.3046,9916.1985,71.5334,HOUSE
```

Figure 5–22

6. Save the text file.

7. In the *Survey* tab, in the current survey database collection, expand **Import Events**, right-click on **Figures-LineCodes.txt**, and select **Re-import**, as shown in Figure 5–23.

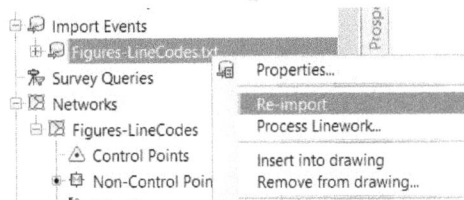

Figure 5–23

8. In the Re-import Points File dialog box, accept the defaults and click **OK**.

9. View the changes as shown in Figure 5–24.

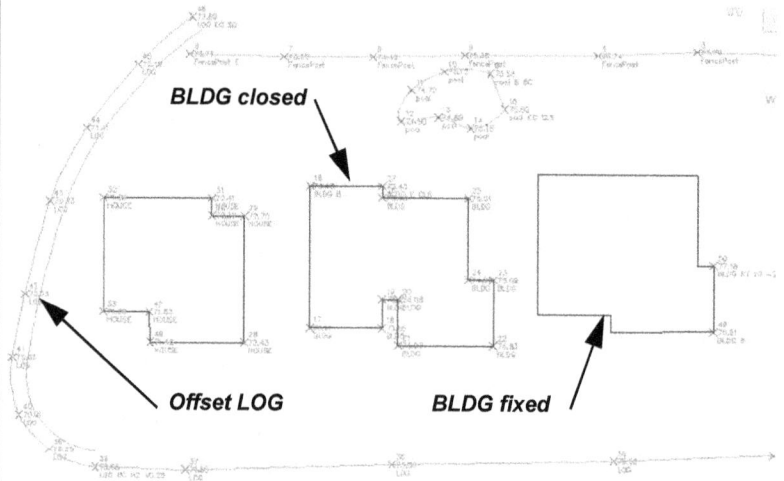

BLDG closed

Offset LOG

BLDG fixed

Figure 5–24

10. Save the drawing.

5.4 Translating a Survey Database

Translating a survey database is used when you need to move all of the data in the survey database from an assumed location to a known location. This is done before the survey data is imported into the AutoCAD Civil 3D software.

To translate a survey database you need to specify a base point, rotation angle, destination point, and elevation (optional). To use data that is based on local coordinates, you need to convert it to a known common coordinate system that is used by everyone in the project team. The team can include many departments in the same company, such as Engineering or Transportation. It can also include consultants from outside the company, such as Contractors or Architects. The AutoCAD Civil 3D software enables you to convert the data using the Translation wizard (shown in Figure 5–25), which applies a **Move and Rotate** command to all of the objects in the survey database project.

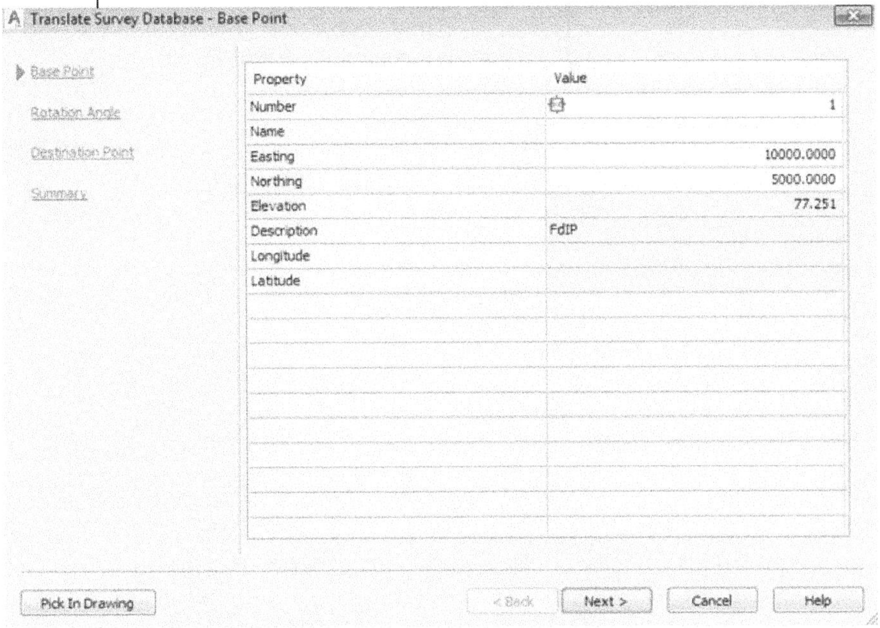

Figure 5–25

Practice 5c

Translating Survey Database

Practice Objective

- Move survey data from an assumed location to a known location using the translation wizard.

Estimated time for completion: 15 minutes

The surveyor has used a local coordinate system for the survey pickup. You will then translate part of the database to the correct coordinates.

1. Continue working with the drawing from the previous practice or open the file **LineCodes-C1-Survey.dwg** from the *C:\Civil 3D for Surveyors Practice Files\Survey* folder.

Refer to Appendix A-1: Open a Survey Database, on how to open a survey database.

2. Continue with the previously opened database or open **Survey Data C**.

   The general coordinates of the current survey: N5000m E10000m. This survey was done using a local coordinate base. Note that if the coordinates for the model are not displayed in the status bar (as shown in Figure 5–26), click

   (Customization) on the status bar and select **Coordinates** at the top, as shown in Figure 5–26.

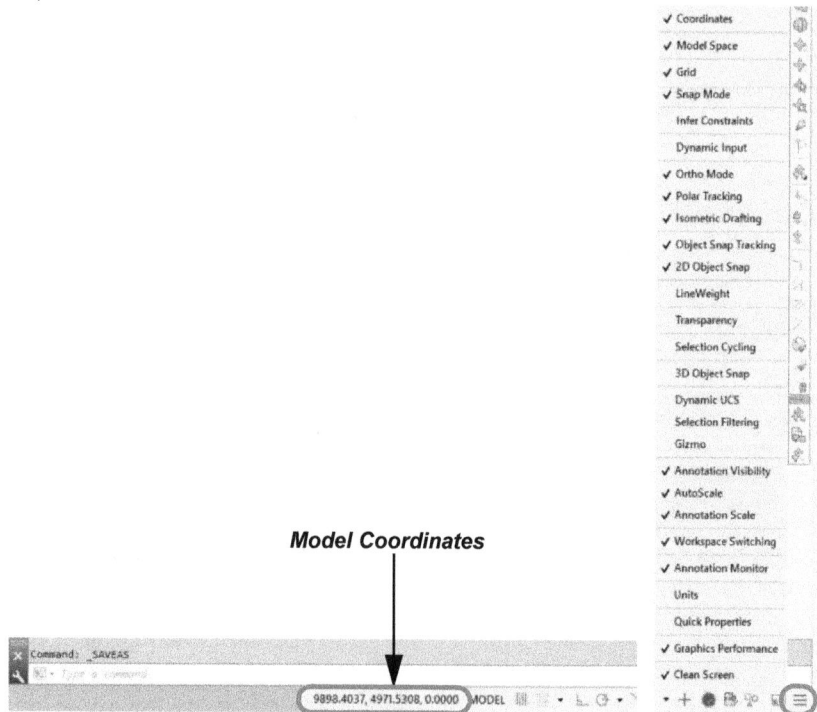

Model Coordinates

Figure 5–26

3. At the Command Prompt, type **ZE** to zoom extents to display all of the objects in the drawing. The original survey and the Base plan are at different coordinates, approximately 6,300,000 units apart and might not be completely displayed in the default view, as a result your Model Space view might seem blank.

4. In the *View* tab, select the **Translating3** preset view. Verify that all the layers are thawed and toggled on. Note that the coordinate of the Base plan is N:620700m E:6256500m.

5. In the *Prospector* tab, select **Points**.

You need to lock the points that you do not want translated.

6. Select points **5** to **10** (hold <Shift> to select them). Right-click and select **Lock**. All other points that we want to stay where they currently are, have been locked previously, in a different practice.

7. In the Toolspace, in the *Survey* tab, right-click on the current opened survey database or open **Survey Data C** and select **Translate survey database**.

8. In the Translate Survey Database dialog box, set the *Number* to **2001** and press <Enter>. The values for *Northing*, *Easting*, *Elevation*, and *Description* are already populated with the base point that the surveyor used as the assumed coordinate base point as shown in Figure 5–27. Click **Next>**.

Property	Value	
Number	⊞	2001
Name		
Easting		10000.0000
Northing		5000.0000
Elevation		77.251
Description	FdIP	
Longitude		-136.05271926
Latitude		26.00231334

Figure 5–27

9. Set the *Rotation Angle* to **0**, as shown in Figure 5–28. Click **Next>**.

Property	Value
Rotation Angle	0.0000

Figure 5–28

10. In the bottom left corner of the Translate Survey Database dialog box, click **Pick In Drawing**.

11. In Model Space, zoom to the property line in the south-west corner of the site and select the intersection point of the property line. This reference point has the correct coordinates, as shown in Figure 5–29. Click **Next>**.

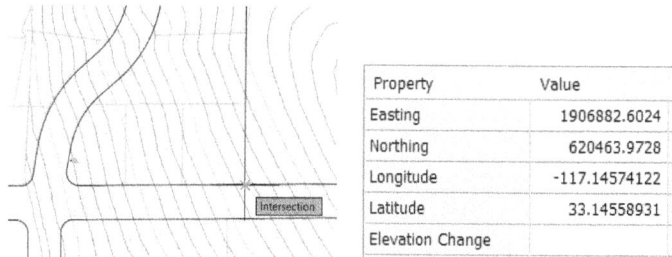

Property	Value
Easting	1906882.6024
Northing	620463.9728
Longitude	-117.14574122
Latitude	33.14558931
Elevation Change	

Figure 5–29

12. The Summary page opens, displaying the information shown in Figure 5–30.

```
- Base Point -
        Easting: 10000.000
        Northing: 5000.000

- Destination Point -
        Easting: 1906882.601
        Northing 620463.974

- Translation -
        Easting: 1896882.601
        Northing: 615463.974
        Elevation: 0.000
        Rotation Angle: 0.0000
```

Figure 5–30

13. Review the results. Click **Finish**.

14. The survey data has now been converted to the correct coordinates as shown in Figure 5–31.

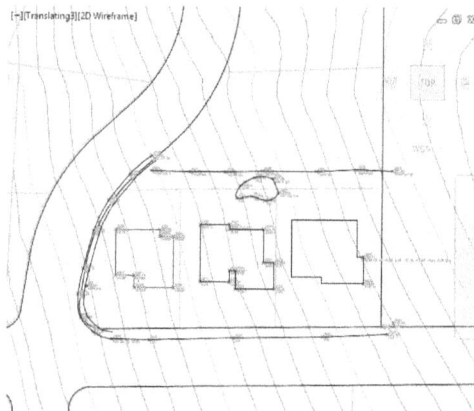

Figure 5–31

15. Save the drawing.

Chapter Review Questions

1. When importing points with connectivity codes, you cannot change to the codes used in the field to define figures.

   a. True

   b. False

2. If the Surveyor forgets to put in a connective code after a point description in the field, how do you create a figure from points in the drawing?

   a. You cannot create a figure after importing survey data.

   b. Select the points in the model, right-click and select **Create figure**.

   c. Right-click on **Figures** in the survey database and select **Create figure interactively**.

   d. Right-click on **Figures** in the survey database and select **Create figure from object**.

3. When would you need to translate a survey database?

   a. When the surveyor provides a file format that the AutoCAD Civil 3D software cannot read.

   b. When you need to move all of the data in the survey database from an assumed location to a known location.

   c. When you need to correct errors in the data caused by varying measurements.

   d. When the Field book file becomes corrupt and no longer usable.

Command Summary

Button	Command	Location
	Create Points	• **Ribbon**: *Home* tab>Create Ground Data panel
	Import Points from File	• **Ribbon**: *Insert* tab>Import panel • **Toolbar**: Create Points • **Command Prompt:** ImportPoints
	Import Survey Data	• **Ribbon**: *Home* tab>Create Ground Data panel • **Command Prompt:** ImportSurveyData
	Survey User Settings	• **Toolspace**: *Survey* tab
	Zoom To Points	• **Toolbar**: Transparent Commands • **Command Prompt:** 'ZTP

Field Book Files

Field book files are unique ASCII files with special coding that connects linework automatically. It is different from point files with connective codes and must be treated differently both in the field and when processing the files. In this chapter, you learn how to import and work with field book files.

Learning Objectives in this Chapter

- Establish horizontal and vertical control for the project by creating a survey network.
- Import a field book file and process linework to automatically display the collected field data in the drawing.
- Modify figures in a survey database to correct errors or add additional linework to the database.
- Filter a survey database to isolate only the points or figures required for the tasks being completed in the current drawing to reduce file sizes.

6.1 Survey Networks

A survey network is a collection of all of the known control points, instrument setups, and directions. They are usually represented by a series of interconnected lines indicating where the instrument was set up and where the side shots were taken. A local Survey Database has one or more networks. You can import one or more field books or point files into a network when the Survey spans more than one field book or point file. For example, networks are usually a day of field work. The larger the area of interest, the greater the number of networks required. At least one network is required when importing fieldbook files to create linework and points.

Before importing a Survey, you create a named network. You can also do so during the importation process. To create a new network, select Survey's network heading, right-click, select **New**, and type the network's name. After creating a named network, Survey creates five nodes below its name: Control Points, Non-Control Points, Directions, Setups, and Traverses, as shown in Figure 6–1.

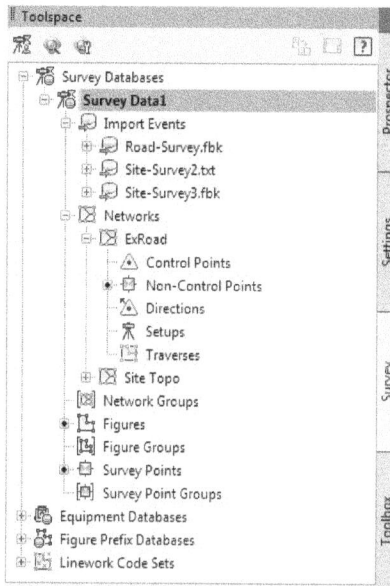

Figure 6–1

You can import one or several fieldbooks or LandXML files into the same network. By default, each import supplements the previous import. When you re-import a file, Survey automatically deletes the information from the original file import and recalculates the observations from the re-imported file.

Importing multiple files with the correct settings creates a single network whose data is a combination of the imported files. This enables you to create traverse(s), or perform a Least Squares analysis from data that spans more than one file.

When importing a file, Survey sequentially processes each line, creating setups and processing the setup's observations. When processing the setup's observations, Survey stores them in the observation database and calculates a point's preliminary coordinates from the observation values.

When toggling on interactive graphics, Survey displays the setups, draws figure linework, and populates the Control Points, Non-Control Points, Directions, and Setups.

When completing the import, Survey populates all or some of the nodes under the *Networks* heading.

Control points are NE or NEZ entries in a fieldbook. Directions are azimuth entries between points used in the stationing process. Survey points are initially calculated coordinates from the file's setups and observations. Any NE SS entries become non-control points. These points have coordinates, but are not control points (not used in a setup or as stationing points). You can promote them to control points by using them as part of a traverse or referencing them as part of a setup.

Non-control points can also be the result of importing a point coordinate file instead of an observation-based file.

6.2 Importing a Field Book

To import a field book, you use the Survey's **Import Events** collection. **Import Events** provides access to an import wizard, which takes you through the steps of creating a survey database, and network, and importing a file. To open the Import wizard, in the *Home* tab>Create Ground Data panel, click 🔌 (Import survey data…).

The Specify Database page (shown in Figure 6–2) sets the survey, creates a new survey, and edits a Survey's settings.

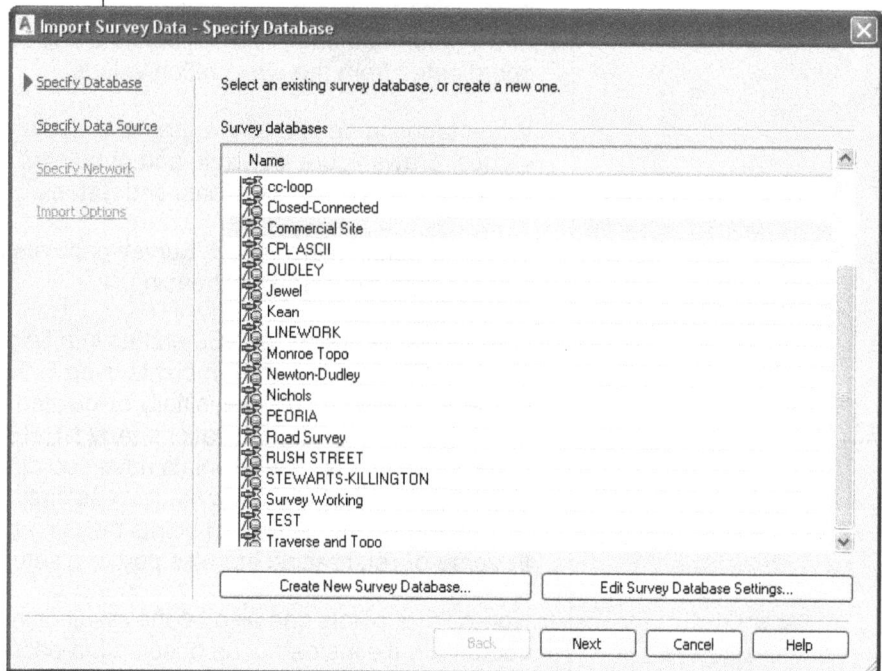

Figure 6–2

Click **Next**. The Specify Data Source page (shown in Figure 6–3) defines the file import type, the file's path, and its format (if it is a coordinate file).

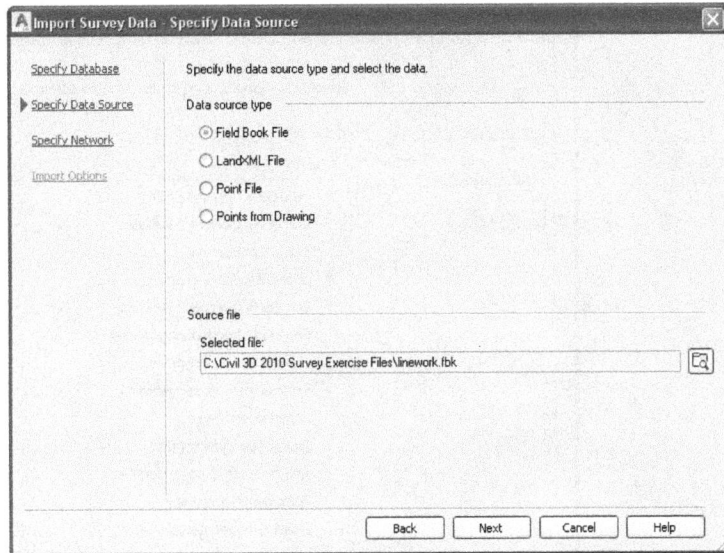

Figure 6–3

Click **Next**. The Specify Network page (shown in Figure 6–4) enables you to change the network or create a new survey network.

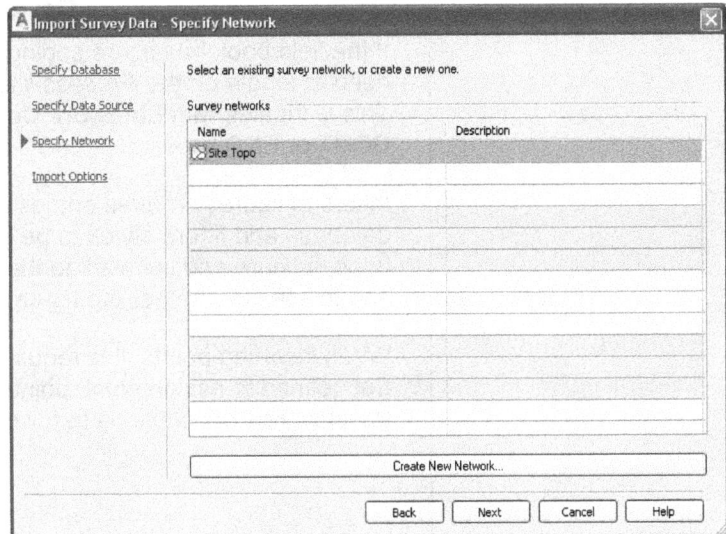

Figure 6–4

Click **Next**. The Import Options page (shown in Figure 6–5) sets the values for the import. These settings affect what the import does and which support files it uses.

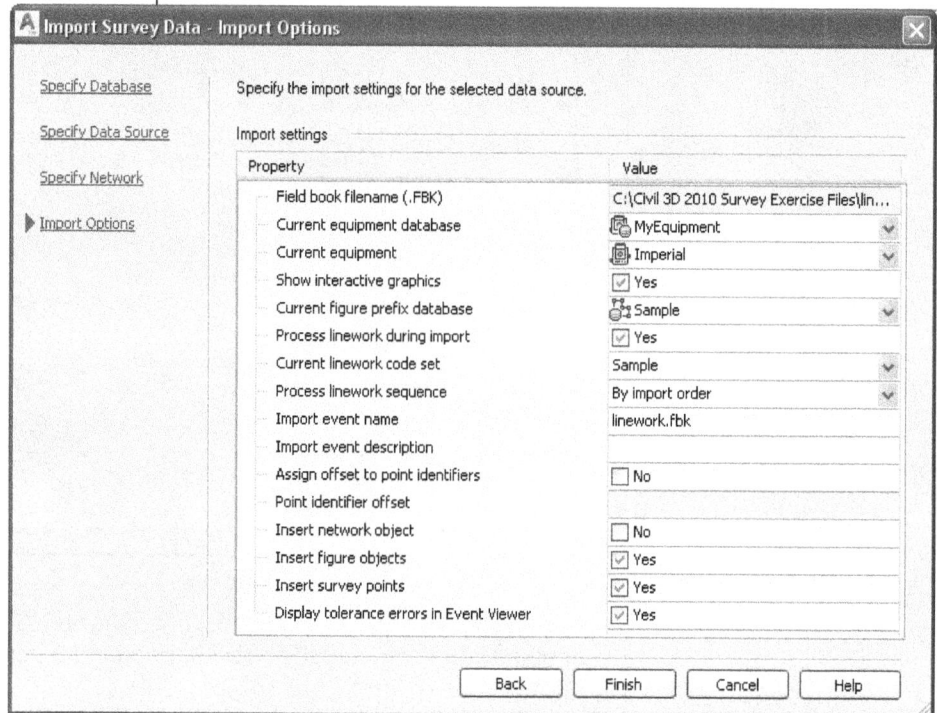

Figure 6–5

If the field book has figure coding from a conversion, you do not need to toggle on the *Process linework during import* property. This is for files with **Linework Code Set** commands and not CONT or END lines.

Inserting figures requires entries to be in the Figure Prefix database and figure styles to be in the drawing. This is required to point figure and linework to the correct layers in the drawing and to specify whether the figure is also a breakline in a surface.

When inserting points, it is required to have a Description Key Set defined to assign point, point label styles, and layers, and to translate raw descriptions to full descriptions.

Practice 6a

Importing a Field Book

Practice Objective

- Import a field book file and process linework to automatically display the collected field data in the drawing.

Estimated time for completion: 10 minutes

Task 1 - Import a field book and create a network.

1. Open **FB-A1-Survey.dwg** from the *C:\Civil 3D for Surveyors Practice Files\Survey* folder.

2. In the *Home* tab>Create Ground Data panel, click 🖳 (Import Survey Data).

3. In the Import Survey Data dialog box - Specify Database page, select **Survey Data**. (If you did not complete the previous practices, select **Survey Data FB-A** instead.) Click **Next >**.

4. Set the *Data source type* to **Field Book File** and click ⌕, as shown in Figure 6–6.

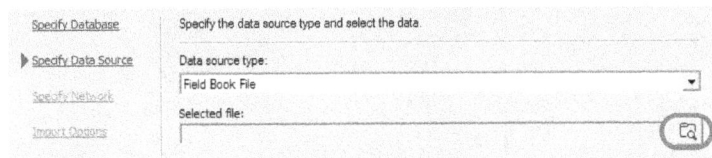

Specify Database	Specify the data source type and select the data.
▶ Specify Data Source	Data source type:
	Field Book File ▾
Specify Network	Selected file:
Import Options	⌕

Figure 6–6

5. For the *Field book filename (.FBK)*, browse to the *C:\Civil 3D for Surveyors Practice Files\Survey* folder and open **Site-Survey3.fbk**. Click **Next >**.

6. In the Import Survey Data dialog box, click **Create New Network**.

7. In the New Network dialog box, set the *Network Name* to **Site Topo**, as shown in Figure 6–7. Click **OK** to create the network. Click **Next >**.

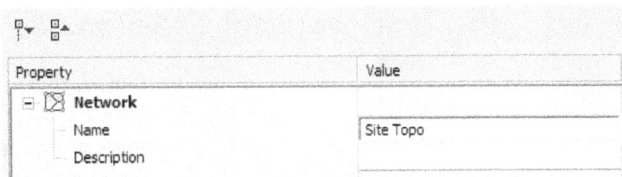

Property	Value
⊟ ◫ **Network**	
Name	Site Topo
Description	

Figure 6–7

8. In the Import Survey Data dialog box, set the following values, as shown in Figure 6–8:

- *Show interactive graphics:* **Yes**
- *Process linework during import:* **No**
- *Insert network object:* **Yes**
- *Insert figure objects:* **Yes**
- *Insert survey points:* **Yes**

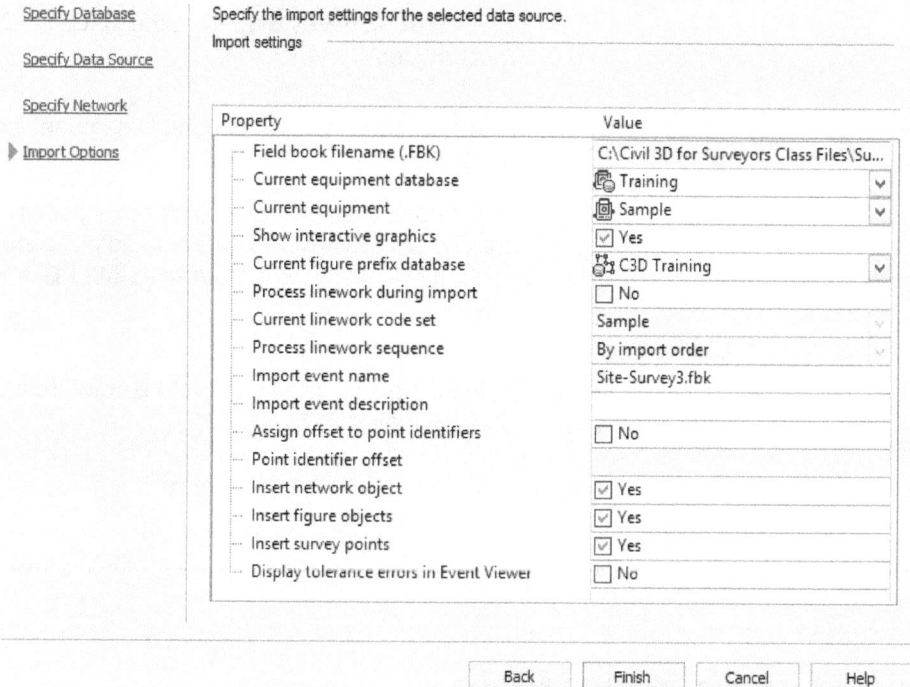

Specify Database

Specify Data Source

Specify Network

▶ Import Options

Specify the import settings for the selected data source.

Import settings

Property	Value
Field book filename (.FBK)	C:\Civil 3D for Surveyors Class Files\Su...
Current equipment database	Training
Current equipment	Sample
Show interactive graphics	☑ Yes
Current figure prefix database	C3D Training
Process linework during import	☐ No
Current linework code set	Sample
Process linework sequence	By import order
Import event name	Site-Survey3.fbk
Import event description	
Assign offset to point identifiers	☐ No
Point identifier offset	
Insert network object	☑ Yes
Insert figure objects	☑ Yes
Insert survey points	☑ Yes
Display tolerance errors in Event Viewer	☐ No

Back   Finish   Cancel   Help

Figure 6–8

9. Click **Finish** to accept the changes when done.

10. In the Survey Network Update dialog box, click **Close**.

Task 2 - Create a new network.

You have now imported the fieldbook file as you created the network, **Site Topo**. In this task you will create a new network and import the field book file into it.

1. Continue working with the drawing from the previous task or open **FB-A2-Survey.dwg** from the *C:\Civil 3D for Surveyors Practice Files\Survey* folder.

2. Continue with the previously opened database or close the currently opened survey database, and open **Survey Data FB-A2**.

3. In the **Survey Databases**>current opened survey database collection, select **Networks**, right-click, and select **New...**, as shown in Figure 6–9.

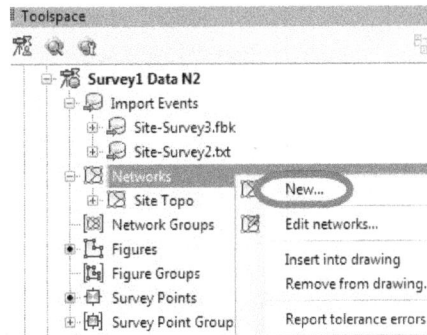

Figure 6–9

4. Set the *Name* to **ExRoad**. Click **OK.**

5. To import the existing road Mission Avenue survey, select the network **ExRoad**, right-click, expand *Import* and select **Import Field Book**.

6. For the *Field book filename (.FBK)*, browse to the *C:\Civil 3D for Surveyors Practice Files\Survey* folder, select **Road-Survey.fbk** and open it.

7. In the Import Field Book dialog box, set the following values:
   - *Show interactive graphics*: **Yes**
   - *Process linework during import*: **No**
   - *Insert network object*: **Yes**
   - *Insert figure objects:* **Yes**
   - *Insert survey points*: **Yes**

8. Click **OK** to accept the changes.

9. In the Survey Network Updated dialog box, click **Close**.

10. Save the drawing.

6.3 Working with Figures

Figures can be surface breaklines. The layer on which they are located on can be toggled off before the final deliverable plots. A figure does not need to be inserted into a drawing to review its location. By selecting a figure from the Survey's figure list, it is previewed in the drawing, as shown in Figure 6–10.

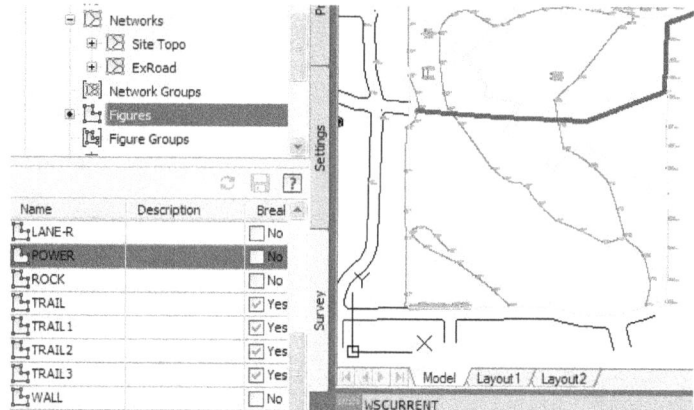

Figure 6–10

Right-click on a selected figure under the **Figures** collections to display a list of options (as shown in Figure 6–11), which enable you to remove the figure from the drawing, display its properties, insert the figure into the drawing, or insert its points into the drawing.

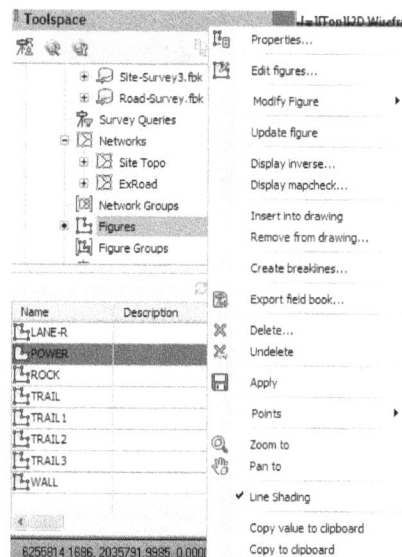

Figure 6–11

- You can access the Panorama's *Grading Elevation Editor* tab by selecting the figure in the drawing, right-clicking, and selecting **Elevation Edit...** Alternatively you can select the figure and click ⬚ (Edit Elevations) in the *Figure* contextual tab>Modify panel. Then, click ⬚ (Elevation Editor) in the *Figure* contextual tab>Edit Elevations panel.

The icons in the editor enable you to raise or lower its elevation for all or single vertices, as shown in Figure 6–12. You can also click in each cell and edit its elevation. The edits made in this Panorama transfer back to the survey when you select **Update Survey Data from Drawing** (select the figure and right-click to access this option).

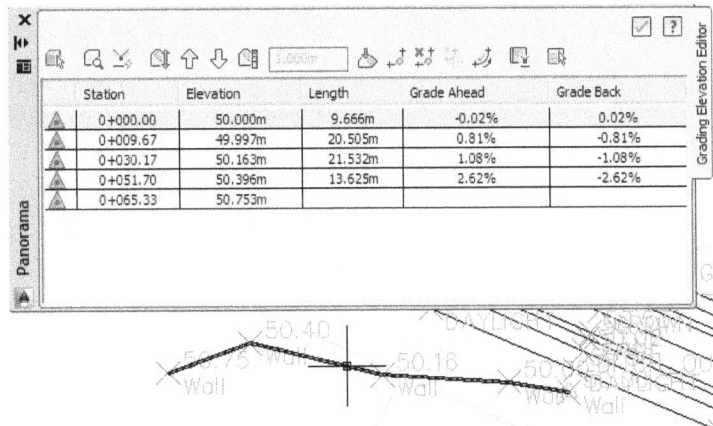

Station	Elevation	Length	Grade Ahead	Grade Back
0+000.00	50.000m	9.666m	-0.02%	0.02%
0+009.67	49.997m	20.505m	0.81%	-0.81%
0+030.17	50.163m	21.532m	1.08%	-1.08%
0+051.70	50.396m	13.625m	2.62%	-2.62%
0+065.33	50.753m			

Figure 6–12

When a figure is selected in the drawing, the ribbon displays all of the tools that are applicable to the figure. If you select the **Edit Geometry** icon in the ribbon, you can also add or remove vertices, and offset figures to create new figures (e.g., top-face-curb from the gutter figure).

Practice 6b

Field Book Edits, Styles, and Figure Prefixes

Estimated time for completion: 15 minutes

Practice Objective

- Edit a field book file by drawing linework and then adding it to the survey.

In this practice you will edit the field book and manually create a figure.

Task 1 - Edit the field book.

1. Continue working with the drawing from the previous practice or open **FB-B1-Survey.dwg** from the *C:\Civil 3D for Surveyors Practice Files\Survey* folder.

2. Continue with the previously opened database or close the currently opened survey database, and open **Survey Data FB-B1**.

3. In the *Survey* tab, select **Figures**. In the preview area at the bottom (shown in Figure 6–13), select **Building1**, right-click, and select **Zoom to**.

4. The survey crew in the field shot the building corners, but some minor work is still required to close the linework in the area shown in Figure 6–14.

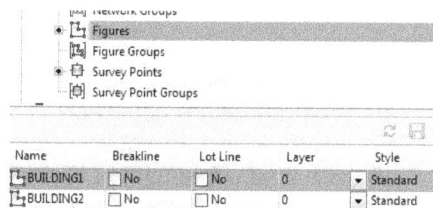

Name	Breakline	Lot Line	Layer	Style
BUILDING1	No	No	0	Standard
BUILDING2	No	No	0	Standard

Figure 6–13

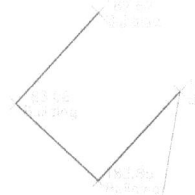

Figure 6–14

5. In the *Survey* tab, expand the **Networks** collection. Select **Site Topo**, right-click, and select **Edit Field Book**.

6. For the *Field book filename (.FBK)*, browse to the *C:\Civil 3D for Surveyors Practice Files\Survey* folder and select **Site-Survey3.fbk**. Open it to display the field book in Notepad.

7. Scroll down to the line containing point number **574**. Note that for Building1 and Building2, you have an *End* for the figure (as shown in Figure 6–15), instead of a *Close*. Change the *End* to **Close**, which will close the figure.

```
Begin Building1                              Begin Building1
NE SS 571 620894.4701 1906908.               NE SS 571 620894.4701 1906908.
NE SS 572 620888.7293 1906903.               NE SS 572 620888.7293 1906903.
NE SS 573 620883.9411 1906908.               NE SS 573 620883.9411 1906908.
NE SS 574 620889.5634 1906913.               NE SS 574 620889.5634 1906913.
End Building1  ◄────────                      Close Building1
Begin Building2                              Begin Building2
NE SS 575 620834.9955 1906904.               NE SS 575 620834.9955 1906904.
NE SS 576 620820.588 1906904.7               NE SS 576 620820.588 1906904.
NE SS 577 620820.588 1906911.                NE SS 577 620820.588 1906911.
NE SS 578 620834.9955 1906911.               NE SS 578 620834.9955 1906911.
End Building2  ◄────────                      Close Building2

NE SS 579 620827.5755 1907112.               NE SS 579 620827.5755 1907112.
NE SS 580 620820.3717 1907112.               NE SS 580 620820.3717 1907112.
NE SS 581 620820.3717 1907105.               NE SS 581 620820.3717 1907105.
NE SS 582 620827.5755 1907105.               NE SS 582 620827.5755 1907105.
```

Figure 6–15

8. Exit Notepad and when prompted, save the edits.

Task 2 - Re-import the field book.

Now that the field book file has been revised in the previous task, you will need to update the drawing.

1. Continue working with the drawing from the previous task or open **FB-B2-Survey.dwg** from the *C:\Civil 3D for Surveyors Practice Files\Survey* folder. Also continue with the previously opened database, or open **Survey Data FB-B2** for editing.

2. Under the **Import Events** collection, select **Site-Survey3.fbk**, right-click, and select **Re-import**, as shown in Figure 6–16.

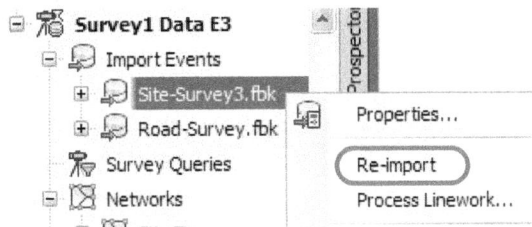

Figure 6–16

3. In the Re-import Field Book dialog box, click **OK** to reset the survey and re-import the network.

4. In the Survey Network Updated dialog box, click **Close**.

5. Select **Figures**. In the preview area at the bottom, double-click on **Building1** and then on **Building2**. As the AutoCAD® Civil 3D software zooms into each of these figures, note that each one is now closed.

Task 3 - Create a figure manually.

1. Continue working with the drawing from the previous practice or open **FB-B3-Survey.dwg** from the *C:\Civil 3D for Surveyors Practice Files\Survey* folder. Also continue with the previously opened database, or open **Survey Data FB-B3** for editing.

2. In the *Prospector* tab, expand the **Point Groups** collection and select the **_All Points** point group.

3. In the preview area at the bottom, scroll to point number **579**, as shown in Figure 6–17. Select it, hold <Shift> and select point number **582**, right-click, and select **Zoom to**.

Figure 6–17

4. Using the AutoCAD® **3D Polyline** command (type **3P** in the Command Line) and the **Node** object snap, draw a polyline connecting the nodes, as shown in Figure 6–18.

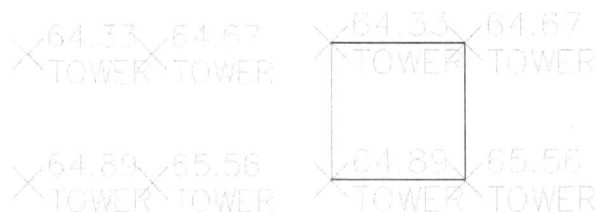

Figure 6–18

5. In the *Survey* tab, under the **Survey Databases**>current opened survey database collections, select **Figures**, right-click, and select **Create figure from object...**, as shown in Figure 6–19. In the drawing, select the polyline that you just drew.

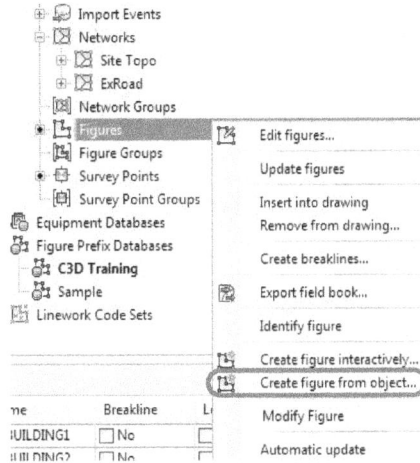

Figure 6–19

6. In the Create Figure From Object dialog box, set the *Name* to **Tower**, as shown in Figure 6–20. Click **OK** to create the new figure. Press <Enter> to exit the command.

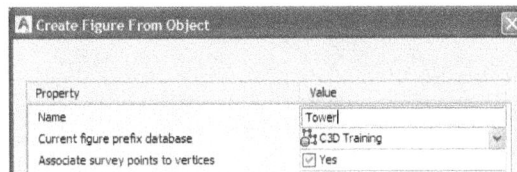

Figure 6–20

7. To update the drawing with the figure, select **Figures**, right-click, and select **Insert into drawing**, as shown in Figure 6–21.

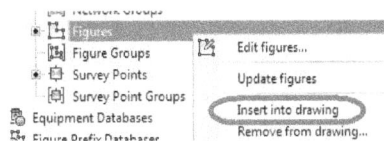

Figure 6–21

Next you will review the figure's properties.

8. In the *Survey* tab, select **Figures**.

In AutoCAD Civil 3D 2017 (R1), it is not required to insert into drawing a figure that you create. Step 7 has been left in to ensure that you know how to insert a figure for other purposes.

9. In the preview window, select the **Tower** figure, right-click, and select **Properties**.

10. Review the figure's properties, as shown in Figure 6–22. If required, change the *Style* to **Buildings**. When done, click **OK** to exit the dialog box.

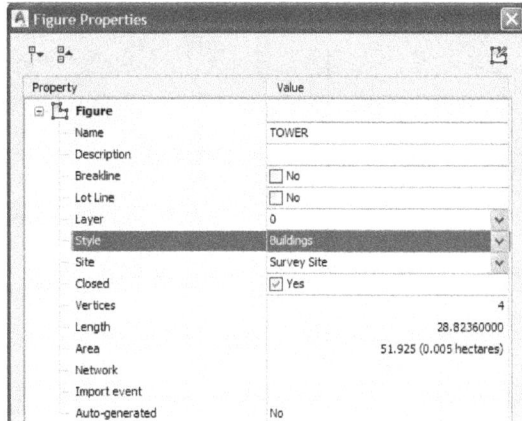

Figure 6–22

11. Save the drawing.

6.4 Filtering a Survey Database

Many civil engineering projects can become quite large depending on the scope of the project or the area that it covers. The larger the project area or scope, the larger the drawing size. This is especially true when designing or modifying long corridor projects, such as trails or freeways. That is why you can filter the survey database and only import the part of the project you are working on into the current drawing. Queries can be defined for both points and figures and can use general properties or extended properties that are either user-defined or imported from LandXML.

General properties available for Points include: elevation, number, description, name, control point, non-control point, station point, easting, and northing, as shown in Figure 6–23.

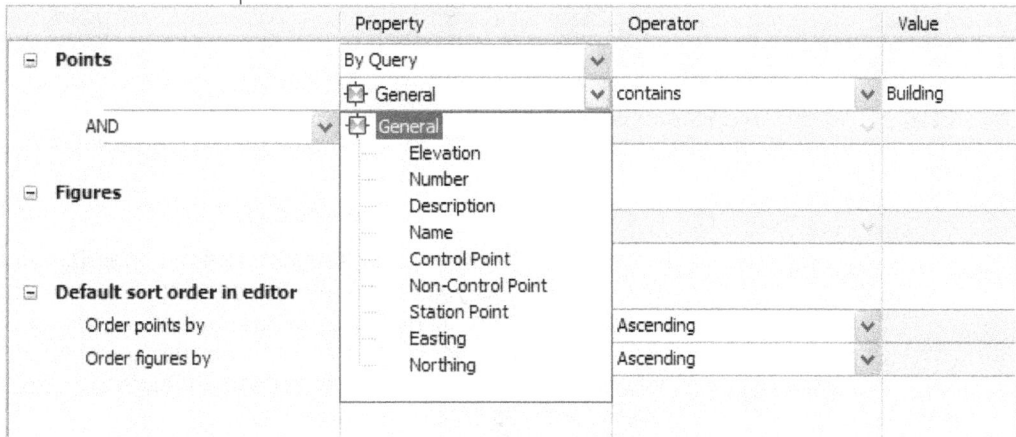

	Property		Operator		Value
⊟ **Points**	By Query	∨			
	⊞ General	∨	contains	∨	Building
AND ∨	⊞ General			∨	
	Elevation				
⊟ **Figures**	Number				
	Description			∨	
	Name				
	Control Point				
⊟ **Default sort order in editor**	Non-Control Point				
Order points by	Station Point		Ascending	∨	
Order figures by	Easting		Ascending	∨	
	Northing				

Figure 6–23

General properties available for Figures include: vertices, description, layer, name, site, style, breakline, closed, auto generated, lot line, first point X and Y, and last point X and Y, as shown in Figure 6–24.

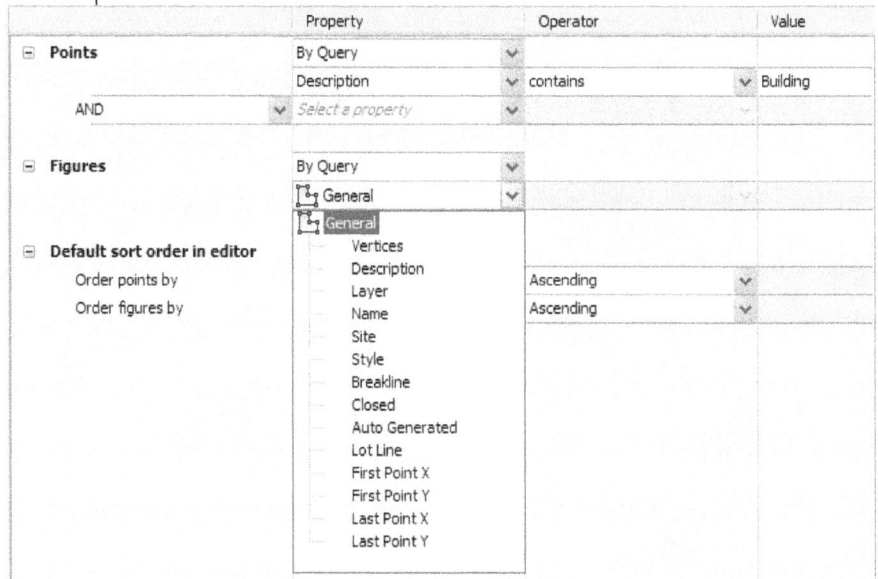

Figure 6–24

Both point and figure queries enable specific operators to help limit the data that you import into the drawing. The operators include: is equal to, is not equal to, is less than, is greater than, is less than or equal to, is greater than or equal to, contains, does not contain, starts with, does not start with, ends with, and does not end with, as shown in Figure 6–25.

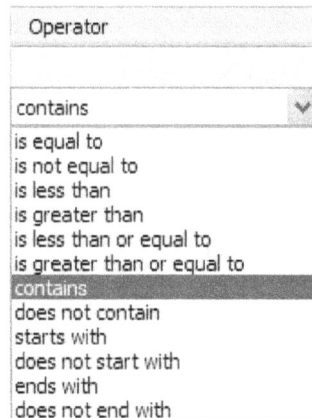

Figure 6–25

You can also include two boolean operators: **And** and **Or**. Each time you create a query, a new line is created below the current line on which you are working, as shown in the top of Figure 6–26. Selecting **And** for the boolean operation limits the data even more because it has to meet both conditions to be included in the query, similar to the results shown in the red area of the two circles on the left in Figure 6–26. Selecting **Or** for the boolean operation expands the included data because can meet either condition to be included in the query, similar to the results shown in the red area of the two circles on the right in Figure 6–26.

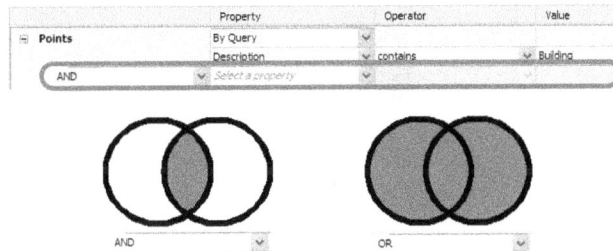

Figure 6–26

Individual survey queries can be saved to QML files that can be opened and reused or imported into another survey database. This can be done in the Survey Query Builder or by right-clicking on the query name under the **Survey Queries** collection and selecting **Save Query to File**.

How To: Filter a Survey Database

1. Expand the survey database in which you are working.
2. Right-click on **Survey Queries** and select **New...**, as shown in Figure 6–27.

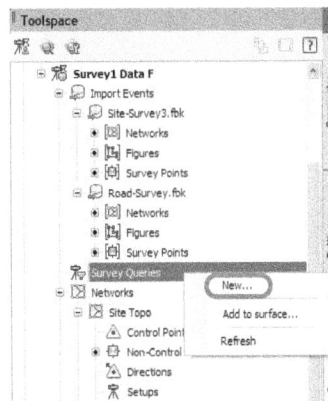

Figure 6–27

3. Select the property that you want to query by under points or figures.
4. Select the operator to use on the data.
5. Type the value that you want the conditions to meet.
6. Add additional conditions using the **And** or **Or** operators to expand or limit the data even more.
7. To ensure that you are getting all of the information you want in the query, you can preview it in the drawing by selecting **Preview in Drawing**, as shown in Figure 6–28.

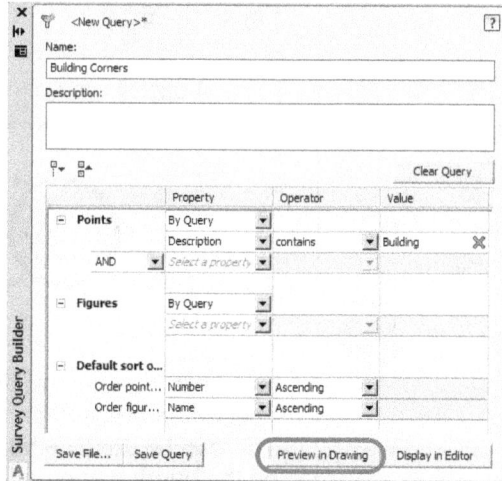

Figure 6–28

8. Finally, save the query for a later use, add the data to a surface, or import it into the drawing. To add it to a surface, right-click on **Survey Queries** and select **Add to surface...**, as shown in Figure 6–29.

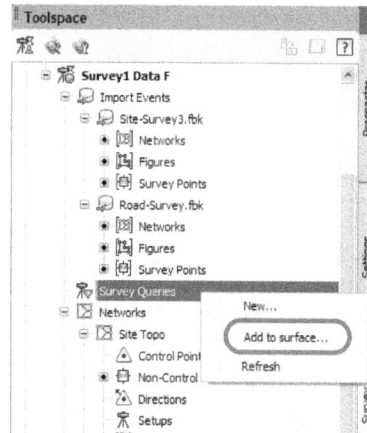

Figure 6–29

Practice 6c

Filter a Survey Database

Practice Objective

- Filter a survey database to isolate only the points or figures required for the tasks being completed in the project to reduce file sizes.

Estimated time for completion: 5 minutes

1. Continue working with the drawing from the previous practice or open **FB-C1-Survey.dwg**, from the *C:\Civil 3D for Surveyors Practice Files\Survey* folder.

2. Continue with the previously opened database. If you did not complete previous practices, open the **Survey Data -FBC** survey database for editing.

3. Expand the survey database, right-click on Survey Queries, select **New...**, as shown in Figure 6–30.

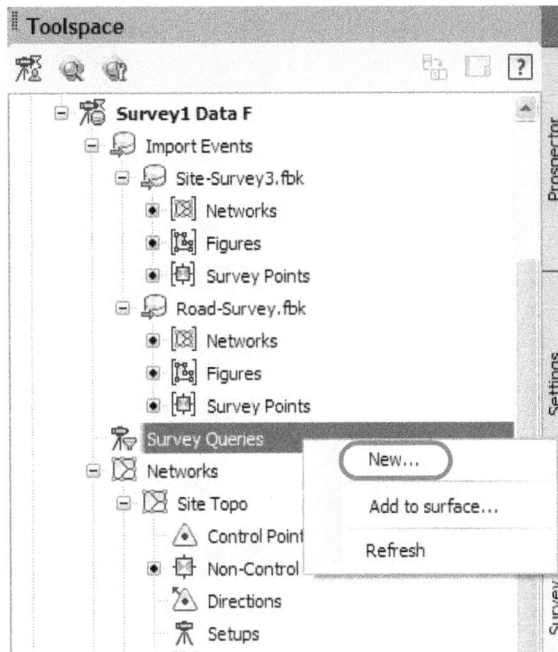

Figure 6–30

4. Name it **Building Corners**.

5. In the *Points* area, set the following:
   - *Property:* **Description**
   - *Operator:* **Contains**
   - *Value:* **Building**

6. Click **Preview in Drawing**, as shown in Figure 6–31.

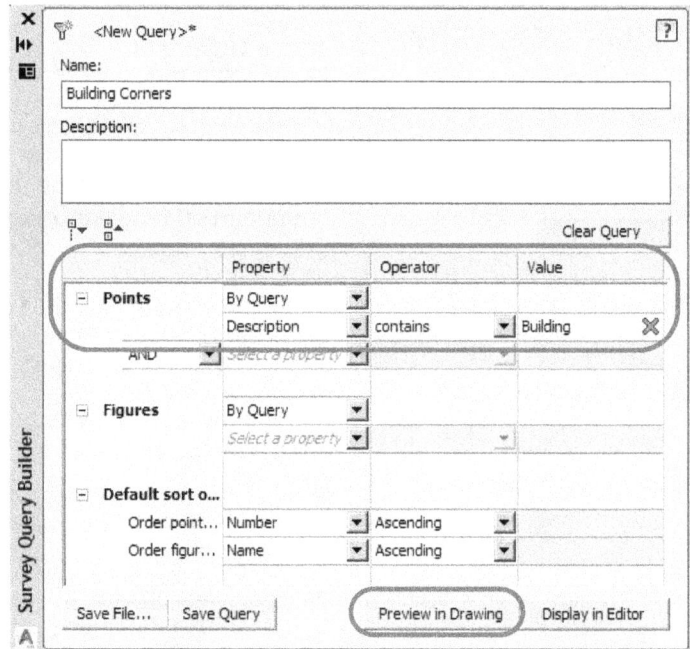

Figure 6–31

7. Click **Save Query** to save the query and then close the Survey Query Builder palette.

Chapter Review Questions

1. If you need to analyze the field data using the analysis tools available in the Survey Database, you must use a field book file rather than a text file.

    a. True

    b. False

2. How many field book files can you import into one network?

    a. One

    b. Two

    c. Ten

    d. Unlimited

3. When modifying a survey to close a figure created from a field book file, you:

    a. Right-click on the figure and select **Close**.

    b. Modify the point code in the field book file.

    c. Modify the field note proceeding the point in the field book file.

    d. You cannot make changes to figures once they are imported.

Command Summary

Button	Command	Location
	Create Points	• **Ribbon**: *Home* tab>Create Ground Data panel
	Import Points from File	• **Ribbon**: *Insert* tab>Import panel • **Toolbar**: Create Points • **Command Prompt:** ImportPoints
	Import Survey Data	• **Ribbon**: *Home* tab>Create Ground Data panel • **Command Prompt:** ImportSurveyData
	Survey Toolspace	• **Ribbon**: *Home* tab>Palettes panel
	Survey User Settings	• **Toolspace**: *Survey* tab
	Zoom To Points	• **Toolbar**: Transparent Commands • **Command Prompt:** 'ZTP

Surfaces

In this chapter, you learn how to create a surface from survey data. Then, you will learn to effectively refine the surface using breaklines, boundaries, and making other edits. Finally, you will analyze the surface and annotate it to communicate the existing conditions.

Learning Objectives in this Chapter

- Learn the steps required to build a surface in the AutoCAD® Civil® 3D software.
- Adjust and edit a surface using surface properties and various commands.
- Add existing contour data to a surface to take advantage of data created by someone else.
- Add drawing objects to a surface to improve the accuracy of a TIN model.
- Add breaklines and boundaries to a surface to improve its accuracy.
- Analyze a surface using a quick profile or the object viewer.
- Label contour elevations, slope values, spot elevations, and watershed delineations to communicate surface information.
- Calculate the volume of cut and fill or adjusted cut and fill between two surfaces.
- Analyze a surface to determine the buildable area for the project conditions.
- Create AutoCAD Civil 3D surfaces from point cloud data files.

7.1 Surface Process

The surface building process can be divided into the following steps:

1. Assemble the data.
2. Assign the data to a surface.
3. Evaluate the resulting surface.
4. Add breaklines, assign more data, modify the data, or edit the surface as required.

1. Assemble data.

The first step in surface building is to acquire the initial surface data. This can be points, contours, 3D polylines, feature lines, AutoCAD® objects, ASCII coordinate files, or boundaries. Each data type provides specific information about a surface.

2. Assign data to a surface.

Acquired data is assigned to a surface. Once assigned, the AutoCAD Civil 3D software immediately processes this data and a surface object is created.

Surfaces are listed individually in the **Surfaces** collection in the *Prospector* tab. Each surface contains content information, as shown in Figure 7–1. The surface content includes **Masks**, **Watersheds**, and **Definition** elements. The **Definition** contains a list of all of the surface data that has been applied, including boundaries, breaklines, and points. The *Prospector* tab displays data for each type of surface data in the list view when one of these types is selected.

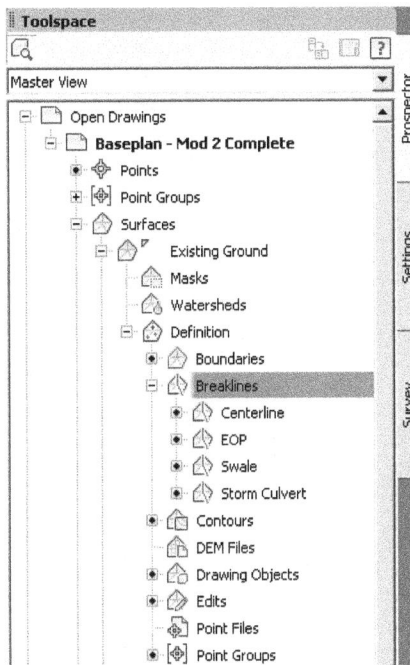

Figure 7–1

The AutoCAD Civil 3D software processes the initial data into one of two types of surfaces. The first type, the **Triangulated Irregular Network** (TIN) surface, is the most common. With triangulated surfaces, surface points are connected to adjacent points by straight lines, resulting in a triangular mesh. Surfaces generated from contour lines have surface points created at their vertices, modified by weeding and supplementing factors. An example of this type of surface is shown in Figure 7–2.

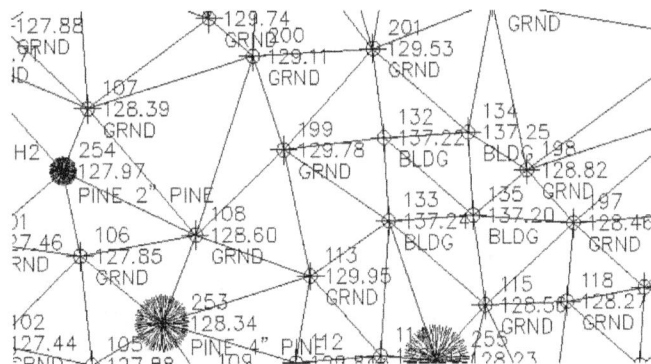

Figure 7–2

The second type of surface is a *Grid* surface. This surface interpolates and assigns an elevation from the surface data to each grid intersection. Most of the elevations at grid intersections are interpolated. **Digital Elevation Models** (DEMs) are a type of grid surface used in GIS applications. An example of this type of surface is shown in Figure 7–3.

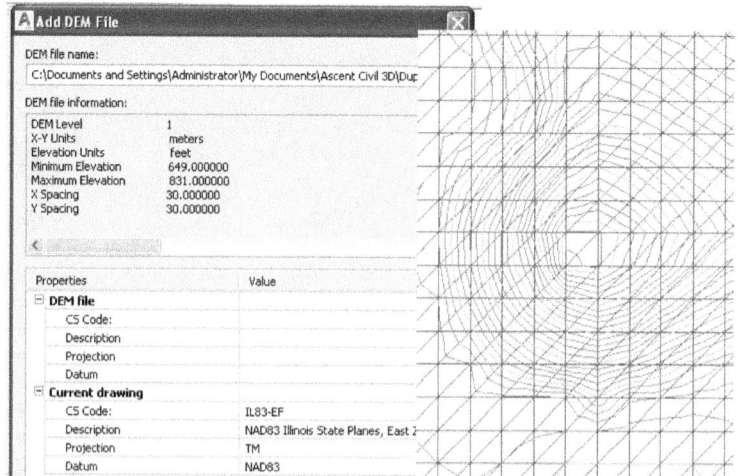

Figure 7–3

3. Evaluate the resulting surface.

Surfaces, especially ones created from points, typically need some attention to represent them as accurately as possible. For any four adjacent surface points, there are two possible triangulations, as shown in Figure 7–4.

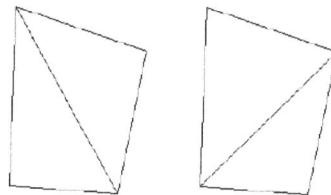

Figure 7–4

The differences can be difficult to envision when viewing the triangles from above, but these two configurations provide entirely different geometries. For example, note the surface shown in Figure 7–5.

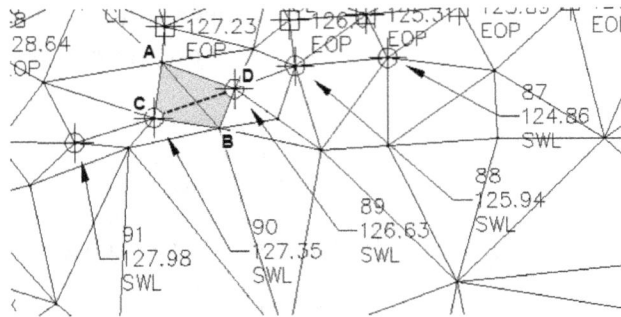

Figure 7–5

The triangulated points A, B, C, and D have a TIN line running from A to B. This configuration ignores the fact that C and D are both part of a continuous swale (SWL), indicated by the dashed line. In a 3D view, this configuration would resemble the example shown on the left in Figure 7–6. The correct triangulation has the triangle line *following* the linear feature rather than *crossing* it, as shown on the right.

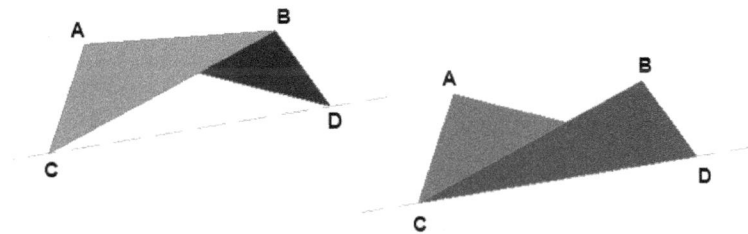

Figure 7–6

When creating surfaces, representing linear features correctly is extremely important. Examples of linear features include road center lines, edges-of-pavement, road shoulders, swales, berms, tops and bottoms of banks, and headwalls. Adding breaklines that follow linear features ensures that a terrain model is triangulated correctly along the features, rather than across them.

Other types of issues to watch out for include bad elevations (blown shots), elevations at 0 where there should be no chance of such elevation values, and points that were surveyed above or below the ground (e.g., the tops of fire hydrants). Unwanted triangles along the edges of the surface might connect points that should not be connected, which could also present problems.

In addition to the casual inspection of the triangles, surfaces can be evaluated by creating contour lines, reviewing the surface in 3D, and using the **Quick Section** command.

4. Add breaklines, assign more data, modify the data, or edit the surface as required.

After you have evaluated the surface, you can add the required breaklines or edit the surface directly to make adjustments. If the triangulation errors are isolated, editing the surface directly might be faster than creating and applying breaklines. For example, the triangulation issue above could be addressed by *swapping* the edge that crossed the swale center line. To do so, right-click on Edits under a Surface's definition in the *Prospector* tab and select **Swap Edge**, as shown in Figure 7–7.

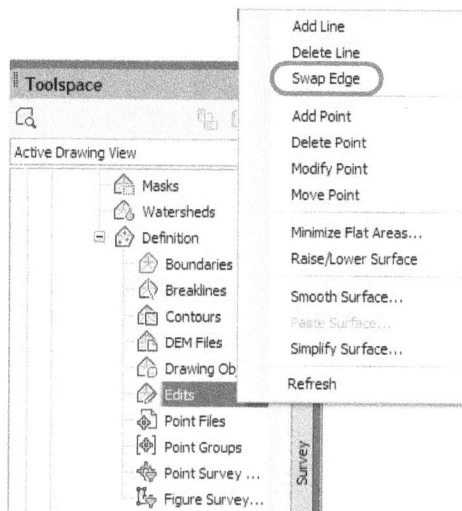

Figure 7–7

Other options enable you to add, move, modify, or remove points from the surface (but not change or erase the point object on which they were based), as well as add or remove triangle lines directly. **Minimize Flat Areas** is a group of algorithms that can be used to minimize the number of flat areas created by contour data. **Raise/Lower Surface** enables you to raise and lower the entire surface by a set amount, and a **Smooth Surface** enables you to smooth surfaces using the **Natural Neighbor** or **Kriging** method. (Contour smoothing is handled through surface styles. These techniques smooth the actual surface geometry.)

7.2 Surface Properties

The *Definition* tab in the Surface Properties dialog box displays the permitted **Build**, **Data**, and **Edit** operations for a surface. The *Operation Type* column is a record of the surface data addition and edits. Using the checkboxes, you can toggle off individual actions in the history and display the resulting changes to the surface. The entries can be toggled on or off no matter where they display in the history. This helps to isolate possible errors or review features (such as surface slopes) that are greatly affected by the addition of a headwall or retaining wall.

You can change the order of items in the list of operations. Operations higher in the list are applied to the surface before items further down in the list. Open this dialog box by right-clicking on the surface name in the *Prospector* (or by selecting the surface in the drawing and right-clicking) and selecting **Surface Properties....**The dialog box is shown in Figure 7–8.

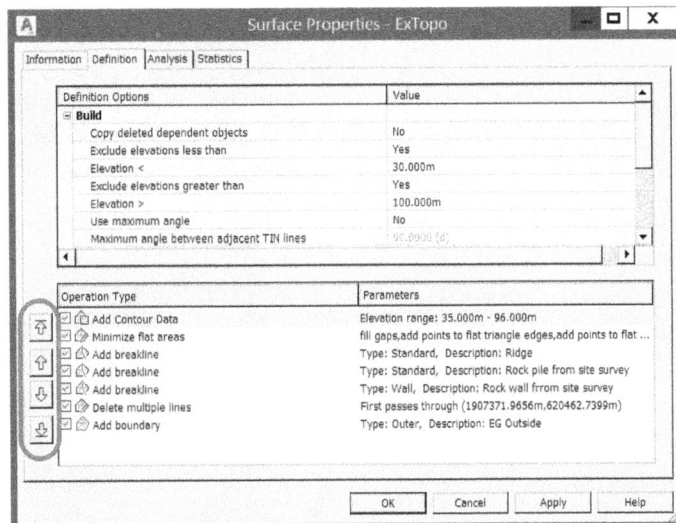

Figure 7–8

The *Information* tab enables you to rename the surface, edit the description, apply a surface object style, and render material, which controls how the surface displays in a rendered view.

The *Statistics* tab displays the current surface slope, elevation, and triangulation. It contains three areas:

- **General:** Provides an overall view of the surface. The **Minimum**, **Maximum**, and **Mean** elevations are the important entries in this area and provide the first hint of bad or incorrect data.

- **Extended:** Reports the **2D** and **3D** surface areas and **Minimum**, **Maximum**, and **Mean** slope values.

- **TIN:** Reviews the number of triangles, minimum and maximum triangle areas, and leg lengths in the surface.

The areas of triangles, along with the minimum and maximum triangle side lengths are indicators of data consistency. Generally, the longest triangles form around the perimeter of the surface. Limiting the length of triangle edges removes these types of triangles from the surface. You can delete these lines rather than try to set an optimum length, or you can create a boundary to prevent these types of triangles from being created.

When surfaces are created, they are assigned properties based on the *Build Options* area in the Edit Command Settings dialog box, as shown on the right in Figure 7–9. To open this dialog box, right-click on the **Create Surface** command and select **Edit Command Settings**, as shown on the left in Figure 7–9.

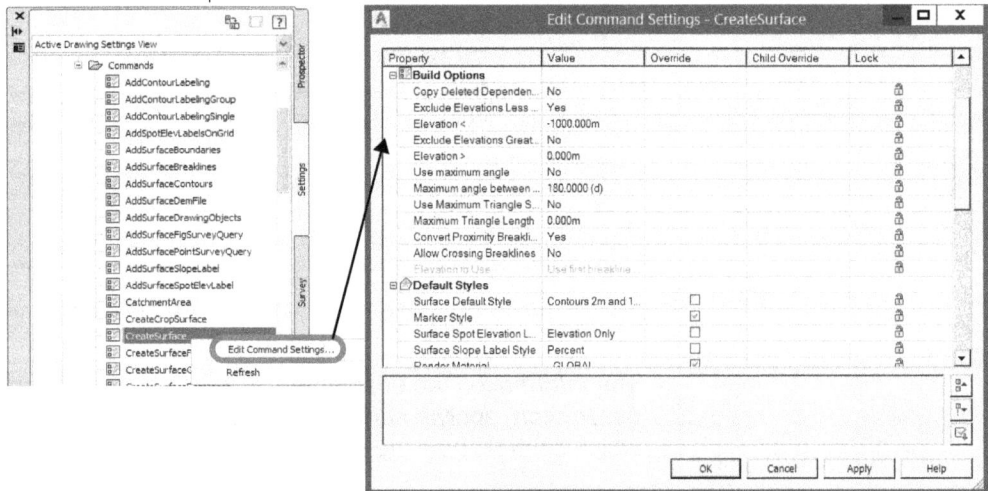

Figure 7–9

Surface Rebuilding

Some surface edits and point modifications can render a surface out of date. At that point, the surface is flagged as being out of date in the *Prospector* tab, as indicated by the **Drawing Item Modifier** icon shown in Figure 7–10.

Figure 7–10

When this occurs, you can right-click on the surface in the *Prospector* tab and select **Rebuild**. This updates the surface to reflect the recent changes. Alternatively, you can right-click on the surface in the *Prospector* and select **Rebuild-Automatic**, which updates the surface automatically without input from you. However, toggling this option on increases the strain on the computer resources and graphics capabilities so it is recommended that you leave it toggled off.

7.3 Surface Data

Contours

In the AutoCAD Civil 3D software, polylines with elevation are useful as custom contour objects. Whether using polylines or AutoCAD Land Desktop contour objects, the AutoCAD Civil 3D software builds a surface by triangulating between contours. The end of each triangle side connects to a vertex of two different contours.

When processing contours for surface data, the AutoCAD Civil 3D software inspects the contour vertices for two conditions: too many data points representing similar data (e.g., 10 vertices on 15 units of contour length in an almost straight line), and not enough data points over the length of a contour.

You can set the values for these conditions in the Add Contour Data dialog box (as shown in Figure 7–11) when you add contour data.

Figure 7–11

Weeding Factors

The *weeding* process removes redundant vertices from contours. The first step in the weeding process is to inspect three adjacent contour vertices, whose overall distance is shorter than a user-specified distance (e.g., three vertices in less than 15 units of contour). When encountering this situation, the weeding process prompts you about the change in direction between the three vertices. For example, does the direction from vertex 1 to vertex 2 change more than four degrees when going from vertex 2 to vertex 3? If not, the vertices are almost in a straight line and are too close. The AutoCAD Civil 3D software considers vertex 2 to be redundant and removes it from the surface data. This process repeats for the next three vertices. If the distance is under 15 units and the change of direction is less than four degrees, the next vertex 2 is removed from the data.

If a contour has three vertices in less than 15 units, and turns more than four degrees, vertex 2 is kept because the change in direction is significant. If there are more that 15 units between the three vertices, the AutoCAD Civil 3D software moves on to the next group.

An important feature of weeding is not what it removes from the data, but what is left over. If not enough data remains, the numbers for the weeding factors should be set to lower values.

Supplementing Factors

When the AutoCAD Civil 3D software inspects contour data, it uses supplementing factors to add vertices to the surface data. The first supplementing factor is the distance between contour vertices. When the distance between vertices is over 100 units, The AutoCAD Civil 3D software adds a vertex to the data along the course of the contour. The second supplementing factor is a mid-ordinate distance for the curve segments of a contour. If curves are distributed throughout the contour data, a setting of 0.1 is a good starting point.

- All weeding and supplementing factors are user-specified.

- Weeding and supplementing does not modify the contours or polylines in a drawing, only their data.

- There is no *correct* setting for weeding and supplementing. Varying the values creates more or less surface data.

DEM Files

Digital Elevation Models (DEMs) are grid-based terrain models primarily used by GIS applications to represent large areas. Since they are large-scale and grid-based, they are generally only used in the AutoCAD Civil 3D software for preliminary design and other approximate tasks.

Drawing Objects

AutoCAD points, text, blocks, and other objects can be used as surface data. Individual AutoCAD Civil 3D point objects can also be selected using the **Drawing Objects** option. Selected objects need to have a valid elevation value.

- All data added as drawing objects is considered point data.

- You can add 3D lines and polyfaces using this method, but each end point is treated as if it were a point object. Linework is not treated as contours or breaklines. The Add Points From Drawing Objects dialog box is shown in Figure 7–12.

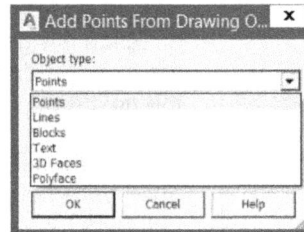

Figure 7–12

Point Files

Points in an ASCII point file can be used as surface data.

- You can use any import/export file format.

- This is an excellent way to create a large surface from a massive number of points, as it bypasses creating point objects, thereby reducing drawing overhead.

Point Groups

Using previously defined points groups in a surface definition enables you to isolate only the points on the ground to ensure that the tops of walls and invert elevations do not distort the surface.

Point Survey Queries

Select points in a survey database can be used as surface data by creating a survey query. The point data is used, but point objects are not created.

- Dynamic references to the points provide a more seamless update if changes to the database or query are made.

- This is an excellent way to create a large surface from a massive number of points, as it bypasses creating point objects, thereby reducing drawing overhead.

- Points from a survey query display under point groups in the surface definition.

Figure Survey Queries

Select figures in a survey database can be used as surface data. The figures are used as breaklines, but 3D polylines are not created in the drawing.

- Dynamic references to the figures provide a more seamless update if changes to the database or query are made.

- This is an excellent way to create a large surface from a massive number of figures, as it bypasses creating 3D polylines and turning them into breaklines, thereby reducing drawing overhead.

- Figures from a survey query display under breaklines in the surface definition.

Practice 7a

Estimated time for completion: 10 minutes

Creating an Existing Ground Surface

Practice Objective

• Add point data to a surface that already exists in the drawing.

The next step in the design project is to create an existing ground terrain model that can be used in the design. In this practice you will define the surface with surface data. You will use this model to create existing ground contours and for reference during the design. You will begin the model with the provided GIS Data surface from contours and the previously created **Existing Ground** point group.

Task 1 - Define surface with point data.

In examining the **GIS Data** surface more closely, note that although the internal site contours correctly reflect the surveyed point elevations, the original contours are out of date or have missing information in the area of the existing road, **Mission Avenue** (the road running east to west at the top of the site). However, you have a detailed survey of the road. Using this data, you will generate a surface.

1. Open **SUF1-A1-Surface.dwg** from the *C:\Civil 3D for Surveyors Practice Files\Surface* folder.

2. Although the point group that you use in this practice has been created, you should change the display order of the point groups to display them clearly. To do so, in the *Prospector* tab, right-click on **Point Groups** and select **Properties**. Move the **_No Display** point group to the top and then move the **ExRoad** point group above it.

3. In the *Prospector* tab, select the **Surfaces** collection, right-click, and select **Create Surface**.

4. In the Create Surface dialog box, set the following:

    • *Surface type*: **TIN surface**
    • *Surface Name*: **ExRoad**
    • *Style*: **Contours 2m and 10m Background**
    • Click **OK** to accept the changes and close the dialog box.

5. Expand the **Surfaces** collection in the *Prospector* tab and expand the **ExRoad** collection.

6. Expand the **Definition** collection, select **Point Groups**, right-click, and select **Add...**, as shown in Figure 7–13.

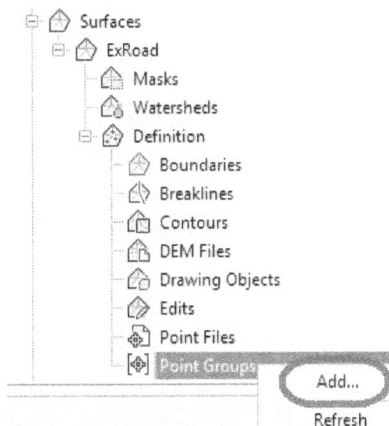

Figure 7–13

7. In the Point Groups dialog box, select the **ExRoad** points group, as shown in Figure 7–14. Click **OK** to accept the changes and close the dialog box.

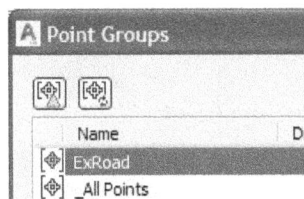

Figure 7–14

8. Save the drawing.

Task 2 - Create a surface contour style.

---

1. Continue working with the drawing from the previous task or open **SUF1-A2-Surface.dwg** from the *C:\Civil 3D for Surveyors Practice Files\Surface* folder.

2. Since there is very little grade change along the road, the frequency of the contours is small, making the surface difficult to see. Expand the **Surfaces** collection, right-click **ExRoad**, and select **Surface Properties**.

3. In the Surface Properties dialog box, in the *Information* tab, expand  to the right of the *Surface style* field and select **Copy Current Selection**, as shown in Figure 7–15.

4. In the *Information* tab, set the style *Name* to **Contours 0.5m and 2.5m (Background)**, as shown in Figure 7–16.

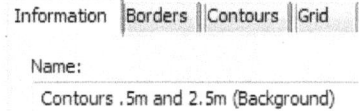

Figure 7–15

Figure 7–16

5. In the *Contours* tab, expand the **Contour Intervals** collection and set the following, as shown in Figure 7–17:

    *   *Minor Interval:* **0.5m**
    *   *Major Interval:* **2.5m**

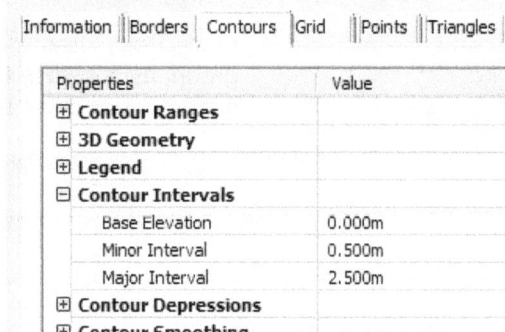

Figure 7–17

6. Click **OK** to accept and close the Edit Style dialog box, and click **OK** to close the Surface Properties dialog box.

7. Zoom into the existing road at the north end of the site and note the detail contours identifying the crown of the road.

8. Save the drawing.

7.4 Breaklines and Boundaries

A surface can include data from boundaries, breaklines, contours, Digital Elevation Model files (DEMs), drawing objects (AutoCAD points, individual AutoCAD Civil 3D points, lines, 3D faces, etc.), manual edits, and point files. The **Boundaries** collection displays above the **Breaklines** collection under the surface's **Definition** (in the *Prospector* tab), as shown in Figure 7–18. However, you should generally add boundaries after adding breaklines to a surface. If you use the Data Clip boundary type, any data that you add to the surface (point file, DEM file, or breakline) is only added to the area within the boundary. In that case, breaklines can be added to the surface after a Data Clip boundary type. Surface edit operations are not affected by the Data Clip boundary.

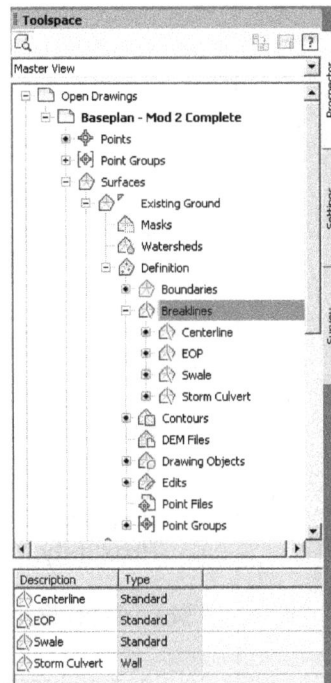

Figure 7–18

Breaklines

Breaklines affect surface triangulation and are important in point-based surfaces. They ensure that terrain models are triangulated correctly along linear features, as shown in Figure 7–19.

Surface before breaklines have been applied along the center line of a road.

Surface after breaklines have been applied along the center line of a road.

Figure 7–19

- When adding a breakline to a surface, the AutoCAD Civil 3D software creates an entry under the **Breakline>Definition** collections, based on a description that you supply.

- When you define multiple breaklines at the same time, the AutoCAD Civil 3D software creates a single entry under the **Breaklines** collection. However, they are listed separately in the *Prospector* tab's List View.

- Breaklines can be defined as one of four types: **Standard**, **Proximity**, **Wall**, and **Non-Destructive**.

Standard Breaklines

A standard breakline is one that has valid elevations assigned at each vertex.

- Standard breaklines can be defined from 3D lines, 3D polylines, survey figures, or grading feature lines.

- The number of points generated along a breakline can be reduced by specifying a *Weeding* factor or increased by specifying a *Supplementing* factor, similar to weeding and supplementing factors for contour data.

- Curves in standard breaklines are approximated through the use of a mid-ordinate distance, similar to the way curved boundaries are resolved.

- For AutoCAD Land Desktop users, tasks that you might have applied to 3D polylines in AutoCAD Land Desktop should use grading feature lines in the AutoCAD Civil 3D software. This is because grading feature lines are more efficient in many ways, including their support of 3D curves.

- When drafting 3D lines, polylines, or feature lines, you can use AutoCAD Civil 3D's transparent commands. For example, using the **Point Object** (**'PO**) transparent command to select a point as a vertex of a 3D polyline prompts the AutoCAD Civil 3D software to assign the point's elevation to the vertex of the polyline.

- Standard breaklines can also be defined from ASCII breakline data files (.FLT file extension).

Proximity Breaklines

Proximity breaklines do not need to have elevations at their vertices. A polyline at elevation 0 could be used as a proximity breakline. When a proximity breakline is defined, the AutoCAD Civil 3D software automatically assigns vertex elevations from the nearest TIN data point, such as a nearby point object or contour line vertex.

- The AutoCAD Civil 3D software can define proximity breaklines from 2D polylines or grading feature Lines.

- The AutoCAD Civil 3D software does not support curves in proximity breaklines. Arc segments are treated as if they were straight line segments.

- One of the default options in the surface *Build* area enables the conversion of all proximity (2D) breaklines into standard (3D) breaklines. After conversion, the breakline is listed as a standard breakline and has the same elevations as the point objects that are at each vertex.

Wall Breaklines

- A wall breakline can be used to represent both the top and bottom of a wall, curb, or other sheer face.

- Wall breaklines are defined by 3D lines, 3D polylines, or feature lines. When defining them from linework, the object itself is meant to define either the top or bottom of the wall.

- The other end of the wall (top or bottom) is defined interactively by entering the absolute elevations or height differences from the defining line.

- If a Wall breakline starts as a 2D polyline or feature line, it can contain curve segments.

- The number of points generated along a breakline can be reduced by specifying a *Weeding* factor or increased by specifying a *Supplementing* factor.

Survey Figures as Breaklines

Figures created by surveyors can be used as breaklines if a connection exists between the drawing and the survey database.

How To: Add Survey Figures as Breaklines

1. Open the survey database for editing.
2. In the *Survey* tab, expand the **Survey Data** collection and select **Figures**. The list of figures in the grid view is displayed at the bottom of the Toolspace.
3. Select the figures, right-click, and select **Create breaklines...**, as shown in Figure 7–20.

Figure 7–20

4. In the Create Breaklines dialog box, select the surface on which to place the breaklines, and then in the *Breakline* column, select the **Yes** option to create the breaklines, as shown in Figure 7–21. Click **OK** to close the dialog box.

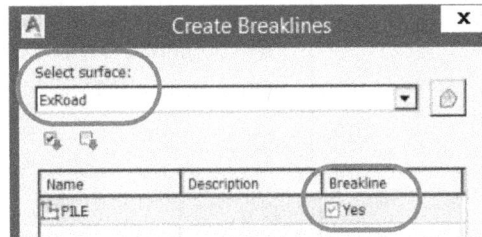

Figure 7–21

Boundaries

Boundaries provide interior or exterior limits to the surface triangulation. Boundaries are typically created from 2D closed polylines. There are four types of boundaries: **Outer**, **Hide**, **Show**, and **Data Clip**. An outer boundary should be one of the last items added to a surface, because adding data outside an existing boundary extends the surface past the boundary.

- An **Outer** boundary hides or excludes data outside its edge.

- A **Hide** boundary hides an interior portion of a surface to delineate features (such as water bodies and building footprints).

- A **Show** boundary displays a portion of a surface within a Hide boundary (e.g., to display an island in a pond).

- A **Data Clip** boundary acts as a filter on all data, including points, DEMs, and breaklines added to the surface after the creation of the Data Clip boundary. If a data clip boundary is used, any data added after it, that falls outside the data clip boundary, is ignored.

A boundary can contain arc segments. To better represent surface elevations around an arc, the AutoCAD Civil 3D software uses a mid-ordinate value to calculate where the triangles interact with the boundary. The mid-ordinate value is the distance between the midpoint of the cord and the arc. The smaller the mid-ordinate value, the closer the surface data is to the original arc. An example is shown in Figure 7–22.

Figure 7–22

A boundary can limit a surface to the data in it. When you want to extend the triangulation exactly to a boundary line, select the **Non-destructive breakline** option in the Create Boundary dialog box. A non-destructive breakline fractures triangles at their intersection with the boundary. The resulting triangles preserve the original elevations of the surface at the boundary intersection as close as possible.

The example in Figure 7–23 shows the following:

1. The surface with a polyline is used as an outer boundary.
2. The boundary is applied without the **Non-destructive breakline** option. This is typically used when the boundary polyline is approximate and not meant to represent a hard edge.
3. The boundary is applied with the **Non-destructive breakline** option. Non-destructive breaklines are often used to create a specific termination limit for the surface (such as at a parcel boundary).

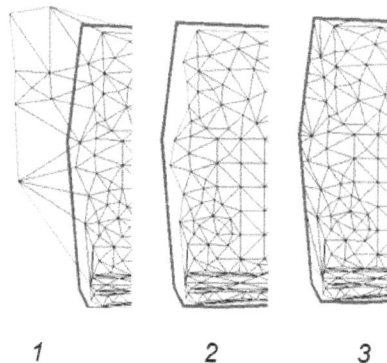

Figure 7–23

Practice 7b

Add Additional Data to an Existing Ground Surface

Practice Objective

- Improve the accuracy of a surface by adding various breaklines, such as standard breaklines, wall breaklines, and breaklines from survey figures.

Estimated time for completion: 20 minutes

Task 1 - Add surface breaklines.

TIN lines are generally created using the shortest distance between points. To further define a surface, you might need to supplement it with breaklines of ridges, ditches, walls, etc., that accurately define the surface. These breaklines prevent the software from triangulating directly between points that are bisected by a breakline. The breakline becomes part of the triangulation between the two adjacent points.

1. Continue working with the drawing from the previous practice or open **SUF1-B1-Surface.dwg** from the *C:\Civil 3D for Surveyors Practice Files\Surface* folder.

2. Select any part of the **GIS Data** surface in Model Space.

The contextual tab displays.

3. In the contextual *Surface* tab>Modify panel, select Surface Properties, as shown in Figure 7–24. The Surface Properties dialog box opens.

Figure 7–24

4. In the *Information* tab, expand the Surface style drop-down list and select **Contours and Triangles**, as shown in Figure 7–25. Click **OK** to close the dialog box.

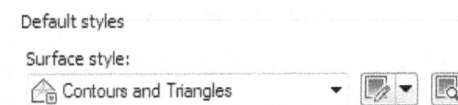

Default styles

Surface style:

Contours and Triangles

Figure 7–25

Now that the triangulations are displayed, you will examine how adding a feature line impacts the surface.

5. In the *View* tab>Views panel, expand the drop-down list and select **Surf-Breakline**. This zooms into the breakline that is located north of the existing road as shown in Figure 7–26. If you do not see the red 3D polyline, turn on the **A-BREAKLINE** layer.

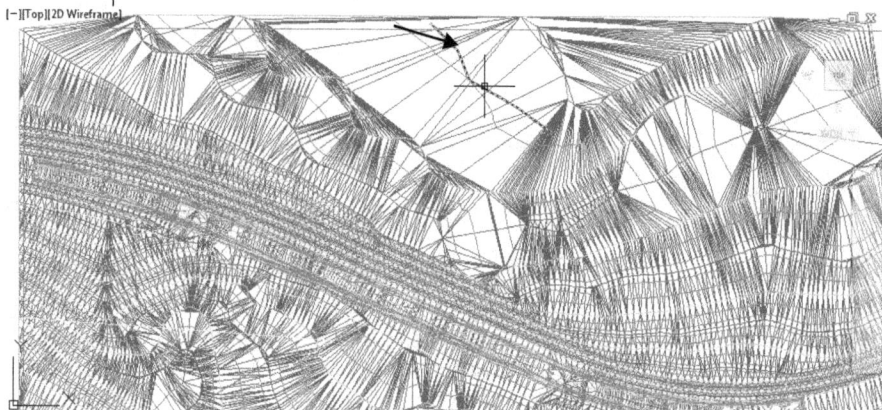

Figure 7–26

The triangulation crosses the breakline.

6. Expand the **Current Drawing** collection in the *Prospector* tab and then expand the **Surfaces>GIS Data>Definition** collections. Select **Breaklines**, right-click, and select **Add**, as shown in Figure 7–27.

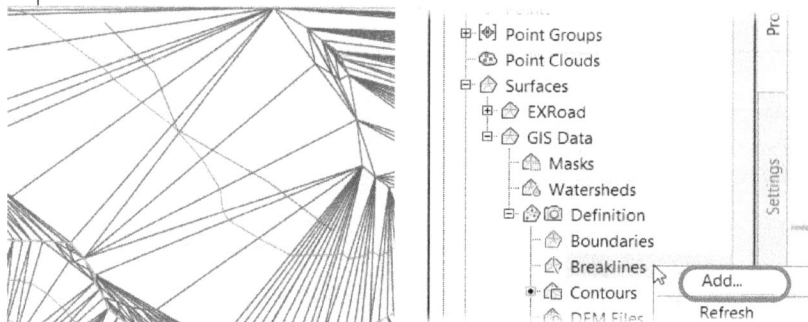

Figure 7–27

7. Set the *Description* to **Ridge**, as shown in Figure 7–28. Accept all of the defaults and click **OK** to close the dialog box.

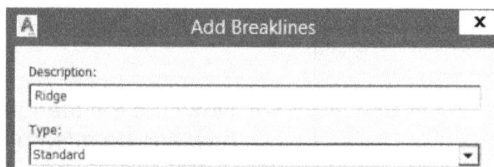

Figure 7–28

8. When prompted to select objects, select the red 3D polyline and press <Enter> to complete the command.

9. The surface should rebuild automatically. Note that the triangulation now takes the breakline into consideration, as shown in Figure 7–29.

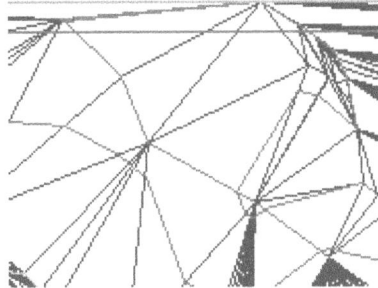

*If the **GIS Data** surface is marked as out-of-date*

*, select the **GIS Data** surface, right-click, and select **Rebuild Automatic**.*

Figure 7–29

10. Save the drawing.

Task 2 - Set up the survey database.

In this practice you will need to incorporate survey data into the surface. To do so, you must first establish a connection to the survey database. If you have not completed the practices in the Survey section you will need to open the survey database **Survey1 Data_Complete** to open the connection.

1. Continue working with the drawing from the previous task or open **SUF1-B2-Surface.dwg** from the *C:\Civil 3D for Surveyors Practice Files\Surface* folder.

If the Survey tab in the Toolspace is not enabled, click in the Home tab>Palettes panel to toggle it on.

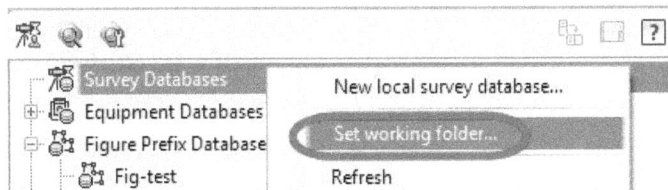

2. In the *Survey* tab>Toolspace, right-click on **Survey Databases** and select **Set working folder**, as shown in Figure 7–30.

Figure 7–30

3. Select the **Survey Databases** folder in the *C:\Civil 3D for Surveyors Practice Files\Survey* folder, as shown in Figure 7–31.

Figure 7–31

4. Select the survey database **Survey1 Data_Complete**, right-click, and select **Open for edit**, as shown in Figure 7–32.

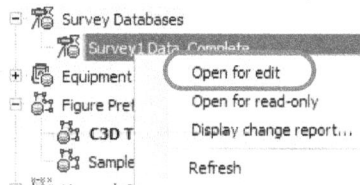

Figure 7–32

Task 3 - Add field book figures as breaklines.

In the task, you will add breaklines to the surface from figures that were created when the field books were imported.

1. Continue working with the drawing from the previous task or open **SUF1-B3-Surface.dwg** from the *C:\Civil 3D for Surveyors Practice Files\Surface* folder.

2. Open the survey database **Survey1 Data_Complete,** if it is not already open.

3. In the *Survey* tab, expand the **Survey Data** collection and select **Figures**. The list of figures in the grid view is displayed at the bottom of the Toolspace.

4. Select the figure **Rock**, right-click, and select **Create breaklines...**, as shown in Figure 7–33.

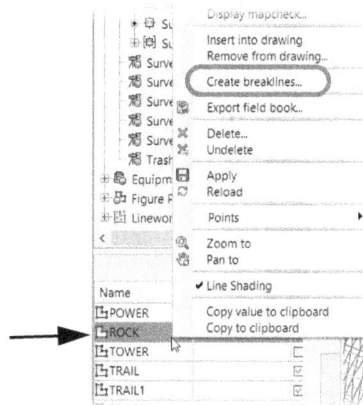

Figure 7–33

5. In the Create Breaklines dialog box, select **GIS Data** for the surface, and select the **Yes** option in the *Breakline* column to create breaklines, as shown in Figure 7–34. Click **OK** to close the dialog box.

6. The AutoCAD Civil 3D software will zoom in to the location of the breakline, and open the Add Breaklines dialog box. Type **Rock pile from site survey** in the *Description* field, and ensure that **Standard** is selected in the Type drop-down list, as shown in Figure 7–35. Click **OK** to close the dialog box.

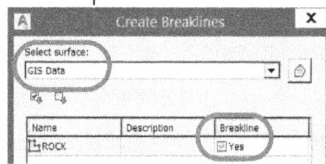

Figure 7–34

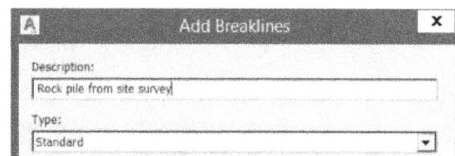

Figure 7–35

The Event Viewer vista in the Panorama opens. You have received a number of errors with crossing breaklines. You can Zoom to the error by selecting **Zoom to** in the far right column. For now you need to clear these errors from the event log file.

7. Click **Action** in the Panorama and select **Clear All Events**, as shown in Figure 7–36.

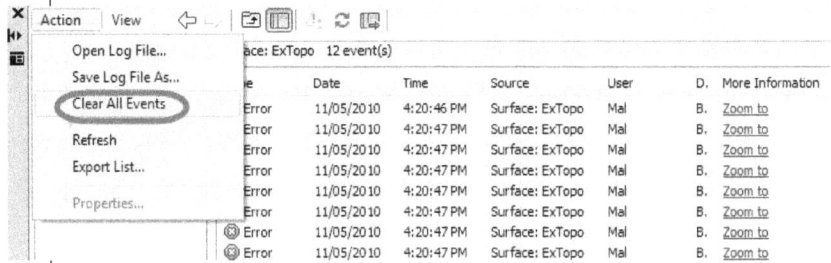

Figure 7–36

8. Close the Panorama by clicking ☑ (checkmark) in the dialog box.

9. In Model Space, select the **GIS Data** surface. The *Tin Surface: GIS Data* contextual tab displays. In the Modify panel, select **Surface Properties** as shown in Figure 7–37.

Figure 7–37

10. The Surface Properties - GIS Data dialog box opens. In the *Definition* tab, expand the **Build** collection and set the value of *Allow crossing breaklines* to **Yes**. Set the value for the *Elevation to use* field to **Use last breakline elevation at intersection**, as shown in Figure 7–38. When you have finished, click **OK**.

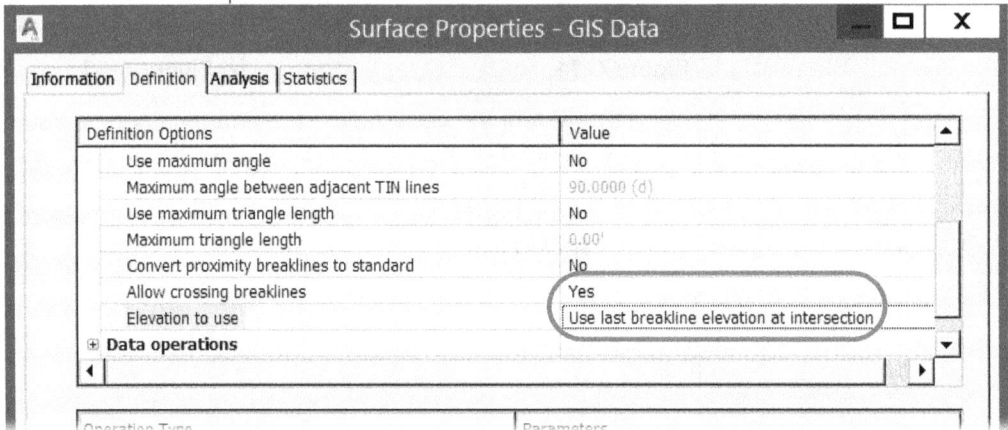

Figure 7–38

11. When prompted to *Rebuild the surface* or *Mark as out of Date*, select **Rebuild the surface**. When you review the surface contours, note that the surface has used the figure as a breakline.

12. Save the drawing.

Task 4 - Add a Wall Breakline.

In the task, you will add a wall breakline to the surface from figures that were created when the field books were imported.

1. Continue working with the drawing from the previous task or open **SUF1-B4-Surface.dwg** from the *C:\Civil 3D for Surveyors Practice Files\Surface* folder.

2. Open the survey database **Survey1 Data_Complete**, if it is not already open.

3. In the *Survey* tab, expand the survey data collection and select **Figures**. Note the list of figures in the grid view at the bottom of the Toolspace.

4. Select the **Wall** figure, right-click, and select **Create breaklines**.

5. In the Create Breaklines dialog box, select the **GIS Data** surface and select the **Yes** option in the *Breakline* column to create breaklines. Click **OK** to close the dialog box.

6. The AutoCAD Civil 3D software zooms in to the location of the breakline, and opens the Add Breaklines dialog box. Type **Rock wall from site survey** in the *Description* field, and ensure that **Wall** is selected in the Type drop-down list, as shown in Figure 7–39. Click **OK** to close the dialog box.

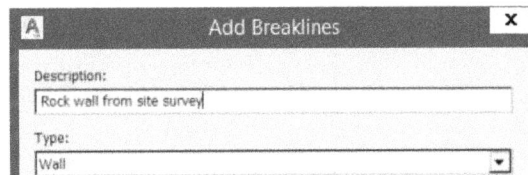

Figure 7–39

7. At the prompt to pick the offset side, select a point to the south of the wall break line, as shown in Figure 7–40.

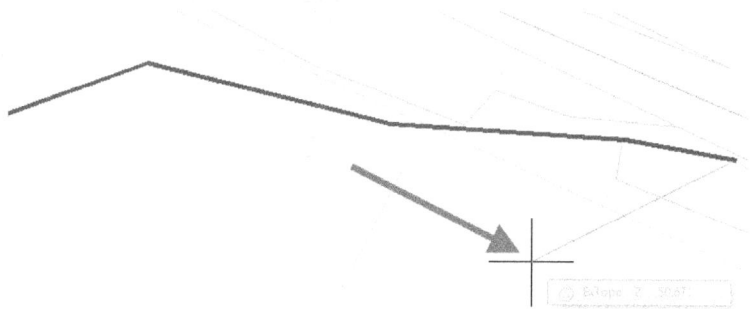

Figure 7–40

8. When prompted to select the option for the wall height, select the default **All** option because the wall has a constant height.

9. When prompted for the elevation difference or elevation, type **0.5** and press <Enter>.

10. Save the drawing.

The wall has a constant height of 1.5' from the base.

7.5 Surface Editing

There are three ways of adjusting surfaces graphically: using lines, points, and area edit tools (such as **Minimize Flat Areas** and **Smooth Surface**). All of these tools are available by right-clicking on the *Edits* heading in a surface's *Definition* area (*Prospector*), as shown in Figure 7–41.

- The AutoCAD Civil 3D software considers each graphical surface edit to be additional data that can be removed later.

- Most surface edits apply immediately. If the drawing item modifier icon displays (as shown in Figure 7–42), then an edit has rendered the surface out of date. When this happens, a surface should be rebuilt by right-clicking on the surface name in the *Prospector* tab and selecting **Rebuild**.

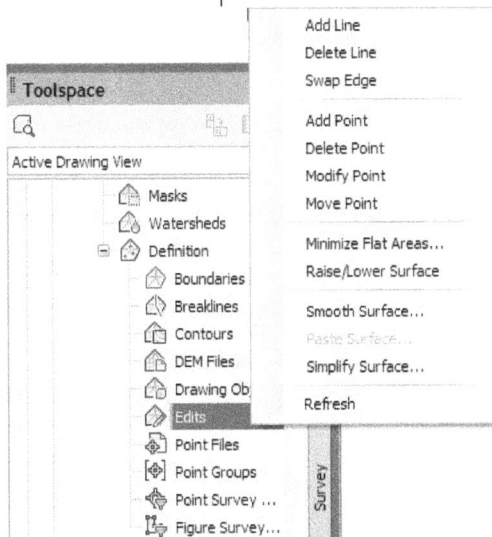

Figure 7–41

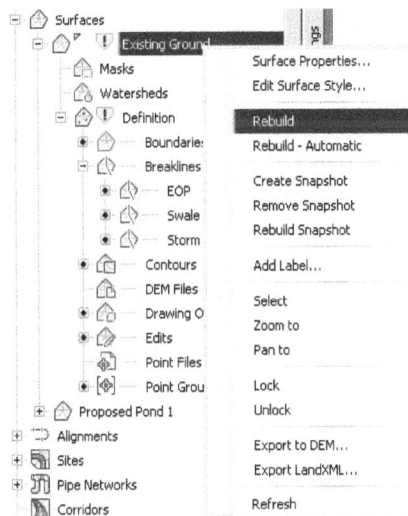

Figure 7–42

- To have a surface automatically rebuild as required, right-click on the surface name in the *Prospector* tab and select **Rebuild-Automatic**. However, toggling this option on increases the use of computer resources and graphics capabilities, so it is recommended that you leave it toggled off.

- To delete an edit from a surface permanently, remove it from the *Edits* list in *Prospector's* preview area or from the *Operations Type* list in the *Definition* tab in the Surface Properties dialog box.

Line Edits

The line editing commands include **Add Line**, **Delete Line**, and **Swap Edge**. The **Add Line** and **Delete Line** commands add or remove triangle lines. The **Delete Line** command is often only applied around the outside edge of a surface to remove unwanted edge triangulation. Deleting lines in the interior of a surface causes both of the triangles next to the removed line to be deleted, leaving a hole in the surface that needs to be repaired by adding another line.

If you are considering deleting a line only to replace it with the opposite diagonal, such as the central line shown in Figure 7–43, using the **Swap Edge** command instead might be more efficient.

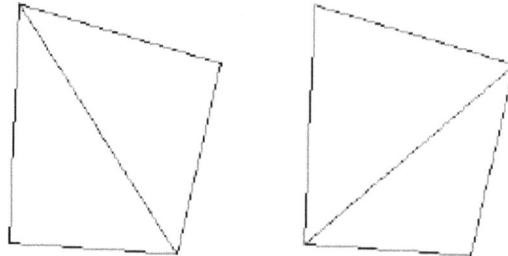

Figure 7–43

Adding an interior line that crosses many existing triangles swaps them where possible to adhere to the geometry represented by the added line. This method can be a good way of swapping multiple edges at the same time.

Point Edits

The Point editing commands can **Add**, **Delete**, **Modify**, or **Move** surface points. They do not affect point objects in the drawing, but rather the surface points created from them. Surface points can be adjusted or deleted as required.

When an AutoCAD Civil 3D point object is adjusted (e.g., moved), the surface containing that point data might not be identified as being out of date nor update automatically. In this situation, you should rebuild the surface.

Simplify Surface

As the collection methods of surface data continue to evolve, yielding significantly larger data sets, the drawing file size increases in proportion to the surface data contained in the drawing. The AutoCAD Civil 3D software has a limit of 2.5 million vertices for a surface. Once it exceeds this limit, the software prompts you to store surface data to an external file with an .MMS extension. The resulting external surface files can be quite large. To avoid this, you can simplify your surface using the Simplify Surface wizard. Extra points can be removed from a surface without compromising its accuracy. Points that you might want to remove include points that are in an external point file or database, or redundant points in areas of high data concentration where the value of this extra information is minimal. There are two simplification methods available.

- **Edge Contraction:** This method simplifies the surface by using existing triangle edges. It contracts triangle edges to single points by removing one point. The location of the point to which an edge is contracted is selected so that the change to the surface is minimal.

- **Point Removal:** This method simplifies the surface by removing existing surface points. More points are removed from denser areas of the surface.

When you simplify a surface, you specify which regions of the surface the operation should address. The region options include using the existing surface border, or specifying a window or polygon. The **Pick in Drawing** icon enables you to select the region from the drawing. If a closed line exists in the drawing that you want to use as the region boundary, you can select the **Select objects** option and then use the **Pick in Drawing** icon to select the boundary. Curves in the boundary are approximated by line segments. The line segment generation is governed by a *Mid Ordinate Distance* value that you determine.

Once you have selected the region, the dialog box displays the *Total Points Selected In Region* value. You can refine the surface reduction options by setting a percentage of points to remove, the maximum change in elevation, or the maximum edge contraction error.

Smooth Contours

Although not a true surface edit, AutoCAD Civil 3D surface contours can be smoothed to reduce their jagged appearance using the Surface Object Style settings. There are two approaches to this: the *Add Vertices* method and the *Spline Curve* method. The *Add Vertices* method enables you to select a relative smoothness from the slider bar at the bottom of the Surface Style dialog box, as shown in Figure 7–44.

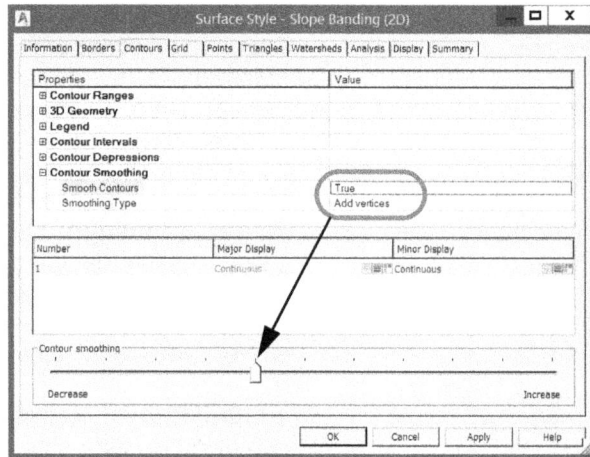

Figure 7–44

The *Spline Curve* method generates very smooth contours, but the contours are more liberally interpolated and might overlap where surface points are close together. This approach is best applied to surfaces with relatively few data points or in areas of low relief, as shown in Figure 7–45.

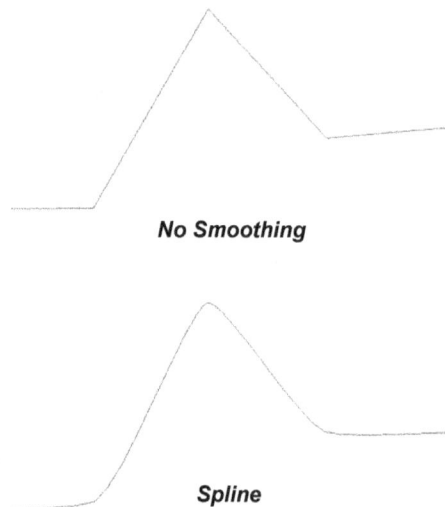

No Smoothing

Spline

Figure 7–45

Smooth Surface

The Smooth Surface edit introduces new, interpolated elevations between surface data. It is used to create a more realistic-looking terrain model, though not necessarily a more accurate one. Generally, surface smoothing works best with point-based surface data.

The AutoCAD Civil 3D software has two smoothing methods: *Natural Neighbor* and *Kriging*.

- *Natural Neighbor* interpolates a grid of additional data points that produce a smoother overall terrain model.

- *Kriging* reads surface trends to add additional data in sparse areas.

Surface smoothing is applied by right-clicking on the **Edits** collection under a surface's *Definition* and selecting **Smooth Surface**. The Smooth Surface dialog box and example of surface smoothing are shown in Figure 7–46.

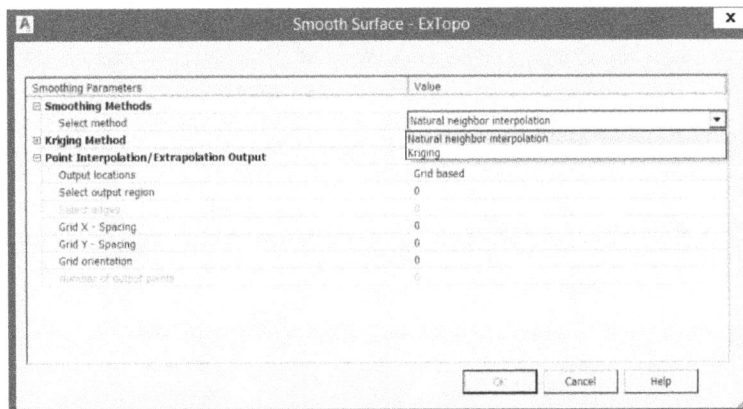

Figure 7–46

Copy Surface

The AutoCAD Civil 3D software does not have a copy surface command, but surface objects can be copied using the AutoCAD **Copy** command (**Modify>Copy**). When copying surface objects, select the same base and then a second point to ensure that the surface is not moved during the copy. After a copy, a duplicate surface is created and is displayed in the *Prospector* tab. The copy has the same name as the original followed with a number in parenthesis, such as (1). These copied surfaces can be renamed as required. Surface copies are independent of each other and can be edited.

Surface Paste

The **Surface Paste** command enables the AutoCAD Civil 3D software to combine multiple surfaces into a single surface. You might want to paste into a copy of a surface if you want to keep the original unmodified. For example, a finished condition surface is required that includes a proposed surface (*Proposed*) along with the existing ground (EG) around its periphery. In this situation, you would first create a new surface and name it **Finished Ground**. In the **Surfaces** collection in the *Prospector* tab, right-click on the Finished Ground surface's **Edit** collection and select **Paste** to merge in the **Existing ground (EG)** and **Proposed** surfaces.

Once the command has executed, the surface's **EG** and **Proposed** surfaces are left unchanged, and the **Finished Ground** surface represents a combination of the two. If you did not create the **Finished Ground** surface, but pasted the **Proposed** surface into the **EG** surface, you would not have the original **EG** surface for reference in profiles and other places. If surfaces are pasted in the wrong order, the order can be rearranged using the *Definition* tab in the Surface Properties dialog box.

Surfaces remain dynamically linked after pasting. Therefore, if the **Proposed** surface changes, the **Finished Ground** surface updates to display the change.

Raise/Lower Surface

The **Raise/Lower Surface** command adds or subtracts a specified elevation value. This adjustment is applied to the entire surface. It is useful for modeling soil removal and changing a surface's datum elevation.

Adjusting Surfaces Through Surface Properties

In addition to the graphical edit methods, you can adjust surfaces by changing their surface properties. Surface property adjustments include setting a *Maximum triangle length* or *Exclude elevations* greater or less than certain values. You can also enable or disable the effects of certain surface data (such as breaklines and boundaries) by disabling them in the dialog box.

To locate these options (as shown in Figure 7–47), right-click on a surface in the *Prospector* tab and select **Surface Properties**.

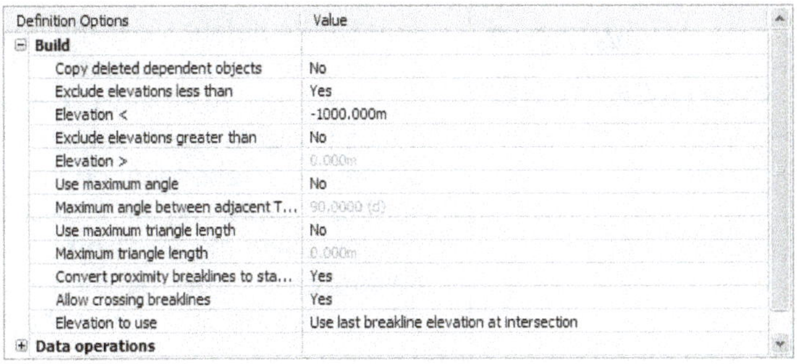

Definition Options	Value
⊟ **Build**	
Copy deleted dependent objects	No
Exclude elevations less than	Yes
Elevation <	-1000.000m
Exclude elevations greater than	No
Elevation >	0.000m
Use maximum angle	No
Maximum angle between adjacent T...	90.0000 (d)
Use maximum triangle length	No
Maximum triangle length	0.000m
Convert proximity breaklines to sta...	Yes
Allow crossing breaklines	Yes
Elevation to use	Use last breakline elevation at intersection
⊞ **Data operations**	

Figure 7–47

Hint: Surfaces from GIS Data

If you have created a surface from GIS data, the surface is dependent on the GIS contours for its definition. However, the contours exist in an external file. Therefore, when you change the surface properties to fix a problem with the contours, the contours are not effected. In cases such as this one, you need to physically edit the surface using surface edit commands instead.

7.6 Surface Analysis Tools

Viewing a Surface in 3D

AutoCAD's default view, the overhead or plan view, is not the only way to view a surface. The AutoCAD **3D Orbit** command and the AutoCAD Civil 3D **Object Viewer** tilt the coordinate space to display a 3D surface model. How the surface is displayed is dependent on the assigned style. You can view a surface in 3D using the Object Viewer or directly in the drawing window using the **3D Orbit** command. Both have similar navigation controls, but the Object Viewer enables you to review your surface in 3D without changing your current view.

Both methods can display a wireframe (3D Wireframe and 3D Hidden), conceptual, or realistic view. By default, a Conceptual display is a cartoon-like rendering without edge lines, while a Realistic display has material styles with edge lines. Both viewing methods use the AutoCAD ViewCube, which uses labels and a compass to indicate the direction from which you are viewing a model.

The Object Viewer method is shown in Figure 7–48.

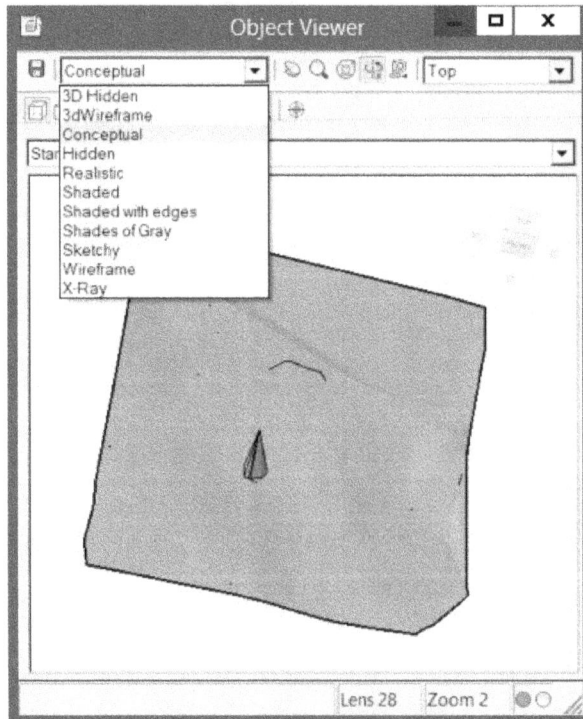

Figure 7–48

Quick Profile

Understanding the affect of breaklines and other data on a surface is critical to generating an accurate surface. The **Analyze>Ground Data>Quick Profile** command enables you to produce an instant surface profile with minimal effort.

A *Quick Profile* is a temporary object, which disappears from the drawing when you save or exit. If you need a more permanent graphic, you should create an alignment and profile.

Quick Profiles can be created along lines, arcs, polylines, lot lines, feature lines, or survey figures, or by selecting points. In addition to the command being located in the *Analyze* tab, you can select one of the previously mentioned objects, right-click, and select **Quick Profile**. Two examples of the Quick Profile are shown in Figure 7–49.

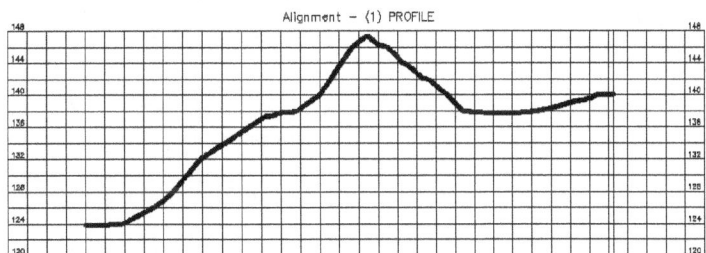

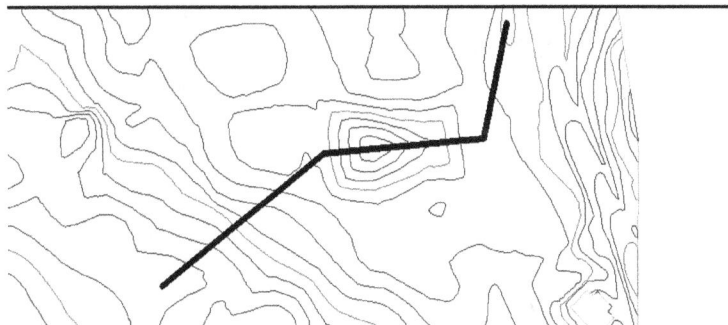

Figure 7–49

Practice 7c

Surface Edits

Practice Objective

- Edit a surface using definition options in the surface properties and commands found in the Toolspace.

Estimated time for completion: 30 minutes

In this practice you will refine a previously created surface. The **GIS Data** surface has some triangulations that are not valid. You will eliminate these TIN lines using three methods: you will set the maximum triangle edge length, delete TIN lines (triangle edges), and add a boundary to the surface. Each of these methods has advantages and disadvantages and should be used appropriately.

Task 1 - Set the maximum triangle length.

*Ensure that the **GIS Data** surface is using the **Contours and Triangles** surface style.*

1. Continue working with the drawing from the previous practice or open **SUF1-C1-Surface.dwg** from the *C:\Civil 3D for Surveyors Practice Files\Surface* folder.

2. Select the preset view **Surf-Edit**, as shown in Figure 7–50.

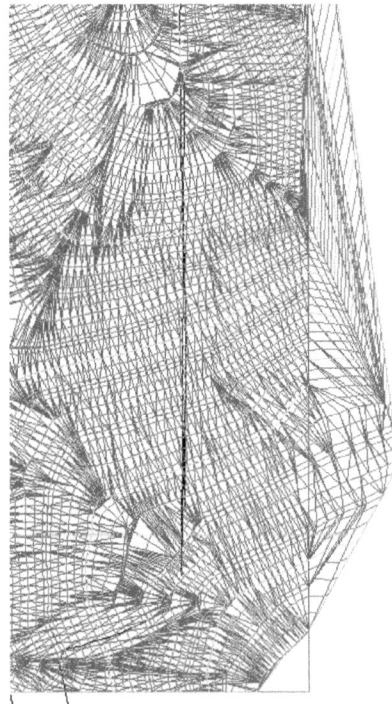

Figure 7–50

3. In Model Space, select the **GIS Data** surface. The *Tin Surface GIS Data* contextual tab will display. In the *Modify* panel, select **Surface Properties**, as shown in Figure 7–51.

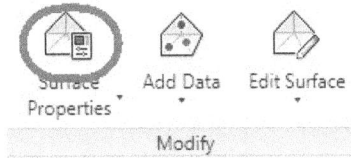

Figure 7–51

4. The Surface Properties dialog box opens. Select the *Definition* tab and expand the **Build** options in the *Definition Options* area.

Although there are invalid triangle lengths that are less than that length in this area, entering a smaller number might remove some valid triangles in the site.

5. Set the *Use maximum triangle length* value to **Yes** and the *Maximum triangle length* value to **100m**, as shown in Figure 7–52. Click **OK** to close the dialog box and accept the changes.

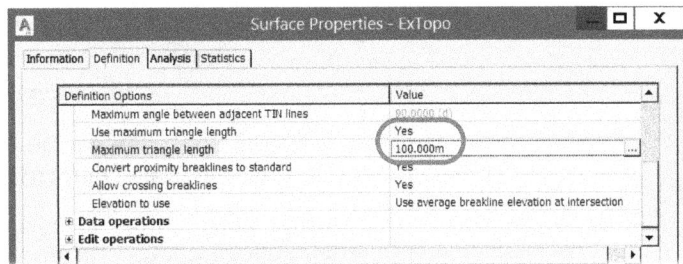

Figure 7–52

All triangles that have edge lengths greater than 330' are removed from the surface.

6. When prompted to *Rebuild the surface* or *Mark the surface as out-of-date*, select **Rebuild the surface**.

7. Save the drawing.

Task 2 - Delete lines.

Although you have eliminated triangle edge lengths greater than 100m, you still have some triangles that you will remove using a scalpel (i.e., deleting selected lines).

1. Continue working with the drawing from the previous task or open **SUF1-C2-Surface.dwg** from the *C:\Civil 3D for Surveyors Practice Files\Surface* folder.

*If you are not still in the drawing view from the previous task, select the View tab>Views panel, and select the preset view **Surface-Edit**.*

Figure 7–53 shows the lines that you will be deleting.

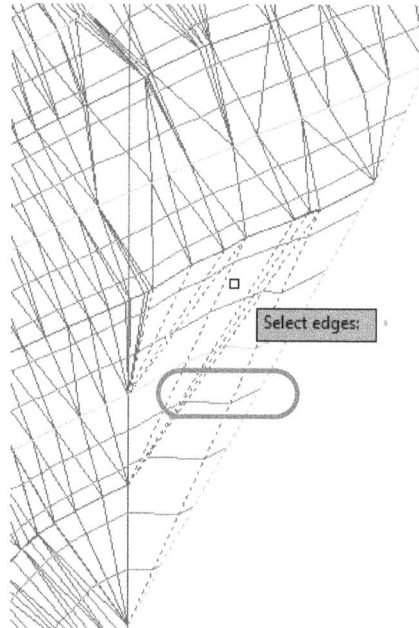

Figure 7–53

2. In Model Space, select the **GIS Data** surface. The *Tin Surface GIS Data* contextual tab will display. In the *Modify*

   panel, expand the ◇ (Edit Surface) drop-down list, and select **Delete Line**, as shown in Figure 7–54.

Figure 7–54

3. Select each of the required TIN lines in Model Space, as shown in Figure 7–55. When you have finished, press <Enter> to end the selection and press <Enter> to end the command.

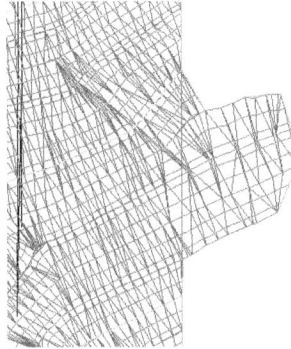

Figure 7–55

4. Save the drawing.

Task 3 - Add a boundary.

The **Delete Line** command can be effective, but might not efficiently clean up the edges of large surfaces. A surface boundary might be useful if you have a well-defined boundary.

1. Continue working with the drawing from the previous task or open **SUF1-C3-Surface.dwg** from the *C:\Civil 3D for Surveyors Practice Files\Surface* folder.

2. If you are not still in the drawing view from the previous task, select the *View* tab>Views panel and select the preset view **Surface-Edit**.

3. In Model Space, select the **GIS Data** surface. The *Tin Surface GIS Data* contextual tab will display. In the *Modify* panel, click ⬠ (Add Data), expand the drop-down list and select **Boundaries**, as shown in Figure 7–56.

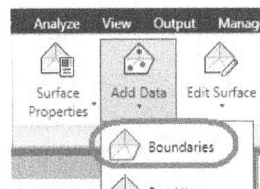

Figure 7–56

4. The Add Boundaries dialog box opens, as shown in Figure 7–57. Type **EG Outside** in the *Name* field, and select **Outer** in the Type drop-down list. Do not select the **Non-destructive breakline** option, because you do not want to trim to this polyline shape. Instead, the dialog box options selected will erase all of the triangle lines that cross or are beyond the boundary. Click **OK** to accept the changes and close the dialog box.

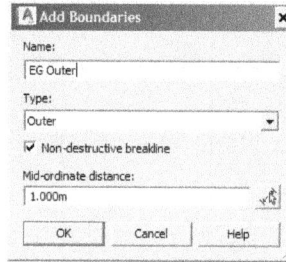

Figure 7–57

You might have to regen the screen to display the boundary.

If the red polyline does not display in the view, turn on the ***A-SITE-BOUNDARY*** *layer.*

5. When prompted to select an object, select the red polyline that represents the boundary, as shown in Figure 7–58.

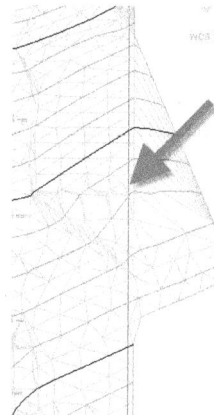

Figure 7–58

6. Examine how this boundary affected the surface. The boundary excluded all data that crossed or fell beyond it. This boundary is a dynamic part of the **GIS Data** surface.

7. (Optional) Select the boundary line and move the grips. Note how the surface expands or contracts to match the change in the boundary. Undo the changes.

8. Save the drawing.

Task 4 - Set the elevation range.

In reviewing the drawing, you need to address an error in the site. The original topographical contour file contains an invalid piece of data that has transferred to the surface.

1. Continue working with the drawing from the previous task or open **SUF1-C4-Surface.dwg** from the *C:\Civil 3D for Surveyors Practice Files\Surface* folder.

2. Select the preset view **Surf Elev Edit**.

3. In Model Space shown in Figure 7–59, select the **GIS Data** surface, right-click, and select **Object Viewer**.

4. In the Object Viewer, click and drag the view to rotate the 3D view to identify the issue, as shown in Figure 7–60.

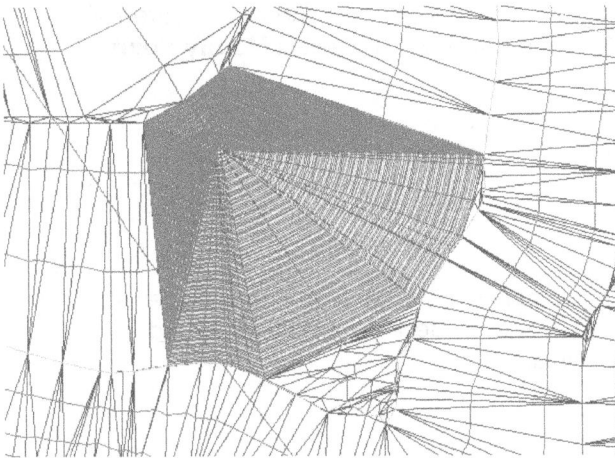

Figure 7–59

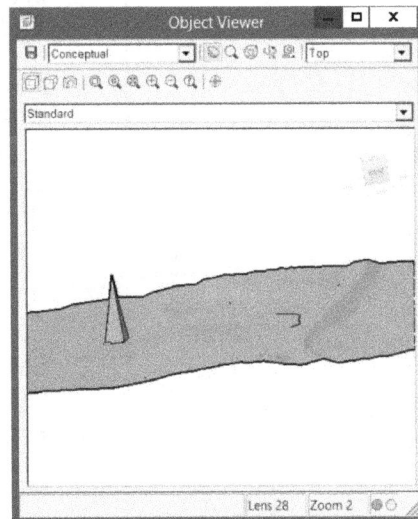

Figure 7–60

5. Close the Object Viewer by selecting **X** in the top right corner of the dialog box.

6. In Model Space, select the **GIS Data** surface. Right-click and select **Edit Surface Style**.

7. In the Surface Style dialog box, on the *Display* tab, click
   (Visible On) next to **Points** to toggle the surface points on,
   as shown in Figure 7–61. Click **OK.**

Figure 7–61

8. In the model, select the **GIS Data** surface again. The *Tin
   Surface GIS Data* contextual tab will display. In the Modify

   panel, click (Edit Surface), as shown in Figure 7–62.
   Expand the drop-down list, and select **Modify Point**.

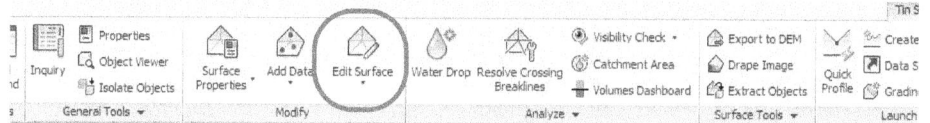

Figure 7–62

9. Select the two points at the center of the spike, as shown in
   Figure 7–63. Press <Enter> to indicate you are done
   selecting points.

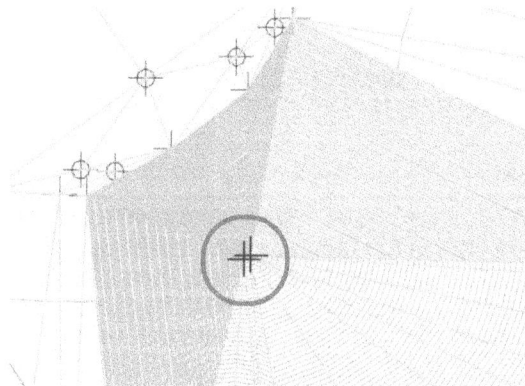

Figure 7–63

10. At the command line, type **60** and press <Enter> for the new elevation for the points.

11. Press <Esc> to end the command.

12. Save the drawing.

Task 5 - Review edits in the *Prospector* tab and the Surface Properties dialog box.

The history of all of the changes made to a surface is saved in the drawing. You can apply and remove these changes selectively to the surface.

1. Continue working with the drawing from the previous task or open **SUF1-C5-Surface.dwg** from the *C:\Civil 3D for Surveyors Practice Files\Surface* folder.

2. Select the preset view **Surface-Edit**.

3. In the *Prospector* tab, expand the **Surfaces** collection and select the **GIS Data** surface. Right-click and select **Surface Properties**. In the Surface Properties dialog box, clear the **Add boundary** *Operation Type* (as shown in Figure 7–64), and click **Apply**.

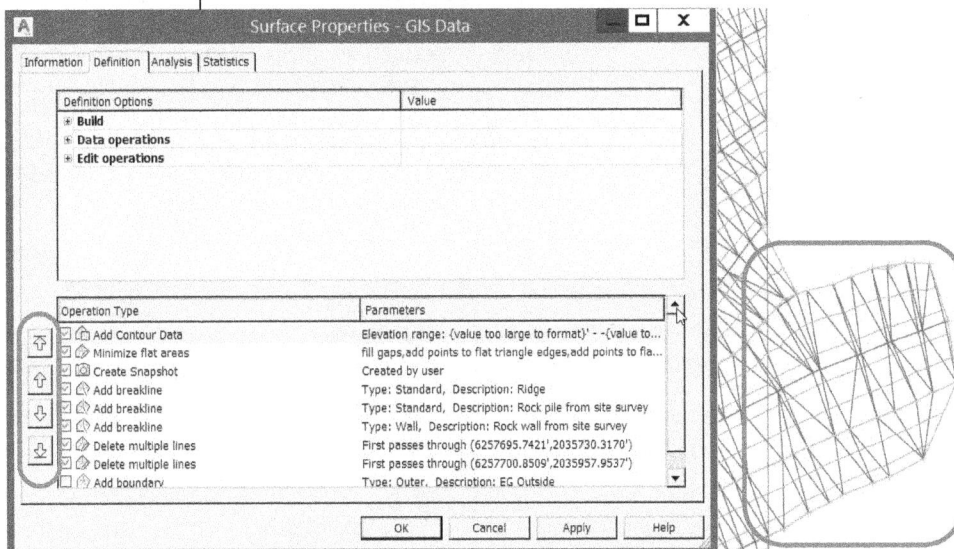

Figure 7–64

4. When prompted, select **Rebuild the Surface** in the Warning dialog box that opens. The boundary is ignored.

The boundary is once again used in the surface definition.

5. Select the **Add boundary** *Operation Type* again and click **Apply**. When prompted, select **Rebuild the Surface** in the Warning dialog box that opens.

6. Save the drawing.

Task 6 - Create a composite surface.

In the preceding tasks, you created a surface from available contour data. However, the data around the existing road, **Mission Avenue** (the road running east to west at the top of the site), was inaccurate, so you surveyed the road and created a surface. You need to create a composite surface that represents the site condition combined with the road.

1. Continue working with the drawing from the previous task or open **SUF1-C6-Surface.dwg** from the *C:\Civil 3D for Surveyors Practice Files\Surface* folder.

2. Select the preset view **Survey Main**.

3. In the *Prospector* tab, right-click on the **Surfaces** collection and select **Create Surface**.

4. Select **TIN surface** for the surface *Type*. Type **Existing-Site** for the surface name and **Composite surface of GIS Data and ExRoad** for the *Description*. Select **Contours 2m and 10m (Background)** for the surface *Style*. Click **OK** to close the dialog box and create a surface.

5. In the *Prospector* tab of the Toolspace, select the Surfaces category. In the preview list area, select the **ExRoad** and **GIS Data** surfaces. Right-click on the *Style* column heading and select **Edit**, as shown in Figure 7–65.

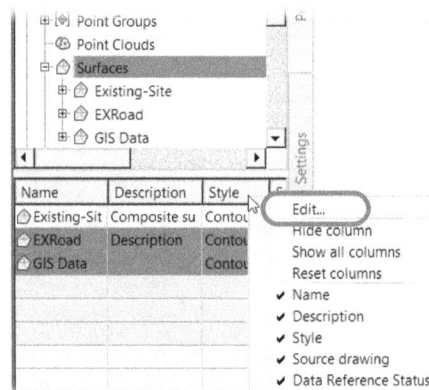

Figure 7–65

6. Set the surface style to **_No Display** and click **OK** to accept the changes and close the dialog box.

7. In the *Prospector* tab, expand the **Surfaces>Existing-Site> Definition** collections for that surface and select **Edits**. Right-click and select **Paste Surface...**, as shown in Figure 7–66.

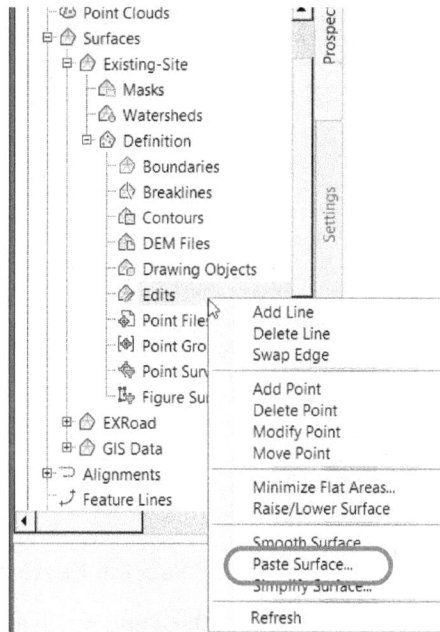

Figure 7–66

To select both surfaces, hold <Ctrl> when selecting the second surface.

8. In the Select Surface to Paste dialog box, select the **GIS Data** and **Ex Road** surfaces, as shown in Figure 7–67. Once selected, click **OK** to close the dialog box.

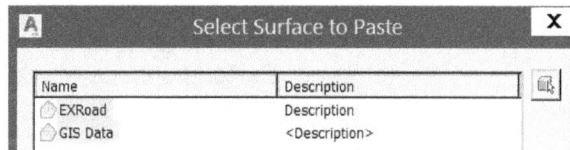

Figure 7–67

Note that the **ExRoad** surface was pasted first, followed by the **GIS Data** surface. In the area of overlap along the road, the **GIS Data** surface data will take precedence. This is not the required result.

9. In Model Space, select the **Existing-Site** surface from the surfaces listed in the **Surfaces** collection in the *Prospector* tab. The contextual tab for the surface object will display. Select **Surface Properties** in the ribbon panel. The Surface Properties - Existing Site dialog box opens. In the *Definition* tab, note the order of the paste operations, as shown in Figure 7–68.

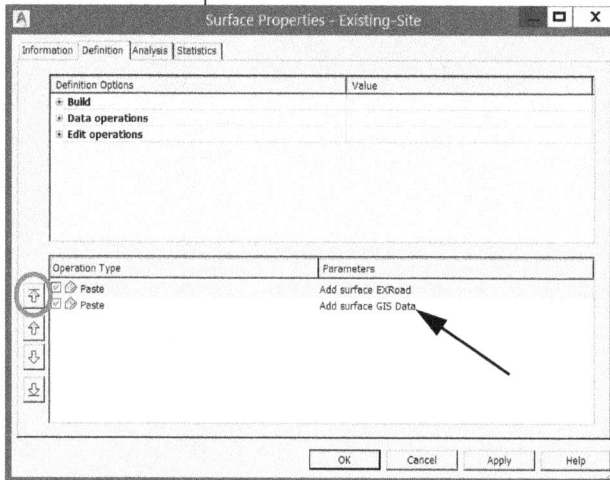

Figure 7–68

10. Select the **Paste** operation with the value **Add surface GIS Data** and move it to the top of the list by clicking ⬆.

11. Click **Apply**. When prompted to *Rebuild the surface* or *Mark the surface as out-of-date*, select **Rebuild the Surface**.

12. Click **OK** to exit the dialog box.

    As a consequence of the AutoCAD Civil 3D software's dynamic abilities, any changes to either the **GIS Data** or **ExRoad** surface will be reflected in the **Existing-Site** surface.

13. Save the drawing.

7.7 Surface Labels

Surface labels can be used to label contour elevations, slope values, spot elevations, and watershed delineations. Label values update if the surface changes.

To create surface labels, in the *Annotate* tab>Labels & Tables panel, expand Add Labels and select **Surface** to access the surface label flyout menu, as shown in Figure 7–69.

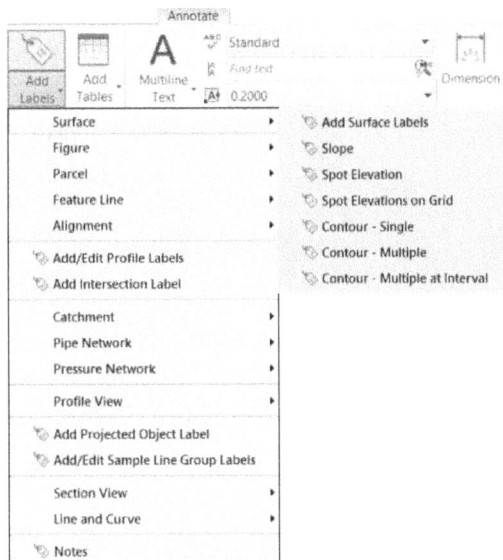

Figure 7–69

You can also click ✎ (Add Labels) to open the Add Labels dialog box, as shown in Figure 7–70. This dialog box enables you to select the feature and label type while being able to control the label style on the fly.

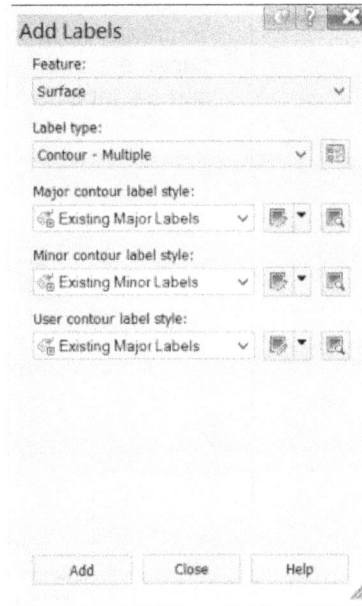

Figure 7–70

Contour Labels

Contour labels can be created individually, as multiples along a linear path, or as multiples along a linear path with repeated labels at a set interval. Multiple contours are aligned along an object called a *Contour Label Line*, which can be repositioned as required, and in turn updates the position of its labels. These label lines have a selectable property that can make them visible only when an attached label is selected. If they are left visible, they should be placed on a non-plotting layer.

Spot and Slope Labels

Spot elevation and slope labels can be created as required to annotate a surface. These are dynamic surface labels and not point objects, although they might look similar to points. Slopes can be measured at a single point or averaged between two points.

7.8 Surface Volume Calculations

You can generate volume calculations in the AutoCAD Civil 3D software in many ways. Surface-to-surface calculations are often used to compare an existing ground surface to a proposed surface to determine cut and fill quantities. In the AutoCAD Civil 3D software, quantities can be adjusted by an expansion (cut) or a compaction (fill) factor. Surfaces representing different soil strata can be compared to each other to determine the volume between the soil layers. There are multiple ways of comparing surfaces to each other in the AutoCAD Civil 3D software.

Volumes Dashboard

In the *Analyze* tab>Volumes and Materials panel, click

 (Volumes Dashboard). The Volumes Dashboard creates a volume surface based on a graphical subtraction of one surface from the other, as shown in Figure 7–71.

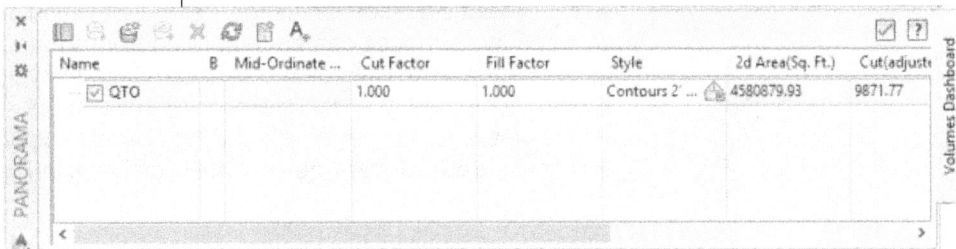

Name	B	Mid-Ordinate ...	Cut Factor	Fill Factor	Style	2d Area(Sq. Ft.)	Cut(adjuste
☑ QTO			1.000	1.000	Contours 2' ...	4580879.93	9871.77

Figure 7–71

The *Net Graph* column color displays in red if the surface difference results in a net cut, and green if it is a net fill. You can have multiple volume entries listed if you are comparing multiple surfaces. If any surfaces change, return to this vista and click

 (Recompute Volumes) to update the calculations. Alternatively, you can add another volume entry. Select the same two surfaces and compare before and after volume calculations.

Bounded Volumes

The area to calculate cut and fill can be limited by clicking

 (Add BoundedVolume). This limits the calculations to the area defined by a polyline, polygon, or parcel.

Volume Reports

The dashboard's cut/fill summary contents can be placed directly into the drawing by clicking A_+ (Insert Cut/Fill Summary) inside the Volumes Dashboard. In addition, you can create a volume report from the dashboard contents to include in specifications or other project documents by clicking

📋 (Generate Volume Report) inside the Volumes Dashboard.

Grid Volume or TIN Volume Surface

This method enables you to assign the surfaces you want to compare as object properties of a volume surface. The volume between the surfaces is calculated and included in the volume surface object properties. The TIN surface calculation is the same one conducted in the Volumes Dashboard. The Grid surface calculation is based on a grid of points interpolated from both surfaces, rather than all of the surface points of both. Grid surfaces tend to be less accurate, but faster to calculate and easier to prove by manual methods.

A grid of spot elevation labels that list the elevation differences between two surfaces can be generated from either a Grid Volume surface or TIN Volume surface. Once the volume surface is created, you can create the labels. In the *Annotate* tab>Labels & Tables panel, expand Add Labels, expand Surface, and select **Spot Elevations on Grid**, as shown in Figure 7–72.

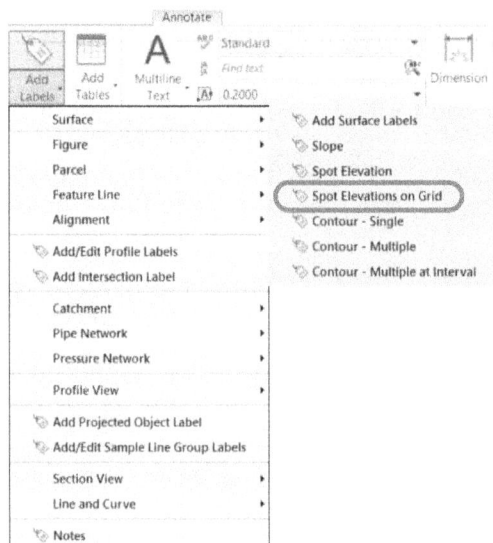

Figure 7–72

3D Solid Surface from TIN Surface

AutoCAD Civil 3D software has the capability to extract a 3D solid surface from any TIN surface. During the extraction process, you can define the vertical properties, the output properties, and which surface to extract.

Vertical Definition

Three options are available for setting the vertical definition of a 3D solid from a TIN surface, as shown in Figure 7–73.

1. The first option creates a solid with a consistent depth across the entire surface. This can be used to quickly calculate the volume of top soil to be removed.
2. The second options creates a solid with a fixed elevation. This option can be used to quickly calculate the water volume of a pond, which will have a consistent water elevation.
3. The last option creates a solid between two surfaces. This could be used to create various solids from soil report point. Doing so provides a solid for each type of material.

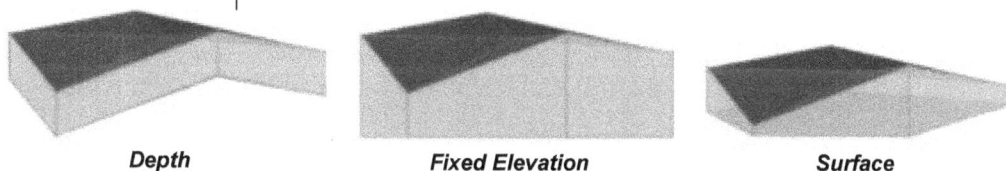

Depth   *Fixed Elevation*   *Surface*

Figure 7–73

Output Properties

Multiple output settings enable you to define where the solid is created during the extraction process. The layer and color for the solid can also be set. Then, you can create the solid in the current drawing or in a new drawing. If you select a new drawing, you can set the file path and name of the new drawing by clicking

(Browse).

How To: Create a 3D Solid Surface

1. In the model, select a TIN surface.
2. In the contextual *Surface* tab>Surface Tools panel, expand

   (Extract from Surface) and select (Extract Solids from Surface).
3. In the Extract Solid from Surface dialog box, shown in Figure 7–74, set the vertical definition and the required drawing output.

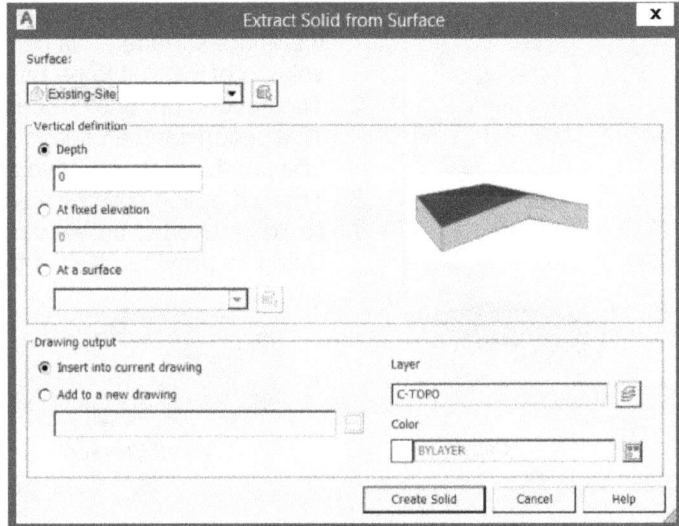

Figure 7–74

4. Click **Create Solid**.

7.9 Surface Analysis Display

The AutoCAD Civil 3D software can calculate and display many different surface analyses. These are described as follows:

Surface Analysis	Description
Contours	This analysis can display contours differently based on their elevation ranges.
Directions	This analysis can render surface triangles differently depending on which direction they face.
Elevations	This analysis can render surface triangles differently depending on their elevation ranges.
Slopes	This analysis can render surface triangles differently depending on their slope ranges.
Slope Arrows	This analysis creates a dynamic slope arrow that points downslope for each triangle, colorized by slope range.
User-Defined Contours	This analysis can display user-defined contours differently based on their elevation ranges.
Watersheds	This analysis can calculate watershed areas, and render them according to area type. The AutoCAD Civil 3D watershed analysis usually results in a very large number of individual watersheds. Although a Catchment Areas command is available to assist in drawing the catchment areas, it is still up to the engineers to draw their own conclusions on how these should be merged together into catchment areas.

- The above analyses are calculated on demand for each surface and their results are stored under the surface's Surface Properties.

In addition, the following separate utilities might be helpful when analyzing surfaces:

- **Check for Contour Problems:** Used to locate problems with the contour data, including crossing or overlapping contours. To access this command, in the *Surface* tab>expanded

  Analyze panel, select **Check for Contour Problems**, as shown in Figure 7–75.

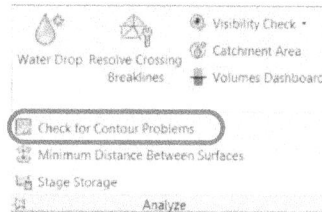

Figure 7–75

- **Resolve Crossing Breaklines:** Identifies and fixes any breaklines that create an invalid condition when two elevations exist at the intersection point of two breaklines. The breaklines can be found in the drawing, in a survey figure, or in the survey database. To access this command, in the *Surface* tab>Analyze panel, click (Resolve Crossing Breaklines).

- **Water Drop:** Draws a 2D or 3D polyline indicating the expected flow path of water across the surface from a given starting point. To access this command, in the *Surface* tab> Analyze panel, click (Water Drop).

- **Catchment Area:** Draws a 2D or 3D polyline indicating the catchment boundary and catchment point marker for a surface drainage area. To access this command, in the *Surface* tab>Analyze panel, click (Catchment Area). You should use this command in conjunction with the **Water Drop** command to determine an accurate placement of catchment regions and points.

- **Visibility Check>Zone of Visual Influence:** Analyzes the line of sight for 360 degrees around a single point. To access this command, in the *Surface* tab>Analyze panel, click

  (Visibility Check>Zone of Visual influence). This command is good for analyzing if towers, buildings, and other objects can be seen within a certain radius.

- **Minimum Distance Between Surfaces:** Identifies the (X,Y) location where two overlapping surfaces are the closest elevation. To access this command, in the *Surface* tab>

  Analyze panel, click (Minimum Distance Between Surfaces). If there is more than one location with the shortest distance between the two surfaces (because it is flat), then the location might be represented by a series of points, a line, or a closed polyline.

- **Stage Storage:** Calculates volumes of a basin from a surface, using either a surface or polylines to define the basin. To access this command, in the *Surface* tab>Analyze

  panel, click (Stage Storage). Either the *Average End Area* or the *Conic Approximation* method, or both are used to calculate volumes for the stage storage table.

Analysis Settings

You apply a surface analysis using the *Analysis* tab in the Surface Properties dialog box. In this tab, you can select the number of ranges and a legend table to be used. All of the remaining analysis settings are located in the *Surface Object* style, including whether to display in 2D or 3D, the color scheme, elevations, range groupings, etc. If you want to change the number of ranges or the range values, use the settings in this tab at any time.

Analysis Data Display

Overall visibility, layer, linetype, and related controls for analysis elements are managed using the *Display* tab in the Object Style dialog box, as shown in Figure 7–76. The component entries for *Slopes, Slope Arrows, Watersheds*, etc., are displayed. These can be set to display different settings and combinations of elements in 2D and 3D.

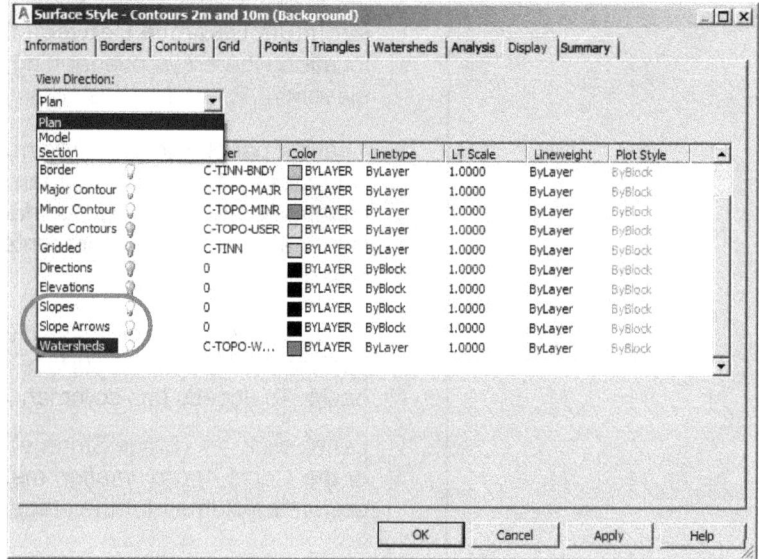

Figure 7–76

Practice 7d

Surface Labeling and Analysis

Estimated time for completion: 20 minutes

Practice Objective

- Communicate information about the surface by labeling and analyzing it.

Task 1 - Add surface labels.

1. Continue working with the drawing from the previous practice or open **SUF1-D1-Surface.dwg** from the *C:\Civil 3D for Surveyors Practice Files\Surface* folder.

2. Select the preset view **Surface Label**.

3. Select the **Existing-Site** surface in Model Space. In the contextual *Surface* tab>Labels & Tables panel, expand Add Labels and select the **Contour - Multiple**, as shown in Figure 7–77.

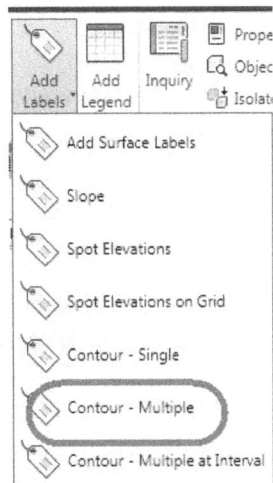

Figure 7–77

4. When prompted to select the first point, specify any point. When prompted for the next point, select a second and third point that creates a line intersecting all of the contours that you want to label, as shown in Figure 7–78. Press <Enter> when done.

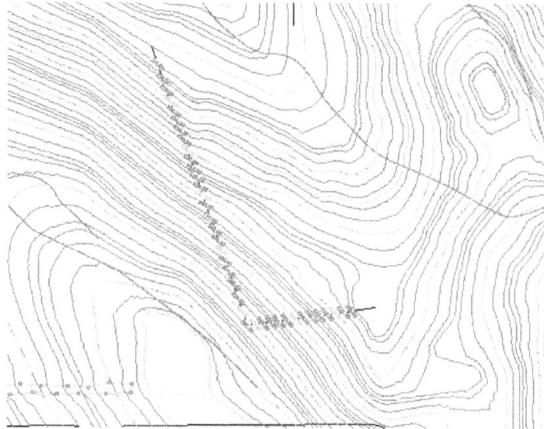

Figure 7–78

5. Move and reorient the contour label line. The labels update.

6. The *Display Contour Label Line* property can be set to only be visible when contour labels are selected. To change the visibility property, select the line in Model Space and select **Properties** in the contextual *Label* tab>General Tools panel. In the Properties dialog box, set the *Display Contour Label Line* property and the *Display Minor Contour Labels* property to **False,** as shown in Figure 7–79.

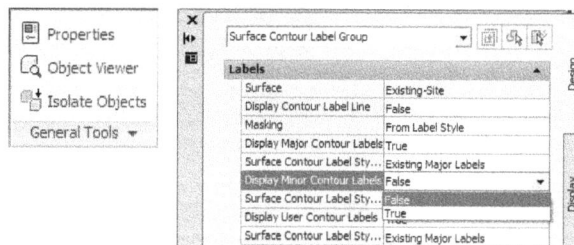

Figure 7–79

7. Close the Properties dialog box and press <Esc> to cancel your selection.

8. To have all of the future contour label lines behave this way in this drawing, select the *Settings* tab in the Toolspace. Select **Surface**, right-click, and select **Edit Feature Settings...,**as shown in Figure 7–80.

Once the grips disappear, the line is no longer displayed. Select a contour label to have the contour label line temporarily display for editing.

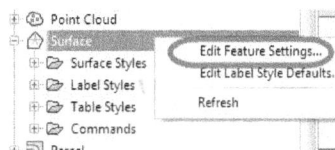

Figure 7–80

9. In the Edit Feature Settings dialog box, expand *Contour Labeling Defaults* and set the *Display Contour Label Line* property to **False** and change *Surface Contour Label Style Minor* to **<none>**, as shown in Figure 7–81. Click **OK** to accept the changes and close the dialog box.

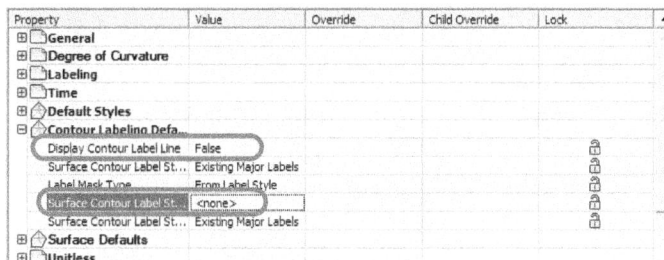

Figure 7–81

10. Select the **Existing-Site** surface again in Model Space. In the contextual *Surface* tab>Labels & Tables panel, expand **Add Labels** and select **Contour - Multiple**.

11. Select two points that will draw a line across some contours and press <Enter> when done. The contour label line and minor contour labels do not display.

12. Select the **Existing-Site** surface in Model Space. In the contextual *Surface* tab>Labels & Tables panel, expand **Add Labels** and select **Slope**.

13. To accept the prompt for the default One-point label, press <Enter>, and select a point in Model Space within the surface boundary. The AutoCAD Civil 3D software will place the slope value at that point. When you finish placing the labels, press <Enter> to exit the command.

14. (Optional) Using the process from Steps 10 and 11, experiment with labeling the surface with spot elevations and two point slopes. Note that you will be able to copy a label and place it at a different location. As the labels are dynamic, the values will change to reflect the surface information at the location of the label.

Task 2 - Perform a slope analysis.

1. Continue working with the drawing from the previous task or open **SUF1-D2-Surface.dwg** from the *C:\Civil 3D for Surveyors Practice Files\Surface* folder.

2. Select the preset view **Surface**.

3. Select the **Existing-Site** surface in Model Space. In the contextual *Surface* tab>Modify panel, select **Surface Properties**.

4. In the *Information* tab in the Surface Properties dialog box, select **Slope Banding (2D)** as the surface style.

The AutoCAD Civil 3D software calculates a range of values to fit within the specified number of ranges.

5. In the *Analysis* tab, set the *Analysis type* to **Slopes** and the number of ranges to use to **5**. Click (Run Analysis).

6. Make the following range value changes, as shown in Figure 7–82:

    - *Range1*: **0-2%**
    - *Range2*: **2-5%**
    - *Range3*: **5-10%**
    - *Range4*: **10-20%**
    - *Range5*: **20-70000%**

7. Change the range of colors for the slope range to match those shown in Figure 7–82. To change the color, click on it to open the Select Color dialog box, as shown in Figure 7–83, and select the required color. Click **OK** to close the dialog box.

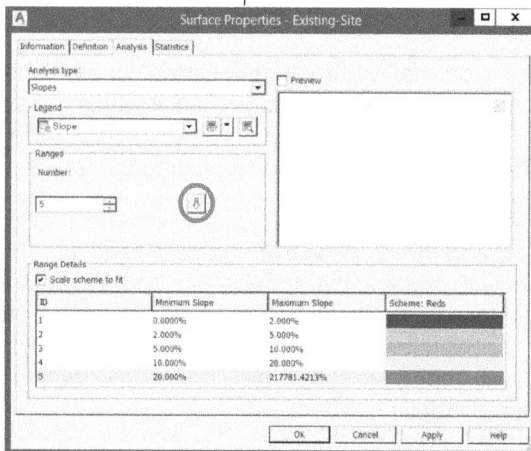

Figure 7–82

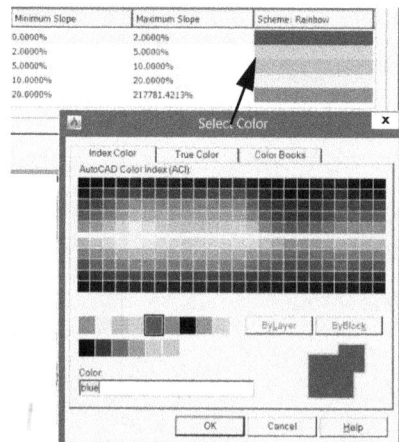

Figure 7–83

8. Click **OK** to close the dialog box and apply the changes. Press <Esc> to exit the surface selection.

9. Review the area that you want to develop. The slope ranges will be an issue.

10. You need to create a slope values table. Select the **Existing-Site** surface in Model Space. In the contextual *Surface* tab>Labels & Tables panel, select **Add Legend**.

11. Select **Slopes** from the command options, and then select **Dynamic** for a dynamic table.

12. When prompted for the top corner of the table (top left), select a location in an open area to the right of the surface, as shown in Figure 7–84. Press <Esc> to exit the selection.

Because this table is dynamic, any changes made to the surface or to the ranges in the analysis will update the table automatically.

Slopes Table				
Number	Minimum Slope	Maximum Slope	Area	Color
1	0.00%	2.00%	48018.14	
2	2.00%	5.00%	70895.06	
3	5.00%	10.00%	136506.91	
4	10.00%	20.00%	166822.56	
5	20.00%	69259.03%	34239.16	

Figure 7–84

13. (Optional) Open the Surface Properties dialog box (Steps 3 to 7) and change the number of slope ranges or the values. The Model Space Legend table will be updated.

14. Save the drawing.

Task 3 - Create a 3D solid.

1. Continue working with the drawing from the previous task or open **SUF1-D3-Surface.dwg** from the *C:\Civil 3D for Surveyors Practice Files\Surface* folder.

2. Select the **Existing-Site** surface in Model Space. In the contextual *Surface* tab>Surface Tools panel, expand

   (Extract from Surface) and select (Extract Solids from Surface).

3. In the Extract Solid from Surface dialog box, shown in Figure 7–85, set the following:

- *Surface:* **Existing-Site**
- *Vertical definition:* select *At fixed elevation:* **30**
- *Drawing output:* select *Add to a new drawing* and save it to **C:\Civil 3D for Surveyors Practice Files\Surface\ 3D-Solid.dwg**.

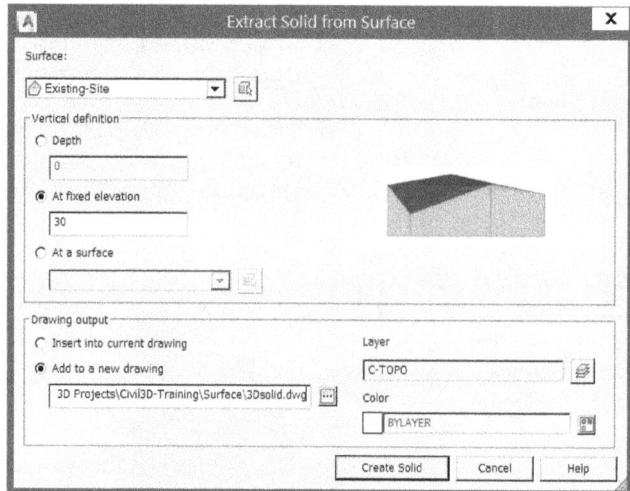

Figure 7–85

4. Click **Create Solid**.

5. Click **OK** when prompted.

6. Open the **3D-Solid.dwg** file from the *C:\Civil 3D for Surveyors Practice Files\Surface* folder. Orbit the model, and verify that the bottom of the solid surface is at elevation **30**, as shown in Figure 7–86.

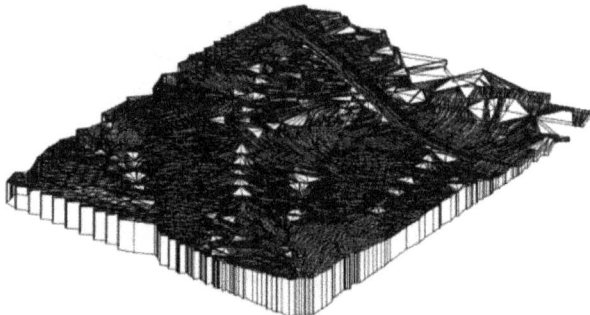

Figure 7–86

7. Close the drawing without saving.

7.10 Point Cloud Surface Extraction

Point Clouds are dense groupings of points created by 3D scanners. The AutoCAD software has been capable of working with point clouds from its previous versions. The accepted point cloud file formats are .RCP and .RCS. They are faster and more efficient than the previous file formats and are created using the Autodesk Recap software.

- As with xrefs, images, and other externally referenced files, you can attach and manage point clouds using the External References Manager.

- Point cloud object snaps have been added to the *3D Object Snap* tab in the Drafting Settings dialog box and the 3D Object Snap options in the Status Bar.

- In a point cloud, you can use the **Object** option in the **UCS** command to align the active UCS to a plane.

- Dynamic UCS now aligns to a point cloud plane according to point density and alignment.

Attach Point Cloud

In the Attach Point Cloud dialog box, you can preview a point cloud and its detailed information (such as its classification and segmentation data) before attaching it, as shown in Figure 7–87. You can also use a geographic location for the attachment location (if the option is available).

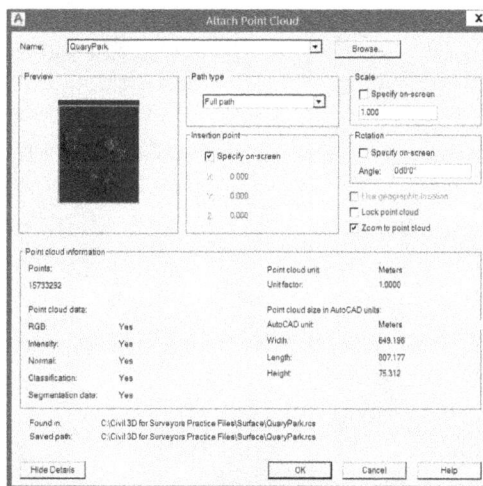

Figure 7–87

How To: Attach a Point Cloud

1. In the *Insert* tab>Point Cloud panel, click (Attach).
2. In the Select Point Cloud File dialog box, expand the Files of type drop-down list and select an option, as shown in Figure 7–88. In the *Name* area, select a file and click **Open**.

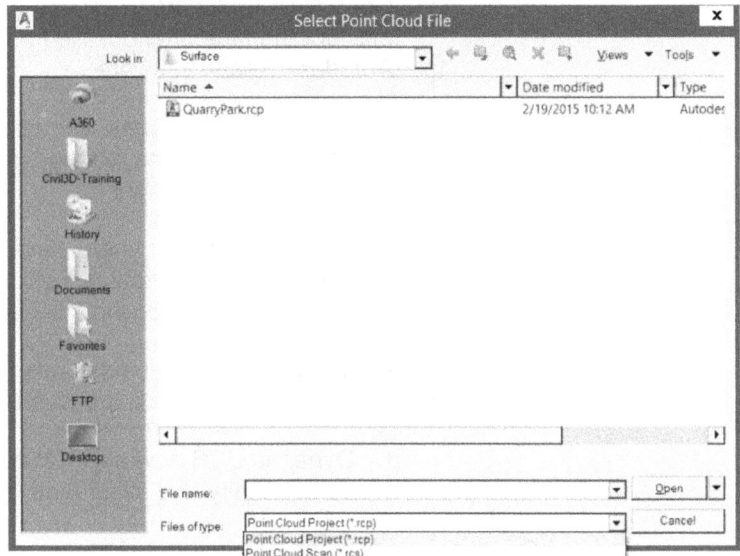

Figure 7–88

- The AutoCAD software can attach Point Cloud Project (RCP) and Scan (RCS) files (which are produced by the Autodesk ReCap software).
- The Autodesk ReCap software enables the creation of a point cloud project file (RCP) that references multiple indexed scan files (RCS). It converts scan file data into a point cloud format that can then be viewed and modified in other products.

3. In the Attach Point Cloud dialog box, click **Show Details** to display the point cloud information

4. In the *Path type*, *Insertion point*, *Scale*, and *Rotation* areas, set the options that you want to use to attach the point cloud, as shown in Figure 7–89. Click **OK**.

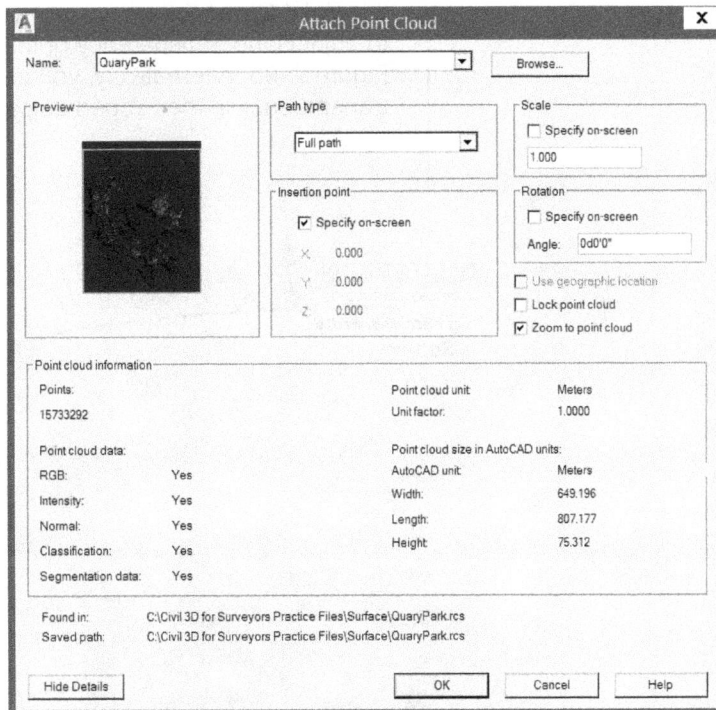

Figure 7–89

5. At the *Specify insertion point* prompt, click in the drawing to locate the point cloud.

Point Cloud Transparency

When point clouds exist in a drawing with other geometry, it can be difficult to see anything behind the point cloud. A new tool in the *Point Cloud* contextual tab>Visualization panel enables you to adjusts the transparency of the point cloud, as shown in Figure 7–90. Alternatively, you can adjust the point cloud transparency in the Properties palette, as shown in Figure 7–90.

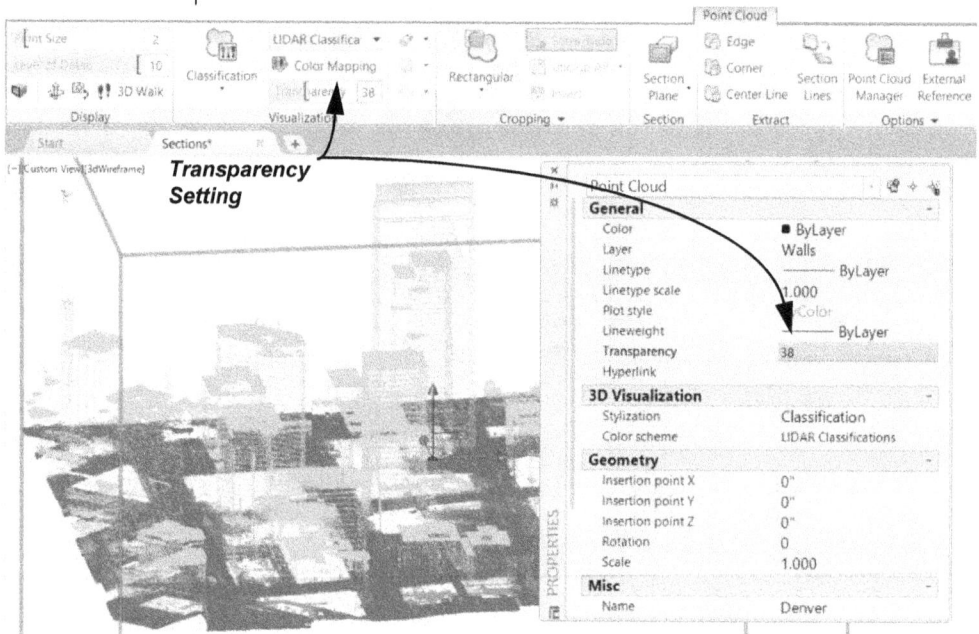

Figure 7–90

Cropping Point Clouds

Displaying the bounding box around the point cloud data enables you to determine its position in 3D space relative to the other objects in the drawing. The cropping tools in the Cropping panel enable you to display only the information that is required for your project, as shown in Figure 7–91. The cropping boundary can be rectangular, circular, or polygonal and is normal to the screen. You can use ⬆ (Invert) to reverse the displayed points from inside to outside the boundary.

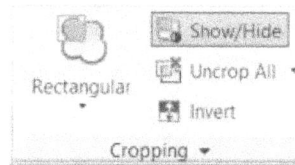

Figure 7–91

A new tool in the Cropping panel (displayed by expanding the panel) enables you to save and restore named cropping states. Both the visibility of the scans and regions as they are displayed and the cropping boundary are maintained in named cropping states, as shown in Figure 7–92.

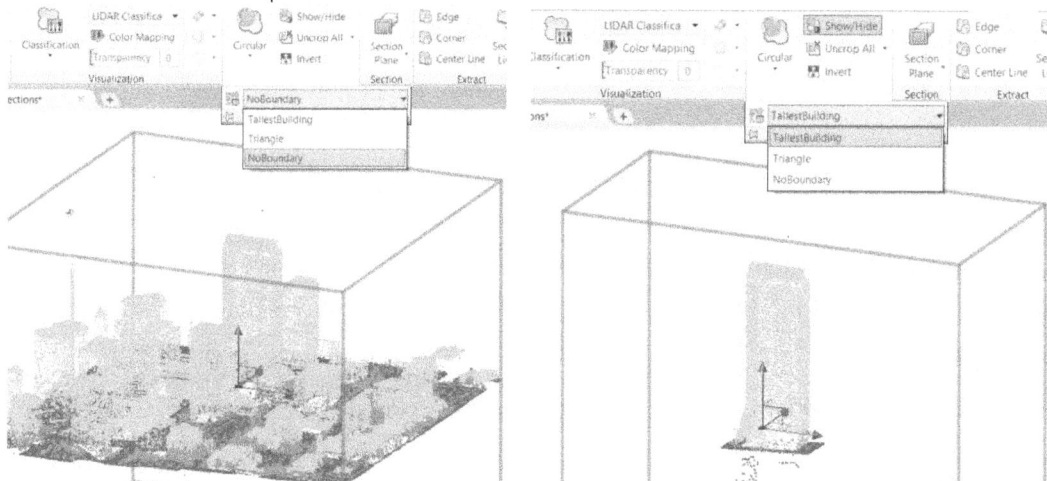

Figure 7–92

Hint: List Crop States

The new command **POINTCLOUDCROPSTATE** can be used to **S**ave, **R**estore, and **D**elete crop states, as shown in Figure 7–93. Using the **?** option will list all of the available crop states.

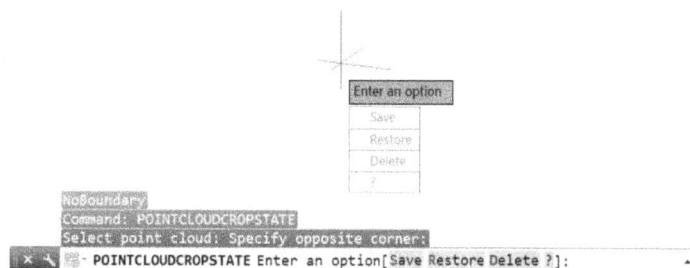

Figure 7–93

How To: Save a Named Crop State

1. Once a point cloud has been attached, select it in the model.
2. In the *Point Cloud* contextual tab>Cropping panel, select an appropriate crop boundary, as shown in Figure 7–94.

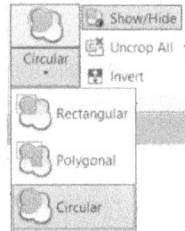

Figure 7–94

3. In the model, pick points to draw the boundary. If a Polygonal boundary was selected, press <Enter> when done.
4. At the cursor, select either **Inside** or **Outside** to indicate which points to keep.
5. Expand the *Point Cloud* contextual tab>Cropping panel, click

   (New Crop State).
6. Enter a name for the new crop state.

Surfaces from Point Clouds

Point clouds can be used to create AutoCAD Civil 3D surfaces. Once a point cloud has been attached to the drawing, it can be used to create a surface. In the *Home* tab>Create Ground Data

panel, expand Surfaces and select (Create Surface from Point Cloud), as shown in Figure 7–95.

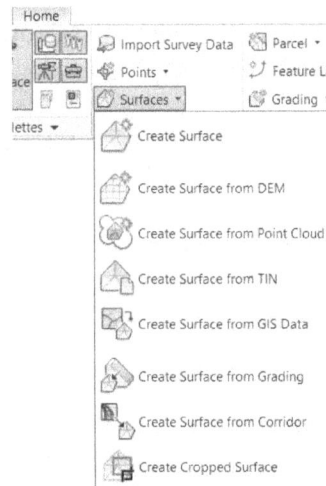

Figure 7–95

The 🌀 (Create Surface from Point Cloud) tool extracts point data from the point cloud to create a TIN surface. During the surface creation process, you can:

- Name the surface.

- Select a style for the surface.

- Select a render material.

- Select part or all of a point cloud.

- Select a filter method for Non-Ground points.

Point Cloud Selection

If there are one or more point clouds in the model, it is important to communicate to the software which points from the point clouds to use in the surface. The three available options for this are described as follows:

- The 🗒 button: Add an entire point cloud

- The 🗒 button: Remove a selection from the list

- The 🗒 button: Add a selected area of a point cloud

Non-Ground Point Filtering

When point clouds are created, they create points on any and every object visible in the scan area. This means that points can fall at the tops of buildings, trees and other structures. To create a surface that represents the ground terrain, the points that are not on the ground must be filtered out.

Three filter methods exist when creating a surface from point clouds:

1. **Planar average:** Predicts the elevation of a surface by finding the average elevation of a plane of points. An example is shown in Figure 7–96.

2. **Kriging interpolation:** Predicts the elevation of a surface by computing a weighted average of the elevations of neighboring points. An example is shown in Figure 7–97. This is usually the most accurate option.

3. **No filter:** Uses the point cloud point elevations for the surface elevations. An example is shown in Figure 7–98.

| Figure 7–96 | Figure 7–97 | Figure 7–98 |

How To: Create a Surface from Point Clouds

1. In the *Home* tab>Create Ground Data panel, expand

   Surfaces and select 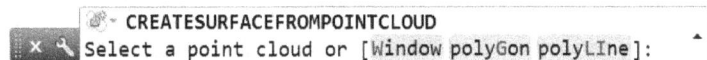 (Create Surface from Point Cloud).

2. In the model, select the point cloud or select any of the following options in the command line, as shown in Figure 7–99.
   - Window
   - polyGon
   - polyLIne

```
    - CREATESURFACEFROMPOINTCLOUD
X   Select a point cloud or [Window polyGon polyLIne]:
```

Figure 7–99

3. In the Create TIN Surface from Point Cloud dialog box - General page, type a surface name, set the surface style, and render material, as shown in Figure 7–100. Click **Next>**.

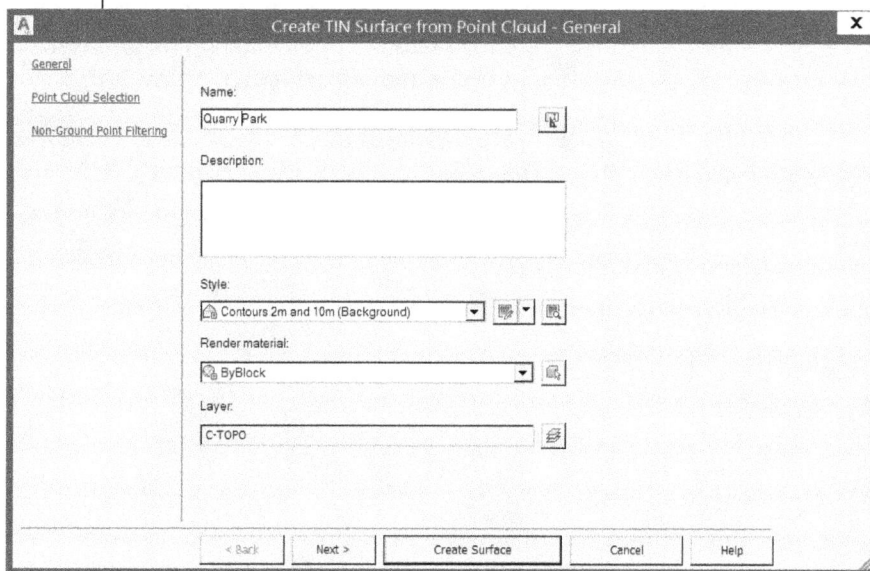

Figure 7–100

4. In the Create TIN Surface from Point Cloud dialog box - Point Cloud Selection page, select the Point clouds or parts of the Point clouds, as shown in Figure 7–101. Click **Next>**.

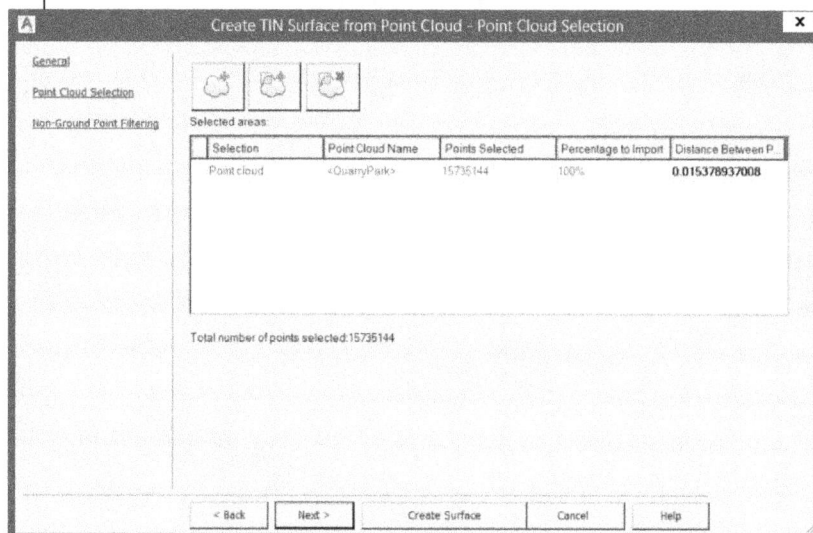

Figure 7–101

5. In the Create TIN Surface from Point Cloud dialog box - Non-Ground Point Filtering page, select a filter method and click **Create Surface**, as shown in Figure 7–102.

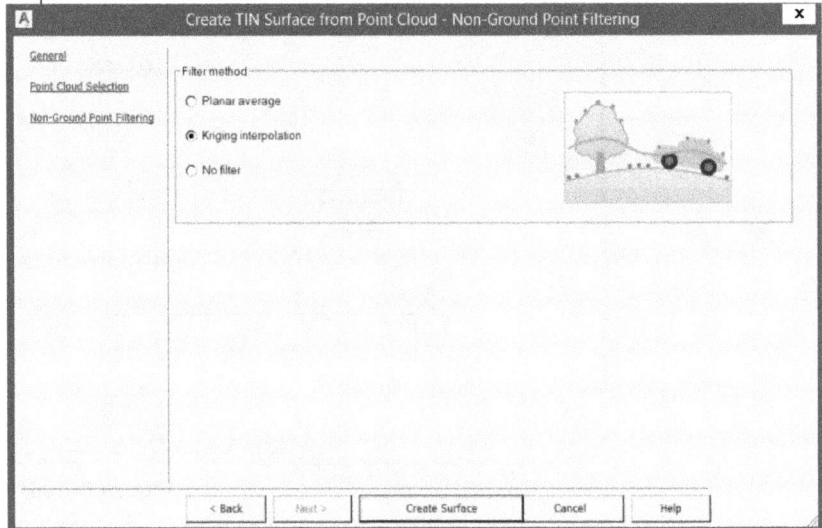

Figure 7–102

6. In the Point Cloud Processing in Background message box, click **Close**.

Practice 7e

Estimated time for completion: 15 minutes

Create a Point Cloud Surface

Practice Objective

- Communicate information about a surface by labeling and analyzing it.

In this practice you will attach a Point Cloud to a new drawing file, as shown in Figure 7–103. You will then create a surface from the point cloud.

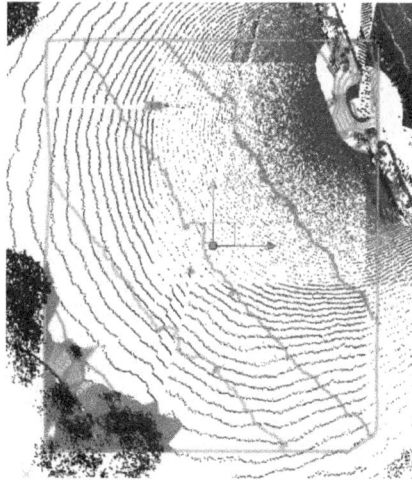

Figure 7–103

Task 1 - Attach a Point Cloud.

1. Start a new drawing from the **_AutoCAD Civil 3D (Metric) NCS.dwt**.

2. In the *Insert* tab>Point Cloud panel, click (Attach).

3. In the Select Point Cloud File dialog box, navigate to the *C:\Civil 3D for Surveyors Practice Files\Surface* folder. In the *Name* area, select **Quarry Park.rcs** and click **Open**.

4. Accept the default options in the Attach Point Cloud dialog box, click **OK**, and use an insertion point of **0,0**.

5. Save the file.

Task 2 - Analyze the Point Cloud.

1. Select the point cloud. In the *Home* tab> Create Ground Data panel, expand **Surfaces** and select (Create Surface from Point Cloud).

2. In the model, select the point cloud.

3. In the Create TIN Surface from Point Cloud dialog box General page, type **Quarry Park** for the surface name. Leave all other defaults and click **Next>**.

4. In the Create TIN Surface from Point Cloud dialog box Point Cloud Selection page, select Point cloud and then click (Remove a selection from the list).

5. In the same page, click (Add a selected area of a point cloud). In the model, draw a window around the area indicated in Figure 7–104, and click **Next>**.

Figure 7–104

6. In the Create TIN Surface from Point Cloud dialog box Non-Ground Point Filtering page, select **Kriging interpolation** and click **Create Surface**.

7. In the Point Cloud Processing in Background message box, click **Close**. It might take a few minutes to process the points.

8. Close the file without saving.

Chapter Review Questions

1. Put the following steps in the order suggested for building a surface.

   a. Add Breaklines, assign more data, modify the data, or edit the surface as required.

   b. Assign data to a surface.

   c. Accumulate data.

   d. Evaluate the resulting surface.

2. What controls how an AutoCAD Civil 3D surface displays (whether it displays contours, TIN lines, or an analysis)?

   a. Surface Style

   b. Surface Definition

   c. AutoCAD Layers

   d. Surface Boundary

3. Where would you set the lowest and highest acceptable elevations for a surface?

   a. In the Create Surface dialog box when you are first creating the surface.

   b. In the *Definition* tab in the Surface Properties dialog box.

   c. In the *Analysis* tab in the Surface Properties dialog box.

   d. Under **Edits** in the surface definition.

4. Select the type of breakline that the following statement defines:
   This type of breakline is a 3D polyline or Feature Line. It does not need a point object at each vertex because each has its own elevation.

   a. Non-Destructive

   b. Proximity

   c. Wall

   d. Standard

5. A Quick Profile disappears when you save or exit a drawing.

   a. True

   b. False

6. What are the types of edits that can be done to a surface? (Select all that apply.)

   a. Line Edits

   b. Point Edits

   c. Simplify Surface

   d. Grip Edit

7. How do you remove an edit from a surface? (Select all that apply.)

   a. Clear it in the Operations Type list in the Surface Properties in the *Definition* tab.

   b. Remove it from the Edits list in the Prospector's Preview.

   c. Select it and press <Delete>.

   d. Delete it from the Operations Type list of the Surface Properties in the *Definition* tab.

8. Which type of boundary would you use to ensure that any data that you add to a surface is ignored if it falls outside that boundary?

   a. Hide

   b. Show

   c. Data Clip

   d. Outer

9. Which of the following is not a surface label that is available out of the box in the AutoCAD Civil 3D software?

   a. Contour Labels

   b. Spot Elevation Labels

   c. Slope Labels

   d. Cut/Fill Labels

10. How do you calculate the volume between two surfaces in a specific parcel?

   a. Bounded Volumes

   b. Grid Volume Surface

   c. TIN Volume Surface

   d. Show Cut/Fill Labels in a grid pattern

11. Which of the following is not a surface analysis that you can run in the AutoCAD Civil 3D software?

    a. Slope Analysis

    b. Visibility Check

    c. Runoff Coefficient Analysis

    d. Water Drop

12. Which of the following are vertical definition options when creating a solid surface from a TIN surface? (Select all that apply.)

    a. Kriging interpolation

    b. Depth

    c. Fixed elevation

    d. Surface

13. Which of the following can be selected when creating a surface from point clouds?

    a. Style for the surface

    b. Render material

    c. Part or all of a point cloud

    d. All of the above.

Command Summary

Button	Command	Location
	Add Data	• **Contextual Ribbon:** *Surface* tab> Modify panel
	Catchment Area	• **Contextual Ribbon:** *Surface* tab> Analyze panel • **Command Prompt:** Catchment Area
	Create Surface	• **Ribbon:** *Home* tab>Create Ground Data panel • **Command Prompt:** CreateSurface
	Create Surface from Point Clouds	• **Ribbon:** *Home* tab>Create Gound Data panel • **Command Prompt:** CreateSurfaceFromPointCloud
	Edit Surface	• **Contextual Ribbon:** *Surface* tab> Modify panel
	Extract Solids from Surface	• **Contextual Ribbon:** *Surface* tab> Surface Tools panel • **Command Prompt:** ExportSurfaceToSolid
	Resolve Crossing Breaklines	• **Contextual Ribbon:** *Surface* tab> Analyze panel • **Command Prompt:** BreaklineTool
	Surface Properties	• **Contextual Ribbon:** *Surface* tab> Modify panel • **Command Prompt:** EditSurfaceProperties
	Volumes Dashboard	• **Ribbon:** *Analyze* tab>Volumes and Materials panel • **Contextual Ribbon:** *Surface* tab> Analyze panel • **Command Prompt:** VolumesDashboard
	Water Drop	• **Contextual Ribbon:** *Surface* tab> Analyze panel • **Command Prompt:** CreateSurfaceWaterdrop

Additional Tools

In the appendix, you learn a little bit more about the Survey Database and how to manipulate it. You are first reminded how to open a survey database, then you will be able to complete a least squares analysis.

Learning Objectives in this Appendix

- Learn how to open a survey database.
- Reduce errors for a more accurate survey by performing a least squares adjustment.
- Create a least squares input file to find the required information for an adjustment.
- Adjust observed point coordinates in a traverse survey without adjusting control points.
- Create and edit a traverse to speed up debugging problem surveys.
- Perform traverse adjustments on multiple field book files.

A.1 Opening a Survey Database

How To: Open a Survey Database for Editing, or As Read-Only

1. To set the working folder for the Survey Database, in the *Survey* tab, select **Survey Databases**, right-click, and select **Set working folder...**, as shown in Figure A–1. Browse and select the *C:\Civil 3D for Surveyors Practice Files\Survey\ Survey Databases* folder, as shown on the right in Figure A–2. When done, click **OK** to close the dialog box.

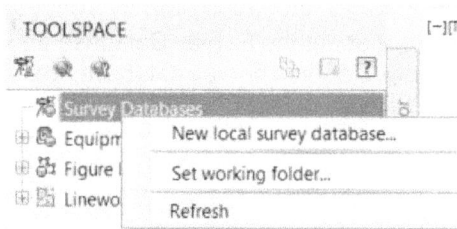

Figure A–1

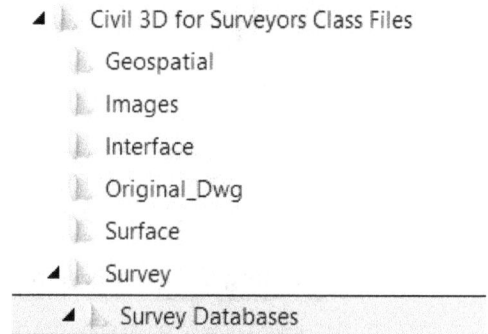

Figure A–2

2. To open a survey database, expand the survey database branch, select the survey database you want to open, right-click and select **Open for edit** or **Open for read-only**, depending on your requirements, as shown in Figure A–3.

Figure A–3

A.2 Least Squares

A survey's observations contain errors resulting from internal instrument errors, an unsteady hand holding the prism, poorly maintained equipment, etc. You must adjust the observations to reduce the errors and produce an accurate survey.

The **Least Squares** adjustment method is a statistical method that resolves a point's statistically most likely location. Observing the same point from different locations produces a slightly different set of point coordinates. **Least Squares** adjust points that have multiple observations from different surveyed locations to resolve the best locations.

A **Least Squares** adjustment minimizes the weighted sum squares of residuals for a point's coordinates. The adjustment calculates a point's location based on the least amount of error from all of the point's various measurements. Each observation from a different location and the observation's error produce slightly different point coordinates. The **Least Squares** adjustment calculates a single (most likely) location for each point from all of the various field observation (angle/distance) measurements and their errors.

A surveyor can apply **Least Squares** to a network or a traverse. A **Least Squares** adjustment can be done on any collection of field observations containing redundant observation values.

- A **Least Squares** adjustment can be in 2D or 3D.

- The survey must contain points with multiple observations (observed from several locations throughout the survey).

- There must be at least one point with known coordinates (a control point).

- Observations can be points outside the survey area, such as towers, antennas, buildings, etc.

The **Least Squares** error estimate values come from the Equipment Database's current instrument values. You should always have an up-to-date instrument database. If you do not have an equipment database, you should have at least one definition that is general enough to accommodate all instruments.

After setting up the network correctly and importing its data, you need to create a **Least Squares** input file. The input file contains all points with redundant observations and breaks down the field book's AD observations to angle and distance measurements. If the data contains elevations, it also includes vertical measurements, such as zenith angles and slope distances.

Practice A1

Creating a Least Square Survey

Practice Objective

Estimated time for completion: 15 minutes

- Prepare to calculate the most probable value for each observation in a survey using the least squares adjustment method.

In this practice you will reduce the survey notes using the **Least Squares** adjustment method. The **Least Squares** method calculates the most probable values for each observation. The values are calculated by adjusting each of the observations simultaneously so that the sum of the squares of the residuals (the difference between measured and adjusted observations) is at a minimum.

Task 1 - Set up a network.

1. Continue working with the drawing from the previous practice or open the file **SUV2-A1-Survey.dwg** from the *C:\Civil 3D for Surveyors Practice Files\SurveyL2* folder.

Refer to Appendix A-1: Open a Survey Database, on how to open a survey database.

2. Continue with the previously opened database or open the survey database **Survey2 Data A**.

3. On the *Survey* tab of the Toolspace, right-click on **Networks** (in the currently open survey database) and select **New**.

4. In the New Network dialog box, set the *Name* to **Control Network**. Click **OK**.

Task 2 - Import a survey.

1. Right-click on **Control Network** and select **Import>Import field book** as shown in Figure A–4.

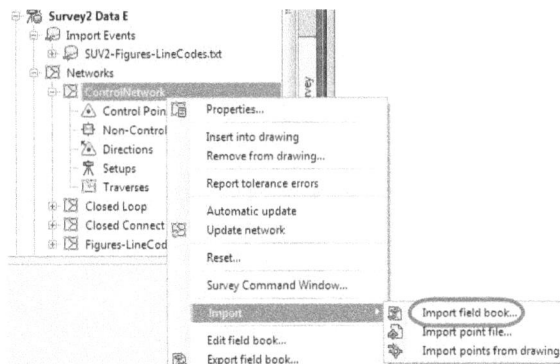

Figure A–4

2. Select the field book file **SUV2-ControlNetwork.fbk** from the *C:\Civil 3D for Surveyors Practice Files\Survey* folder and click **Open**.

3. In the Import Field Book dialog box, ensure that **Assign offset to point identifier** is not selected. All other checkboxes should be selected as shown in Figure A–5. Click **OK**.

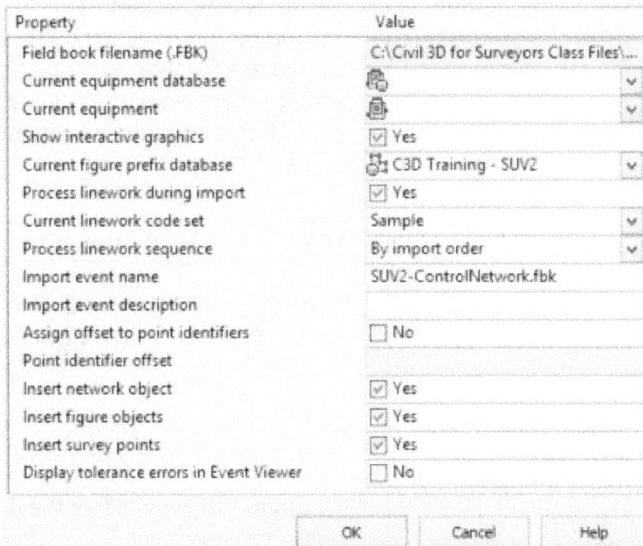

Property	Value
Field book filename (.FBK)	C:\Civil 3D for Surveyors Class Files\...
Current equipment database	
Current equipment	
Show interactive graphics	☑ Yes
Current figure prefix database	C3D Training - SUV2
Process linework during import	☑ Yes
Current linework code set	Sample
Process linework sequence	By import order
Import event name	SUV2-ControlNetwork.fbk
Import event description	
Assign offset to point identifiers	☐ No
Point identifier offset	
Insert network object	☑ Yes
Insert figure objects	☑ Yes
Insert survey points	☑ Yes
Display tolerance errors in Event Viewer	☐ No

OK   Cancel   Help

Figure A–5

4. In the Survey Network Updated dialog box, click **Close**.

5. In the *Prospector* tab, right-click on the point group collection and select **Update**. Because you have previously created your point groups, the correct points are assigned to the point groups.

6. Save the drawing.

You might need to zoom extents when the import process completes so that you can see what has been imported.

Task 3 - Review the survey data.

1. Continue with the previous drawing or open the file
   SUV2-A3-Survey.dwg from the *C:\Civil 3D for Surveyors
   Practice Files\SurveyL2* folder.

2. In the Survey toolspace, in the Networks list, expand the
   ControlNetwork collection, right-click on the **Control Points**
   heading and select **Edit** to review the control values as
   shown in Figure A–6.

Number	Name	Easting	Northing	Elevation	Description
6000		1906881.1352	620764.5945	61.878	CM-1501E
6002		1907103.6422	620464.4649	75.281	CM-1150A
6003		1906984.1313	621001.8114	50.581	CM-8716X
6004		1906792.8281	620448.2614	70.545	CM-2718A

Figure A–6

3. After reviewing the survey control points, click **X** in the upper
   left or right corner of the dialog box to exit the Panorama.

4. In the Survey toolspace, in the Networks list, expand the
   ControlNetwork collection, right-click on the **Setups**
   heading and select **Edit** to review the control values as
   shown in Figure A–7.

Station Point	Backsight Point	Backsight Direction	...	Bac...	Bac...	Instru...	Instrumen...	Easting
5001	6000	228.0015				0.000	53.871	1907018.8737
5002	5001	268.0629				0.000	55.031	1907276.4596
5003	5002	1.2747				0.000	60.163	1907271.8413
5004	5003	98.2329				0.000	69.059	1907102.9298
5005	5004	74.3345				0.000	68.062	1906889.3886

Figure A–7

5. After reviewing the survey setups points, click **X** in the upper
   right corner of the dialog box to exit the Panorama.

6. In the Survey toolspace, in the Networks list, select the
   ControlNetwork network, right-click and select **Remove
   from drawing**. When prompted whether you are sure, click
   Yes. Note that the network has been removed.

7. In the Survey toolspace, in the Networks list, select the
   ControlNetwork network, right-click and select **Insert into
   drawing**.

8. Save the drawing.

A.3 Creating a Least Squares Input File

When a survey contains redundant point observations and possibly no traverse, you can create a **Least Squares** input file that contains the information required for an adjustment. The input file has two parts. The first part lists the control points and the points to be adjusted. The second part breaks down the angle/distance observation values into angle and distance entries. Each entry has a standard deviation (quality estimate) based on the Equipment Database's current instrument entry.

For example, the following **Least Squares** data file contains Angle and Distance values and their error estimates.

!

!	From	At	To			Angle	Distance
!	Point	Point	Point	Angle	Distance	Std Error	Std Error
SD		1153	100		392.761		0.020
VA		1153	100	90.43379		3.9	
A	1151	1153	100	247.30410		9.5	
SD		1153	100		392.761		0.020
VA		1153	100	90.43409		3.9	
A	1151	1153	100	247.30330		9.5	
SD	101	100			440.099		0.022
VA	101	100		90.03042		2.8	
SD	101	100			440.089		0.022
VA	101	100		90.03112		2.8	
SD	101	102			1208.698		0.060

- The angle error is in seconds and the distance error is in feet.

- Control Points with known coordinates are not adjusted.

- All observed points with redundant observation data are floating points (points to be adjusted).

- Floating points have a question mark at the beginning of their NEZ line.

- You can make a floating point into a control point by removing its question mark.

- You can add data to the file and enter the estimated error values.

- You can exclude data by placing an exclamation point before the line of data.

Points that are going to be adjusted are listed at the top of the **Least Squares** data file and display a question mark at the beginning of their NEZ lines. Points without a question mark are not adjusted. You can change the status of a point by adding or removing the line's question mark.

The following example includes points that are marked to be adjusted.

!3D Input File

!	Least Squares Input File			
!	Generated By Survey			
!	Point	Northing	Easting	Elevation
?NEZ	100	17634.989383	22353.319301	129.766957
?NEZ	101	17472.296414	22762.231891	129.966290
NEZ	1153	17761.182578	21981.405937	134.759730
?NEZ	129	17376.379315	23374.803904	135.564365
NEZ	1151	17622.054456	21859.470581	134.359731
?NEZ	131	17435.520588	23219.865323	133.633393
?NEZ	132	17647.452902	23504.541614	137.079584

Adjustment Analysis

When selecting a **Perform** analysis in the Least Squares flyout, the AutoCAD® Civil 3D® software creates data, analyzes the survey, and updates the survey database.

You can perform a preliminary adjustment analysis without affecting the current survey. This enables you to review potential changes and fix any errors or remove data from the analysis.

Right-click on a network name and select **Least squares analysis>Create input file**, **Process input file**, or **Display output file** (as shown in Figure A–8) to analyze a survey and review its results.

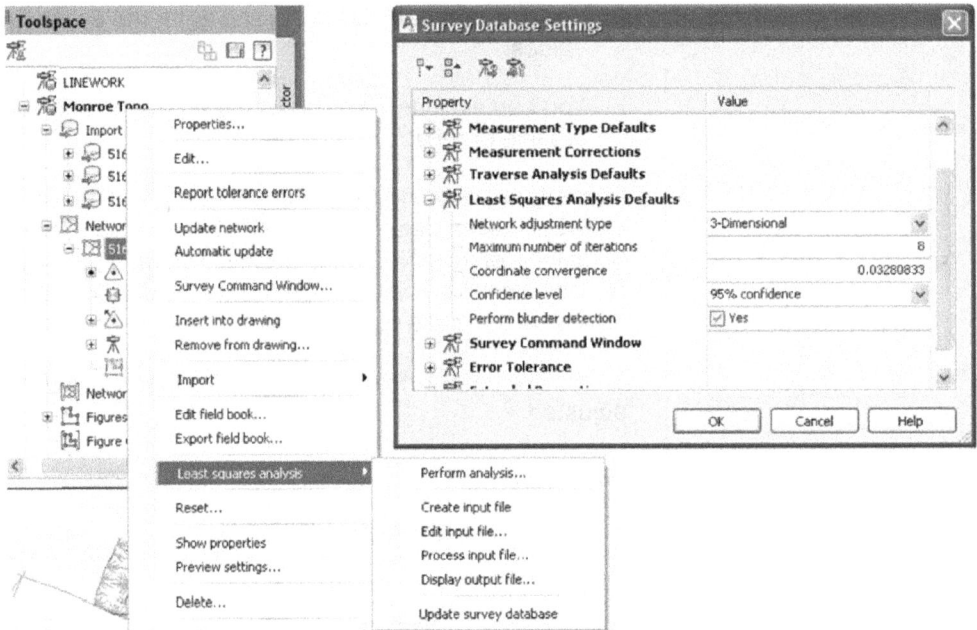

Figure A–8

To adjust the network, right-click and select **Least squares analysis>Update survey database**. Select the file **Network.adj**.

*   When adjusting a survey that contains figures, update the figures after adjusting the survey.

Blunder Detection Analysis

The *Blunder Detection* area of the adjustment identifies the failed measurements because of their high statistical residuals. They indicate errors in the survey that need to be addressed before you continue.

For example, a Blunder Detection analysis includes the following:

****

Blunder Detection/Analysis

****

Reliability Tests

Type	Pnt1	Pnt2	Pnt3	Adjusted	Resid	Redun	Estimate	Marg	Ext
—	—	—	—	—	—	—	—	—	—
SD	101	102		1208.705	0.007	0.956	-0.008	P	P
VA	101	102		89-53-51.06	5.562	0.896	-6.204	P	F
VA	101	102		89-53-53.06	6.562	0.896	-7.319	P	F
ANG	100	101	102	181-00-48.86	1.855	0.525	-3.534	P	P
SD	103	102		1461.861	0.001	0.833	-0.002	P	P
VA	103	102		90-12-07.07	10.367	0.833	-12.440	F	F
SD	103	102		1461.861	-0.009	0.833	0.010	P	P

The adjustment does not affect the control points when you are adjusting a survey. However, it promotes the observed and occupied points to derived control points. All points that were observed from a station and were not promoted to control points, remain as observed points (sideshot points) as shown in Figure A–9.

Figure A–9

Updating the Survey

After tweaking and correcting the observations in the data, you must update the survey with the analysis results. This is done from the shortcut menu that was used to create and process the survey.

The update routine moves the points to the correct location and adjusts their elevations, if a 3D analysis was done. When updating the survey, the figures become out of date. You must update the figures to their new point attachment locations.

Practice A2

Creating a Least Square Input File and Adjustment

Practice Objective

Estimated time for completion: 10 minutes

• Perform a least squares analysis of the surveyed network.

In this practice you will use imported data to perform a **Least Squares** analysis of the surveyed network.

Task 1 - Create the least squares input file.

1. Continue working with the drawing from the previous practice or open the file **SUV2-B1-Survey.dwg** from the *C:\Civil 3D for Surveyors Practice Files\SurveyL2* folder.

Refer to Appendix A-1: Open a Survey Database, on how to open a survey database.

2. Continue with the previously opened database or open **Survey2 Data B**.

3. Right-click on the survey database and select **Edit Survey database settings**.

4. In the **Coordinate Zone** group, select **Browse**. In the *Zone* area, set the *Categories* field to **USA, California** and the *Available coordinate systems* to **NAD83 California State Planes, Zone VI, Meter**.

5. In the Survey Database Settings dialog box, scroll down to the *Least Squares Analysis Defaults* branch and set the *Network adjustment type* to **2-Dimensional**, as shown in Figure A–10. Click **OK**.

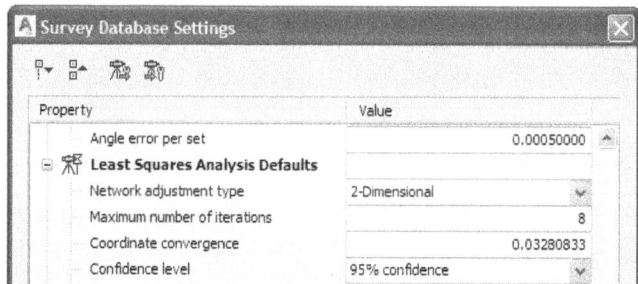

Property	Value
Angle error per set	0.00050000
⊟ 絣 **Least Squares Analysis Defaults**	
Network adjustment type	2-Dimensional
Maximum number of iterations	8
Coordinate convergence	0.03280833
Confidence level	95% confidence

Figure A–10

6. In the currently opened survey database, expand the **Networks** collection, right-click on the **ControlNetwork** and select **Least squares analysis>Create input file,** as shown in Figure A–11.

*If you are prompted that a Network file already exists, click **Yes** to overwrite the file.*

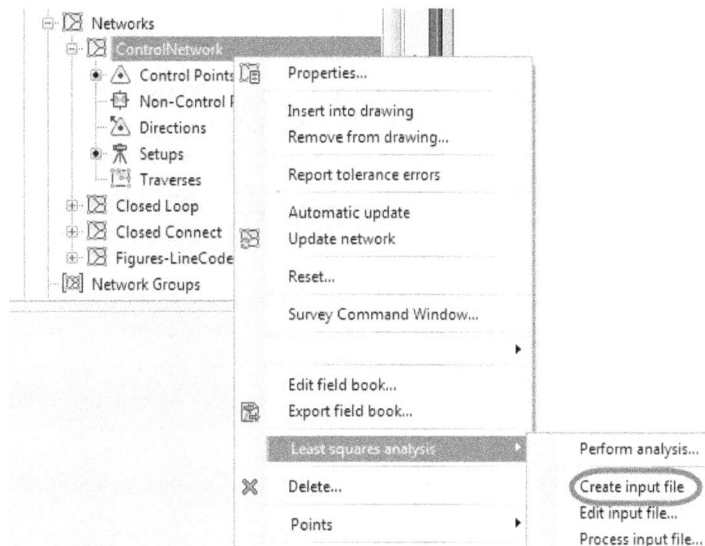

Figure A–11

7. In the currently opened survey database, in the **Network** collection, right-click on the **ControlNetwork** network and select **Least squares analysis>Edit input file**.

8. Review the points that need to be adjusted, and the angle (horizontal and vertical), and distance (horizontal and slope) values as shown in Figure A–12.

Figure A–12

9. Close the **Network.lsi** in the Notepad file and save the drawing.

Task 2 - Perform a least squares adjustment.

1. In the currently opened survey database, in the **Network** collection, right-click on the **ControlNetwork** network and select **Least squares analysis>Process input file**.

2. In the **Network** collection, right-click on the **ControlNetwork** network and select **Least squares analysis>Display output file**.

    *   Note the Measured and Adjusted values as shown in Figure A–13.

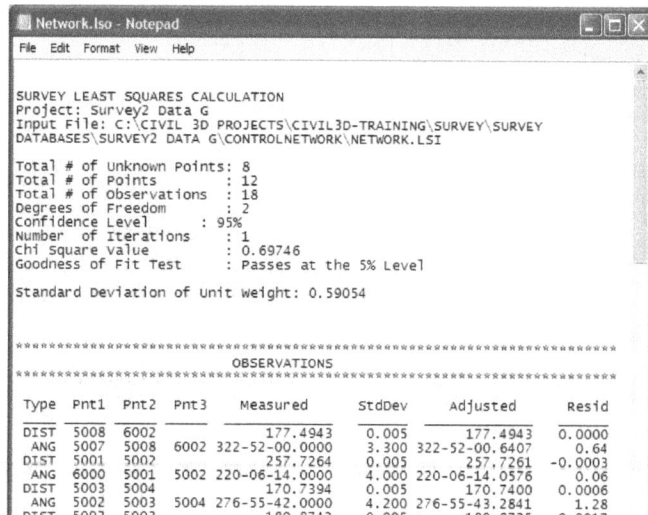

Figure A–13

3. Save the drawing.

Task 3 - Update a survey and figures.

1. In the **Network** collection, right-click on the **ControlNetwork** network and select **Least squares analysis>Update survey database**.

2. In the default folder *C:\Civil 3D for Surveyors Practice Files\Survey\Survey Databases\Survey2 Data B\ ControlNetwork*, select the file **Network.adj** and click **Open**. Note that the default folder path is based on the currently opened survey database.

3. A warning dialog box might open prompted you to process the linework. Close the dialog box. To process the linework, in the Import event, select **SUV2-ControlNetwork.fbk**, right-click and select **Process Linework**, as shown in Figure A–14. Click **OK**.

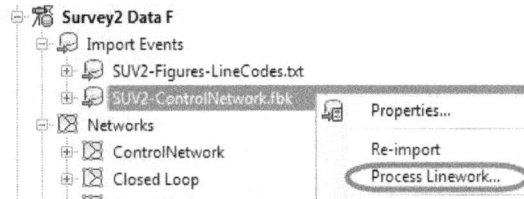

Figure A–14

4. In the **Network** collection, right-click on the **ControlNetwork** network and select **Insert into drawing**.

5. Each adjusted point will display an error ellipse in Model space. To view the point, in the *Survey* tab, select the **Survey Network Control Points** collection. In the list view, right-click on **point 5001** and select **Zoom To**. The drawing zooms to the point and ellipse.

6. Save the drawing.

A.4 Traverse Basics

A traverse is a systematic method of collecting field observations. It is used to accurately locate a parcel's boundary, but there are also other uses for the traverse methodology. You can observe two types of traverses: Open and Closed.

Open Traverse

An Open traverse begins at a control point (with known coordinates) and ends at a location relative to the starting point. The only available observations are forward and back to the points along the survey path. There are no other measurements with which to check the survey's errors.

Closed Traverse

A Closed traverse is the most common type of traverse. It starts at a known location and ends at the starting location. The initial backsight is an azimuth or a second known point. Traditionally, this point is not a point in the traverse.

Closed Connected Traverse

The Closed Connected traverse is a variation of the Closed traverse as shown in Figure A–15. It starts at a known points and ends at known points that are not the beginning points. The ending points have known coordinates, which are not affected when the traverse is modified. The traverse report notes the location error of the points and adjusts the survey's observations to that the traverse ends at the known coordinates of these points. The error is in the observations from the known starting points to the first last known point.

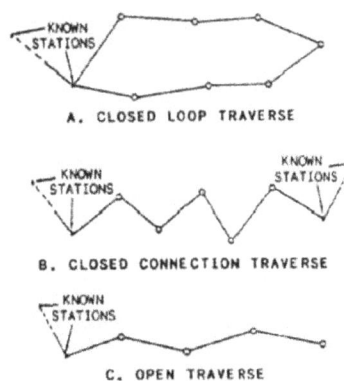

A. CLOSED LOOP TRAVERSE

B. CLOSED CONNECTION TRAVERSE

C. OPEN TRAVERSE

Figure A–15

One problem with the traditional traverse is that its data is limited to observations made between the current, last, and next stations. No observations are made to other traverse points across the loop or to external points that are viewable from other traverse points (e.g., antennas, water towers, etc.). These observations would help to define a better calculated shape because they add another dimension to the traverse data. The **Least Squares** adjustment at the Network level is the only method that analyzes a survey containing traverse and redundant cross or external observations.

All Network traverses use traditional adjustment methods and only use forward and backsight measurements. The traditional traverse adjustment methods are: **Compass**, **Crandall**, **Transit**, and **Least Squares**.

- The **Compass** rule assumes that the coordinate error is distributed in proportion to the traverse leg's distance and that both the angle and distance values contribute to the survey error. The largest error occurs along the longest distances.

- The **Transit** rule assumes that the coordinate error is distributed in proportion to the amount of coordinate change between points and that the surveyor's error is due to distance rather than angle. The greater the amount of coordinate change, the more errors there are in the observations.

- **Crandall's** rule distributes the error throughout the traverse and makes adjustments to the distances in the traverse.

- Traverse **Least Squares** adjusts the point coordinates based on the traverse's foresight and backsight observations.

Traverse Data in a Field Book

Depending on the field crew and the survey task, a traverse can be easy to identify or have portions in non-sequential setups (stations). Some field crews execute the traverse first and then return to the stations to collect additional data. These new observations are known as sideshots. Some field crews execute the traverse and sideshots at the same time. They have to research the observations from each station to validate and edit any possible errors. A large error is easily detected, while small errors are harder to locate.

A.5 Defining a Traverse

A traverse is often part of the initial survey. In some surveys, the traverse is interspersed throughout the observations. In others, the traverse is the survey. The 5199 field book contains the topography and a traverse. The survey stations also represent the traverse stationing. The initial and final foresight stations are at **point 1** (the only control point) and **point 26** is the initial backsight. When defining a traverse, you need to enter its definition as shown in Figure A–16. Since you call out the initial station, you do not include it in the traverse stations list. If you include the initial station, you cannot adjust the traverse.

Property	Value
Name	CLTraverse
Description	
Initial Station	5001
Initial Backsight	6003
Stations	102-105
Final Foresight	5001

Figure A–16

When reviewing each station's observations, you should look for observations to the previous station and to the next occupied station. If these observations are missing, you are at the end of the traverse. If you are near the end or at a point around the perimeter of the site, the traverse data set is probably broken.

Traverse Editor

The Traverse Editor's primary function is to enable you to manually enter a traverse. It understands the data requirements for the traverse and prompts you for the correct values as you enter the data.

The Traverse Editor can also be used to debug problem traverses. It displays where a traverse breaks and enables you to edit or add data.

Least Squares Traverse

Using **Least Squares** on a traverse implies that it contains redundant observation data. Although the traverse data might include observations across and outside the traverse's course, these observations are ignored and only foresight and backsight data are analyzed. To analyze a traverse with outside or across observations, you must use network-based **Least Squares**, not traverse-based **Least Squares**.

Traditional traverse data and adjustment techniques produce an approximate point along the course of the traverse. Because the analysis does not contain any across or outside data, you might not end up in the correct place when walking from one side of the traverse loop to the other.

Adjustment Reports

When a traverse adjustment is processed, it displays four Notepad reports. Each one contains specific adjustment results.

- The **Raw Closure.trv** report lists the traverse quality and any possible traverse problem locations.

- The **Balance Angle.trv** report lists the original raw coordinates from the traverse observations on the left. The application of an angle correction to each observation's angle is displayed on the right. The accumulated error is displayed on the far right and a new traverse precision from correcting an angular error is displayed at the bottom. The report lists the improved precision and might also display a value that passes when the initial traverse fails.

- The **Traverse Name.lso** report is similar to the **Balance Angle.trv** report, except that it uses the angular correction and the selected rule to do the final traverse adjustment.

- The **Vertical Adjustment.trv** report lists the amount of vertical adjustment that is done using the selected adjustment method. The report displays when you select a vertical adjustment method.

Practice A3

Estimated time for completion: 30 minutes

Refer to Appendix A-1: Open a Survey Database, on how to open a survey database.

Creating a Network Traverse

Practice Objective

- Perform traverse adjustments on multiple field book files.

In this practice you will import a number of different field book files and perform a traverse adjustment.

Task 1 - Import the traverse.

In this task you will import your Closed Loop field book file into the Closed Loop network.

1. Continue working with the drawing from the previous practice or open the file **SUV2-C1-Survey.dwg** from the *C:\Civil 3D for Surveyors Practice Files\SurveyL2* folder.

2. Continue with the previously opened database or open **Survey2 Data C**.

3. Expand the currently opened survey database collection and the **Networks** collection. Right-click on the **Closed Loop** and select **Import>Import field book** to import the field book file, as shown in Figure A–17

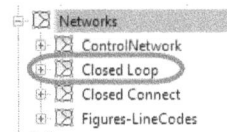

Figure A–17

4. Select **SUV2-ClosedLoop.fbk** from the *C:\Civil 3D for Surveyors Practice Files\Survey* folder and click **Open**.

5. In the Import Field Book dialog box, set the **Assign offset to point identifier** and **Process Linework during import** options to **No**. All of the other checkboxes should be selected. Click **OK**.

6. Save the drawing.

Task 2 - Define a traverse.

1. In the currently opened survey database, in the **Networks** collection, expand the **Closed Loop** collection. Right-click on the **Traverses** branch and select **New** as shown in Figure A–18.

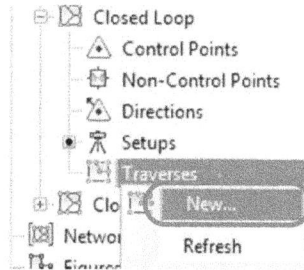

Figure A–18

2. in the New Traverse dialog box, set the following, as shown in Figure A–19:

- *Name:* **CLTraverse**
- *Initial Station:* **5001**
- *Initial Backsight:* **6003**
- *Stations:* **102-105**
- *Final Foresight:* **5001**

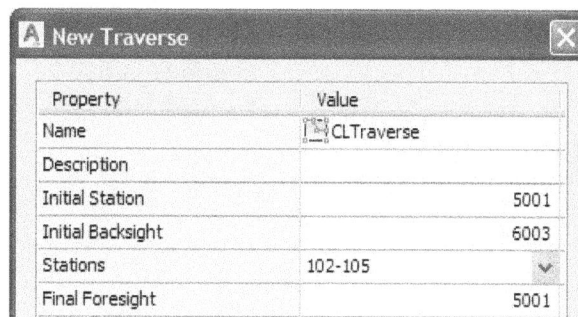

Figure A–19

3. Click **OK** when done.

4. Save the drawing.

Task 3 - Review the traverse and station observation.

1. In the currently opened survey database verify that the appropriate Zone has been set for the survey database. Right-click on the survey database and select **Edit survey database** setting. In the coordinate *Zone* area, click **Browse**. In the *Zone* area, set *Categories* to **USA, California** and set *Available coordinate systems* to **NAD83 California State Planes, Zone VI, Meter.**

2. In the *Networks* collection, expand the **Closed Loop** collection. In the **Traverses** branch, right-click on **CLTraverse**, as shown in Figure A–20. Select **Edit Traverse**.

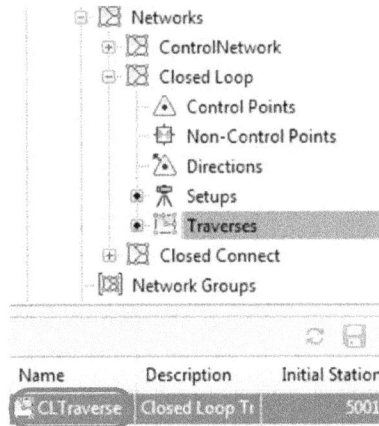

Figure A–20

3. In the Traverse Editor panorama, review the Traverse as shown in Figure A–21. Click ✖ to close the panorama.

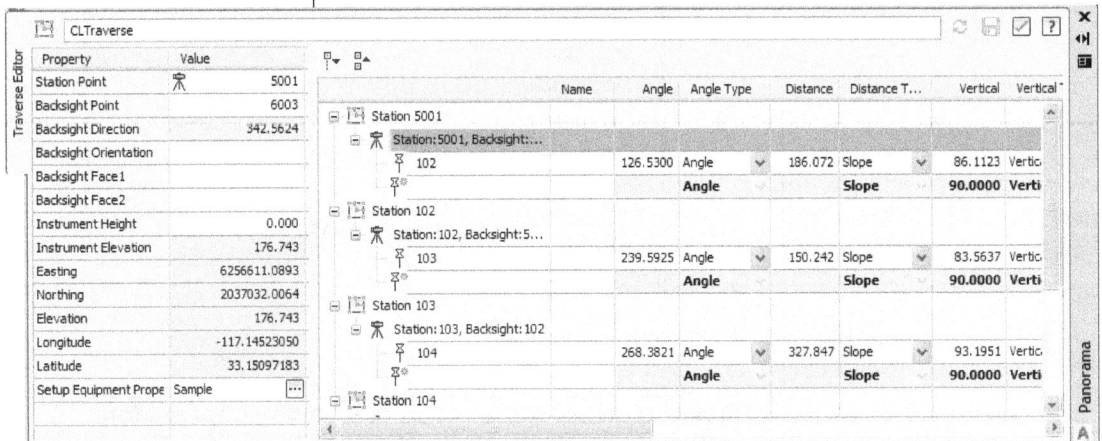

Figure A–21

4. In the currently opened survey, in the **Networks** collection, expand the **Closed Loop** collection and select the Setups branch. Right-click on **Station Point 103**, as shown in Figure A–22. Select **Edit Observation**.

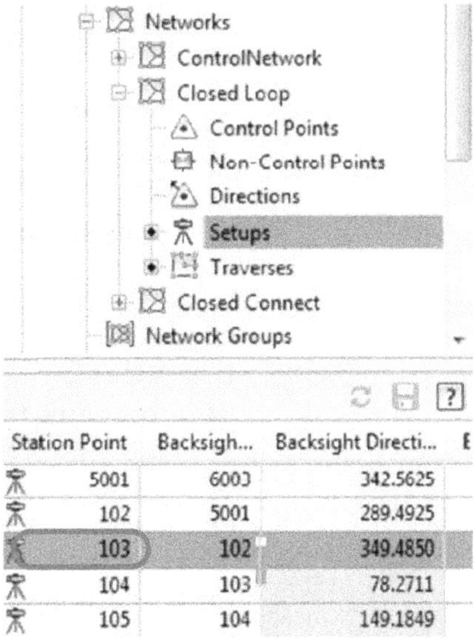

Figure A–22

5. In the Observation Editor panorama, review the Observation as shown in Figure A–23. Note that in the graphics view, the AutoCAD Civil 3D software will zoom to the selected setup point. Click ✖ to close the panorama.

Number	Name	Angle	Angle ...	Distance	Distance ...	Vertical	Vertical T...	Target H...	Target T...	Scale F...	Description	Easting	
104		268.3821	Angle	327.847	Slope	93.1951	Vertical Ar	0.000	Prism	000000000	STA4	6256491.5022	20367
200		48.0401	Angle	43.130	Slope	90.1100	Vertical Ar	0.000	Prism	000000000	PINE 3	6256838.6534	20368
201		101.4333	Angle	93.940	Slope	83.0343	Vertical Ar	0.000	Prism	000000000	BLDG	6256905.3896	20368
202		136.2924	Angle	48.248	Slope	84.1135	Vertical Ar	0.000	Prism	000000000	PAD	6256850.8542	20367

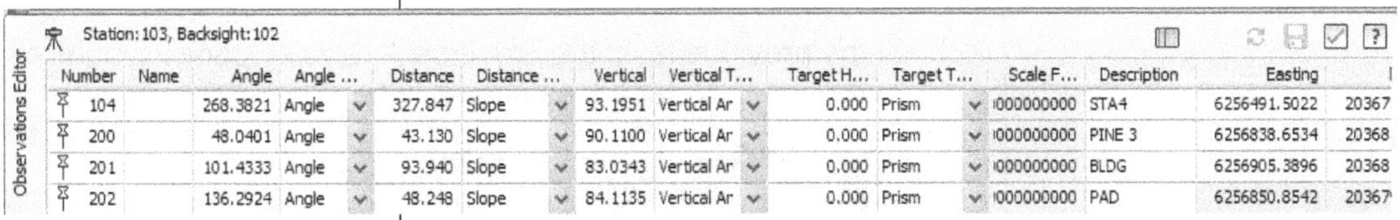

Figure A–23

6. Save the drawing.

Task 4 - Adjust a traverse.

1. Continue working with the previous drawing or open the file **SUV2-C5-Survey.dwg** from the *C:\Civil 3D for Surveyors Practice Files\SurveyL2* folder.

2. Continue with the previously opened database or open **Survey2 Data C5**.

3. In the currently opened survey, in the **Networks** collection, expand the **Closed Loop** collection and select the **Traverses** branch. In the panorama window at the bottom, right-click on **CLTraverse** and select **Traverse Analysis**.

4. In the Traverse Analysis dialog box, set the following, as shown in Figure A–24:

- *Horizontal adjustment method*: **Compass rule**
- *Vertical adjustment method*: **Length weighted distribution**
- *Update survey database:* **No**

Property	Value
Do traverse analysis	☑ Yes
Do angle balance	☑ Yes
Horizontal adjustment method	Compass rule ▼
Vertical adjustment method	Length weighted distribution ▼
Horizontal closure limit 1:X	15000.00000000
Vertical closure limit 1:X	15000.00000000
Angle error per set	0.00050000
Update survey database	☐ No

Figure A–24

5. Click **OK** to review the adjustment values.

6. Save the drawing.

Task 5 - Review the preliminary results.

1. In the previous task, the Traverse Analysis opened a number of reports in Notepad, as shown in Figure A–25

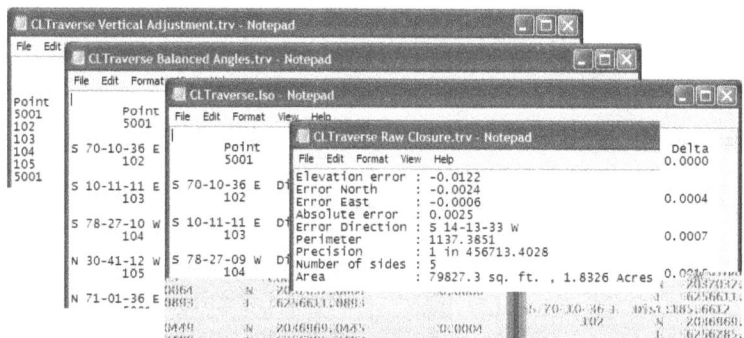

Figure A–25

2. In the Notepad file list, select the file **CLTraverse Raw Closure.trv** and review its values. The traverse passes. Close the file.

3. In the Notepad file list, select the file **CLTraverse Balance Angles.trv** and review its values. Angle Balance slightly increased the traverse's values. Close the file.

4. In the Notepad file list, select the file **CLTraverse.lso** and review its values. The file contains the results of balancing angles and the **Compass** rule adjustment. Close the file.

5. In the Notepad file list, select the file **CLTraverse Vertical Adjustment.trv** and review its values. The file lists the vertical changes in the adjustment. Close the file.

6. Use the **Crandall** and **Transit** adjustments to run a preliminary adjustment on the **Boundary** traverse again. Try using a different vertical adjustment as well to display any differences in the results.

7. Use the **Least Squares** method to create a preliminary adjustment on the **Boundary** traverse. Review the results.

Task 6 - Apply the survey adjustments.

1. In the **Networks** collection, expand the **Closed Loop** database and select the **Traverses** branch. Right-click on **CLTraverse** and select **Traverse Analysis** to apply the **Survey** adjustments to the traverse.

2. In the Traverse Analysis dialog box, set the following, as shown in Figure A–26:

   • *Horizontal adjustment method:* **Compass rule**
   • *Vertical adjustment method:* **Length weighted distribution**
   • *Update survey database:* **Yes**

Property	Value
Do traverse analysis	☑ Yes
Do angle balance	☑ Yes
Horizontal adjustment method	Compass rule ▼
Vertical adjustment method	Length weighted distribution ▼
Horizontal closure limit 1:X	15000.00000000
Vertical closure limit 1:X	15000.00000000
Angle error per set	0.00050000
Update survey database	☑ Yes

Figure A–26

3. Click **OK** to apply the adjustment values to the traverse.

4. The Notepad reports open. Read and close each one to continue adjusting the traverse loop.

5. Click **Save** to save the drawing.

A.6 Multiple Network Surveys

A survey might contain traverses that depend on control points from an initial site survey. For example, for a site with multiple phases, each succeeding survey builds on the previous survey's control points.

Survey Points

Each network in a survey contributes to an overall list of survey points. Any control point in the list is available to any network that needs to use the point for its control. For example, Network 1 is a boundary traverse. The survey's initial control point is added to the survey points list. The traverse's observed, occupied, and adjusted points become control points because of their adjustment. Their survey icons change from observed/occupied (a tripod symbol) to an adjusted control point (a control point triangle with a prism) as shown in Figure A–27. The icon indicates that the point's origin was an observation, which was occupied and part of a traverse adjustment.

Number	Easting	Northing	Eleva
62	50109.6590	47577.6550	287.
900	50335.4657	47494.8700	286.
901	50306.1782	47091.1730	279.
902	50238.5935	46846.4988	274.
903	50100.4441	46696.3428	274.
904	49939.4508	46774.5546	291.
905	49931.6317	46453.4611	283.
906	49765.3417	46853.1628	347.
907	49618.1853	46967.5125	360.
908	49634.2577	47132.9177	359.
909	49624.7361	47516.5026	356.
910	49621.9607	47714.2345	349.
911	49700.3305	47637.9537	353.
912	49869.4677	47638.5499	323.
1100	50289.2425	47262.3073	285.
1101	50292.8135	47350.8579	286.
1102	50361.2921	47851.5299	299.
1105	50259.0043	46967.9543	276.

Number	Easting	Northing	Eleva
62	50109.6590	47577.6550	287.
900	50335.4895	47494.9345	286.
901	50306.3093	47091.2419	279.
902	50238.7898	46846.5581	274.
903	50100.6809	46696.3729	274.
904	49939.6699	46774.5490	292.
905	49931.9276	46453.4502	283.
906	49765.5430	46853.1185	347.
907	49618.3597	46967.4362	360.
908	49634.3919	47132.8504	359.
909	49624.7772	47516.4442	356.
910	49621.9537	47714.1812	349.
911	49700.3441	47637.9236	353.
912	49869.4832	47638.5677	323.
1100	50289.3328	47262.3586	285.
1101	50292.8785	47350.9102	286.
1102	50361.2140	47851.6018	299.
1105	50259.1680	46968.0108	276.

Figure A–27

Once a point becomes a network control point, it also becomes a control point in the survey points list. The point is available to any other network in the survey as a control point.

Closed Connected Traverse

A closed connected traverse starts and ends with control points. Although it starts at a known location, the traverse observations do not arrive at the same coordinates as the ending point(s). This is because the field observations contain errors. With observations that have errors, the traverse has to be adjusted to make the observations arrive at the correct coordinates.

- When a survey's starting and ending points are control points, the traverse adjustment only adjusts the observed points and not the control points.

The AutoCAD Civil 3D software does not change the control point coordinates when they are part of a traverse. The adjustment changes the survey's observation values so that the survey arrives at the control point coordinates. The adjustment result arrives at the control point coordinates after correcting the observation errors.

Field Book Edits

If a field book contains control point NEZ entries that are duplicates of existing control points, they must be removed from the field book. This prevents duplicate points and the redefining of existing control error messages when you are importing the field book.

The field crew might also use different point numbers for the closed loop control points. If this is done, you have to find these observation point numbers and change them to the actual control point numbers.

For example, you can facilitate this by having the field crew include the new and old point numbers in the point descriptions. They can enter the new point number and include the original control point number in the description as follows:

!NEZ 902 46846.5179 50238.6309 274.7200 ""PIN/C(s) TRAV""

!NEZ 903 46696.3614 50100.4920 274.8600 ""D.H.(S) TRAV""

!NEZ 934 47714.2556 49621.9667 349.8000 ""AKA910""

!NEZ 935 47637.9849 49700.3467 353.4600 ""AKA911""

…

AD VA 934 290.11250 142.093 83.07180 "AKA910/65"

STN 934 5.28

BS 933 0.00000

PRISM 5.33

AD VA 935 185.0222 109.427 88.0343 "AKA911"

To have the field book calculate the traverse closer, the coordinates entered in the field book need to be commented out. When importing the field book, the control point's coordinates in the Survey Points point list are used. The last five lines of the example require that the point number be changed to 911 and that the observation before and the stationing point number should change to 910. The field book import then uses the coordinates from the point numbers 910 and 911 in the Survey Point point list.

Practice A4

| | |

Estimated time for completion: 15 minutes

Refer to Appendix A-1: Open a Survey Database, on how to open a survey database.

You might need to zoom extents to see the results.

Closed Connect Traverse

Practice Objective

• Import and adjust open, closed, and closed connected traverse surveys.

In this practice, you will import and adjust the three different types of traverse: **Open**, **Closed**, and **Closed connected traverse**.

Task 1 - Import the traverse.

In this task you will import your Closed Connected field book file into the **Closed Connect** network.

1. Continue working with the drawing from the previous practice or open the file **SUV2-D1-Survey.dwg** from the *C:\Civil 3D for Surveyors Practice Files\SurveyL2* folder.

2. Continue with the previously opened database or open **Survey2 Data D**.

3. In the currently opened survey database collection, expand the **Networks** collection. Right-click on **Closed Connect** and select **Import>Import field book** to import the field book file as shown in Figure A–28.

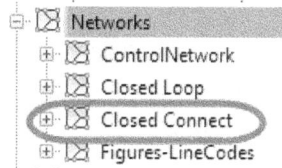

Figure A–28

4. In the *C:\Civil 3D for Surveyors Practice Files\Survey* folder, select the field book file **SUV2-ClosedConnected.fbk** and click **Open**.

5. In the Import Field Book dialog box, if not already selected, set the **Assign offset to point identifier** to **No**. All of the other checkboxes should be selected. Click **OK**.

6. Save the drawing.

Task 2 - Define a traverse.

1. In the currently opened survey, expand the **Networks** collection, expand the **Closed Connect** collection. Right-click on the **Traverse** branch and select **New** to create a new traverse.

2. In the New Traverse dialog box, set the following, as shown in Figure A–29:

   • *Name:* **CC Traverse**
   • *Initial Station point number:* **5005**
   • *Initial Backsight:* **6000**
   • *Stations:* **106,107**
   • *Final Foresight:* **5007**

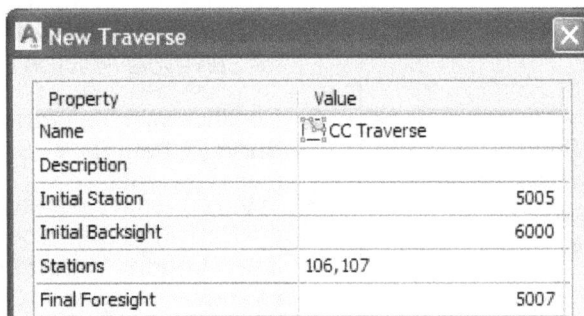

Property	Value
Name	CC Traverse
Description	
Initial Station	5005
Initial Backsight	6000
Stations	106,107
Final Foresight	5007

New Traverse

Figure A–29

3. Click **OK**.

4. Save the drawing.

Task 3 - Apply the survey adjustments.

1. In the currently opened survey, expand the **Networks** collection, expand the **Closed Connect** collection and select the Traverses branch. In the panorama window at the bottom, right-click on **CC Traverse** and select **Traverse Analysis** to apply Survey adjustments to the traverse.

2. In the Traverse Analysis dialog box, set the following, as shown in Figure A–30:

   - *Horizontal adjustment method*: **Compass rule**
   - *Vertical adjustment method*: **Length weighted distribution**
   - *Update survey database*: **Yes**

Property	Value
Do traverse analysis	☑ Yes
Do angle balance	☑ Yes
Horizontal adjustment method	Compass rule ▼
Vertical adjustment method	Length weighted distribution ▼
Horizontal closure limit 1:X	15000.00000000
Vertical closure limit 1:X	15000.00000000
Angle error per set	0.00050000
Update survey database	☑ Yes

Figure A–30

3. Click **OK** to apply the adjustment values to the traverse

4. A Warning box opens, indicating that the survey does not meet the user-specified limits. Click **OK** to continue. In the Notepad report list, select **CC Traverse Raw Closure.trv** to review its values.

5. The Notepad reports display. Read and close each one to continue adjusting the traverse loop.

6. Click **Save** to save the drawing.

7. Close the drawing and the survey database.

AutoCAD Civil 3D Certification Exam Objectives

The following table will help you to locate the exam objectives within the chapters of the *AutoCAD® Civil 3D® 2017 (R1): Fundamentals* and *AutoCAD® Civil 3D® 2017 (R1) for Surveyors* student guides to help you prepare for the AutoCAD Civil 3D Certified Professional exam.

Exam Topic	Exam Objective	Student Guide	Chapter & Section(s)
Styles	Create and use object styles	• AutoCAD Civil 3D Fundamentals	• 1.6 • 4.3
		• AutoCAD Civil 3D For Surveyors	• 1.6
	Create and use label styles	• AutoCAD Civil 3D Fundamentals	• 1.6 • 4.2 & 4.3
		• AutoCAD Civil 3D For Surveyors	• 1.6
Lines and Curves	Use the Line and Curve commands	• AutoCAD Civil 3D Fundamentals	• 3.1
		• AutoCAD Civil 3D For Surveyors	• 3.6
	Use the Transparent commands	• AutoCAD Civil 3D Fundamentals	• 3.1 • 6.3 • 7.6
		• AutoCAD Civil 3D For Surveyors	• 3.6 • 4.5

Exam Topic	Exam Objective	Student Guide	Chapter & Section(s)
Points	Create points using the Point Creation commands	• AutoCAD Civil 3D Fundamentals	• 4.5
		• AutoCAD Civil 3D For Surveyors	• 4.4
	Create points by importing point data	• AutoCAD Civil 3D Fundamentals	• 4.7
		• AutoCAD Civil 3D For Surveyors	• 4.7
	Use point groups to control the display of points	• AutoCAD Civil 3D Fundamentals	• 4.8
		• AutoCAD Civil 3D For Surveyors	• 4.8
Surfaces	Identify key characteristics of surfaces	• AutoCAD Civil 3D Fundamentals	• 5.2
		• AutoCAD Civil 3D For Surveyors	• 7.2
	Create and edit surfaces	• AutoCAD Civil 3D Fundamentals	• 5.3 to 5.6
		• AutoCAD Civil 3D For Surveyors	• 2.4 • 7.3 to 7.6
	Use styles and settings to display surface information	• AutoCAD Civil 3D Fundamentals	• 5.2
		• AutoCAD Civil 3D For Surveyors	• 7.2
	Create a surface by assembling fundamental data	• AutoCAD Civil 3D Fundamentals	• 5.1
		• AutoCAD Civil 3D For Surveyors	• 7.1
	Use styles to analyze surface display results	• AutoCAD Civil 3D Fundamentals	• 5.10
		• AutoCAD Civil 3D For Surveyors	• 7.10
	Annotate surfaces	• AutoCAD Civil 3D Fundamentals	• 5.8
		• AutoCAD Civil 3D For Surveyors	• 7.8
Parcels	Design a parcel layout	• AutoCAD Civil 3D Fundamentals	• 3.3 & 3.4
	Select parcel styles to change the display of parcels	• AutoCAD Civil 3D Fundamentals	• 3.2
	Select styles to annotate parcels	• AutoCAD Civil 3D Fundamentals	• 3.2, 3.5, 3.7, & 3.8
Alignments	Design a geometric layout	• AutoCAD Civil 3D Fundamentals	• 6.3 & 6.4
	Create alignments	• AutoCAD Civil 3D Fundamentals	• 6.3 & 6.4

Exam Topic	Exam Objective	Student Guide	Chapter & Section(s)
Profiles and Profile Views	Create a surface profile	• AutoCAD Civil 3D Fundamentals	• 7.3
	Design a profile	• AutoCAD Civil 3D Fundamentals	• 7.5 & 7.6
	Create a profile view style	• AutoCAD Civil 3D Fundamentals	• 7.2
	Create a profile view	• AutoCAD Civil 3D Fundamentals	• 7.4
Corridors	Design and create a corridor	• AutoCAD Civil 3D Fundamentals	• 8.1 to 8.3
	Derive information and data from a corridor	• AutoCAD Civil 3D Fundamentals	• 8.6 & 8.7
	Design and create an intersection	• AutoCAD Civil 3D Fundamentals	• 8.5
Sections and Section Views	Create and analyze sections and section views	• AutoCAD Civil 3D Fundamentals	• 8.7 • 11.1, 11.2, & 11.4
Pipe Networks	Design and create a pipe network	• AutoCAD Civil 3D Fundamentals	• 10.3, 10.4, & 10.7
Grading	Design and create a grading model	• AutoCAD Civil 3D Fundamentals	• 9.1 & 9.3
	Create a grading model feature line	• AutoCAD Civil 3D Fundamentals	• 9.2
Managing and Sharing Data	Create a data sharing setup	• AutoCAD Civil 3D Fundamentals	• 2.3
Plan Production	Create a sheet set	• AutoCAD Civil 3D Fundamentals	• 12.5
	Use view frames	• AutoCAD Civil 3D Fundamentals	• 12.2 & 12.4
Survey	Identify key characteristics of survey data	• AutoCAD Civil 3D Fundamentals	• 4.2
		• AutoCAD Civil 3D For Surveyors	• 3.2
	Use description keys to control the display of points created from survey data	• AutoCAD Civil 3D Fundamentals	• 4.6
		• AutoCAD Civil 3D For Surveyors	• 4.6
	Create a boundary drawing from field data	• AutoCAD Civil 3D Fundamentals	• 4.7
		• AutoCAD Civil 3D For Surveyors	• Ch. 5 (all) • Ch. 6 (all)

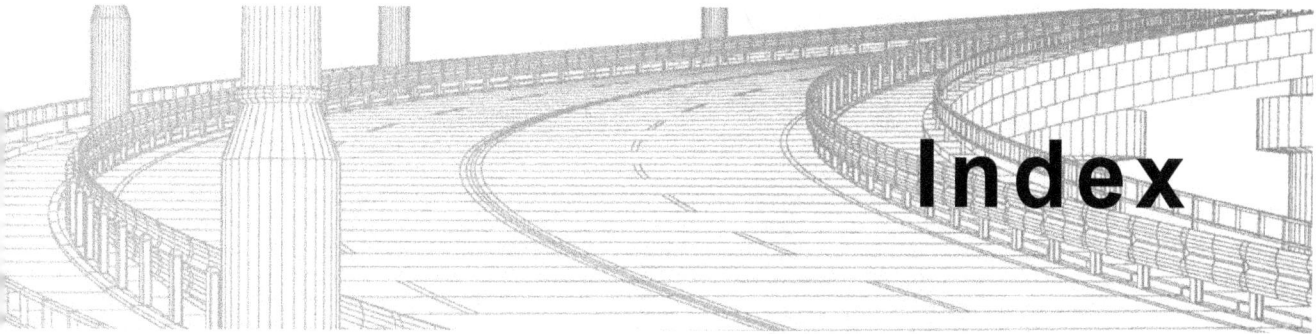

Index